INHALING THE MAHATMA

Christopher Kremmer

INHALING THE MAHATMA

HarperCollins*Publishers*

Fourth Estate
An imprint of HarperCollins*Publishers*, Australia

First published in Australia in 2006
by HarperCollins*Publishers* Australia Pty Limited
ABN 36 009 913 517
www.harpercollins.com.au

HarperCollins*Publishers*
25 Ryde Road, Pymble, Sydney, NSW 2073, Australia
31 View Road, Glenfield, Auckland 10, New Zealand
77–85 Fulham Palace Road, London, W6 8JB, United Kingdom
2 Bloor Street East, 20th floor, Toronto, Ontario M4W 1A8, Canada
10 East 53rd Street, New York NY 10022, USA

National Library of Australia Cataloguing-in-Publication data:

Kremmer, Christopher.
    Inhaling the Mahatma.
    Includes index.
    ISBN 0 7322 8092 3.
    ISBN 9 7807 3228 0925.
    1. Kremmer, Christopher – Journeys – India. 2. India –
    Description and travel. 3. India – Social life and customs –
    21st century. I. Title.
915.4053

Cover and internal design by Marcelle Lunam
Cover image by Palani Mohan
Internal cover photo montage by John Webber
Author photograph by Jason Michael Lang
Internal images by Palani Mohan (pp. xii, 54); Jason Michael Lang (pp. 122, 286);
and Christopher Kremmer. Photo p. 141 courtesy Maya Bahadur.
Typeset in Bembo 11.5/16 by Kirby Jones
Printed and bound in Australia by Griffin Press on 70gsm Bulky Ivory

5 4 3 2 1   06 07 08 09

One has to dare to believe.
Mahatma Gandhi[1]

CONTENTS

Part Five

PREFACE

One in every six people on our planet is an Indian, and the nation they inhabit is conducting the world's largest and most important experiment in democracy. Can a deeply religious society of more than one billion people with a large Hindu majority sustain a secular government under which people of all faiths are treated equally? If it can work in a developing country as populous and diverse as India, it can work anywhere.

In just sixty years, the power of ordinary Indians to determine who governs them has revolutionised a once demoralised colony of Britain, breaking down feudalism and caste discrimination, and making enormous strides in reducing poverty and illiteracy, famine and disease. In 1947, the average Indian had a life expectancy of thirty-two years, and only one in five people could read or write; today's Indian lives twice as long on average, is better off than ever, and two out of every three people are literate. India's information technology boom has buried its image as a timeless, caste-ridden place teeming with paupers, snake charmers and maharajas. The world is doing yoga, wearing pashmina and reading Indian authors, not to mention enjoying spicy Indian cuisine and being entertained by the pulsating output of the Bollywood cinema.

Yet at the very moment of India's emergence as a force in the world, the secular democracy that made this possible has come under threat from within. As elsewhere in the post-Cold War world, politicians have sought to garner votes by appealing to old caste and religious prejudices, exploiting the large pockets of poverty and ignorance that inevitably exist in a developing country. There have been moments when the great Indian experiment has failed, as occurred in the western state of Gujarat four years ago, when some 2000 people, mainly Muslims, died in sectarian riots fomented by militant Hindus. There have also been times when those who spoke loudest in the secular republic's defence betrayed by their actions its nobler aspirations.

My portrayal of India's momentous struggles focuses mainly on the past fifteen years, which marked a decisive stage in the nation's progress. While India's experience is unique, it should cause us to reflect on the consequences in any society when religion is exploited by vested interests, including politicians and the media. But it also demonstrates how a republic, wisely constituted on the basis of law and equal rights for all citizens regardless of race, region, faith, education, language or poverty, is the best guarantee against appeals to extremism.

India is a work in progress, a painting on a shifting canvas. In Hindi, the word used for yesterday, *cul*, is the same word used to describe tomorrow. My story shifts frequently between past and present, and a timeline and glossary of Indian terms is included at the back of the book to help readers follow the sequence of events. Rather than rendering it in dry, historical terms, I have chosen to tell India's story in the context of my own changing life there, which began as a young reporter on his first foreign posting in the early 1990s, and deepened when I met my wife, Janaki. The experience of living within a Hindu family on the fringes of Old Delhi, more than anything else, allowed me to discern the fundamental difference between the tolerant Hinduism of the majority and the less appealing kind practised by power-hungry politicians. Indeed, as will become clear to the reader, I have been personally moved and inspired by the Hindu faith and philosophy, and fully expect it increasingly to influence the world in the twenty-first century. As India changes, it will continue to draw strength from its traditions. Its ancient wisdom and modern ambitions can walk hand in hand towards what I am sure will be a brighter future.

Jai Hind!

Sydney

March 2006

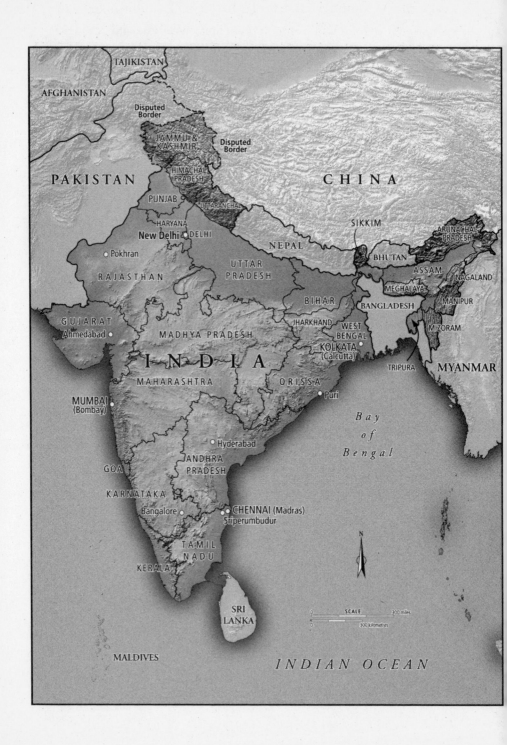

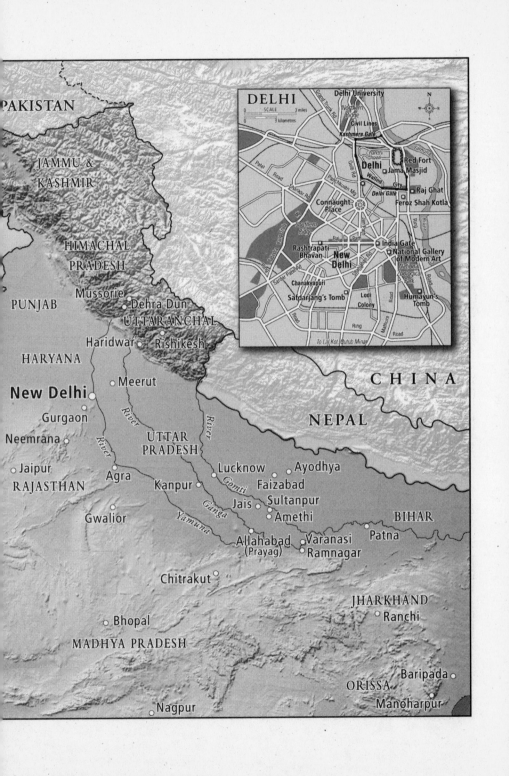

Part One

1

The Hindi Lesson

'Come along now,' said Hari Lal, removing his shoes and calmly massaging his toes, as if the shuddering steel assemblage of interstate bus was not swerving maniacally at night on an unlit road in northern India. 'You want sugar. What will you say?'

He means to break me, this gentlemanly creature, relic of a bygone era of humanities and languages, when knowledge was not entirely technical and people still had time for each other. In the murky half-light, road signs warned of 'Work in Progress' and 'Dead Slow'. But the driver — who obviously could not read English, or perhaps read at all — paid no heed. Oblivious to the danger, Hari Lal braced himself for one final assault on my ignorance. He would drive the demon ignorance from my body and force me to speak in tongues.

'*Accha* [Good], now,' he said, grinding his teeth, a trademark of frustration. 'Let's say you want to know the price of a kilogram of sugar. What would you say to me?'

Two rows ahead of us a woman in a cheap cotton sari was heaving, having earlier partaken of the same spicy snack I'd enjoyed at a roadside *dhaba*. The wind that caught her retches and blew them back at us was full of heat and dust, and the acrid odour of burning cow dung, among other things. The heavy glass window panes of the bus rattled in their frames, as if foretelling some terrible disaster. An insistent boy seated across the aisle kept saying 'Hallo' and 'What is your good name?' A couple of choice epithets in the vernacular died on the tip of my tongue. Hari would not approve.

The Hindi alphabet, an alien script of vowels and consonants piled one upon the other like top-heavy turbans, flashed before me, and I thought I might die of language training. Some of the sounds were familiar but the word order was scrambled and the conjunctions took your tongue to secret, slightly illicit places. Descended from Sanskrit it belonged to the Indo-European family of languages, like Gaelic and Greek, and had we not been hurtling towards oblivion in an overheated rattletrap somewhere in Uttar Pradesh I might have heard familiar echoes in words like *mata* and *pita* — mother and father. But amid the clamour of the nocturnal bus journey, on a pitilessly hot night somewhere between Delhi and Haridwar, all I could do was hazard a guess.

'Well, I suppose that would be *kimat. Kya kimat* . . . what price?' I ventured. 'What price of — *kya kimat ki?* — and, one kilo — *ek kilo* — of sugar . . . that's *cheeni*. So, I'd say, *Kya kimat ki ek kilo cheeni?*'

Hari's ear, placed conveniently close to my mouth, did not look satisfied.

'Not quite *pukha* [right],' he said, polite to a fault in the face of adversity. 'The noun comes before the post position — *chinni ki kimat*. Then comes the interrogative — *kya hai?* Say it.'

'*Chinni ki kimat kya hai?*'

'*Shabash!* Well done. Now listen to this and see what I'm saying. *Mai Hindi bol rahaa hum*.'

'I am speaking Hindi,' I said, in English.

'*Accha, theek hai!* [Good, okay!]' Hari clucked approvingly. 'You see, you know more than you think. I'm telling you, Chris-ji, a few words of Hindi will take you a long way in this country.'

I'd heard it all before, and it was all true. For more than a decade, Hari had been my sporadic but indefatigable tutor, and throughout those years we had teetered agonisingly close to the brink of fluency. Then I would disappear for a year or two, to places where people spoke Sinhalese or Arabic or Vietnamese, and return with the fruits of our progress erased from my memory. We'd had more false starts than a lawn mower, but failure was a word that Hari Lal would not recognise in any language.

At the Inter-State Bus Terminal beside Old Delhi's Kashmere Gate that afternoon, he'd fought like a lion to secure us the best seat on the bus. The bus terminal was a *jungly* place, full of pimps and touts, pickpockets and homeless persons, who somehow survived in the grimy hellhole of a once presentable public facility. Our journey had begun with a tragi-comic episode of miscommunication by mobile phones, as Hari waited patiently in the lower-level departure bays, among clouds of sooty black diesel smoke and the sound of gnashing gearboxes, while I looked for him on the upper concourse. When finally I spotted his sinewy frame and trademark *jhola* shoulder bag he was standing in the doorway of a bus, like one of those touts who bark destinations in the hope of attracting tired pedestrians.

Of all the battered conveyances in the terminal he had chosen this particular vehicle, discerning some hallmark of quality that eluded me. On the phone that afternoon he'd spoken of the new air-conditioned private coaches that now plied the highways of India, offering levels of service not previously seen or enjoyed by the much put-upon travelling public. But the hulking behemoth we boarded was in no way different from hundreds of other dilapidated juggernauts you saw careering everywhere on India's roads, steel shells without the hint of a cushion, carrying their hapless passengers towards a death less dignified than a crash test dummy's. I'd read somewhere that 80,000 people died on India's roads each year, with 300,000 seriously injured. To make matters worse, the sweet spot favoured by Hari — two seats on the left that were less exposed to oncoming traffic, and situated beside a steel pole that would act as a roll bar should we overturn and plunge down a ravine — was already taken by a pair of students, who by rights should have got up and offered them to their elders, but didn't.

Barely had this shambling conveyance charged out of the terminal and crossed the bridge over the Yamuna River than we came upon an accident. The body of a woman fallen from a scooter lay on the road, surrounded by thousands of poorly dressed stickybeaks, helpers, know-alls, lechers and wannabes, all chipping in with excuses, explanations and blame for what had happened. The crowd's desire for vengeance was palpable, but the offending driver had fled, leaving their anger to congeal in the outrageous heat.

Never ones to miss an opportunity, roadside vendors piled onto the bus to hawk salty *namkeen* snacks and plastic sachets of ersatz mango juice and water from a dubious spring. Then the conductor, whose life seemed less pleasant than the sweat-soaked towel that hung around his neck, pressed his crotch against my shoulder and arduously wrote out our tickets in duplicate, showering us with a thick cough as he tore off the perforated coupons with fingers blackened by carbon paper. Snatching my hundred-rupee note, he promised to give me change later — an old ruse designed to ensure that we both forgot about it — and could barely conceal his animus when I remembered. We'd been gridlocked for half an hour on a flyover, the metallic ark perched above a sea of grunge, overlooking cruddy rooftops littered with bricks, car tyres and black plastic water tanks. A blood-red sun drowned in the grey polluted haze that passed for air in a city of fourteen million people. When we got under way again, it was only to crash into the bus beside us, prompting a new dispute to erupt between the drivers.

'Oh God, Delhi is a *pagal ghar* [madhouse] these days,' murmured Hari, sucking on a fruit sachet, adding that no two buses had ever collided in the thirty years he'd been travelling to and from Delhi, a comforting self-delusion.

It was a relief when the drivers' argument ended inconclusively, and the breeze of forward motion dried our cloying perspiration. An hour out of Delhi, beyond the Hindon River, patches of countryside appeared and text messages on our mobiles welcomed us to the state of Uttar Pradesh, population 170 million. Night fell, illuminated by the acetylene torches of roadside garages and the flashing headlights of oncoming trucks and buses. Freed from urban constraints, our surly driver — with shocking disregard for the lives of his passengers, his own life, or indeed life in any form — immediately accelerated and claimed the full width of the road, daring oncoming vehicles to crash into us. A trumpeting horn heralded our madcap progress and arrival in the Cow Belt of northern India. Behind us, a group of card players was becoming increasingly voluble.

'Typical Haryanvis,' said Hari, whispering in my ear in a haughty tone, referring to a state of the Indian Union just north of Delhi. 'I can tell by the way they laugh. *Haw haw haw!* Uneducated fellows.'

The mention of education reminded him that we had not yet concluded mine. It would take more than a bunch of vocal yokels to distract the relentless Hari Lal.

'It will come. It *will* come,' he insisted, undeterred by my inability to grasp some verbal conjugation. 'One day you will be listening to me, and suddenly it will burst forth. You shall speak beautiful Hindi!'

In the early 1990s Hari Lal had arrived at my door in New Delhi's genteel Chanakyapuri neighbourhood, an itinerant purveyor of language services. For a teacher of Hindi, Urdu, Persian and English, the enclave of diplomats, correspondents and wealthy Indian families provided rich pickings. Every Monday Hari Lal Dhingra would leave his home in Dehra Dun, a quiet town nestled in a valley in the Himalayan foothills, and journey by road or rail down to the overheated, self-important capital, there to spend the week trekking by auto rickshaw and on foot between the homes of clients whose names he carefully noted in a tiny spiral-backed notebook which, despite its seeming fragility, had served him for years.

Hari Lal was a saver, a keeper of people and things, whose frugal nature was forged during the holocaust the Indians called Partition, when his family had lost everything. They were Hindus in what became Muslim Pakistan, with sizeable tracts of land around Hazro, near the Indus River midway between Peshawar and Rawalpindi and owned a factory in Muzaffarabad that processed tobacco from Peshawar and Mardan into snuff. Hari Lal was sixteen years old, preparing to continue his studies at Lahore University, when war broke out and Pashtun raiders from the North-West Frontier Province entered Muzaffarabad in divided Kashmir, killing many Hindus and taking the survivors hostage. When eventually a ceasefire was arranged, they made it to a refugee camp in Kurukshetra. Hari's maternal grandfather, who'd fled earlier to India and become a mercer in the old hill station of Mussoorie, took them in. Life began again with little more than a few rupees and the gold chain around young Hari's neck.

After the chaos of Partition, in which up to a million people are thought to have died, the peaceful foothills provided a haven where the Punjabi Dhingra family could set about rebuilding their lives, pooling their meagre funds to establish small businesses and educate their children. At Dehra Dun, Hari Lal completed his Bachelor's and Master's degrees in Law, then moved to Meerut to work in a legal practice. But the life of the law did not suit his gentle temperament, and he drifted into odd jobs, teaching Hindi to Christian missionaries, becoming a travelling agent selling thread, and later, a consular officer in the British High Commission in New Delhi. By the 1970s, he'd saved enough money to build a home for himself and his wife, Kamlesh, in Dehra Dun. Whatever else he'd made had been spent educating and marrying off his three daughters.

When we'd first met he was approaching retirement age, but having no pension was compelled to continue plying his trade as long as the years and health would allow. He spoke and taught an elegant Hindustani, refusing to submit to the slang-strewn crudity that characterised life in post-independence India. He had read the American motivational guide *How to Win Friends and Influence People* by Dale Carnegie, and manners were his forte. If he asked for a discount on some small item in the bazaar, as is the custom in India, he would be careful to avoid any suggestion that the vendor's price was too high.

'I will say, "The price is all right. But if possible, could you make it a little less. We don't have much money." When speaking to lowly persons you should always be polite, and when speaking to those in high places it should not appear that you are an uneducated person. The lowly will love you, and the mighty will respect you. Speak down, and you get the worst. Speak well, and it brings out the best in people.'

It was rumoured that Hari Lal had once rejected the offer of a glittering appointment. The prime minister's family had been looking for a Hindi teacher to tutor their new Italian daughter-in-law, Sonia, and a family friend had put out feelers. But Hari was in no rush to enter politics.

'It's dangerous to get involved with political people. You get too close to them and you suffer the consequences,' he warned me, but I ignored him. As a young correspondent on my first foreign posting, I could hardly avoid political leaders.

He was visiting me three times a week in those days, sitting in the downstairs living room with some photocopied sheets of phrases and grammar that had stood the test of hundreds of hopeless pupils. Unaccustomed to servants, I would make his tea, an unconscious courtesy that won me Hari's enduring esteem and affection.

My first home on Malcha Marg resembled a displaced ski lodge, with gabled ceilings and a large stone fireplace, incongruous given Delhi's predominantly hot climate. Long-horned Brahmin bulls the colour of old bones towed antique grass cutters across the neighbourhood's common. The city of New Delhi, designed by Edwin Lutyens and Herbert Baker during the final years of the Raj, was a work in progress. Wide boulevards devoid of traffic connected a handful of grand public buildings separated by acres of open ground, the complete antithesis of the teeming walled city of Shahjahanabad, or Old Delhi, situated just north on the banks of the Yamuna River. Although imbued with Asian touches including Buddhist *stupas*, Islamic cupolas and Hindu temple 'bells' frozen in mute stone, New Delhi's classical colonnades still resembled something from Europe. Lutyens's Delhi was an elegant, but rather empty, showcase of an order that had collapsed just sixteen years after it was inaugurated in 1931. Like previous royal follies in the subcontinent, it had barely been occupied before being abandoned in 1947, when Gandhi, Nehru and the rest of the freedom fighters moved in. This Indian Persepolis, shimmering like an exotic, slightly useless spoil of battle, became independent India's capital.

My first weeks in Delhi were spent trawling through government offices in a quest for various accreditations and permissions from a bureaucracy grown sluggish with complacency and power. Most afternoons I'd wander into the spokesman's office at the Ministry of External Affairs, where an august, cigar-smoking gentleman gave briefings. Seated behind his desk, he would elongate his vowels like an Indian Noel Coward, issuing statements at dictation speed to a clutch of venerable reporters, some of whom had been around since Partition. These crusty scribes recorded the spokesman's every utterance in spidery longhand, slurping the government's *chai* and coffee and nibbling its *biscoots*, as their source enunciated India's firm resolve to mobilise world opinion against the nefarious designs of Pakistan, and rejected as false and malicious all allegations of Indian interference in the affairs of neighbouring countries. India's first prime minister Jawaharlal Nehru's noble vision of non-alignment and Indian moral leadership had collapsed into a doddering funk that saw New Delhi supporting the Soviet invasion of Afghanistan, sitting on the fence when Iraq invaded Kuwait, and cheering when communists tried to crush the Soviet Union's reform movement.

India in the early 1990s was a nation in waiting. The Green Revolution had produced hardier and more productive crops, all but eliminating famines, and modern medicine slashed the mortality rate. But state socialism and failed birth-control strategies had produced the worst-case scenario — too many people fighting for a share of too little wealth. Almost 40 per cent of India's 850 million people were officially classed as paupers and just on half the population was illiterate.

Gandhi's clarion call for *swadeshi*, or self-sufficiency, produced a fortress economy unable to manufacture the things people wanted. Prevented from owning a majority share in their subsidiaries, big multinationals like IBM and Coca-Cola had left the country in the 1970s, after the government pressured them to reduce their equity and demanded the secret recipe for Coke.[1] If an Indian businessman wanted to manufacture something, he needed a licence. What he produced was determined by government-set quotas, and the government also determined the price at which the product could be sold. The 'Licence Raj', as the system was known, was riddled with corruption. Gurcharan Das, the author and former CEO of Procter & Gamble India, captured the mood in his book on the period, *India Unbound*.

> Bank managers who advance loans want a share, factory inspectors will not give clearances for new equipment without a bribe, the engineer of the State Electricity Board would not connect the power without a cut. The boiler inspectors had to be paid. The labour inspector wanted his cut. The excise inspector requested a fee to give them an excise number without which they could not begin production. The minister threatened to change the rules to prevent them supplying their wares until he was given a share of the company. An entrepreneur has to bribe twenty to forty functionaries if he wants to do business.[2]

While happy to torture businesses, the government refused to let them die. The *Industrial Disputes Act* made it unlawful for private firms employing 100 or more people to close without the permission of the government, a process which, on average, took eleven years. Industries were located to satisfy political rather than economic imperatives and those lucky enough to work for them enjoyed subsidised housing, hospitals, schools and transport. Yet these enterprises, starved of capital and competition, were strangers to profit, and had to be bailed out by the state. The phenomenon Indians call 'industrial sickness' became an epidemic and, by 1989, around 160,000 'sick units' were being propped up.

Under Nehru's daughter, Indira Gandhi, vast swathes of the economy, including aviation, banking and coal mining, fell under state control. Subsidised factories produced subsidised fertiliser which was then sold to farmers at subsidised prices. Four decades after independence, the country's share of world trade had dropped from 2.4 per cent to 0.5 per cent, and per capita income was on a par with that of sub-Saharan Africa.

Ensconced in my ski lodge, I had inherited a staff assembled by my predecessors over twenty years. They were all Christians from South India, drivers, laundrymen, book-keepers and scribes, who apparently were considered more user-friendly than North Indian Hindus. To their number I added a housekeeper, a bubbly mother of seven called Margaret whose family had fled the troubles in Burma. The book-keeper, a young Tamil named Peter, had taken to sleeping beside the fax machine, jumping up in the middle of the night whenever a call came through to switch it on, the fear being that if the machine was left on overnight it would overheat and start a fire. The locally employed journalist was Edmond Roy, later to become a well-known broadcaster, who taught me not to believe anything the local politicians told me and, more important, how to use my fingers as cutlery. Indian food — especially a good vegetarian *thali* — tastes better if you eat it with your hands.

When it came to non-veg food, the local mutton turned out to be goat meat, delivered by a furtive-looking Muslim who concealed it in a cloth to avoid offending Hindu sensibilities. No matter what I ate, bouts of 'Delhi Belly' were frequent, and I was at all times stuffed to the gills with a variety of prophylactics designed to prevent me getting typhoid, cholera, meningitis, malaria, polio and encephalitis. My tender belly was further protected by washing virtually everything I ate in an iodine solution known as 'pinky water'. Despite all these precautions I was hospitalised twice with different ailments.

All the staff, from the driver to the *dhobi* (laundry worker) insisted on calling me 'Sir' or 'Sahib', which I quite liked, all except Edmond, who was something of a Sir-Sahib himself. We clacked away on antique typewriters, fighting the urge to sleep off our huge lunches, coping with erasers that smudged rather than erased, and relying on battery-powered desk fans when the power failed. When it rained, as it did through July and August, the telephones ceased to function and, even when it didn't rain, calling overseas required hours of fruitless dialling. Although it was difficult to find a light fitting that didn't electrocute you, the landlord demanded two years' rent in advance paid in dollars into a foreign bank account, and insisted that all repairs were our responsibility. Television and radio channels were state-controlled, the only competition coming from a widely distributed news program on video cassette that was delivered door-to-door each week like some clandestine newsletter. In times of national crisis, Indians tuned to foreign short-wave radio news broadcasts, so limited was their faith in their own national broadcaster. Forty years after they'd kicked out the British, the BBC was still their most trusted source of broadcast news. Only the newspapers retained the defiant spirit of the Freedom Struggle.

★ ★ ★

One morning over breakfast I read about a new scheme the government was introducing to give low-caste Hindus much improved access to public-sector jobs. It sounded like a good idea, given the fact that they accounted for at least one-quarter of the population and had been discriminated against for at least 2500 years.

The original Hindu social order of priests, warriors, merchants and labourers had over centuries generated thousands of occupational sub-castes. Hundreds of these *jatis*, including leather workers, boatmen, laundrymen and cleaners, were considered to be 'Untouchable', outcasts from society. Gandhi, himself a high-caste Hindu, regarded the Jati system as an abomination. At a Congress Party conference in Calcutta at the turn of the twentieth century, he noted the way high-caste Tamil Brahmin delegates set up their camp as far away from the rest as possible; apparently fearing that even the sight of anyone of lower birthright during a meal would spoil their digestion.[3] Gandhi called the outcastes Harijans, or Children of God, and campaigned relentlessly to raise their status. But, wary of splitting India's Hindu majority at a time when evicting the British was his main priority, he refused to denounce hereditary caste *per se*, enraging fellow Congressmen like Dr Bhim Rao Ambedkar, a Harijan who later converted to Buddhism in protest at caste oppression. Under Ambedkar's leadership, the panel that drafted independent India's new Constitution banned Untouchability, and 22 per cent of central government jobs were reserved for the so-called Scheduled Castes and Tribes. The Untouchables and the poor, who accounted for a quarter of the population, would eventually become a powerful political force. They took on a new, more militant name, the Dalits, or oppressed.

But caste proved to be resilient; even India's Muslim, Christian and Sikh communities practise it in some areas. Even among Harijans, caste consciousness can be acute, with barbers and laundry workers considering themselves above sweepers. Urbanised, affluent Hindus who no longer need the advantages of their high caste are reluctant to renounce it entirely, much as the descendants of Irish émigrés honour their heritage. Despite two centuries of social reform, the matrimonial columns of the Sunday newspapers are still full of notices about fair-skinned Brahmin boys seeking genetically similar girls. Fear as much as habit sustains this staunch traditionalism. When a daughter marries, she generally leaves the family home to live with her husband's family. Horrific tales of abuse and even murder of young brides by in-laws disgruntled at an insufficient dowry regularly appear in the newspapers. Terrified by such a prospect, even the cosmopolitan Hari Lal had gone so far as to choose grooms for his daughters who were not only fellow Kshatriya (ruler) caste, but members of his own extended family.

'The idea is that if we know the people, then the daughters will never suffer. That's the main thing,' he told me.

Ironically, job quotas for the lowest castes triggered a flood of claims for similar help from those who, while not Untouchable, were not high caste either. The so-called Other Backward Castes (OBCs), often farmers who owned their own land but saw government jobs as an avenue of social mobility, formed a potentially lucrative 'vote bank' for any politician prepared to give them their due. That August of 1990, just a fortnight after I'd arrived in India, they found an unlikely messiah in the person of Vishwanath Pratap Singh, a high-caste Thakur and scion of a former royal family who the previous year had defeated the Congress Party and become prime minister. Singh's ambitious plan was to reserve a further 27 per cent of all public-sector jobs for OBCs, with similar quotas to follow in university admissions. V.P. Singh justified job quotas by dusting off the decade-old report of a government inquiry, the Mandal Report, which had recommended just that, but which had been ignored by the previous Congress Party government of Rajiv Gandhi.

A few weeks after Singh announced his plan to implement the report's recommendations, Edmond arrived at the office in a breathless state, saying there was a disturbance outside the All India Institute of Medical Sciences. Rushing to the scene, we found one of the capital's main intersections transformed into a battleground.

Police wearing padded khaki vests and carrying bamboo shields were firing their antique rifles into crowds of young men, who responded with volleys of rocks. Pools of blood had formed on the pavements where some of the casualties — mainly upper-caste students protesting against the government's decision — had fallen. Caste politics had produced caste war, and the students who were leading the rebellion had used garbage skips and burnt-out vehicles to block Aurobindo Marg, a major boulevard. A traffic-control box lay overturned and smouldering on the sidewalk where they had taken control of nearby residential colonies and were mounting hit-and-run attacks on the armed police. They had commandeered and demobilised buses by letting down their tyres, smashing their windows for good measure. Families and friends, even some of their teachers, supplied food and first aid like a well-trained auxiliary. The air was thick with the smoke from burning vehicles interspersed with the sound of gunfire. Crouching behind a concrete ventilation shaft within range of the shooting, I saw that the police were shooting to kill. I'd never seen people trying to kill other people before and it sickened me. There were rumours that the army had been called out.

V.P. Singh was onto something. He'd come to power on an anti-corruption platform, but his coalition government was falling apart, and his middle-class support base was too narrow to ensure political longevity. The politician who could win the intermediate castes' backing would have a secure future. All that stood in his way were the students, but for them too it was a battle for survival. With private enterprise deliberately constrained by the state, their employment prospects rested heavily on the public sector, which provided a total of some twenty million jobs, the vast majority already taken and tightly held. Increasingly desperate about their futures, some students resorted to the extreme step of self-immolation in protest against the new policy. A photograph of a young New Delhi man, Rajiv Goswami, swathed in flames that almost killed him became the iconic image of the rebellion.[4] In the face of students self-immolating and being shot by police, V.P. Singh made no concessions.

In October, barely two months after the government unveiled its plan, the Supreme Court ordered a stay on the implementation of the policy and the violence abated. V.P. Singh, once the darling of the middle class, was now widely reviled. Even his intended beneficiaries, while happy to accept their new job quotas, seemed strangely ungrateful to him. Eleven months after defeating Rajiv Gandhi at the polls, V.P. Singh's government — only the second non-Congress administration in the forty-three years since independence — collapsed and his political career effectively ended.[5]

My Indian education had begun in a blaze of self-interest and self-destruction. Gandhian non-violence was no longer in vogue, and the once simple struggle for freedom from colonial rule had become a bloody civil war for a poor country's scarce resources.

2

Instant Karma

The night bus to Haridwar had carried Hari Lal and me across the wellspring of Indian civilisation, the ancient Doab, literally the land of two rivers, the Ganga and Yamuna, between which the ancient Aryan-speaking people lived.

Seven thousand years before Christ, members of the species *Homo sapiens* were growing wheat and barley and raising sheep and goats on the banks of the Indus River in what is today Pakistan. The rich alluvial soils of the valley, and early trade in precious commodities, including the blue gemstone lapis lazuli, generated prosperity and by 2500 BC large towns of brick buildings on a grid pattern of streets had sprung up. The two biggest towns whose remains have so far been uncovered, at Mohenjodaro and Harappa, book-ended the 1600-kilometre-long valley, but around 2000 BC their civilisation went into decline, posing several great mysteries. Who were the people of the Indus Valley and what caused the destruction of their way of life? Were they the ancestors of the Aryan people who later settled in the Doab, or did the Aryans come from elsewhere? We don't know because the Indus Valley script remains undeciphered. Unlocking it could settle one of ancient history's greatest arguments. Did the fair-skinned, cow-herding Aryans bring their Indo-European language and culture to India as invaders? Or did the civilisational traffic flow the other way?

Whether they created or destroyed the Indus Valley civilisation, the Aryans are widely accepted as the progenitors of the Hindu culture of northern India. They worshipped the militant god Indra with offerings made via the god of fire, Agni. Indra, although not as popular as he once was, is still worshipped with fire in India today, and one of the country's nuclear-capable missiles is named after Agni. The Aryans' sacred scriptures were the Vedas. Collated and written down in the first millennium BC, the Vedas outlined the original caste system. Brahmins, who were the priests in Vedic society, held a monopoly on Sanskrit and religious ritual, while the Kshatriyas' job was to win wars and govern. Their struggles are canonised in India's twin epics, the *Ramayana* and *Mahabharata*. The Vaishyas, also high caste, were the producers — farmers, artisans and merchants mainly — and the Shudras, low caste but not Untouchable, were manual labourers.

The Aryans would preside over the rise of one of the world's great civilisations in the melting pot of races, creeds and languages that is India, home today to more than one-sixth of humanity, with a population exceeding one billion people. But by the sixth century BC, opposition to Vedic Hinduism's celebration of war, ritual and social hierarchy crystallised in the life of a young prince, Siddhartha Gautama, who embraced non-violence and renunciation — and became the Buddha, founder of a new faith. His spiritual quest also inspired soul-searching and reform among Hindus, who eventually accepted him as an incarnation of one of their own gods, Vishnu, and adopted renunciation as the appropriate final stage in a caste Hindu's life.

Great debates raged alongside rapid economic and technological development. Cities like Varanasi and Taxila formed thriving centres of trade and culture along the Grand Trunk Road, still northern India's main thoroughfare. By the first century AD, Indian Buddhist monks were spreading the faith to Sri Lanka, Afghanistan and China.

In the land of its birth, Buddhism would enjoy royal patronage for centuries, and when the Chinese pilgrim Faxian (Fa Hsien) visited India in the years AD 399–414, he found that the faith dominated a vast area from Mathura, near today's capital, to the Bay of Bengal. But by the time another adventurous Chinese pilgrim, Xuanzang (Hsuan Tsang), arrived in AD 630 and stayed for fifteen years before returning to China, Indian Buddhism had gone into steep decline and Hinduism was again in the ascendant.

It was after midnight when a tired Hari Lal and I disembarked from the Uttar Pradesh State Transport Company bus in the pilgrim's town of Haridwar. No sooner had we stepped down than a tribe of cycle-rickshaw-*wallahs* began fighting over our meagre luggage, the way starving people fight over food rations. Deciding to settle the issue by carrying the bags ourselves, we set off on foot into the dark alleys where small hotels charged only a few hundred rupees per night for a room.

At the Hotel Sunita next morning, I awoke to the sound of Hari Lal mildly snoring. He slept well, for a man of his years, no doubt due to the kilometres of walking he clocked up on his rounds in New Delhi. Normally, he would have been snoring in his own bed in Dehra Dun, about 50 kilometres away, but he had agreed to my request for the detour to Haridwar. He knew the town well. It was a frequent destination for family holidays when India was still undivided and a Hindu family from the Muslim-majority northwest could visit the rest of India without hindrance. The family holidays were more like pilgrimages. Hari's family were passionate *yatris*, pilgrims, who would happily journey long distances to visit the holy sites of other faiths, just as Westerners do today. But Hindu catholicity went much deeper than that. From an early age, Hari Lal had been taught to read the works of the Sikh gurus in their original Gurmukhi dialect, and he was still an avid reader of the Sikhs' holiest book, the *Guru Granth Sahib*. Sikh holy sites like the birthplace of Guru Nanak were as important to his family as were such Hindu places of pilgrimage as

Haridwar and Rishikesh. Some Hindu families would even choose one of their sons to be raised as a Sikh, a testament to the fellow feeling of many members of both faiths. It was still the practice of the Dhingras to visit a Sikh *gurdwara* once a week. Whenever Hari Lal passed a mosque, or a Christian church, or a Buddhist shrine, as he did often on his return trip to Dehra Dun every Friday by bus or train, he would bow his head and whisper a small prayer.

So in the summer of 2004, when I returned to India on a yatra, or pilgrimage, of my own, an expedition into memory, it was unthinkable that Hari Lal should not join me. I knew enough Hindi to get around without his help. What I wanted was his company at the beginning, that small but essential part of any journey, when you most need to hold someone's hand. Instead of continuing direct to Dehra Dun from Haridwar, we would take the national highway to Rishikesh, a picturesque town of ashrams and yoga centres some 20 kilometres away, where the Ganga leaves the mountains to begin its long traverse across the north Indian plain. But at that early hour it seemed wrong to disturb him, and I decided to take a walk before breakfast.

The narrow lanes leading down to the Ganga were already alive with activity. The *dhobans* — women wielding massive charcoal-fired irons — pressed away the neighbourhood's creases, their ironing tables further narrowing the navigable limits of the alleys, while men sat cross-legged on their stoops reading newspapers. The neighbourhood belonged to Haridwar's 'sacred zone', and the easiest way of finding the river was to follow the *sadhus*, or holy men, who made their way towards it holding their stainless-steel *tiffin* carriers (lunch containers) and rolled-up black umbrellas. In deference to religious injunctions, the civic authorities banned consumption of meat and alcohol in the town, which seemed cleaner than most in India, sluiced by the frigid torrent of the Ganga even on the hottest day. The river's name meant 'that which moves swiftly' but its perpetual spate at this point was an engineers' trick, achieved by rerouting it along the Upper Ganga

Canal, giving Haridwar a waterfront instead of a distant, shallow stream rippling across a wide expanse of gravel.

For thousands of years, Hindus have scaled the Himalayas of the soul, and invested the Indian landscape with sacred meaning. In the *Rig Veda*, the earliest known composition in Sanskrit or any other Indo-European language, all the earth's rivers rise in heaven, and life on earth began with their release. When a Hindu pours water over the stone phallic symbol known as a *lingam*, they are re-enacting that first downpour. If the mountains are home to their gods, their seven sacred rivers receive their prayers and wash away their sins and ashes. Seven towns — Haridwar, Varanasi, Mathura, Ayodhya, Kanchipuram, Ujjain and Dwarka — are honoured as sites where spiritual release, or *moksha*, is most readily obtained. By their devotions, Hindus lay claim to the land, not always to own or govern it, but certainly to worship it, and no government in Indian history has successfully prevented them from doing so. The land is too big, the faith too deeply embedded in the people's consciousness.

From the elevated bank of the Ganga in Haridwar, I could see the river rushing towards a rose-coloured bridge. Pilgrims were strolling beside the fast-moving stream, enjoying the cool of the morning while temple priests clanged heavy brass bells to welcome the day. A low-caste man pushed sweepings into a neat pile beside a woman who emerged modestly from the water in a wet sari. Turning her back towards me, she proceeded to fill a small steel container with Ganga *jal* — Ganges water, considered sacred — then drizzled it back into the source, an action she performed repeatedly. A second woman passed an oil lamp before an idol of the elephant-headed god Ganesh — a ritual known as *arti* — while beside her a bare-chested man wearing the holy string of a Brahmin looped over his left shoulder stood waist-deep in the water with his hands clasped. He was reciting a prayer, I guessed the Gayatri Mantra, twenty-four syllables that play on the lips of millions of Hindus every morning — a 3000-year-old invocation that asks God to enlighten the human mind. Though they may worship the world's largest pantheon of gods, Hindus believe in a single creator, whose precise nature cannot be grasped by humans. All the other gods are *avatars* (incarnations) of that Almighty power. On the main bathing *ghat* in Haridwar, maximum Hinduism was on show. Young boys were hurling themselves off bridges, knowing that if they failed to catch hold of the slippery chains suspended from the next bridge downriver they would probably drown. Unwashed, naked ascetics with hair in dreadlocks dragged heavy sacks behind them as a form of penance, all the while squeezing rupees and dollars from anyone foolish enough to photograph them.

But on this quiet southern stretch of the river, the ordinary Hindus and pilgrims of Haridwar lived their faith more simply, collecting holy water for domestic uses.

In the enervating heat, the water looked irresistibly inviting, and seating myself on the bank, I rolled up my trousers and eased my legs into the icy stream. An Australian childhood had given me one thing in common with most Indians — a deep love of water. In the upper reaches of the Ganga, where the forests come down to river's edge and pristine sandy beaches line the shore, I had once taken a dip. But downstream of any major town or city, the river was heavily polluted. No power on earth would make me dunk my head in the Ganges anywhere between Haridwar and the Indian Ocean.

★ ★ ★

'The food is good, isn't it?' chirruped Hari Lal, restored by his slumbers. 'Nowhere else will you find such food.'

We'd chosen a typical town dhaba for breakfast before heading for Rishikesh, the 'abode of the sages'. The fare was simple but filling — fried *paranthas*, or flat bread, stuffed with vegetables, smeared with ghee, toasted on a griddle and served with tangy pickle and curd — and washed it down with several cups of sweet chai. The tea stained your teeth and the ghee encouraged heart disease but, apart from that, it really set you up for the day.

Hari Lal's blue-rimmed eyes were not as clear now as they'd once been. Veins bulged in his temples, and a curtain of lank hair skirted his bald dome. Yet like the rest of his countrymen and women, he had survived epochal events and the everyday graft of life in India. Like many Indians he wore several tattoos; the mystic syllable *Om* was stamped on the back of his right hand, and his initials, 'HLD', were inked on the skin of his inner right forearm. The 'Om' would help protect him, and if it didn't, the initials would help identify him, a happy Hindu with one foot in this world and the other in the next.

Our mission was simple: to drive to Rishikesh. We had no business there; it was the road that mattered, the way it rose gradually but inexorably towards Hindu holy places; the forests that flanked its progress and scented the air; the bitumen embedded with memories. With our stomachs filled we hired a taxi and set out for the town, a hundred kilometres or so from the Chinese border.

The Himalayas are India's Holy Land, where the clean, crisp air and temperate climate have for centuries provided a retreat for gods and pilgrims. Instead of continuing direct to Dehra Dun from Haridwar, where the Ganga enters the plains, we would take the national highway to Rishikesh. India's wealthy have always appreciated the need for spiritual insurance, lavishing religious institutions with endowments, and some of the retreats looked more like five-star hotels than humble ashrams. There was more traffic along this road, and more visible human habitation and industry than the first time I'd travelled it, which shouldn't have surprised me; the population of India had grown by 150 million since then.

The foothills bordering China had once been part of India's most populous state of Uttar Pradesh but had been transferred by an act of parliament to the new mountain state of Uttaranchal, the logic being that smaller, more discrete, entities might be easier to manage than a gargantuan state like UP. Most people thought it was a step forward, the Indian federation being tailored to better serve the people. But no one had asked our driver Ram Chandra about it.

'We're not all *Pahari* [hill people],' he complained, expectorating a mouthful of blood-red betel juice in an Olympian squirt that arched across oncoming traffic and landed on the opposite side of the road. 'Our clothes are different. Our living standards are different. We're plains people.'

Much as I sympathised, we *were* heading uphill, and I was beginning to recognise the landscape.

In the summer of 1991, covering my first election in India, I had travelled this same road. The caste card played by V.P. Singh had destroyed his government and destabilised the country, which had had three prime ministers in just over a year. The man considered most likely to succeed was Rajiv Gandhi, who Singh had hounded out of office with a slew of corruption allegations after he quit Rajiv's Cabinet. Rajiv was on the comeback trail, launching a gruelling 30,000-kilometre political yatra across India, travelling by plane, helicopter and car in a desperate effort to reclaim his mandate. He would average two hours' sleep a night in the course of the campaign, addressing dozens of rallies a day. It wasn't a good time to arrange an interview, but a mutual friend, Suman Dubey, was running the media side of the campaign. Suman had said that if I followed the leader's convoy he would try to get me a few minutes with him.

Rajiv Gandhi was Indian political royalty. Since independence, Indian history and the history of his family had been inextricably entangled. As a baby, he had been cradled in the arms of the Mahatma, and as a child he had shaken hands with Lord Louis Mountbatten, the last viceroy. Everything he did was photographed. His mother had been prime minister of India, his grandfather Jawaharlal Nehru also, and in 1984, at the age of forty, Rajiv had become the country's youngest ever leader, inspiring people with his charm and modern ideas. He had spoken of telephones and laptop computers, driven his own car, polished his own shoes, and had promised to wipe out endemic corruption. He was Mr Clean and Mr Uncomplicated, Mr Idealism and Mr Hope.[1] Those who knew him said he was slow to anger, but when angered quick to repent. There was more sunshine than shadow in his character. He loved Fellini films and jazz, which, like Indian classical music, celebrates improvisation, and he was sensitive to beauty in nature, which he photographed as a hobby. He was good with his hands, kind to animals and had doted on his mother. He was also an adventurous spirit who flew planes and had married a foreigner.

But Rajiv Gandhi had squandered his priceless inheritance. There had been scandal and infamy, and more than a whiff of corruption, and acts of folly and revenge for which thousands of Indians had paid with their lives. In 1984, his mother, Indira, sent the Indian Army to flush out militants sheltering in the Sikhs' holiest shrine, the Golden Temple of Amritsar, an operation in which the death toll topped 600 and the shrine was badly damaged. When Indira was shot dead the same year by her own Sikh bodyguards in revenge, Rajiv was immediately sworn in as prime minister. On the streets of the capital, armed mobs of Congress Party supporters began attacking Sikhs — a two per cent minority, but one of India's most productive communities — but for reasons that he never fully explained, Rajiv took no timely action to quell the violence, which went on to claim the lives of some 3000 Sikhs.

Later in his term, his government purchased Swedish-made Bofors artillery guns for the Indian Army, and $50 million in illegal kickbacks allegedly went into secret bank accounts controlled by family friends. Then there was the reckless and ill-fated 1987 Indian 'peace-keeping' mission into neighbouring Sri Lanka, which Rajiv had personally ordered and which resulted in the deaths of more than 1000 Indian soldiers and damaged the army's morale. It also turned a former Indian ally, the leader of Sri Lanka's separatist Tamil Tiger guerrillas, Velupillai Prabhakaran, into a sworn enemy.

Prabhakaran claimed to have been held incommunicado in a New Delhi hotel on Rajiv's orders until he agreed to the intervention.

In five years as prime minister Rajiv reshuffled his Cabinet twenty-four times. If it sounds amateurish, it's because it was. Before being drafted into politics by his mother, who'd lost her preferred heir, Rajiv's younger brother Sanjay, in a recreational flying accident, Rajiv had been a commercial airline pilot with no interest in government. Now, at forty-seven, with a young family to look after, he was searching for a job — India's top job — again.

Following Suman's advice I had made my way to a dusty *maidan*, or common, on the outskirts of Haridwar, where Rajiv's convoy had paused long enough to allow the leader to clamber onto a bamboo podium and make a speech. Since losing power in 1989, Rajiv's security cover had been reduced, and in the surging crowds there were just two plain-clothes security men flanking him, one of whom I recognised as the sturdy, eagle-eyed Pradip Gupta. Along with his mother's political legacy, Rajiv had inherited his father Feroze's good looks, with large black eyes and full lips that curved easily into a shy smile. His charm and youthful energy remained the principal political asset of the Congress Party, one of the world's oldest political organisations, which had gradually been transformed into a family keepsake. It was Day Two of the campaign and Rajiv was telling the crowd, whose numbers were rather thin, that only the Congress could provide India with a stable government, all other parties being incompetent or socially divisive. It was a simple speech in Hindi, both because Cambridge-educated Rajiv's grasp of the vernacular was rudimentary, and because half the electorate were illiterates who could only identify the different parties by their symbols.

'I urge you all to vote for the hand symbol of the Congress,' Rajiv appealed to them, and his audience, most of them peasant women trucked in from nearby villages and paid thirty rupees each for attending, cheered on cue.

Scanning the periphery of the crowd, I caught sight of Suman, looking elegantly crumpled, arms folded and casting glances at his watch like a preoccupied parent at a school function. He and Rajiv had hardly slept, returning from the first day of the campaign in Rajasthan to Delhi early that morning. With barely enough time to shower and change, let alone sleep, they'd then boarded a chartered plane to Dehra Dun, joined a road convoy south to Haridwar, and were now tracking northeast towards Rishikesh. While Rajiv's job was to meet the people, Suman's was to arrange press opportunities along the way. Standing there, hot and harassed by the perpetual lateness of the schedule, he did not look like he was enjoying it, and it was a relief when I caught his eye and his face lit up in recognition. When the speech was finished and Rajiv was settled back in his car next to the driver, Suman took me by the arm and shoved me into the rear seat, slamming the door behind me as he ran off to another vehicle. Then a swarm of motorcycle outriders converged in front of the car and we were on our way to Rishikesh.

In the cramped confines of the white Hindustan Motors Ambassador sedan I had my first close-up look at the one-time leader of the world's largest democracy; it was the back of his head, the bald patch to be precise. Seated in the passenger seat in front of me, he was wiping the perspiration from his brow with a handkerchief drawn from the pocket of his *kurta*. Beside me in the back seat was a man of silvery eminence wearing a starched white Gandhi cap, Narain Dutt Tiwari, a Congress stalwart and former chief minister of Uttar Pradesh, whose smile of greeting was so flinty that his face barely moved. The driver, by contrast, was a fit young man whose dark hair and moustache were neatly trimmed and whose taut body suggested that he might double as a bodyguard.

The Ambassador — not the world's niftiest car — was labouring severely, at first I thought due to the hilly terrain. But later I realised it must have been bomb-proofed with heavy armour. As we drove towards Raiwala Junction, Rajiv kept his left hand on the dashboard, as if the road to Rishikesh might crumble and plunge him into some terrible vortex. Several times when a vehicle rounded a bend ahead of us or pedestrians strayed close to the road, he would utter a brief caution to the driver.

So there we all were, out for a midweek drive in the Himalayan foothills on a beautiful, albeit hot, summer's day. Popping a lozenge into his mouth, Rajiv turned to offer me an ice mint, and I introduced myself. I was about to put a question to him when a boisterous clutch of supporters carrying tricolour banners of the Congress flagged us down with cries of 'Rajiv Gandhi *zindabad*!' (Long live Rajiv Gandhi.) We couldn't have been in the car more than five minutes, but at the sight of them, Rajiv motioned to the driver to stop, excused himself, and stepped out to be garlanded, felicitated, confided in, encouraged and touched. The garlands piled up around his neck like rope quoits on a peg, and had he not kept tossing them back they would have buried him. The heat was incredible, forty in the shade, but Rajiv had only one thing on his mind — mass contact. If enough people — say 200 million — could grope him, victory might be assured. For illiterate voters, manifestos meant little. But to touch the wheatish skin of a Gandhi was something you could tell your grandchildren about. All he had to do was endure a few more weeks of this, and the voters might forgive him. Fuelled by porridge, *jalebis* (sweetmeats), mints and toffees, he was revelling in the close encounters. Every garland was a vote, every handshake another step closer to redemption.

Suman had said I might be hauled out of the car at any moment on security grounds, so when Rajiv resumed his seat I quickly asked him about his arduous campaign schedule. 'One doesn't feel it's taxing,' he replied, choosing his words and modulating his vowels as you'd expect from a product of the Doon School, India's most prestigious boys college in Dehra Dun, also known as the Harrow of the Himalayas. But again, even before he'd finished answering the question, another clutch of supporters appeared who must, at the very least, be waved to. On one occasion he even left the car and walked to a roadside dhaba, sitting with the locals over chai to discuss their priorities and problems.

The constant interruptions, together with my own uncertainty about how long I would be in the car, disrupted my carefully prepared line of questioning. I'd wanted to ask in detail about Rajiv's prescription for solving the sectarian troubles in Punjab and Kashmir, about how he would balance the urgent need for economic reform with his party's traditional commitment to socialism, even about relations with Australia. But in the end I had to rush across my brief like a skater on a melting ice rink. His answers were qualified, not unusual for a politician on the campaign trail, hedged with clauses like 'if I can put it that way' or 'if I remember correctly'. At least he was still embarrassed by the need to obfuscate; a small twinkle would appear in his eye and he'd apologise and say, 'That's politics.' But despite the constraints of time and circumstance, he did come across clearly on one thing: he would resume the course of economic liberalisation he'd begun in the 1980s.

'The old methods of development just are not open any more, because the resources are not available. So new ways will have to be found, which really means that government will have to concentrate in those areas which are really essential ... you can't have the government in every field,' he said.

As the road climbed into Rajaji Forest — still home to the odd wild elephant — *adivasi* (tribal) women gathering wood would straighten their backs, turn towards the sound of the car approaching and flash the most dazzling smiles at the brief intrusion of this glamour into their lives. The simple ritual of democracy was what I remember most about that day, when people briefly were the rajas, and the candidate was a beggar.

At Shampur, Rajiv visited the building that housed the local *panchayat*, or people's representative body, and made a brief speech mocking his nemesis, V.P. Singh. Although Singh had been deposed by another socialist six months earlier, he was still in the running and still the focus of Congress's wrath as a traitor to the party and nation. Singh, he told the crowd, had done more to divide India on the basis of caste and religion than even the British. In the upheaval of the caste riots, long-suppressed religious tensions had also raised their ugly heads, and right-wing Hindu nationalists were vying for upper-caste votes. The previous year, one of their leaders, Lal Krishna Advani, had launched a cross-country yatra aimed at whipping up support for Hindu claims to a Muslim shrine in the pilgrim town of Ayodhya, which they believed had been built on the ruins of an important Hindu temple deliberately destroyed on the orders of a Muslim emperor. That an event that allegedly happened almost 500 years ago could be political dynamite said something about modern India. Advani had stirred tensions wherever he'd gone, with hundreds of people killed before his caravan of death was finally halted by police before it reached Ayodhya.[2]

'On the social tensions side much of the problem will get solved just by a change in government,' Rajiv said, in a tone so mild and reassuring that I found myself nodding in agreement. But in reality, the Congress, led by the Nehru–Gandhi family, had spawned its fair share of violence. Mahatma Gandhi had wanted his party to disband after achieving independence but the allure of power persuaded his colleagues to ignore him. The marriage of Nehru's daughter Indira to the Parsi (Zoroastrian) journalist Feroze Gandhi — no relation to the father of the nation — had given Rajiv's family rights to the most marketable name in the country. Rajiv was not of a mind to question its legitimacy. All that mattered to him was what the Congress stood for, not what it had done. Its opponents, he told me, were 'by their very character, provoking these disturbances, in some instances deliberately. But even where it's not deliberate, it happens because of the character of the government.'

The road kept rising, crossing bridges over dry creek beds where cattle grazed before the annual deluge of Himalayan snowmelt. The car seemed to be slowing and, when Rajiv asked why, the driver pointed at more supporters lining the route ahead.

'*Log*,' he said.

People. The people who would decide his destiny.

We had reached the outskirts of Rishikesh, where the mountains close in on the road. The motorcycle outriders who had gone ahead of us now fell back and, as the car came to a halt, the door beside me opened and the familiar bearded face of Suman Dubey appeared. The end of our time together had come and, without taking his leave, Rajiv plunged back into the crowds.

★ ★ ★

A few weeks later I decided to throw a party in New Delhi. It had been a good year workwise — not so good for India. The world's media had flown in for the first day of voting in the elections, and it was my birthday, so all friends and colleagues were invited. The previous day I had watched Rajiv cast his ballot, accompanied by his wife, Sonia, and his daughter, Priyanka, a stunning young woman whom I would have liked to invite to my party had not courage failed me. They were a handsome family.

That night, as Delhi's dauntless and desperate crowded into my downstairs apartment, there were journalistic triumphs to toast, and girls to chase, and a feeling that somehow I had survived and made a mark in India, if not on India. The music was loud, the conversation frivolous and the party was in full swing when the phone rang. This particular call, however, was different. It was a subeditor at head office, calling from Sydney, wanting another story on the election. I thought I'd covered it adequately, and said so, but according to the caller there had been a fresh development so astonishing that I was convinced she was playing a birthday prank. Reluctantly, I agreed to go upstairs to my office and check the report. Climbing the stairs I had to steady myself, having had quite a few drinks, and when I reached the bank of newsagency teleprinter machines just inside the door to the office, I took a second or two to focus on the copy:

FLASH
RAJIV GANDHI ASSASINATED.
UNI WS SR CG AKK2315
DELHI 23:17
NNNN

Three words — two of them the name of the man I'd travelled with just a few weeks earlier, the other misspelt and written in haste. The brief sentence included none of the usual disclaimers that journalists use to distance themselves from their sources, no 'reportedly' or 'allegedly'. It said he was dead, murdered, and suddenly I noticed that my heart was beating faster with a kind of fear and disbelief that I had never felt before.

It was Big Fear, the kind that makes you feel very small. There was not even a hint of the excitement that can mark a reporter's reaction to even the most terrible news. I so wanted it *not* to be true. Perhaps it was simply because I'd met him, been charmed by him to a degree, or because of the brutal symmetry of India's political violence. Mahatma Gandhi had fallen to an assassin just months after leading the nation to freedom. Then Indira Gandhi; now her son. What kind of country was it that could bear so much violence?

Looking at the second teleprinter, sourced from a different agency, I hoped to see some hint of contradiction, but there was none, only the added note that the assassination had happened in the southern state of Tamil Nadu, and the assassin was thought to have been a Tamil.

It was past 11 p.m. and Delhi was cloaked in darkness. I had a houseful of guests, many of them foreigners on their first visit to India, and a staff comprised mostly of Tamils. When a Gandhi dies, nobody is safe. Suspended in a surreal state somewhere between disbelief and shock, I walked downstairs and told everyone that the party was over.

Rajiv's final journey had taken him to India's southern state of Tamil Nadu. He'd flown to Madras, then driven to the small town of Sriperumbudur, 40 kilometres to the southwest, an hour late for a night rally in support of a local candidate. Until that night the town had been known only as the birthplace of an influential Hindu philosopher, Ramanuja, born around AD 1000, who had argued that far from being an illusion, as the Vedas taught, the physical world was an actual manifestation of God.

Ten thousand people were on the steamy maidan, waiting to see India's leading political celebrity. Leaving his car, Rajiv had walked past huge, luridly coloured cutouts of himself towards an elevated dais constructed of timber and bamboo, stopping to chat and be garlanded by supporters. It was a ritual he'd performed hundreds of times during the three-week campaign and fireworks burst in celebration of his arrival. Twenty metres from the stage, he had paused to hear a schoolgirl in plaits read a poem she'd composed in his honour, and when she was done, he had leant towards a bespectacled woman in a green and orange *salwar kameez* holding a garland of flowers. Bending to touch his feet in respect, the dark-skinned woman flicked a switch wired to her leg, triggering a powerful explosion.

'Suddenly it looked like crackers were being burst where Rajiv was,' Suman Dubey would later recall, having been following his friend at a distance of only 30 metres or so when the bomb exploded. 'When I turned, I saw people falling apart in slow motion ... I rushed to the dais. I was looking for white, as Rajiv wears white. Most of what I saw was black, charred stuff.'[3]

The suicide bomber had detonated a charge of plastic explosives embedded with nuts and bolts strapped to her body, killing seventeen people and injuring fifty others standing within a 20-metre radius. As dazed survivors staggered around in shock, someone cried, '*Thalaivar enge?*' (Where is the leader?) They found one of his bodyguards, Pradip Gupta, still alive among the mangled bodies, but he died from his injuries the moment someone spoke to him. Lying across his body was another corpse; face down in the bloody mud, identifiable by the imported running shoes and a bald patch on the back of the head. It was Rajiv. When they turned him over, they saw that most of his face was missing.

The mortal remains of India's Prince Charming were loaded into a police van, into which Suman also climbed to escort the body back to Madras, shattered and slumped beside his old friend. The massive explosion had ripped through Rajiv's brain and intestines with devastating force yet had barely damaged the bamboo crowd-control barriers that still stood on the killing field. Only one of the people who died that night, a young Tamil woman from neighbouring Sri Lanka, was never positively identified. Her body had been completely dismembered, and wires, springs and a battery were found embedded in her torso. Her head, with facial features still perfectly intact, was found 16 metres away. Her name — probably an alias — was Dhanu, derived from the Sanskrit word for bow, the preferred weapon of war among the ancient Hindus.[4] Although there were 300 police on duty at the venue that night, no one had frisked her.

It would be several days before police could determine the motive for the murder. Rajiv had been killed by a Hindu in an act of instant, yet premeditated, *karma*. She had been sent by the Liberation Tigers of Tamil Eelam (LTTE) as an act of revenge for Rajiv's decision four years earlier to militarily intervene in Sri Lanka's civil war, and the humiliating circumstances in which their leader, Velupillai Prabhakaran, had been held in New Delhi in order to secure his agreement to the mission. Soon after returning to the island in 1987, Prabhakaran had declared war on the Indian Peace Keeping Force, giving them a bloody nose. Now he had given Rajiv much more than that. For his trouble, Prabhakaran and the LTTE would be branded as a terrorist organisation by the United States and other countries around the world. They fought on alone against what they saw as oppression at the hands of the island's Sinhalese Buddhist majority. Rajiv's mother, Indira, had secretly armed the LTTE during her term in office, ensuring that India would have a say in the outcome of the island's conflict. Now they had killed her son.

Like Kalaratri, the Hindu goddess of time who destroys the world at the end of each age, the assassin was dark-skinned and blood-spattered. And like the assassins both of Mahatma and Indira Gandhi, she had bowed respectfully before her quarry before murdering him. The crows feasted on her handiwork the following morning.

★ ★ ★

When I'd left Rajiv on the outskirts of Rishikesh thirteen years before, he'd had nineteen days to live. He'd spent it on the road, chasing a dream. Now, standing on the road where I'd left him, I paid off the driver, Ram Chandra. Hari Lal and I walked past the roadside stalls bulging with lychees and peaches, plums and pomegranates. Then, we strolled down to the river, which remained as nature had made it, shallow rapids rippling over a wide gravel bed. On the drive from Haridwar, I'd spoken to Hari about that first year in India, how some things had never left me, some of them painful. On the drive from Haridwar he had been patient as I'd struggled to recognise various landmarks, hopping in and out of the car with me to ask locals whether they remembered the day when Rajiv had passed through. I'm not sure he understood my need for a companion on the journey. But he must have sensed my feelings because standing beside the river he told me something deeply personal; something I have never forgotten. He told me how he prayed.

'When I pray,' said Hari Lal, 'I take the names of all ten of the Sikh gurus, and all ten of the Hindu incarnations of Vishnu. I take the names of the Lord Jesus and Mother Mary, and the Prophet Mohammed. I take the names of my five brothers and my sister, and the names of all their husbands and wives and children, and of course, my own wife and children's names. There must be eighty people whose names I mention when I pray, that's in addition to the names of the gods. There are so many people and gods in my prayers that I have to count them off on my fingertips. When I've named all of them, I ask God to give them health, wealth and happiness, and to all their relatives also.

'Every day, morning and night, I say these prayers. If any of my friends is in trouble, I ask, "Please God, help them." If I know anybody who needs work, or anyone who is sick, I ask, "Dear God, please give them a job, please make them well again." And you would be surprised how often my prayers are answered. So, my friend, if you want something, either for yourself or for others, with no harm or hurt to anybody, you should ask God's help. Maybe he will be too busy to assist you on every occasion, but if you ask all the gods, one of them might have time. When Mohammed-sahib came, when Rama came, when Jesus came, they all came with the same purpose — to help people find the right path. Remember the truths that all these gods gave us, but don't just focus on gods. Be kind to people. Some of my students have been quite big people, important people, but they have been very considerate to me, very kind to me. You respect those people. You love those people. You never know about the future. In Delhi, crossing the road, you might die one day by accident, or a sickness might befall you. Nobody is immune. So while you're here, be kind to your relatives and friends. It's no use crying about people when they're gone.'

Then Hari Lal walked to the bus station and took the next bus to Dehra Dun.

Back to the past on the road to Rishikesh, my journey to India's future had begun.

3

The Raja Remembers

The object of our public life is to serve the visible god, that is, the poor.
Gandhi[1]

'It was like everything had come to a stop,' Suman recalled, his sad, sensitive eyes locked onto a tea cup as he returned it to its saucer. 'It must be a manifestation of shock. Everything came to a standstill at that particular moment.'

Back in New Delhi after my visit to Rishikesh, I had gravitated towards him the way a lost dog finds its way home. No one understood better the peculiar aura of hope and tragedy of that long-gone summer of 1991, thirteen years before, the consequences both personal and political, than Suman Dubey. After Rajiv's assassination, he had gone back to journalism, and was now working on the management side for Dow Jones out of a new building designed to be in keeping with the old mansions along Sikandra Road. It was a sunny kind of place with banks of computer screens, light pine furniture and good phone lines; the kind of office you could find everywhere in Delhi these days, unlike when I first lived there. The road outside was named after Alexander the Great, the Macedonian general who spent eighteen months in India after crossing the Beas River in 326 BC. Alexander never achieved his dream of seeing the Ganga. He lost his beloved horse Bucephalus in battle and, according to some historians, after abandoning his efforts to conquer India died of wounds he received there. Judging by Dow Jones's confident corporate interiors, the company had no fear of tragic history. The *chowkidar* who buzzed me through the glass and aluminium doors wore the uniform of a global security company. As I waited in reception flipping through a magazine, I overheard Suman's secretary telling New York about problems she was having finding accommodation for one of the company's employees about to be posted to New Delhi. The new arrival was a Singaporean, surely an inoffensive nationality, but Delhi's landlords had a problem with her: she was Indian by origin.

'We've told them she's coming alone. But they think that the moment she finds accommodation the husband and family will descend on the place and they won't be able to get them out. It's the mentality of Indian landlords. Like, reverse racism,' the secretary said. Where else would outsiders be more trusted than locals, I wondered.

In an office decorated with small mementos of friends and family — a picture of a favourite mutt took pride of place on Suman's computer screen — Rajiv's old friend welcomed me warmly. He'd lost a little weight and his grizzled silver beard drooped like an old lion's mane, more unruly than I remembered. But his voice retained a beautiful timbre that was wasted in print media, and his self-deprecating, economical manner reminded me a lot of Rajiv. They had both attended the Doon School, and were at Cambridge together where Rajiv had met Sonia, the daughter of an Italian building contractor, from the town of Orbassano, near Turin. Suman was there at their wedding, had eaten more meals prepared by Sonia than he could remember, and the Gandhi children Rahul and Priyanka used to attend his own children's birthday parties before high school scattered them. Their friendship had endured and grown, but as Suman often hastened to point out to me, 'with a family like the Gandhis, or the Kennedys, for example, I don't think anyone from outside can ever really be like "family"'.

In the summer of 1991 India had been transfixed by horror. All the newspapers published uncensored photographs of the unseemly carnage at Sriperumbudur, as well as images taken moments before the blast, recovered from the camera of a local photographer who'd unwittingly been engaged to document the attack for LTTE training purposes, and who had also died in the explosion. The schoolgirl in plaits reading poetry to the Congress leader in the presence of her proud mother had thus been immortalised, as had been the murderess and her co-conspirators lurking ominously on the periphery. Indian philosophy teaches that the things we perceive as real are actually *maya*, an illusion concealing the reality that lies behind appearances. The photos taken that dark night in Tamil Nadu seemed to confirm it.

Suman exhaled deeply from a wellspring of grief that seemed inexhaustible. 'When I look back on it,' he said, shaking his head sadly, 'there's a tremendous air of unreality about what I saw. A *tremendous* air of unreality ... But obviously it happened.'

Long-lost summers are always hotter. Maybe I'd just acclimatised, but Suman too remembered the inferno, and the insane schedule the entourage maintained, more physically demanding than the mountain-climbing he did for recreation. Having scaled the endless crowds, and the lack of sleep which was the worst torture, he and Rajiv had believed they would reach the summit, a second term for the former prime minister. Next thing he knew he was slumped beside a mangled body in a wooden crate at Meenambakkam airport in Madras. Had he not been walking a short distance behind the candidate when the bomb exploded, he might well have had a box of his own. He waited at the airport until Rajiv's wife and daughter arrived the following morning, and then took the unspeakable flight back to Delhi with them, Sonia shattered and inconsolable, Priyanka composed and stoic. No one could count their losses.

'This is the land of Gandhi and Gautama Buddha, and the pacifist religion that Hinduism is,' said Suman, smiling that slightly squeezed smile one associates with a certain class of Englishman. 'But the fact that Gandhi preached non-violence, and succeeded in his own way in getting the British to leave doesn't mean that we've not been a violent society. We've been a nation of caste prejudice, and from prejudice to violence is a short step.'

Through India's long history of invasions and fighting, and the competition for land and resources stretching back to Aryan times, power derived from the sword and the bow. Long before it was ever a country, India had been colonised and, in the process, enlightened and brutalised, enriched and impoverished. In the dying decades of Muslim rule, and under the British, it became poorer, and by the time freedom came was rich principally in one thing: people. More people, fewer resources. Fewer resources, more intense competition. The struggle was endless. Social churning, Indians call it.

But the long view obscured the individual choices that are the milestones of fate. Had Rajiv chosen not to drink from the poisoned chalice of politics, or drifted perilously close to the shoals of corruption, he'd probably still be alive. His decision to send the army to Sri Lanka had been touted as a moral act protecting the island's Tamil minority, but was seen by both sides of the conflict there as an overbearing flex of Indian military muscle. Similarly, after the fall of V.P. Singh, Rajiv had backed a new minority government, only to withdraw his support on a pretext a few months later when he judged his re-election prospects to be optimised. Having wrecked the government, he campaigned on the theme that only Congress could provide stability. Had he been more patient, and bided his time, the crowd-surfing campaign — during which he had ignored advice from the security services to limit his exposure to the risk of assassination — might not have been necessary. To Suman, my speculations probably seemed like wisdom after the event. He listened politely, just a hint of a raised eyebrow, waiting for me to finish before responding.

'There were regrettable decisions. I felt that at the time,' he conceded. 'But it's not that Rajiv *ignored* security. It's that he was not *given* security.'

In every tragedy there must be a villain, real or imagined. In the hours after the assassination, Congress mobs chanted the name of V.P. Singh and burnt him in effigy. It was Singh's claims about the Bofors scandal that had cost Rajiv the prime ministership in 1989. Then, having defeated him and in an alleged act of pettiness, Singh had downgraded Rajiv's security cover, despite at least two previous plots to harm the former prime minister.

Suman was a man who liked to keep control of his emotions, especially negative ones. But for an instant, a flash of disdain crossed his usually equable features.

'I think V.P. Singh was basically promoting himself,' he said, striving to suppress what looked very much like anger. 'He was a betrayer.'

★ ★ ★

It is not possible to live justly in an unjust society, unless of course you renounce it. Since the time of the Buddha, India has confronted well-meaning humanists with a dilemma: unless you give away everything you own, you are still better off than most people. It is impossible to be at once moral and comfortable. If you enjoy even a modicum of prosperity and security, it means you occupy a privileged place in a monstrous hierarchy. That man there lying on the pavement is somebody's son, husband, brother, father. You walk right by him. The same dilemma exists in all societies to an extent — we sleep soundly while others suffer — but in India, the co-existence of wealth and poverty, of glamour and squalor, education and illiteracy is colossal. Imagine being a passenger on a plane that is falling out of the sky when you discover that there simply aren't enough parachutes to go around. It's a high-stakes grabbing game in which most people are losers.

Indian society reserves its highest honours for the renunciates, those who embrace *tyag*, or sacrifice. It counts among its greatest scoundrels, politicians; the more self-righteous, the more debased. Perversely, hypocrisy on a massive scale also appeals to the Indian psyche, for much the same reasons that the dance and drama spectacles of the Bollywood cinema appeal: it's all a damn good show. The politician who jumps ship from his party and principles more frequently than he changes his underwear is acclaimed as a genius; the leader who archly renounces power just before it unavoidably slips from his grasp is said to have superb timing. Lust for power and a ruthless determination to hold onto it are seen as normal, partly because they reflect the desperation of the vast majority. Everyone except mahatmas (great souls) imagine that they would like to rule India, despite ample evidence that the job destroys all who touch it.

It had been more than a decade since Vishwanath Pratap Singh had enjoyed the limelight — and infamy — that he once enjoyed in Indian public life. No sooner had his star risen than it exploded. In one, tumultuous year the political career that had taken a lifetime to build was ruined, as his coalition collapsed around him.

Born in 1931, he'd been adopted at the age of five into one of India's oldest royal families. The rajas of Manda were high-caste Thakurs who'd been in the business of power for at least a thousand years, with extensive landholdings near Allahabad on the Ganga. Vishwanath's early childhood was marred by the death of his adoptive mother and his adoptive father's incurable tuberculosis, which meant that the two could not spend more than five minutes together due to fear of contagion. Starved of normal parental attention and love, the young prince drifted towards his custodians. But with turnover among the staff quite high, he became withdrawn and developed an interest in painting and writing.

At the age of eleven, when the raja died, he inherited the lands and royal obligations of the fortieth Raja of Manda. On his eighteenth birthday he assumed the title but a title was all it was. In the new democracy, rajas had no more rights than commoners, apart from a modest privy purse, or pension. In the case of V.P. Singh, it was no great hardship. Swept up in the Gandhian spirit of the times, he donated 75 hectares of his newly inherited lands near the village of Pasna in Uttar Pradesh to lower caste labourers. It was the sort of populist gesture that could put a former royal in the good books of the new ruling family of India, the Nehrus, and for V.P. Singh it led to a political career in the Congress Party.

In 1969, Indira Gandhi moved to strip the former maharajas of their privy purses. Two years later, V.P. Singh was elected on a Congress ticket to the parliament, and began a rapid rise as chief minister of UP, followed by several senior ministries in Indira and Rajiv's governments. When, in 1987, he fell out with them, the family again provided him a political opportunity. At the subsequent polls in 1989, he ran with the slogan 'In every alley they are shouting that Rajiv is a thief', sending the Congress to its worst-ever election defeat. This erstwhile raja with a social conscience became the first former royal to lead independent India.

Nothing that happened in India in the 1990s would have been possible without the enigmatic, controversial Vishwanath Pratap Singh. The left had run out of answers and the Congress had run out of leaders. With the backing of the Supreme Court, job quotas were eventually implemented by his successors. In the vacuum created by his defeat and Rajiv's murder, a new politics would emerge based on caste and religion, rather than the secular socialism of Gandhi and Nehru's time.

A hospital for the rich is an unlikely place to find a messiah of the poor, but when I'd called the raja's private secretary seeking an appointment, he had directed me to a private room at New Delhi's Apollo Hospital, where three times a week Singh was undergoing dialysis for malfunctioning kidneys.

The road to India's most exclusive hospital passes squatter camps with television antennae sprouting from makeshift roofs. Children play on swings made from car tyre inner-tubes while sleek black buffalo float on ponds under billboards for 'New Lifebuoy' soap. In the midst of it all rises a gleaming monument to modern medicine and money, a five-star facility named after a god, but not an Indian one. Apollo Hospital is a luxurious hotel in which all the guests are ill. Towering doormen in cummerbunds, stacked turbans, and uniforms festooned with braid, bow deeply before the affluent and important who throng its grand portals. Memsahibs in Prada and Chanel crowd its cavernous pale apricot central hall, where white-coated doctors with stethoscopes move purposefully back and forth like extras on a movie set. The din resembles that of a railway platform where porters convey bandaged, plastered and intravenously fed passengers to and from private suites. Indian newspapers revel in gruesome tales of forgetful surgeons who occasionally leave entire cutlery services sewn up inside their patients. But if such things have ever happened at Apollo, then the media must have overlooked them. It is, quite simply, a pleasure to be unwell there. Middle-class Indians no longer travel to Varanasi to die; they come to Apollo to live.

Entering the West Wing, I took the lift to an upper floor where Vishwanath Pratap Singh, once briefly the ruler of all he surveyed, lay prostrate. Over a decade since his prime ministership, the mere mention of his name could still provoke some middle-class Indians to froth and curse. But generally people accepted that politicians, like gods, played by different rules, and the minuscule number of *netas* (leaders) hauled up before the courts on corruption charges seemed to suggest that it was true. When a lower caste Indian falls ill, they usually die in abject poverty; when a political messiah of the lower castes sickens, they get five-star life-support. Ultimately, however, they are both mortal, as the dialysis machine that was keeping V.P. Singh alive testified.

'This damn machine is part of my life now,' he joshed, welcoming me to his bedside. 'It's my hobby.' Propped up in his bed with a towel draped around his neck, he was engaged in some good-natured bantering with a doctor who was conducting a routine blood-pressure test.

'Prime ministers may be powerful, but our lives are in doctors' hands. So it must be doctors only who have higher powers, isn't it?' he said, twisting his hand like a fruit picker, in answer to his rhetorical question. With a pair of half-frame eyeglasses perched mischievously low on his nose, he smiled and waggled his head approvingly, as the doctor pumped up the arm band. The physician was either genuinely charmed, or intent on looking so.

'One-twenty over seventy,' he announced with theatrical solemnity.

'*Accha, theek hai*,' clucked V.P. Singh, satisfied, and then turning to me with his snaggle-toothed grin added, 'Now. Tell me,' the Indian version of 'You were saying?' or 'Next question'.

I wanted to know whether he regretted playing the caste card. Had the battle for social justice compromised good administration and economic growth? Had he, as many observers claimed, used caste as a ruthless ploy simply to checkmate other political players?

Lying in his hospital bed, the former prime minister folded his hands over his chest and looked down his nose at me, as if I should know better.

'Now you see, reservation is nothing new in Indian society. The caste system meant reservations for various sections for thousands of years. Brahmins got the education, Kshatriyas got the ruling positions, Vaishyas monopolised business, and Shudras had the manual jobs. What is all that other than reservation?'

It was the first time I'd heard of job quotas being justified by reference to Vedic Hinduism. Even so, it wasn't a bad line, and Mr Singh had more contemporary authorities to quote as well.

'The first reservations for the Scheduled Castes and the Backward Classes were introduced by Nehru and the Congress. Later on, a government formed by the left and Hindu nationalist elements introduced the Mandal Commission, which recommended more reservations. Within a month of coming to power, I declared our intention to implement the report. There was nothing like this talk of using it to acquire a new political base, or checkmating of other leaders. All that kind of talk is nonsense. I implemented it and the Supreme Court endorsed my action, and now the Congress talks of extending the system to the private sector. So who all is criticising? Nothing new happened during my time.'

As the violent reaction to the policy had spread, and students had been shot by police or took the extreme step of self-immolating, V.P. Singh had remained serene, seeming to his critics to be revelling in the disorder he'd unleashed. As a former student politician himself, he could have reached out and called a moratorium to settle things down before moving to the negotiating table. He had sons of his own. Why had he sat like Buddha contemplating the anarchy?

'I issued orders to the police that no bullets should be issued to those on duty so there would be no firing. Afterwards, it did happen because certain orders were passed at the Home Ministry without my knowledge. Then I told them, "Unless the students attack your life, don't fire back. Let them destroy as much property as they want. Let it be, because they are children." I went on TV and said, "Children, even if you have to fight me, live. Why do you have to commit suicide?" I know what it means, because I lost my brother and my nephew in an unnatural death, killed by *dacoits* [outlaws]. I know what a family suffers.'

One of the students who had tried and failed to self-immolate, Rajiv Goswami, had only recently died, having spent fourteen years coping with the legacy of his injuries. How did V.P. feel about that, I wondered.

'That was very tragic, very tragic. I worked with his mother too, you know. Both of them assassinated,' he said.

Goswami assassinated? And his mother? I realised that he'd confused Rajiv Goswami with Rajiv Gandhi. 'Some people blame you for his death as well,' I said. 'They blame you for reducing his security cover.'

The raja grimaced and raised his finger disapprovingly.

'You see, during my tenure he went about half a dozen times to Tamil Nadu, and came back safely. He went all over India. And I put the top people of the intelligence, the RAW [Research and Analysis Wing], the IB [Intelligence Bureau] and some of the officers who were appointed by Rajiv himself, they were in place. I asked the Home Ministry to provide full cover to him. But an act of parliament which Rajiv himself had passed denied SPG [Special Protection Group] cover to ex-prime ministers. It was a law that was made by him! I gave cover to him for three months, then the SPG took objection. They said we will be prosecuted if something happens. So I said, "All right, in the present circumstances give the best cover." And all the intelligence people sat down and gave a scheme which worked very well. After I demitted office, the government of Chandrashekhar that replaced mine was virtually a Congress-controlled government. If they wanted changes, the Congress could have had them then. Obviously they were satisfied with it, now in hindsight they use it.'

Forced out of office, Rajiv had had to adjust to life as a mere mortal. He'd died under a cloud of suspicion, and the rainmaker was V.P. Singh. But why hadn't the raja produced the evidence as promised? Where was the list of bank accounts containing the Bofors loot that Singh claimed to possess?

'I never said personally that Rajiv Gandhi has taken money,' said Singh with breathtaking panache, given the 'Rajiv is a thief' slogan that won him the election. 'I said illegal money has been transferred, and it must be investigated. So my stand even now has been vindicated. Swiss courts are still investigating, they realise that illegal monies have been given. I said I had an account number into which illegal monies were paid, and illegal money was paid into that account. Journalists had given me copies of the actual bank documents. But I never said Rajiv has taken money.'

For a man in failing health, V.P. Singh still had a formidable political immune system. When I asked again about Rajiv Goswami he said the young man's self-immolation attempt was a stunt aimed at winning student representative council elections. When I asked what he considered to be his most lasting achievement, he answered without hesitation, 'Mandal!'

'That was the most powerful thing. It changed the political centre of gravity, because what is a political revolution if not a shift of the power centre? From the social strata that used to enjoy power, the power shifted to those sections which did not have a share, and that's what a political revolution is.'

Picking up the remote control to lower the room temperature, his face did not look like that of a man who'd just claimed to have led a revolution. He was smoothing the sheets, almost pouting. At the peak of his power, V.P. Singh had been called a genius at managing contradictions, now he merely contradicted himself. First he'd said job quotas were nothing new; now, they were a revolution. Then, just as suddenly, he admitted to having reservations about reservations.

'The vision we had was that all the deprived sections should come together, but it has *degenerated* into the dynamics of caste politics, and that has led to conflict,' he said. 'I tell people, "For five years you are a farmer. But on voting day, you are your caste! If your caste fellow is the candidate, even if he is a villain, you will vote for him. But if the candidate is not of your caste, he may be Buddha but he will not get your vote. You have made your own development irrelevant by this caste politics!"'

Hypocrisy aside, it was a valid point. Apart from opposing Untouchability, Mahatma Gandhi had shied away from caste wars because he needed Hindu unity to oust the British. It was only with the coming of democracy that modern politicians like V.P. Singh discovered the electoral potential of caste politics. Yet not being low caste themselves, they handled the issue with a feudal lack of concern for its impact on the lower orders, like spoilt children playing with dispensable toys. Before Singh's reign, India had chipped away gradually at caste injustice. In 1965, Untouchables occupied less than 5 per cent of senior civil service positions. By the early 1990s, it was 20 per cent,[2] roughly proportionate to their numbers overall. But the fiery rhetoric of caste politics tended to polarise rather than manage the issue. 'We are ruled by an upper-caste Hindu raj. Hang V.P. Singh, but give the deprived justice. Otherwise this country will go beyond anyone's management,'[3] the raja had once thundered, and now in parts of the country it is not uncommon for caste relations to resemble civil war. In response, high-caste voters switched their support to the Hindu nationalists, the lower castes rallied in their own defence, and V.P. Singh fell through the cracks, discarded by the voters. Now he wanted to sound statesmanlike about it. 'What we have been suffering is the politics of birth,' he said, making it simple for me.

'Religion — on which the Hindu nationalists harp — is birth. So is caste. So is the Gandhi family. All birth politics! Nobody who was born in this country can be denied, but in the process of removing caste victimisation, don't create new victims. I've never told the lower castes to hate the upper castes. When democracy came, the Dalits used the strength of their numbers. Now, power is coming to them. They have become the engine. They should carry everybody with them.'

Gadflys are always hard to pin down, but the 'betrayer' label that Suman had given Mr Singh didn't quite fit. The raja who became a high-caste Congressman, then a low-caste messiah, was more like a political hitch-hiker looking for his next ride, disowning his inheritance, then his party, and now finally his own revolution. So clever was he that people found it hard to trust him. Did he even trust himself, I wondered?

'People always suspect,' he said, allowing himself a small chuckle. 'Even if you do something very honestly, the press tries to find out a deeper plan. I don't blame them, because you see how our leaders behave.'

Suddenly, the unmistakeable refrain of 'Für Elise' was heard. It seemed to come from the dialysis machine, but then V.P. picked up his mobile phone.

'Hallo? Hallo?' he said, in that slightly panicky tone that still characterised all telephone calls on India's once rickety network. Beside the bed, the glass face of the dialysis machine showed a wheel constantly turning, like a Buddhist *chakra* or the mind of a politician.

'Now. Tell me?' he said again when he got off the phone.

Did he have any regrets, I wondered.

'One big regret,' he said. 'I joined politics. I should have been painting and writing.'

Surely it was in his blood: the dusty, uproarious elections, his name on millions of lips, the high-stakes gamble of public life in India.

'Politics is a sea,' he said, allowing his head to roll back on his pillow. 'Now it's better to stroll along the shore than go sailing. I won't go away, but I won't be in it. I'll enjoy this stroll along the sea. India will survive without V.P. Singh. In spite of all the stresses and strains that a new democracy can be put through — war, emergency, assassination of leaders — we survived it all, and retained our ballot box. In spite of all the ups and downs, we have failed to lose our bounce.'

He'd paid Indian democracy the highest compliment that a politician could think of — it had survived leaders like him.

4

Reflections on a Samadhi

Professional swimmers will find a watery grave.
Gandhi[1]

Leaving the chilled halls of Apollo, hospital of the gods, I was suddenly engulfed by a tidal wave of hot, thick, spicy air. Half the patients, I realised, were only there for the air-conditioning.

Glancing towards the hospital's crowded driveway, I saw Lovely Singh standing defiantly beside his battered black Ambassador with the yellow roof of a taxi. While the other drivers sat with engines running, blasted by frigid air-conditioning in their imported luxury cars, Lovely wiped the brow of his turbaned head with a handkerchief as he waited in the sun. A proud young Sikh, he was working long shifts for a taxi stand in North Delhi, making the money that would transform his engagement to a Punjabi girl into a marriage.

A country boy himself, he was impatient with everything in the city: Delhi's congested traffic; his turban (wearing an instant hat-like version that needed no tying); his bachelorhood; and with me, insisting that I tell him in advance of the exact duration of my every engagement. The only time he wasted came at the end of my journeys, when instead of telling me the fare, he would gesture blankly and say, 'As you like', which I didn't like at all. I never saw his meter, which remained permanently cloaked by a hand towel.

A languid charm sometimes balanced Lovely's impatience and stubbornness. One day I agreed to his request to visit an emporium where he got a commission. Pleased with this scam, he leant across the taxi's bench seat and smilingly confided, 'You are my lovely customer', earning his nickname. Now, keen to distract attention from my chronic lateness, I climbed back into the car and told him I had just met a former prime minister. But the information raised barely a shrug from shoulders that normally danced to tape-deck *bhangra*, and sighing loudly he guided his old jalopy back along the Ring Road.

The Yamuna River is shallow and turquoise in the Himalayan foothills. She waltzes past the Taj Mahal in Agra, and in Brindavan, Krishna is said to have played on her banks with his beloved milkmaids. In Delhi, as in most towns along its course, the river is heavily polluted, but behind the walled city of the Mughal emperor Shah Jahan, its manicured banks are home to the *samadhis*, or cenotaphs of independent India's leaders, preserved in verdant parklands as national memorials. The samadhis mark the spot where each was cremated and contain no human remains. *Samadhi* is also the Sanskrit word denoting the enlightened soul's final, conscious departure from the body to merge with God in an ocean of love. I asked Lovely to take me there.

On the hottest day I have ever known, the body of Rajiv Gandhi had been brought to Raj Ghat, the King's embankment, like those of his mother Indira and grandfather Nehru, and before them Mahatma Gandhi. For the previous three days it had lain on a bier, draped in the Indian tricolour to hide its horrific injuries, in the lofty entrance hall of Teen Murti Bhavan, the prime minister's residence during Nehru's time, where Rajiv had played as a child and which now was a museum. On the floor beside the bier, dressed in the white cotton sari of a Hindu widow, Sonia Gandhi was weeping. Her flooding grief came in waves, subsiding and then welling up again in impossible quantities from the depths of her soul. In the distance, from beyond the mansion's gates, the wretched voices of her uninvited supporters screeched, 'The murderers of Rajiv — cut them to pieces!' and 'V.P. Singh *hai hai*!' (Down with V.P. Singh!). They were the Congress rent-a-mob, people whose passions were visceral and easily directed, as the mob's passions had been after Indira's death in 1984. Fortunately this time the Congress was not in power; and its street support enjoyed no sanction from the state.

Before the cremation I had dropped by the Raj-period bungalow on Akbar Road that was the Congress Party's headquarters to find the gnomish spokesman Pranab Mukherjee alone in his office. He looked lost, the telephone strangely silent, his thick Bengali accent, which turned decision into 'deshizion', gazette into 'gajette' and government into 'gowerment', no longer played with words. After Indira's death, Pranab had vied for the top job against Rajiv but, like all such pretenders to the throne, was sidelined and forced out of the party. Eventually, seeing the futility of challenging the system, he came back and since then had been a loyal servant of the family.

'Those who want to destabilise and make violence as a cult do these things,' Pranab said, referring to the assassination, and clearing his throat with his trademark retching sound. 'Congress is the biggest stabilising factor in this country, and Rajiv was the most important stabilising element in the party. Mandal [caste] and *mandir* [temple] created the atmosphere of violence. This is the reality. This is the cold fact.'

In the searing heat of May it was difficult to imagine anything being cold — facts or corpses — and the ice blocks brought to stem the decomposition of Rajiv's body kept melting as fast as they could be replaced. The only cold thing in Delhi that summer was the Congress leadership's calculation that public sympathy for the widow would sweep the party to victory when the election process resumed. With no mature heir, and fearing an interregnum, the All India Congress Committee had unanimously elected Sonia as party president, even though she was not a party member. Without a member of the family at the helm, the Congress power brokers believed, the party would collapse under the weight of its own mistakes and internal rivalries.

After the assassination and before the funeral, when Pranab fronted the media to announce Sonia's election, he'd been confronted by unexpectedly tough questioning.

'Has she agreed?' one reporter asked.

'She will be informed in due course,' the spokesman answered officiously.

'How would you respond to the charge that you're having a foreigner to rule?' asked another scribe.

'No queshtion of foreigner,' Pranab fobbed him off. 'She's a wife of, housewife of, Gandhi-Nehru family.'

'Is there any question of her refusing the post?' another voice called.

'No queshtion of her refusing,' said Pranab.

Deep in mourning and insulted by their insensitivity, Sonia *had* declined the position. Masking her feelings, she issued a statement of breathtaking restraint:'I am deeply touched by the trust placed in me by the Congress Working Committee,' it said. 'However the tragedy that has befallen my children and myself does not make it possible for me to accept presidentship of the Congress Party.'

Sonia stayed by Rajiv's body, sobbing into her *dupatta*, or headscarf. It was her third violent bereavement in just over ten years. First, Rajiv's brother, Sanjay, had died in a plane crash in 1980, plunging her husband reluctantly into politics. Then, in October 1984, she had been at home in New Delhi, preparing to bathe, when from the garden she had heard what sounded like firecrackers bursting to celebrate the festival of Diwali, but it was the sound of Sten guns emptying bullets into her mother-in-law. Sonia had cradled the dying Indira on their way to the hospital. Now a nightmarish reprise was unfolding. From Italy her own family urged her to return home, but she told them she'd become too Indian to live there. The Catholic girl from Orbassano, who had once hated Indian clothing and food, was now removing her jewellery, a true Hindu widow commencing forty days of mourning.[2]

On the morning of 23 May 1991 she went to Raj Ghat and chose a site for Rajiv's samadhi, and soon afterwards the labourers arrived to mow the grass and lay the bricks. That day, her only son, twenty-year-old Rahul, had arrived from the United States where he'd been studying, and went directly to Teen Murti Bhavan to join his mother and sister beside the bier.

At two o'clock the following day, Rajiv's corpse was loaded onto a gun carriage and began its final journey, arriving at the cremation platform at 3.30 p.m. Rahul helped India's service chiefs carry the body to the platform where, with the help of Hindu priests, he constructed a pyre of sandalwood logs over the body and doused it with ghee. The painstaking process took hours in the mind-numbing summer sun, and the earth radiated heat. The priests' droning Sanskrit dirge cast a hypnotic spell over the crowd, and rose petals rained from a cloudless sky, a miracle arranged by Indian Air Force helicopters. Then a bugler played the Last Post. Handed a flaming oil torch, Rahul mounted the platform and walked three times around his father's body, then bent low and lit the pyre. The flames were ravenous, leaping high into the air with an elemental force fed by logs and ghee. Standing a short distance away, I watched Rahul, who resembled an Indian Harry Potter, bespectacled and forlorn in white *kurta pajama*, retreat from the blistering heat to cradle his broken mother.

At Raj Ghat, where today's tourists surrender their shoes at a sign that says 'Free Service (At your own risk)', an eternal flame flickers above a polished, black stone platform. Etched in the bunker-like walls are the Mahatma's sayings in Indian languages, including his 'Seven Social Sins' — Politics without Principles, Wealth without Work, Pleasure without Conscience, Knowledge without Character,

Commerce without Morality, Science without Humanity, Worship without Sacrifice. His last words — *Hey Ram* (Oh God!) — grace his black stone samadhi. Rajiv Gandhi's cenotaph — known as Vir Bhumi, or place of the brave — is sculpted in swirling motifs that mimic the flames that consumed his body that day, and an unusual timber walkway, or *parikrama*, surrounds it. As I wandered around what was now a green and landscaped place, a blue turban caught my eye. It was Lovely Singh. Normally content to wait near his car, he had followed me onto the memorial grounds, an oddly cold expression in his eyes.

'Why would you come here?' — his face said it all — and I knew instinctively that he was thinking about 1984, and Rajiv's failure to save the Sikhs. 'There are always tremors when a great tree falls,' Rajiv had said later, seeming to justify the killings, after his party's goons had roamed the streets crying, 'Blood for blood.' The Sikh victims are not commemorated by any memorial. Yet acres in New Delhi are devoted to the memory of Rajiv Gandhi.

In May of 1991, with the embers of Rajiv's funeral pyre still warm, a violent electrical storm lashed the capital, and police guarding the cremation site scrambled to cover the ashes with sheets of tin to prevent them from being blown away. At dawn the following day, Rajiv's son returned to the site, and assisted by the priests, performed the final rituals. In intermittent rain and wind gusts — most unusual in May — they swept the ashes into thirty urns that were transported to Teen Murti Bhavan, where the people of Delhi paid their last respects. On the following day, a special train departed from New Delhi railway station headed for Prayag, at the *sangam*, or confluence, of the Yamuna and Ganges rivers near the city of Allahabad. On board were members of the Gandhi family and their friends, Congress Party leaders, and one of the urns containing Rajiv's remains. The train travelled through the night, stopping at many stations, where police tried to hold back the crowds who came to say farewell.

'Sonia said, "Let them come,"' Suman recalled when I went to see him so many years later. 'The family members were shattered, but you know, they're very strong people, very tough. They know duty, and this is a duty. To grieve in the public eye is very hard, but they did it. And they didn't sleep on the train. I went and dozed off for an hour, but for them it was unrelenting.'

By entering politics, Rajiv had answered the call of his *dharma*, Hinduism's natural law of individual conscience and social responsibility. Right and wrong are not absolute, but depend on the situation and the person confronting it. Dharma challenges believers not with a predestined fate, but a fateful choice. Get it right, and you achieve salvation. Get it wrong and you return to earth to try again. Hinduism has no Hell. Rajiv had made his choice, and paid the price. What choice would Rahul make, I wondered.

At Prayag, the family joined a small armada of boats which carried them to the sangam, where Rajiv Gandhi's ashes and, perhaps, his legacy were committed to the river.

Part Two

Siege of the Red Fort   The Blood-Dimmed Tide
Breakfast at Civil Lines   An Indian Wedding

5

Siege of the Red Fort

Hindus and Muslims of India are not two nations.
                                                                Gandhi[1]

The walled city of Shahjahanabad, now known as Old Delhi, is a sanctuary so teeming with life that it feels like a work of nature. When I first lived in New Delhi, I would cross town and pass through its gates with a childlike sense of wonder. Now, years later, Lovely Singh had driven the short distance from Raj Ghat, and eager as always to moonlight with other customers, insisted on being told exactly how long I would stay. Informed that I might be a decade, he gave me his 'cell phone' number and told me to call when I needed him.

In the seventeenth century, when the city with its fourteen gates was constructed as the new capital of the Mughal emperor Shah Jahan, creator of the Taj Mahal, Shahjahanabad was the last word in technology and style. The waters of the Yamuna were diverted to fill its moat and the channel that ran down the centre of the richest bazaar in all India. Off its main street, Chandni Chowk, ran a capillary system of *galis*, passages barely wide enough for two people to pass one another. The channel is gone now, but the walled city remains a living link to a time when India enjoyed prosperity while England was mired in civil war. The traders of Dilli, as the old city is known to its stalwarts, still cluster together in guilds to conduct their ceaseless commerce, strength in numbers producing lanes in which all the shops sell similar things, jewellery in one gali, bolts of cotton or car parts in the next. In the confined spaces, the *tring* of bicycle bells is more common than the blare of car horns, and steam and smoke define the slanting rays of sunlight that penetrate this realm. In a dusty bric-a-brac store you might find an antique Leica or Rolex, while a few doors down huge vats of goat curry will be simmering towards the same tenderness appreciated by the Mughal emperors. Penetrating the crenellated defensive walls designed to protect all things fine from invaders, I would spend hours happily lost there, exploring the spice and silver markets, and occasionally stumbling into private courtyards where I might find a long-horned bull turning an old stone mill. Here, people of all of India's major faiths lived and worked side by side, the *azan* and the temple bells both echoing through the same galis.

Every few years, communal trouble in some far-off part of India would spread to the walled city. The police, mainly Hindus, would impose a day curfew, shutting down businesses and confining people to their homes. Packs of mongrel dogs would roam the deserted galis, while in Muslim neighbourhoods the tension between police and residents suggested that Partition was a state of mind, not some distant tragedy. After a day or two, the curfew would be relaxed briefly, a few brave traders would raise their shutters and householders emerge to buy food and essential supplies, and gradually life in the old city would regain its normal bustle.

Emerging back onto Chandni Chowk, I'd retrace my steps to the Lal Qila, or Red Fort, a walled palace within the walled city, where the fabled Peacock Throne once stood. It was carted off by the eighteenth century Persian raider Nadir Shah, who sacked and razed the city before departing. The British garrisoned their troops at the Red Fort after narrowly surviving the Indian Rebellion of 1857, and the leaders of independent India scale its ramparts every year to deliver their annual address on the state of the Indian Union.

On 15 August 1947, the day a new democracy was born in the subcontinent, Nehru unfurled a new flag from the barbican, in the process releasing a shower of rose petals. Ever since, Indian prime ministers have repeated the ritual, after explaining themselves to their billion bosses. The ceremony concludes with the release of gas-filled balloons and pigeons, which fly high into the monsoon sky watched by the children of the capital.

In the aftermath of Rajiv Gandhi's assassination and his widow's rejection of the leadership in 1991, the Congress Party narrowly won the postponed election and resigned itself to finding a leader from outside its First Family. The post fell to a crusty veteran from India's south, Pamulaparthi Venkata Narasimha Rao, who was sworn in as prime minister a few days before his seventieth birthday. Narasimha Rao, it was said, could speak ten languages — and prevaricate in all of them — and had undergone a surgical procedure feared by all politicians, the charisma bypass.[2] He had no political base, nor even a seat in parliament, having decided just before Rajiv's death to retire from politics. In the court of the dynastic Congress, no second-run leader could ever grow tall. But the Gandhi family interregnum meant that the new stop-gap leader — chosen only because the rival ambitions of the real power brokers cancelled each other out — would have to soldier on.

When news spread that Rao would get the job, I decided to try my luck by showing up at his residence to meet him. While requests for formal interviews could be tied up for years in bureaucracy, the *darshan* culture in which politicians, like gods, are expected to show themselves frequently to their followers worked in my favour. Arriving at his bungalow, I found Mr Rao seated in his living room, a jowly, irascible man who refused to answer any questions beginning with the word 'if', and who once told an interviewer that in India 'the past has a dominant role to play'.[3] Asked on another occasion to explain his apparent indecisiveness, he replied, 'Any decision for which the time is not right or ripe, needs a clear-cut decision of non-taking, either express or silent.'[4]

Despite his crotchety character and classical instincts, Rao would prove to be a godsend for India in at least one respect. Unlikely to survive for long, and with no particular political constituency to serve, he was uniquely placed to dismantle rather than merely tinker with the Licence Raj. In one of his first moves as prime minister, he appointed a respected Sikh economist, Dr Manmohan Singh, as his finance minister. Singh's early budgets promised an end to the stifling restrictions that suffocated economic activity. He allowed the value of the rupee to fall, making exports cheaper and imports dearer, scrapped industrial licensing and liberalised the financial sector. Foreign investors were permitted to take a larger stake in Indian companies, and when private cable TV operators began wiring Indian cities in contravention of the government monopoly on broadcasting, Rao turned a blind eye. Investment rose exponentially, inflation declined and foreign reserves recovered to US$5 billion at first, then went higher. The unlikely partnership of Rao and Singh achieved something the Gandhi family could never have managed — a complete break with the shibboleths of the past. Mr Rao was too old to worry about getting re-elected and too self-effacing for a personality cult or a Raj Ghat samadhi.

Just over a year in the job, Mr Rao was scheduled to report on progress and outline his vision for the future from the ramparts of the Red Fort. It had taken me two days of grovelling and hectoring to obtain a pass for the ceremony, which advised that guests must be seated by 6.45 a.m. sharp. Kites in the colours of India's flag dotted the dawn sky that morning, as khaki-clad policemen self-importantly directed traffic with shrill blasts of their whistles, and Sten-gun wielding paramilitaries stood guard at 20-metre intervals along the roads. At the fort, boardwalks provided paths across lawns soggy with recent rains, and a scratchy public address system fluttered and trilled with the voice of an Indian diva singing patriotic songs, backed by *tabla* and swirling orchestra. Schoolchildren had been bussed in by the thousand and sat cross-legged and bored in the shadow of the fort, providing the kind of vast crowd that always looks good in official photos.

Anniversaries are ambiguous occasions. The events they commemorate can be joyous or terrible. Birthdays are meant to be happy, yet they mark the passing of another year of life, and the commemoration of wars mixes grief with pride. On their national day, Indians celebrate the departure of the British, but they also mourn Partition, when some fifteen million people were forced to migrate in one of the largest instances of human displacement in history. In a matter of months, Delhi's population doubled. A Mughal city steeped in Muslim culture became a largely Punjabi city, dominated by Sikhs and Hindus, as the refugees raced to occupy properties abandoned by the Muslims who fled to Pakistan.

Having forgotten to bring binoculars, I sat at the base of the fort, straining to see the VIPs perched high on the ramparts. A brass band started up, all thumping drums and clashing cymbals, horns trumpeting like a herd of somewhat tired elephants. An announcement heralded the arrival of the prime minister, who stepped out of a white Ambassador sedan to a fanfare and a 21-gun salute. Taut-bodied guards from the National Security Group stalked around him, eyeballing the crowd suspiciously.

From behind a bullet-proof screen atop the barbican, Narasimha Rao could see the city of Shah Jahan laid out before him. To his left, the minarets of the Jama Masjid, India's largest mosque, soared skywards, its three bulbous domes inflated like onion-shaped hot-air balloons. All seemed orderly here in the industrious heart of the walled city, with schoolchildren and police assembled in ranks on the parade ground. But the calm, as Mr Rao knew, was deceptive. Seven hundred kilometres to the east, trouble was stirring in a small town bordered by farmlands and huddled in the bend of a lazy river. A dispute over a few acres of land, and another old mosque, older even that the Jama Masjid, was threatening to impose itself on the Indian imagination.

Constructed in the Hindu temple town of Ayodhya in 1528 by order of the first Mughal emperor, Babur, the mosque allegedly stood on the ruins of a temple destroyed by order of the Muslim ruler. This temple, it was claimed, had honoured the birthplace of a man called Rama, whom Hindus believe became the incarnation of the god Vishnu, the preserver. No conclusive evidence for this claim about the temple was ever presented, but historical accounts suggested that ownership of the site had been disputed for centuries, and not just between Hindus and Muslims. There was no consensus among Hindus in general as to the precise birthplace of Rama — numerous sites in Ayodhya itself laid claim to the distinction — and Jains and Buddhists could also claim prior historical connections with the area. Nevertheless, the claim alone served as a rallying point for the Hindu nationalists, whose adherents view all non-Hindu rulers of India as illegitimate, regardless of their achievements.

The small mosque at Ayodhya wasn't the most extravagant structure in the land, more a utilitarian prayer hall erected when India was a collection of warring fiefdoms. Forced out of his native Samarkand, Babur and his warriors had drifted south, winning their battles and finding riches beyond their wildest dreams. The Mughals founded one of India's greatest empires, providing the region with a unity and stability it had not enjoyed for centuries. Most of its rulers were born in India, but their ancestral home was Central Asia, which they tried and failed repeatedly to reclaim. Their spiritual allegiance was to Mecca and under their patronage Islam put down deep roots in India, giving birth to a renaissance that to some degree blended Hindu and Muslim cultures, although efforts to forge a hybrid religion failed. While talented Hindus found employment at the highest levels in government, power ultimately vested in the Muslim monarchy. Armed uprisings against its power — in some cases by rival Muslim warlords — were commonplace. Force was the currency of power.

During the Raj, British courts had inconclusively arbitrated the dispute at Ayodhya, but two years after independence, a 'miracle' reignited the Hindu cause. On the night of 22 December 1949, idols of Rama and his consort Sita mysteriously appeared inside the mosque beneath its central dome. India at that time was a country changed irrevocably by Partition. Muslims, who before the exodus to Pakistan formed a quarter of the population, now represented a 10 per cent minority, further weakened by the departure of most of their elite. The Muslims who remained tended to vote as a bloc, clubbing together in order to defend their interests. It was a successful strategy, but one that exposed the community to criticism that it was self-obsessed and separatist, and also empowered orthodox imams, who used their clout to defend archaic social practices.

The day before the appearance of the idols, dawn *namaz* (prayers) were said inside the mosque for the last time. As religiously minded Hindus flocked to the site after the miracle — which police reports confirm was nothing of the kind — the outnumbered Muslim faithful who tried to approach it were pelted with shoes and stones. The government's response was to proclaim the premises a disputed area and lock the gates. The district magistrate was ordered to remove the idols, but declined on the grounds that doing so would lead to bloodshed.[5] Ever since, with the full cooperation of the authorities, Brahmin priests employed by the government had been maintaining the idols and performing *puja* before them, while Muslims — although maintaining their claim to the site — stayed away. In 1986, a local magistrate ruled that the gates be opened to Hindus wishing to worship at the site. The Indian judiciary had sanctioned the creeping takeover of a place of worship, but still unsatisfied, Hindu activists were demanding the demolition of the mosque and construction of a grand Rama temple on the site.

India today is a secular state grafted onto a deeply spiritual society. In most cases religion determines a person's name, clothing and food preferences; it influences their choice of marriage partners and how they greet one another, whether with a *namaste* for Hindus, a *salaam aleikum* for Muslims or a *sat sri akal* for Sikhs.

Indian secularism — generally understood to mean equality of all religions before the state — is supposed to ensure that, unlike in Pakistan, all citizens are treated equally regardless of their religion. The Constitution precludes a theocracy, and protects individuals' freedom to 'profess, practise and propagate religion'.[6] It does not, however, establish a Jeffersonian 'wall of separation between Church and State'. Government holidays mark religious anniversaries, and private schools and religious institutions enjoy access to state funding. However, secularism in India has never been unambiguously defined by either the Constitution or the courts. This combination of a vaguely defined official secularism, the citizenry's strongly held but diverse religious beliefs, and intense political competition in a democracy, contribute to the persistence of communal violence in India. On average, 233 people are killed in communal riots each year, which seems few given the huge population, but the figures obscure the fact that the violence occurs in major spasms.[7]

By 1992 the conflict over the Babri Masjid, as Babur's Mosque is also known, was a powder keg waiting to explode and its fate a litmus test for India's commitment to the principles upon which it was founded.[8] The last thing Mr Rao needed was a religious war. The Congress Party's long dominance rested on retaining both Hindu and Muslim votes, so he did what he did best — he prevaricated — expressing empathy for Hindu aspirations but pledging the might and reputation of the Indian state to the defence of the disputed structure. 'We want a temple at Ayodhya, but masjid must not be broken,' he said, standing atop the forbidding red stone walls of the fort. The Mughals had built it, the British had used it as a garrison, and now it was the symbol of India's secular democracy. But, like all forts, it invited a siege.

★ ★ ★

While pilgrimage to holy places is a Hindu passion, Ayodhya does not rank with Varanasi, Haridwar, Ujjain and Puri as such a magnet. Some historians have even questioned whether the existing town, a scruffy backwater of yoga and Ayurveda centres and sweet shops, is the same place mentioned in the *Ramayana* (Travels of Rama). Attributed to the sage Valmiki, writing in Sanskrit around 300 BC, the epic's adaptation into early Hindi by Goswami Tulsidas (1532–1623) electrified the Indian imagination. The story would be translated and reinterpreted in dozens of regional variations, its fame spreading to South-East Asia. In the nineteenth century, it was translated into English by F.R. Growse, but perhaps the more accessible English version was produced by the Bengali intellectual Romesh C. Dutt, whose abridged translation cuts away much of the detail in the original 24,000 verses to reveal its full power and glory.

Every Indian child, no matter what their religion, is familiar with the story of Rama, his wife, Sita, and brother Lakshman, exiled from their rightful kingdom through the manipulations of an ambitious queen. The Ayodhya of the *Ramayana* is a civilised place of truth, prosperity and beauty:

> *And this town like Indra's city,*
> *Tower, dome and turret brave,*
> *Rose in proud and peerless beauty*
> *On the Sarayu's limpid wave,*
> *Peaceful lived the righteous people,*
> *Rich in wealth and merit high,*
> *Envy dwelt not in their bosoms,*
> *And their accents shaped no lie.*[9]

The good burghers of Ayodhya are swathed in gems, gold and sandalwood paste. Their arms are clasped in bracelets and their necks decorated with baubles. Their daughters are winsome and their sons athletic, and 'Impure thought and wandering fancy stained not holy wedded life'. The poor — who clearly have been around forever — 'fed not on the richer'. Society functioned seamlessly on caste lines:

Kshatriyas bowed to holy Brahmins,
Vaishyas to the Warriors bowed,
Toiling Shudras lived by labour,
Of their honest duty proud . . .

Pure each caste in due observance,
Stainless was each ancient rite,
And the nation thrived and prospered,
By its old and matchless might.

Nonetheless, the people of Ayodhya, even its wise king Dasaratha, are human and therefore fallible. The king's four wives bear him four sons. Rama — or Ram, as his name is pronounced in Hindi — is the eldest, an archer of Olympian skill who wins the hand of Sita in a contest organised by her father. They unite in marriage by pacing seven times around a sacred fire, but a cruel fate awaits them; palace intrigue denies Rama the throne and he is condemned to a fourteen-year exile, an unjust order that he accepts with equanimity. Sita stands by her husband, and his irrepressible and inseparable younger brother Lakshman cheerfully tags along, as if fourteen years in the demon-infested jungles is no more than a walk in the park. But Ayodhya is plunged into mourning as the townsfolk watch them go:

And they parted for the forest,
like a long unending night,
Gloomy shades of grief and sadness,
Deepened on the city's might.

Mute and dumb but conscious creatures,
Felt the woe the city bore,
Horses neighed and shook their bright bells,
Elephants returned a roar.

Man and boy and maid and matron,
Followed Rama with their eye,
As the thirsty seek the water,
When the parched fields are dry.

As a pledge of renunciation and loyalty, Rama's half-brother, Bharat — whose mother, Kaikeyi, has engineered the whole crisis — puts a pair of Rama's sandals on the throne to await the rightful heir's return. But the exiles' odyssey takes them to the far corners of India, lands as dangerous as they are beautiful. South of the Vindyas the ten-headed demon king of Lanka, Ravana, conspires to kidnap Sita, provoking a mighty war in which all India, from the monkeys to the gods, joins forces to rescue the princess and destroy the demon king.

After the battle, Rama and Lakshman eventually return to Ayodhya where Rama takes the throne he has been denied. But they never see their father again. Dasaratha has died a broken man during their exile. Rama's rule, delayed but not denied, outshines even his father's. Tulsidas's most revered version, the *Ramcharitamanas*, gives readers a reassuring ending with Rama and Sita living happily ever after, but only after Sita has endured Rama's misplaced suspicion of her infidelity with Ravana, and undergone a terrible trial by fire to prove her purity. Some regional variations that end with Rama's rejection of Sita can be viewed as parables of kingly duty: with dissension over Sita dividing Ayodhya, Rama must put the unity of his kingdom ahead of his own feelings. Others see in the couple's misfortunes the unfailing laws of karma. Fearing that Rama has been mortally wounded during the battle with the demons, Sita had turned against Lakshman, accusing him of conspiring to take his elder brother's wife. Sita's foul and unjust suspicion of loyal Lakshman — like Rama's suspicion of her — is born of love.

Romesh Dutt — writing when India was still a colonised nation of 200 million people — observed that:

> Sita holds a place in the hearts of women in India which no other creation of a poet's imagination holds among any other nation on earth. There is not a Hindu woman whose earliest and tenderest recollections do not cling round the story of Sita's sufferings and Sita's faithfulness, told in the nursery, taught in the family circle, remembered and cherished through life. Sita's adventures in a desolate forest and in a hostile prison only represent, in an exaggerated form, the humbler trials of a woman's life; and Sita's endurance and faithfulness teach her devotion to duty in all trials and troubles of life.[10]

Importantly, Dutt adds that unlike those of ancient Greece, where the ideal of life was joy and beauty, ancient India's ideals were piety, endurance and devotion. 'The creative imagination of the Hindus has conceived no loftier and holier character than Sita,' he wrote.

In one version of the epic, Rama eventually recognises his own grievous error and beseeches the story's author, Valmiki, to give back his beloved wife. Witnessing the scene from afar, Sita's heart bursts with love, as she is taken to the bosom of the earth on a golden throne held aloft by sacred serpents 'as the leaves enfold the rose'. Rama's happy days are over, but his sons are said to have founded the great cities of Taxila and Pushkalavati in the Indus Valley. In time, Rama and his brothers leave Ayodhya, cross the River Sarayu, depart this life and attain moksha, or release from the endless cycle of reincarnation.

If, as some believe, Rama was a real prince who ruled a real kingdom, then his historians served him ill. The extent of the epic's historicity has drowned in devotion, and may never be determined. Instead, Rama's story is an ode to loyalty, bravery, compassion and nobility, and a homage to the wild beauty of the land of the Himalayas, the Vindyas and the Ganga. His jungle exile is a metaphor for the challenges we all face in this life, and as India has become more corrupt and crowded, so Indians have become increasingly dependent for moral sustenance on their *Odyssey*. Mahatma Gandhi regarded the *Ramcharitamanas* of Tulsidas as 'the greatest book in all devotional literature'. Devoid of hectoring, it inspires with beautiful characters and sentiments. Even the villains display such manifestly human flaws as to earn the sympathy of some readers.

The *Ramayana* is an irresistible song — but not for everyone. In southern India, the epic is often seen as a parable of northern, high-caste domination over peninsular India. Tamil politicians in the south have been known to publicly burn copies of the book, regarding it as patronising of them. But regional political rivalries aside, the story's universal message is that life is fleeting but deeds are immortal. We sense in ourselves the weakness of a Dasaratha, the calculating greed and envy of a Kaikeyi, but hope that when our own moment of truth comes we can find within us the strength and loyalty of a Sita, the sheer immortal bravery of a Rama. The *Ramayana*'s contagious optimism, its conviction that the hard road is often the best road, has shaped the character of Hindus, helping them to retain hope and good humour even in their darkest hours. Those who claim that the faith lacks moral foundations have not read or understood the story. Those of us born into different traditions are the poorer for having been denied its riches.

★ ★ ★

Indian nationalism is a broad church. Debate over what kind of country independent India should be had a long provenance, stretching back to the start of the nineteenth century. New modes of travel and communications were making the world a smaller place, challenging such archaic Hindu customs as Untouchability, child marriage, widow burning and the prohibition on crossing the oceans. Indians educated in Britain during the Raj were influenced by modern ideas of democracy and secular government, and together with Indian philosophers such as Swami Vivekananda, Swami Dayanand Saraswati and Sri Aurobindo participated in a broad Hindu reform movement that became known as the Bengali Renaissance. A passionate interest in new ideas and a solid faith in ancient ones formed the two banks between which the river of Indian nationalism flowed.

By the 1920s, the intellectual and spiritual Hindu revival of the nineteenth century had split into two main factions — Gandhi's broad-based Congress Party, and an organised Hindu supremacist movement represented by such groups as the Hindu Mahasabha and Rashtriya Swayamsevak Sangh (RSS), or National Volunteer Association.

The RSS's longest serving leader, Madhav Sadashiv Golwalkar, summed up their views in his 1939 book *We or Our Nationhood Defined*:

We repeat: in Hindusthan, the land of the Hindus, lives and should live the Hindu Nation ... Consequently only those movements are truly 'National' as aim at re-building, revitalizing and emancipating from its present stupor, the Hindu Nation ... All others are either traitors and enemies to the National cause, or, to take a charitable view, idiots.[11]

Mahatma Gandhi was a Hindu and a nationalist, but he was not a Hindu nationalist. His assassin, Nathuram Godse, was. While Gandhi used the Hindu ideal of Ramrajya — God-given government on earth — to convey his ideas of self-reliance and non-violence, he nonetheless believed that all citizens and religions of India should be equal in a secular state. He left no doubt about his feelings on this:

... In no part of the world are one nationality and one religion synonymous terms; nor has it ever been so in India.[12]

This view made Gandhi some dangerous enemies. Sectarian nationalists like Godse saw him as a compromiser whose generosity towards Muslims caused the Partition of their motherland. The thinker who most influenced Godse was Veer Savarkar, an admirer of Hitler and Mussolini, who was jailed by the British colonial authorities as a threat to law and order. Savarkar longed for Hindus to be tougher and less accommodating of minorities and outsiders. At the age of twelve he committed his first political act, leading his schoolmates in throwing stones at a village mosque:

We vandalized the mosque to our heart's content and raised the flag of our bravery on it. We followed the war strategy of Shivaji completely and ran away from the site after accomplishing our task.[13]

Ironically, the Hindu nationalists took a dim view of Hindus, seeing them as lazy, corrupt, disloyal and selfish people who had betrayed India. At its training camps the group sought to instil discipline through rigorous physical drills designed, according to a former member, Des Raj Goyal, to ensure 'total surrender of the individual personality to what the RSS establishment [calls] "the ideal".'[14] They also considered European and Islamic civilisations as 'debased', and were inclined to view Nazi Germany in a positive light. In *We or Our Nationhood Defined* Golwalkar wrote:

To keep up the purity of the Race and its culture, Germany shocked the world by her purging the country of the Semitic Races — the Jews. Race pride at its highest has been manifested here. Germany has also shown how well nigh impossible it is for Races and cultures, having differences going to the root, to be assimilated into one united whole, a good lesson for us in Hindusthan to learn and profit by.[15]

As commentator Sitaram Yechuri wryly noted, 'Western concepts and civilisational advances are condemned as "alien", except for fascism!'[16]

Because of its differences with Gandhi and Nehru, the RSS largely stayed out of the Freedom Struggle. Its strategy, according to Goyal was to 'curry favour with the British'. When the struggle ended in Partition, the nationalists claimed to have been vindicated, and vilified Gandhi as the 'Father of the [Pakistani] nation'. After Partition, in which Hindu-Muslim violence is estimated to have claimed up to one million lives, containing sectarian politics was literally a matter of life and death for Indians, and for India as a nation. Gandhi's murder at the hands of a Hindu nationalist sympathiser made the RSS a political pariah. Nevertheless, while committed to the destruction of secular democracy, it was able to use the democratic space afforded by the new Constitution to ensure its survival. A series of political parties and social organisations were formed which came to be known as the Sangh Parivar, or 'united family'. By the early 1990s, the RSS — although it kept no formal records — boasted a membership of several million, with political and religious front organisations, the Bharatiya Janata Party (Indian People's Party, or BJP) and Vishwa Hindu Parishad (World Hindu Council, or VHP). Their principal demands were for a uniform civil code (denying Muslims the right to practise polygamy), a ban on slaughtering cows (forcing Muslims and Christians to observe the Hindu religious practice in this regard), abolition of the special status of Jammu & Kashmir (India's only Muslim-majority state, which had a modest degree of autonomy), and relocation of Babur's Mosque 'with due respect' and the construction of a Hindu temple on the site. While their grassroots supporters loudly called for payback against the once powerful Muslim minority, their leaders insisted that the only purpose of such policies was to strengthen India as a nation. They even claimed to be secular; indeed, some of them were not very religious.

While official secular histories imagined the Indian story as a kind of extended love-in between people of different faiths, the nationalists took refuge in an equally fanciful saga of all-pervasive Muslim oppression. Deeply divided by caste, it was difficult to imagine unity among Hindus, but symbols like the lotus flower and a saffron flag would point the way. The *trishul* — a trowel-sized pitchfork — would be the trademark of their militant defence of a 'threatened' Hindu way of life. The nationalists saw that the Ayodhya temple campaign could be the rallying point.

Throughout 1992 a dialogue between the nationalists and Narasimha Rao's government sputtered and revived, confounded by mutual recriminations and distrust. Eventually, the nationalists set a deadline, 6 December 1992, when they would play their trump card, deploying huge numbers of *kar sevaks*, or volunteers, at the disputed site in Ayodhya to begin construction of a Rama temple on the site. In the last week of November, one of the Sangh Parivar outfits, the Bajrang Dal, announced that its suicide squads were ready to demolish the mosque. The dispute had the potential to provoke widespread violence in India, and — reluctantly — I made arrangements to travel to the town to report on the issue should things get out of hand.

It seemed like a normally quiet Sunday morning when I arrived at Lucknow's Amausi Airport and hired a taxi to the temple town. The route to Ayodhya was devoid of the significant army or police presence that might have indicated a serious problem in the making. Beyond Faizabad, once capital of the Muslim princely state of Awadh (Oudh), the roads narrowed and became more crowded. In the unfamiliar town, the crowds of young men thronging the street confused and disorientated me. The taxi driver had taken a back route to avoid the bulk of the congestion, and before I could figure out where I was, his old Ambassador emerged onto open ground at the base of a steep hill directly behind Babur's Mosque. High on the hill, with its back turned obstinately towards the distant Saryu River, the distinctive triple-domed structure partially obscured by large trees looked more imposing than it really was. Across the open ground below, groups of young men wearing headbands in various shades of orange, red and yellow streamed towards the monument. I was still getting my bearings when a knot of kar sevaks approached chanting 'Jai Sri Ram!' (Hail Lord Rama). As they passed me, headed for the mosque, a tall youth among them turned around, and I noticed that his eyes were quite bloodshot.

'Patraka murdabad!' (Death to the journalists) he screamed at the top of his lungs, raising his fist towards me and then walking on with his friends, who congratulated him.

Nobody had ever said anything like that to me before in India, or for that matter in Pakistan, Afghanistan or Kashmir. Once, during a massive anti-American protest in Pakistan, a wild-eyed Muslim who'd been shouting 'Death to the infidels' in front of me rendered a heartfelt apology after he accidentally lost balance and stepped on my foot. But the mood in Ayodhya as noon approached and the temperature rose was worryingly different. Before I could ponder my next move, I saw a young Indian woman in the crowd whom I recognised. Natasha Singh was the daughter of an army family who'd migrated from India to the United States. She had grown up in California before returning to the land of her birth to try her hand as a freelance journalist. She was paying off her taxi driver when I reached her, not yet aware of the hostile element in the crowd. Natasha was bubbling with excitement, sharing news of her recent adventures and mutual friends as we ascended a path that led around the northern side of the mosque. As we neared the disputed structure, the noise of the protestors grew ominously loud, and I had to lean down to Natasha to hear what she was saying.

At the top of the path, the source of the commotion was revealed. In the 50-metre gap between Babur's Mosque and an old guesthouse opposite known as Manas Bhavan, a highly unusual scene was being played out. It was common in India to see police confronting demonstrators. In Parliament Street in New Delhi, where I used to do my banking, such confrontations were a daily ritual. But here, at the physical epicentre of one of the country's most dangerous flashpoints, responsibility for security had been delegated to the main Hindu nationalist organisation, the RSS, I could only assume as a result of some deal with the state government which the BJP controlled. Volunteers had come from across the Hindi-speaking heartland of northern India to help build the temple, cramming the galis and creating a bottleneck at a rickety boom gate that separated them from the mosque. There were a few police standing around, but most of them were behind the steel barricades that had been erected on the walls of the mosque itself.

Sitting in lofty isolation on a nearby rooftop and maintaining a stream of encouragement and invective were a group of nationalist leaders. They were an odd collection of elderly fair-skinned English-speaking men, and a few firebrand saffron-and-vermilion-clad women. Over loudspeakers they were decrying the mosque as a symbol of slavery and an insult to all Hindus. 'See the power of the Hindus. The end of meekness and subjugation,' the volatile BJP mascot Uma Bharti was heard to shout.[17] Their exhortations electrified the crowd, mostly made up of young men wearing jeans and T-shirts, not *dhotis*, and smiling amid the life-threatening crush. Nobody really knew how many of them were in the town, but estimates ranged from 150,000 to 400,000, far outnumbering the resident population. They were perched in the branches of trees, brandishing staves and tridents, and using conch shells as trumpets of war. Occasionally those on the front line would break through the cordon, scrambling onto the open ground in front of the mosque.

In the intricate legal and political manoeuvring that had preceded the event, the Supreme Court had sanctioned a peaceful gathering at the site to sing hymns, but had stipulated no disturbance to the status quo. Instead, a vast mob had assembled, egged on by leaders such as the BJP party president, Lal Krishna Advani, who days earlier had reportedly said that the *kar seva*, or social work, would be performed 'with bricks and shovels', a statement he later denied making.

In the din surrounding the mosque, I could not make out what the assembled Hindu leaders were saying to their followers. But police intelligence reports released years later quoted Advani as saying, 'The Hindus of Hindustan have woken up. We don't need any support. A temple for Ram Lala, who represents the religious beliefs of Hindus, will be constructed at any cost through kar seva. No power can stop it.'[18]

Conspicuous by his absence was the party's parliamentary leader, Atal Bihari Vajpayee. Asked a few days earlier whether the gathering at Ayodhya would be peaceful, he had replied, '*Asha hai, aur ashanka bhi*' (There are hopes, but also doubts).[19]

Now the shouts of the individual kar sevaks were growing into an awesome roar, drowning out the speeches from their leaders. Before clambering over the barricades, with the help of some stewards, Natasha and I had stopped at a small stall selling bandanas printed with slogans hailing Lord Rama. Buying two, I handed one to Natasha, urging her to keep it handy just in case things turned nasty. Stumbling around amid the growing tumult, I tried to talk to a few nationalist organisers, who blithely insisted that everything was proceeding as planned, oblivious to the impending anarchy. The kar sevaks were chanting the name of Ram and blowing whistles in time, and the fingers of fear were tightening their grip on me. I kept asking the nationalist officials if everything was all right.

'*Koi baat nahin*,' they told me. No problem.

6

The Blood-dimmed Tide

Just before noon, standing beside the old mosque, I turned on my tape recorder. The recording would later be tucked away for safekeeping; I did not want accidentally to erase it. Twelve years after the event, before embarking on my yatra, I retrieved it from the bank vault where it was held and listened to it.

The fear in my voice was palpable. 'A huge roar going up,' I heard myself say. 'A huge roar going up, because one of the Hindu volunteers has managed to get inside. More than one ... They're standing on top of one of the three domes of the mosque raising their fists in the air.'

Thousands of kar sevaks had burst through the security cordon and were streaming onto the site. Almost simultaneously, large brick fragments began raining down on the area, apparently hurled by catapults towards the mosque. As chunks of masonry thudded into the ground frighteningly close to me, I saw Ashok Singhal, leader of a Sangh Parivar organisation, wielding a stave in a somewhat stagey effort to make the mob stand down. For a moment, some of the volunteers responded, vacating the area, but then another volley of bricks was unleashed and Singhal disappeared. Another deafening roar drew my attention back to the mosque where, clearly visible on one of the domes, a handful of young men were raising a flag the colour of marigolds, firing the rest of the mob to frenzy. The trickle of intruders turned quickly to a flood, as they ran towards the building and began scaling the barricades protecting it. Those on top, meanwhile, had begun hacking away at its surface with iron bars and hammers.

'You can see them,' the voice on the tape, my voice, said. 'They've got some sort of pick, just any sort of steel implement and they are breaking the mosque ... There are hundreds of Hindus climbing over the barbed-wire fence. The saffron flag of Hinduism is raised ... and the police, well, I just can't see the police now. They're standing inside and they don't appear to be doing anything.'

Heading for Ayodhya were some 25,000 armed police and paramilitary troops, but only a hundred or so were inside the mosque and they were trapped. They could start shooting and risk being killed when they ran out of bullets, or accept a humiliating defeat at the hands of the mob and flee. Instead they did neither, merely huddling inside. Having become separated from Natasha I'd drifted back towards the northern entrance to the mosque. On the eastern side, kar sevaks had begun attacking journalists and breaking their cameras, but where I was their anger was focused solely on the disputed shrine. As I stood there surrounded by chaos, the simple act of talking into a microphone seemed to insulate me, instilling a measure of confidence, and I decided to follow the kar sevaks through the fallen barricades and into the mosque.

Reaching the low outer perimeter wall near an arched gateway on the northern side, for the first time I touched the time-worn structure speckled with age. Beside me, a young Hindu man was hacking at the wall with a spike, the mortar breaking to reveal the sandy loam inside. Reaching into the wound, I took a handful of the material — it felt gritty in my palm. It had been standing there for over 400 years, one of the first things the Mughals ever built in India, completed only thirty-six years after Columbus reached

America. It had become for Hindu nationalists a symbol of a thousand years of Muslim oppression. By attacking it, they were driving a stake into the dignity of an entire religious community. I didn't know it then, but columns of smoke had begun rising over Ayodhya as Hindu militants who were unable to reach the mosque began torching Muslim homes, killing the inhabitants if they emerged, and leaving them to be incinerated if they didn't.

Standing beside the outer perimeter wall of Babur's Mosque, I turned to survey the scene. There were now thousands of people rushing backwards and forwards, as if caught up in some kind of splendid emergency. Some were elated, radiant with religious ecstasy, speaking in tongues of worship — 'Jai Sri Ram!' Others, more worldly, were organising volunteers into gangs to carry off the rubble. They were turning back the clock, erasing one history to build another, humbling one god to honour their own, and I realised they were capable of anything in God's name. Turning back towards the mosque, my path was blocked suddenly by an elderly half-dressed sadhu, or religious ascetic, who had emerged through the gateway leading a group of uniformed men away. They were the Provincial Armed Constabulary members who'd been holed up inside the building. There were at least two dozen of them, walking in single file with rifles slung low and heads bowed, carrying their useless bamboo riot shields. As they filed out, the saffron-clad sadhu was hectoring and pushing them, completely comfortable in his new authority. A minute or two later, I heard a voice thick with emotion shouting something unrecognisable in Hindi behind me, and before I could make out what was happening, felt the shoulder strap of my tape recorder being tugged violently. Grabbing the strap to avoid losing my equipment, I turned and saw the old sadhu grappling with the recorder. Then, just as suddenly as he'd started, he let go and returned inside the mosque. At that moment, a large chunk of brick crashed into the wall, rebounding onto the ground in a hail of dust particles, narrowly missing my head. I heard a hollow, metallic sound and saw a group of kar sevaks toppling a police post, clearing a path for the thousands of volunteers who poured forth from the alleyways. Meanwhile, one of the kar sevaks near me had produced a sizeable pickaxe and began hacking into the masonry above the entrance. His manic zeal — or the shower of masonry chips his pick was producing — caused me to pause on the threshold. Whether out of a sense of fear, or self-preservation, or revulsion, I decided against proceeding into the building. A few hours later, several kar sevaks were killed when the central dome collapsed on top of them.

Gandhi once observed that 'So long as there is sympathy between you and the mob, everything goes well. Immediately that cord is broken, there is horror'.[1] He thought the authorities should use music to calm riotous crowds. Now fear had finally gotten the better of me, and I felt very alone. 'The blood-dimmed tide', as W.B. Yeats put it in 'The Second Coming', was loosed, 'and everywhere the ceremony of innocence is drowned; the best lack all convictions, while the worst are full of passionate intensity.' Placing the tape recorder in my day pack, I took one of the bandanas I'd purchased that morning, tied it around my head in the style of the militants, and walked away, taking the same narrow path that Natasha and I had entered by that morning. Behind the mosque I came upon a large group of uniformed police who'd taken shelter under a neem tree. Several of them were trembling visibly, and one young constable was drenched at the crotch. The sight of these men, armed yet terrified, frightened me more than anything else I had seen that day. Shocked and disorientated, I turned right and headed east, the wrong direction entirely. Instead of escaping Ayodhya I was heading into its heart, where the lanes were in the hands of the militants.

The road rose initially — providing a wider view of the demolition in progress, holes appearing in the domes — then descended into a narrow, blue-walled bottleneck through which thousands of young men heading for the mosque created a terrible crush. Many of them were wearing headbands like mine, pouring towards the maelstrom, an army of fanatics. As I tried to squeeze past, close enough to smell their sweat, they raised their fists and cried 'Jai Sri Ram!' and I smiled and returned the call. To have done otherwise would have been suicide, though I almost choked on the words, disgusted by their flagrant misuse of the phrase and humiliated by my own need to humour them. Increasingly desperate, I was clinging to the memory that Ayodhya had a railway station. In the midst of a national emergency, the idea that the trains would be running was completely absurd, but the folly somehow sustained me, preserving hope and warding off unmanageable fears. Then, an elderly gentleman dressed in a jacket and tie — and one of the few people I saw attempting to leave — asked if I needed help.

'Where is the railway station?' I asked in Hindi.

'Come. I'll take you,' he replied.

Half an hour later we were still walking in circles and I realised that the kindly old man was as much a stranger to Ayodhya as I was. All seemed lost, but relief arrived in the form of a *tonga*, or horse-drawn trap, that rounded a bend and headed straight towards us. My anxiety must have been obvious because the bearded young man seated on the open trap beside the driver asked in good English whether I was all right. When he said he was headed for the adjacent town of Faizabad and that I was welcome to join him, I thanked the old man and leapt onto the cart.

My rescuer was the son of Indian émigrés who'd settled in Australia. He was loosely involved with the Hare Krishnas, now known as ISKON, and seemed to have drifted into Ayodhya out of curiosity, but appeared to have seen enough. When I told him I was also from Australia he responded politely, but was quite guarded in his comments and focused on the path ahead. Perhaps he was also scared, or had reasons for concealing his own background in Australia or business in India. Content to be leaving Ayodhya, I resisted the temptation to ask anything more of him. The horse retraced the path I'd taken in error, until we were back on the high ground east of the mosque, where we caught a glimpse of thousands of kar sevaks teeming over the crumbling structure like ants on an ant hill. Passing in silence, the driver turned the cart right onto a dirt track and we proceeded to Faizabad along sugar-cane lined lanes. Little was said on the return journey, the three of us watchful lest stragglers from the greater mob attack us in God's name. Nothing seemed certain any more, except the bone-jarring ruts on the dirt road out of Ayodhya.

★ ★ ★

Prime Minister Narasimha Rao was reportedly having an afternoon nap at his official residence in New Delhi when the mosque was demolished. By 5 p.m. all three domes had collapsed, the rubble, mortar, cement and stone crumbling as quickly as law and order. All through the following day the Hindu militants worked undisturbed to clear the site, erecting a small pink tent over a bamboo frame on the levelled ruins. Concerned that the Hindu idols might be damaged in the chaos, priests had entered the shrine soon after it was seized and removed them for safekeeping, reinstalling them later in the makeshift tent temple. On the second night of the occupation, in the early hours of 8 December, the government finally ordered four battalions of Rapid Action Force paramilitary troops to retake the site. In the darkness before dawn, the kar sevaks brick-batted the troops from positions atop the guesthouse Manas Bhavan and other points, but by five o'clock that afternoon the troops had secured the area using only tear gas, baton charges and warning shots, with no loss of life.

Security forces then fanned out across Ayodhya, clearing the town of the militants and forcing them onto 150 buses and nineteen special trains. That morning, All India Radio — concerned to suppress rumours that might fuel more violence — announced that 'a structure which was being built and the idols placed inside are safe'. Hindus among the troops sent to secure the site were soon praying before the idols, removing their shoes out of respect before entering the shrine. Like Germans collecting souvenir pieces of the Berlin Wall, the kar sevaks carried off pieces of the mosque to the far-flung corners of India. Thousands of young Hindu men — nobodies when they left for Ayodhya — were heroes when they returned home. They spoke with shining eyes of how a new army of a million volunteers would complete the job of demolishing 3000 mosques allegedly built on the ruins of mandirs destroyed by Muslim emperors.

Across the country, the violence in Ayodyha encouraged outbreaks elsewhere, with some 2000 deaths attributed to communal rioting triggered by the demolition, the vast majority of victims being Muslims. Only a tiny fraction of Hindus indulged in such atrocities, but in a country as large as India, even aberrations get magnified. From their perch on the nearby building, Hindu nationalist leaders including Mr Advani, the former physics professor Dr Murli Manohar Joshi, and young firebrand women like Uma Bharti and Sadhvi Rithambara had watched the demolition all day. India's Central Bureau of Investigations later gave evidence that speeches made from the dais had incited the violence. As each dome fell, sweets had been distributed in celebration among the leaders present, some of whom embraced in jubilation, the Allahabad High Court was told.[2]

After a brief incarceration on charges of inciting communal hatred, Mr Advani declared that 'Ayodhya has had a salutary effect on the country's unity.'[3] Prime Minister Rao, who had washed his hands of the mosque, heaped blame on the perpetrators, accusing the BJP-controlled government of Uttar Pradesh of being party to a conspiracy to demolish it. Individual RSS members would later admit that the operation was meticulously planned.[4]

On Independence Day the following year, Narasimha Rao again scaled the ramparts of the Red Fort in Delhi and declared,

'Whatever has been demolished, we will build it — rebuild it.' Instead, his government established a judicial inquiry and referred the issue of whether a Rama temple had existed on the site before Babur's Mosque to the Supreme Court, the repository of many a politically intractable problem. But for the Congress Party, his failure to manage the issue would have catastrophic political consequences. Muslims and high-caste Hindus both turned away from the Congress in droves. Muslims were disgusted by the party's failure to protect the mosque, while many Brahmins gravitated towards the BJP's more muscular form of Hindu nationalism. The ideal of a single political party representing different economic, ethnic and religious interests of Indians was buried in the rubble at Ayodhya. The day after the demolition, the staunchly secular Calcutta-based newspaper *The Statesman* looked to an earlier, more noble leader, Mahatma Gandhi, for guidance:

> If the father of the nation were alive today, he would ask that the Masjid be rebuilt, preferably by the Hindus who destroyed it, and suggest that the temple of Lord Ram be built nearby and urge Muslims to help with it.[5]

The only blood relative of the Mahatma I knew at the time was Rajmohan Gandhi, and a few weeks later I contacted him, hoping his true Gandhian compass might provide bearings for a way forward. In January 1948, twelve-year-old Rajmohan had stood at Birla House in New Delhi beside the body of his assassinated grandfather, and later helped to collect his ashes from Raj Ghat. On the train that carried Gandhi's remains to Allahabad for immersion in the Ganges, Rajmohan's childish mind half expected, half hoped that the Mahatma would burst forth from the urns at any moment. Rajmohan had grown up to become a Gandhian thinker and author, and was working at the Centre for Policy Studies near Malcha Marg when I stopped by there to see him. Tall and elegant in a scholarly way, he was in a gloomy mood. Not only had the Mahatma not risen from the dead, India seemed to have turned its back on his legacy.

'We're looking at the past, not at the future. We're looking at bitter things. We're looking for people to blame, for whole communities to blame. We're committing terrible acts of violence,' he told me sadly, reflecting on India's wasted opportunities. 'The idea that one group should be at the top, and all those who are not Hindus should not be equal citizens is something that will eventually destroy Hindu society. After all, Hindus also belong to various categories and it's the easiest thing in the world to promote clashes and conflicts within the Hindu community. So, if you start dividing people, that's the end of India and of Hindu society as well.'

The end of my time in India was drawing near, and there was talk of a new posting in Vietnam, where people seemed fed up with past conflicts and determined to build a better future. Despite everything that had happened, my three years in Delhi had been the most stimulating and enjoyable in my career. I had survived, and Rajmohan was certain that India would too.

7

Breakfast at Civil Lines

It was a routine interview, a chat with one of India's most passionate human rights defenders, Ravi Nair, at his basement office in Green Park. There was a lot to discuss — disappearances in Punjab, the dirty war in Kashmir, and the looming confrontation in Ayodhya. It was November, early winter, a few weeks before the demolition, and Ravi was on the phone when I arrived, so I took a seat in the outer office where his interns, usually students of law or journalism, researched the South Asian Human Rights Documentation Centre's voluminous reports. There was only one other person there that morning, a slender girl with a mop of black hair, tapping at a computer keyboard while her feet were warmed by a one-bar heater. Her skin was pale, almost lighter than mine, and I wondered if it was the cold, or just the 'wheatish' skin prospective grooms were always searching for in the matrimonial columns. She had a mischievous face, with large eyes, and was wearing a dark pullover and jeans and a stylish pair of brown leather boots. She'd been living in New York, she said, interning at *The Nation* after completing a few degrees in English literature, philosophy and journalism. She was twenty-eight, single, had worked at the *Washington Post*'s New Delhi office, and was helping Ravi finish a few reports while figuring out what she wanted to do next.

Fascinated, I was almost disappointed when Ravi got off the phone and invited me to take a seat at his desk.

A week after meeting her I bumped into Janaki again, this time at a party at the home of the *New York Times* correspondent. It was a manic evening, a gathering of the South Asian correspondents who, although we lived in the same city, saw more of each other in Kabul or Colombo than we did in New Delhi. There were lots of stories and gossip to catch up on, and an edge of desperation among the assembled gypsies, who lived hard and played hard. She was standing with Ravi, a good human rights defender keeping her out of harm's way. I remember becoming uncomfortable with the behaviour of some friends, who seemed suddenly boorish, wolves in camera vests and instant experts prognosticating on the imminent demise of vile, absurd India. Had they read my thoughts they would have wasted no time in exposing my hypocrisy. Amid the all too intense socialising, the well-educated young Indian woman appeared an island of poise, a little too well bred for carousing and not at all the tomboy I had imagined. She drank, but only a little; danced, but kept her balance. Acutely conscious of guilt by association, I made an effort to appear more thoughtful and sober than I actually was, managing by this ruse to obtain her telephone number.

She was staying with her family in the Civil Lines, a quiet quarter of the capital squeezed between the forested Ridge and the banks of the Yamuna, just north of the walled city. She'd topped her year at Delhi University and then, like her mother before her, gone off to the United States to continue her studies. Her father was managing director of a family-run finance company that specialised in providing credit to independent truckers. Now I knew who was responsible for putting all those multicoloured hulks emblazoned with 'OK TATA' and 'HORN PLEASE' onto India's roads. Her brother was a manager with the company, and her only other sibling — a sister — had married an American and lived outside Boston. As a schoolgirl, Janaki had played hockey badly, but was a voracious reader and later an enthusiastic thespian with the well-regarded Yatrik theatre company. This talent for drama ran in the family; her aunt Madhur Jaffrey had acted in Merchant Ivory films before becoming a well-known author and broadcaster on Indian food.

All of this made Janaki better educated, better read and better connected than me, but I like a challenge and began inviting her out, showing up at official functions and social gatherings with a partner instead of solo. At thirty-four, I had just about everything I wanted: a career based on travel and writing; even the odd, quite glamorous Indian girlfriend, which had earned me the undying envy of some of my peers. Things were so good, there seemed no need to change anything. But things changed anyway and I became a frequent visitor to a whitewashed bungalow on a quiet lane near the Old City.

Three Commissioner's Lane was more than just an address — it was the centre of Janaki's universe. It sat on over an acre in the Civil Lines, protected by high brick walls and surrounded by verdant grounds dotted with large neem and mango trees. It was a Sunday, late autumn in 1992, and I'd been called for breakfast. It was an odd time to show up in an unfamiliar household, the timing determined more by the dictates of my unpredictable schedule than anything else. I'd driven myself, becoming hopelessly lost, and by the time the high wooden gates of the compound rolled open and I drove onto the ochre gravel drive, Janaki and her father were pacing the lawns, having checked several times with the chowkidar for any sign of their guest.

Krishen Bans Bahadur was a dapper man of medium stature in his late sixties, and I immediately recognised a striking family resemblance in the aquiline nose, thin frame and shy smile that played on his lips. Normally on a Sunday morning he'd have been relaxing at home in his white cotton kurta pajama, enjoying a respite from the stresses of running a business in India. But that morning he'd gone to the trouble of donning trousers and a pullover. Janaki introduced her father as 'Abba'.

'Did you lose your way?' he asked, with a look of concern that soon turned to a resigned smile and handshake. 'Never mind. Kutu! Go tell Ma your friend has come.'

My initiation into life at the Civil Lines had begun. Nobody there called Janaki by her proper name. To the family, she was 'Kutu', a nonsense name. To the gatekeeper and other servants she was 'Choti Baby', being the youngest of her siblings. Krishen Bans, meanwhile, was known to his children as 'Abba', father in Urdu, the language of India's Muslims, which he knew better than Hindi, even though he was a Hindu. To Abba's sisters he was 'Bhaiya', or brother, a term his wife also used. While I was still digesting the nomenclature, another voice, this one with a slightly nasal American twang echoed along the veranda.

'Hi there! Welcome!' said Maya Bahadur, an elegant woman with a radiant smile wearing a sari and cardigan. 'Do come in, won't you.'

Maya's accent, I learnt, was a legacy of five years in the United States just after World War II, when the young Maya Deb studied at Smith College in Northampton, Massachusetts. Learning, it appeared, was something of a fetish in both her family and her husband's, with Krishen Bans also having completed a Master's at Delhi University before joining the family business. Janaki was the fourth generation in her family to study overseas.

The Civil Lines was an area steeped in history, within sight of the walled city, the scene of intense fighting during the Indian Rebellion of 1857. Cycle rickshaws outnumbered motorised ones, and the narrow lanes were bounded by listing red-brick walls. 'Civil lines' was a generic term for the neatly laid-out residential neighbourhoods built in many towns and cities across northern India during the Raj. They were designed to be green and restful retreats from the heat and dust of India. Old lithographs show Delhi's Civil Lines as the first such model town to spring up north of Kashmere Gate.

The bungalow at Number Three resembled a mouldering fortress, its metre-thick stone-and-mortar walls built in 1911, the year Delhi succeeded Calcutta as capital of the Raj. Designed on a cruciform plan, the house had verandas on three sides, and curved colonnades of a distinctly Islamic influence. Repeated coats of lime wash had softened the building's edges, and a patina of various stains and moulds from successive monsoons lent an air of antiquity. Inside, it was cool and dark with towering ceilings surmounted by skylights. A number of such bungalows built in the time of Janaki's great-grandfather dotted a small grid of lanes on the high ground west of the Yamuna between Qudsia Bagh — a garden that had been the scene of discreet liaisons since Mughal times — and the imposing edifice of the Maidens Hotel, one of Delhi's two top hotels during the Raj, now owned by the Oberoi family. Commissioner's Lane ran east from the castellated offices of the Delhi administration towards the Ring Road. Most of the early bungalows along its course belonged to the one family. Krishen Bans was born in Number Seven, and moved into Number Three in the late 1950s, as his family expanded and divided and the house passed down and sideways through the Bahadur clan. Most of the people living in the area belonged to the caste of scribes known as Mathur Kayasths. Street names like Raj Narain Marg and Maharaja Lal Lane recalled their ancestors.

At the breakfast table, Abba concentrated on his food while Maya cross-examined me about my thoughts on India. As she pumped me for information about the growing communal divide, Maya's staunch secular viewpoint was apparent. She was a proud Brahmo, a descendant of a Bengali Hindu family that spurned all religious rituals. They hailed from Calcutta originally, epicentre of the Bengali Renaissance that produced Ram Mohan Roy, a Brahmin who had been expelled from his family after publishing a book attacking orthodox Hinduism. Roy, considered to be the founder of the reformist Brahmo-Samaj, campaigned vigorously against such backward Hindu practices as widow burning and child marriage, seeing the British presence as an opportunity to revive India's greatness, and create a new Indian politics based on principle rather than brute force. However, that morning at the breakfast table in Civil Lines, Maya's efforts to enlighten me about all this were sabotaged by Janaki, who kept up a stream of inane remarks aimed at amusing everyone. She was the only one of her siblings living at home, still occupying her childhood bedroom, and slipped easily into the role of precocious baby of the family, even leaving food on her plate, which greatly irritated her mother. There was some code embedded in their badinage that I found impenetrable. Were they an argumentative family? Or was it all just affectionate teasing? One minute Maya would be cross with Kutu, then in the next, she would grace me with her quite beautiful smile and ask, 'Now. Where were we?'

After breakfast, Maya joined us on a tour of the home, and when we came to a hallway decorated with framed photos of her children as youngsters, the stern memsahib and earnest intellectual almost melted with nostalgia and affection.

From that first meal on, the family were entirely themselves in my presence, without airs or graces and comfortable in their own skins, chiding one another in a ritualised, deeply homely manner. Later, Janaki got out the family photo album, and I saw a much younger Krishen Bans, fly-fishing in Kashmir, shooting in Rajasthan, and suited and booted with his ravishing young bride. Theirs was a different Delhi from the city of politicians, *babus* (bureaucrats), media people and expats that I inhabited, and a world away from the caste, political and religious violence I had seen. By the end of the morning I knew that I had found a group of special people, in a special place, and felt that I had known them my entire life.

★ ★ ★

I knew a man who owned a fort. It was a 500-year-old citadel that sprawled over 10 hectares and nine levels on a spur of the Aravalli

Range on the edge of the Rajasthan Desert. Francis Wacziarg — a Frenchman who'd taken Indian citizenship — and his partners were slowly renovating the old ruin, hoping to turn it into a hotel. I'd stayed there a couple of times and thought Janaki might find it interesting, but a bit spartan for her taste. So, wanting to have a quiet weekend away together after the trauma of Ayodhya, I'd chosen a former royal hunting lodge reasonably close to the Rajasthan capital, Jaipur, for our accommodation, with the option of dropping in at the fort on the way back to Delhi. To ensure our privacy, I would be doing the driving.

Rajasthan is a dream in sand and saltbush, a martial desert where a mountain is not just a mountain, but a natural fortress. The Rajputs are a proud but mellow people with a culture of puppetry and balladeering. Their confidence is rooted in their role as warriors, whose ancestors acquitted themselves honourably during centuries of defiance against Muslim, Hindu and Sikh invaders. They also cut deals, notably with the Mughal Empire, which they served as governors and military commanders. The men are burnished and swaggering, with flamboyant moustaches and earrings; and the women dress like nomad princesses, even those who labour on the roads. To clothe themselves in this harsh wilderness the Rajasthanis prefer colours that stand out — shades of scarlet and electric yellow, royal blue and neon green — a vivid wardrobe distinguishing friend from foe amid the earth tones.

The dry creek beds and parched ribs of Rajasthan reminded me of Australia, as we sped along the Jaipur road, dodging trucks, buses and camel carts, and discussing the aftermath of the demolition of Babur's Mosque. I was still a bit shaken by what I'd seen, jumping to conclusions about what it meant for India, while Janaki seemed to take it all in her stride. She'd lived through a variety of crises, from war with Pakistan to the Sikh pogrom following Indira Gandhi's murder, and while concerned, believed things would settle down again. It went without saying that she abhorred the chauvinism and violence of the rioters. Members of her own cosmopolitan Hindu Kayasth clan had intermarried with foreigners and Muslims without fear of caste pollution, and her mother's Brahmo roots meant she had not been raised in an atmosphere of religious devotion. She was a Hindu, but left a blank on forms that asked one to declare a religion. We listened to each other's different perspectives — hers based on a lifetime of experience of the way India muddles through, and mine based on having looked into the abyss that beckoned — and realised that no firm conclusions were possible.

No sooner had we arrived at the hunting lodge than my hopes of a romantic weekend evaporated. It was a gloomy place where all the wildlife was stuffed and mannequins stood dressed in chain mail. Tacky mementos gathered dust in display cases. The lake which our suite overlooked had all but evaporated and the cold desert night winds howled in the chimneys. Asking for anything, from a cup of tea to a laundryman, would produce a conga line of bearers whose shambling inefficiency complicated the smallest request and made for many tragi-comic episodes. When I wanted a bath and found the taps not functioning properly, they formed a human chain stretching from the downstairs kitchen to our bathroom, passing scores of buckets of steaming hot water that never seemed to fill the enormous tub. When I eventually blew up at the bearers, my rage was defused by Janaki's fits of laughter.

'You're like Basil in *Fawlty Towers*!' she said, doubled up on the bed.

We all laughed then — her, me and the conga line of bearers. Our disastrous weekend was not so disastrous any more. We talked late into the night, the conversation turning towards our future. Had she ever thought about leaving home and setting up her own place in Delhi, I asked. It seemed an odd suggestion to her. She had lived for several years away from home, but that was overseas. In India, it went without saying that she would live with her family at home until the day she married. Even then it would depend on whether she and her husband could afford to live on their own. Janaki was smart, well educated and strong-willed, but challenging tradition for its own sake wasn't her style. She would wait and see what happened, but as for becoming someone's live-in partner? In Delhi?

'Never,' she said, no longer joking. 'Socially, in my family, it would simply be impossible. Anyway, why would I want to do that?'

The clock was ticking ahead to my expected departure from India the following year. Why not join me in another country on my next posting, or back in Australia? See where things led? But again, my modern Western ideas seemed far-fetched to her. It just wouldn't feel right. Driving back to Delhi the following day the cultural differences between us seemed unbridgeable. I was happy as a global gypsy, she was rooted firmly in an Indian family.

We were nearing Shahjahanpur late in the afternoon, everything bathed in a golden light, when I saw Neemrana, the fort owned by my friend. It was a few kilometres east of the highway, but despite the distance, looked imposing, a stronghold that had never once been attacked, let alone conquered. Situated on a stark spur, it clung to the mountain, a mute witness to earthly and celestial spectacles. The Rajput Hindus who built the fort were feudal lords of the Kshatriya, or soldier caste, descended from the Chauhans who held sway from Ajmer to Delhi in the twelfth century. With the death in 1192 of Prithviraj Chauhan, their empire went into terminal decline. By the time Neemrana was built in 1464, its raja could barely defend the village below it, let alone vast swathes of desert, a fact reflected in the name of the place which meant half king.

In 1947, the last prince to occupy the fort, Raja Rajendra Singh, shifted to a modest bungalow on the outskirts of the village. Emboldened by the victorious Freedom Struggle elsewhere in India, the villagers looted the palace right down to the doors and windows, and the raja sold off some iron support girders, causing part of the structure to collapse. In the 1980s, it was relinquished for a pittance to Francis Wacziarg and his artistically inclined group of friends from Delhi.

Turning off the highway, we drove along a rutted, rising track towards the sheer walls of the fort, pulling up at a massive arched gateway more than 6 metres high. Tall wooden doors embedded with spikes — the kind used to ward off attacks by war elephants — creaked theatrically as we entered to find ourselves in a walled garden of fan palms and bougainvillea. A series of steeply raked walkways climbed through more formidable doorways and dimly lit passages decorated with old frescoes. Finally, we emerged onto an open terrace and met the familiar face of Vipal, one of Wacziarg's managers, whose welcome was so effusive that I'm sure Janaki thought I was paying him. Insisting we take tea, Vipal suggested we tour the fort first and inspect the twelve rooms they'd managed to renovate so far.

As we wandered through the maze of streets and courtyards, Janaki and I found the place almost entirely deserted. The fort had grown organically over centuries, new rooms of eccentric shape and size grafted on according to the rajas' needs. Soon after buying the fort, the new owners realised that extensive repairs were required to prevent parts of it collapsing, and decided to rent out rooms as a way of funding the repairs. In the fifteenth century, the fort had been built to ward off invaders. Now it would welcome guests. Working wall by wall and room by room with a local *mistry*, or chief mason, they gradually resurrected the galleries and courtyards, revealing a host of unsuspected charms. It had taken them a year to clear the rubble, and five years to open the first suite, but what they lacked in finance they made up for with a sense of history. Discreet stairwells once used by clandestine lovers were restored to link the different levels, and vernacular window frames and doors were resized in an on-site atelier to provide views over the village. For decoration, the new owners relied on traditional block-printed textiles and scoured Shekhawati district and towns as far away as Gujarat for period furniture to re-create an environment of beauty and pleasure. The rooms and niches were filled with lohar hanging lamps from Jodhpur, old moneylender's desks, even washbasins from decommissioned train compartments.

The restoration itself was memorialised in framed architectural floor plans hung in the rooms, and 'before and after' photographs that showed how the builders had worked up from the foundations — like blind men groping for the original form. Portraits of the old kings graced the walls, and the rooms were named after figures from Hindu mythology: Krishna Mahal stared amorously at Radha Mahal across a small courtyard named after the poet of the *Ramcharitamanas*, Tulsidas. The torture chamber — a tough reminder of medieval times — became a gift shop. At night blackouts often plunged the narrow streets inside the fort into darkness, and you were advised to tread carefully or risk plunging to your death from the ramparts. But in those first few months, before word of what was happening leaked out, it was easy to believe that the entire fort was your own private domain.

Climbing a precarious staircase to the highest point on the western rampart, above the open pavilion known as the Hawa Mahal, or Wind Palace, we found afternoon tea laid out and waiting for us on the upper terrace. From our lofty perch we could look down on the roofs and courtyards of the village below, and catch words and phrases carried aloft on warm air rising from the desert floor. As the molten orb of the sun descended, it painted the facades of the palace in a succession of colours, from cream to wheat, and gold to red, and finally brown to grey, and the yowl of peacocks echoed in the ravines outside the fort walls. Then, right on cue as the sun subsided, a full moon rose over the mountain behind us, so clear that you could see its plains and craters.

The planets were in alignment, a vital element in any big decision in India. Janaki and I had been dancing around the issue for weeks, almost since the day we'd met. Common sense suggested waiting, getting to know one another better, thinking through the consequences. But while caution is laudable, risk also has its place. Babur's Mosque had stood in Ayodhya for centuries, but had I delayed a single day I would never have seen it. Suddenly, I felt resolved, and before courage could fail me, I knelt before Janaki, took her hands and asked her to marry me.

★ ★ ★

In India marriage is not something people rush into. Finding a suitable mate and negotiating the terms of the 'alliance' normally take months or even years. When I asked Janaki later why she had accepted my proposal there on the ramparts at Neemrana, she said simply that 'it seemed right'. We'd known each other for all of six weeks, and for reasons that neither of us really understood, were in a terrible hurry. Perhaps it was the uncertainty of the times, but moving from meeting to marriage within three months was sure to give her parents heartburn.

Returning from Rajasthan to Delhi after dark, we stopped to buy jonquils — Janaki's favourite flower — then called to tell her parents to expect us. When we arrived, they were seated together on the sofa, not separately in their favourite chairs as usual, and were dressed somewhat too formally. Did they sense something? The bearer, Munawar, brought nuts and poppadums, and we made polite conversation about the fort and the terrors of the Jaipur Highway, in those days regarded as the country's most dangerous road. Then I announced that I had proposed, and that Janaki had accepted, and that we wanted their approval to marry as soon as possible.

Maya's eyebrow lifted worryingly high on her forehead and she pursed her lips. Krishen Bans emitted a small, strangled sound that was half laugh, half gasp. Both of them appeared momentarily befuddled, exchanging anxious glances. Then Abba raised his hand in that way Indians do, begging the obvious.

'What's the rush?' he said.

It seemed a reasonable question. Or was it a wily play for time? But reckless honesty had served me well so far that day, so I replied with the first thing that came into my mind. I was concerned, I said, that if we delayed, something or someone might snatch her away from me.

Maya stared goggle-eyed at her husband as if that was the most ridiculous thing she had ever heard. Then a piece of poppadum caught her throat, triggering a gagging reflex. Abba looked like he'd just taken a mouthful of sour tamarind. It's never the right time to lose your youngest daughter.

'Well …' he said, sighing heavily and abandoning the sentence.

But words never failed Maya. 'This is *crazy*!' she said, but she was smiling, the brilliant, radiant smile I'd seen in the family photos. And before we knew what was happening, the tension gave way to relief and we were all laughing and embracing. Crazy was good! Crazy was India!

'This calls for a drink,' said Abba, cracking open a bottle of his best Scotch. But like everything else in the country, from the composition of a government to the price of a lemon, our marriage would be the subject of extensive and intricate bargaining, among ourselves and even with the authorities. Because I was a foreigner, there were lots of forms to fill in and guarantees to provide — a 'certificate of no objection' from the Australian diplomatic mission, health checks and police reports stating that we were not criminals. Then came the negotiations over the arrangements. Janaki, a Hindu who'd never prayed in a temple, shocked everyone by announcing her desire for a big church wedding. The fact that she might have to convert to Roman Catholicism didn't seem to bother her.

'This is what comes of sending children to convent schools,' said Maya, faking a stare of disbelief at her mad daughter.

'Actually, I had something smaller in mind. Perhaps a registry wedding,' I interrupted, thinking it might save money, but that went down like a stale jalebi.

'Better not to go to the courthouse,' cautioned Abba, his face squeezed into a painful frown. 'Those bureaucrats will cause lot of headaches. We can arrange for a magistrate to come to the house if you wish. Main thing is the reception. You must invite everyone to a big reception.'

In the coming days we would argue about the merits of a church wedding versus a registry wedding versus a big reception, eventually making a compromise. I would get my moment in court with a registry office marriage; Janaki would get her moment in church with a 'blessing' by an Anglican reverend, who was less finicky about these things than his Catholic counterpart; and the parents would get to celebrate our union at a big wedding reception before the entire Bahadur clan, Abba's business associates and our friends and colleagues, on the sprawling lawns of Number Three. There would be no *purohit*, or family priest, chanting Sanskrit *shlokas* that nobody understood. No white horse and no brass band with Petromax lamps. No fire and no seven steps around it. The dowry I received was more than sufficient; it was my wife. In short, it was to be a typical Indian wedding — an expensive, drawn-out ordeal so onerous and complicated that you would never wish to repeat it. Marriage would be simple by comparison. But just when we thought we'd arranged the perfect compromise, the whole thing hit a snag. In India, there is one thing you should never take for granted — India.

8

An Indian Wedding

Winter in Delhi is the marriage season. Between November and February, it was not unknown for as many as 14,000 weddings to take place in the capital on a single day. Getting hitched was a huge business, with an average ceremony and reception costing $10,000. All over the city, brass bands with members dressed like grenadiers parade to and from wedding parties in the white glare of lanterns, producing a noise that would wake the dead. There are lots of parties, lots of alliances and lots of bankruptcies.

Going about my business in the city — which now consisted of buying rings and getting a suit made — I would see numerous *barats* (grooms) dressed in *zari* turbans and Nehru jackets riding meekly on white horses to their destinies, blasted into marital orbit by clamorous combos. Seeing these often terrified young men and their equally morose brides, I experienced mixed feelings. On the one hand I was grateful that I would not have to wear a turban and ride a horse; on the other hand I wondered whether I could cope with the stability of marriage. Fortunately, there was little time to brood.

Two weeks after my proposal and Janaki's acceptance, the communal rioting that had abated after Ayodhya erupted again, this time in Bombay, India's largest and most cosmopolitan city, famous for its rambunctious 'Bollywood' cinema. The death of a Hindu family in a fire triggered general lawlessness in which thousands of slum hutments were razed by supporters of the Shiv Sena, another militant Hindu group which also campaigned against outsiders coming to the city and taking residents' jobs. The Sena was named after the legendary seventeenth-century Hindu warrior Shivaji, who was known for his respect of all religions. Not so the Shiv Sena leader, Bal Thackeray. The violent reaction targeting Muslims was fuelled by provocative statements by the former cartoonist, who had written in the group's newspaper that 'We have to teach them a lesson'.[1]

Arriving in the balmy city on the morning after the riots started, I found the airport terminal entrance, which normally seethed with taxi drivers vying for customers, deserted and not a single taxi driver interested in my fare. Seeing a couple of drivers with their vehicles some 50 metres away, I walked across to hire one, only to be rebuffed.

'Bombay burning,' said one of the drivers. 'No going there.'

It took $100 — ten times the normal fare — and a guarantee to pay for any damage to the car to persuade the other driver to take me. No sooner had we departed than I began to doubt the wisdom of the deal. In India's financial capital — home at the time to over ten million people, headquarters of the country's largest companies and its main bourse — law and order had collapsed. Burning cars blocked the entrances to side streets where mobs could clearly be seen dragging loot from apartment houses. Police and fire crews were conspicuous by their absence, and my driver — probably quite wisely — refused my request to stop and investigate.

Closer to town he relaxed a little and we visited the *bastis* (squatter hutments) that bore the brunt of the worst violence, where families squatted shell-shocked outside the smoking ruins, the assailants having long since fled. On ritzy Malabar Hill, Muslim families had removed the nameplates from their apartments, terrified of being targeted by Hindu mobs. In Worli, I visited a foundry that was busy forging trishuls, the symbolic trident of the Hindu god

Shiva, which the mobs were using as lethal pitchforks. Youth caught up in the violence quickly learnt to improvise. A car inner-tube slung between light poles could launch bottles of acid hundreds of metres. Two hundred thousand people, most of them Muslim, fled the city, turning Victoria Terminus railway station into an unofficial refugee camp. Others took shelter in places like the shrine of Haji Ali, perched on a small island linked to the mainland by a causeway. Crossing the causeway at low tide, I found some of the men had armed themselves with home-made weapons, ready to pay with their lives rather than bow down to the mob.

For a week or so I remained in India's seaside capital of money and hope, a city now traumatised by its horrific alter ego. Communal violence on such a scale was an unpleasant fact of life in parts of the country, but in Bombay it was unprecedented. Despite this, the police responded in a thoroughly communal manner, suggesting that Indian secularism was a thin veneer for much older enmities. On the rare occasions that the mainly Hindu police force did intervene, it was usually to crack down on Muslims who tried to stage protest marches against the attacks on their community. The Committee for the Protection of Democratic Rights recorded police radio transmissions in which officers on duty advised their colleagues to let Muslim properties burn.[2]

Once the violence began, it was quickly exploited by an unholy alliance of criminal gangs and land developers, who seized the chance to drive squatters off prime building sites. Muslim men were being dragged from their cars and stripped to confirm their circumcision, before being necklaced with burning car tyres. Amid the horror, there were many acts of compassion — Hindus saving Muslims and Muslims sheltering Hindus in their neighbourhoods. The former Indian Test cricket captain Sunil Gavaskar intervened to save a Muslim family being attacked on the street; but most of the city's population retreated to their homes, and quite a few sympathised with the perpetrators.

In a conversation with one well-off Hindu family who lived on Malabar Hill, the familiar list of grievances against Indian Muslims was aired: their 12 per cent bloc vote, which allegedly had given them undue influence over the Indian government; their women being trapped in a medieval system of Muslim personal law; their militants using violence to give Kashmir to Pakistan; even their support for the Pakistani cricket team when it played India. It seemed shocking to me that educated, comfortable Hindus could coolly enumerate the failings of a minority group of fellow Indians who, at that moment, on the streets of that very city, were being butchered by the worst elements in Hindu society. An official inquiry found that the riots were the result of a deliberate and systematic effort to incite violence against Muslims. Seven years later Bal Thackeray was arrested and charged, but a magistrate threw out the case on a technicality. Of thirty-two police officials indicted, not one would be convicted, and one became Director-General of Police in the state.[3]

As the death toll in the post-Ayodhya rioting rose into the thousands, I found myself questioning the wisdom of marrying into India. The torment I was witnessing was no longer just another story full of tragedy and adrenaline; it was personal. The Bahadur family too must have had their doubts, as their prospective son-in-law went missing in action at an important time in the life of the family. Trapped between the personal and the professional, I was relieved when, after a week or so, the rioting in Bombay died down. One more flare-up and the wedding might have to be postponed; I needed a plan. If I could wrap up the story, say, by returning to Ayodhya and filing a comprehensive report from the source of the troubles, I might still be able to attend my own wedding, and even get a honeymoon. But my return to Ayodhya only further complicated matters.

Travelling with my friend and cameraman Christophe de Neuville, we had completed shooting the story and were returning from Ayodhya via Lucknow on the afternoon flight to Delhi, IC 810. Cabin service was just beginning when a commotion erupted across the aisle. A short, quite dark Indian man wearing a pullover and scarf with a daub of orange *tilak* on his forehead stood up and began shouting in Hindi and raising his fists in the air. At first I thought he was complaining about the service — 'Give me more Scotch!' or 'Why no vegetarian food?' — but when I heard the telltale words 'Jai Sri Ram!' I realised that something very unpleasant was happening. It was Hindu nationalism at 20,000 feet above sea level. The young man, who turned out to be only nineteen years old, was brandishing two small spheres, one in each hand, which he claimed were some kind of explosive. Unless the pilot turned back to Lucknow immediately, he threatened to blow the plane out of the sky. It appeared we had been hijacked.

Satish Chandra Pandey was a face from the crowd, a young Brahmin farmer from the Hindi heartland of Uttar Pradesh who feared being left out of the Ayodhya action. In 1990 he'd tried and failed to join Advani's yatra to the town, and was frustrated that he'd been unable to attend the more recent demolition of Babri Masjid. Now he was demanding that all those arrested be released, that a ban imposed on Hindu nationalist organisations after the demolition be lifted, and that a Rama temple be built on the rubble of the mosque. Leaving his seat, Pandey paced the aisles, pumped up with adrenaline, watching the passengers closely for signs of defiance. As he stalked around he issued a stream of slogans and threats, interspersed with claims that Hindus were fed up and would take no more of anybody's nonsense. He was hardly the glamorous hijacker you see in movies, so pint-sized that I reckoned we had a fair chance of overpowering him. But when I whispered my idea to a middle-aged man seated across the aisle from me, he reacted with horror. 'Do that and you'll endanger the lives of everyone on this aircraft,' he told me in no uncertain terms. 'You'll be no better than the hijacker. Let the crew handle it.'

He was probably right, but at the time, a dissertation on Gandhian non-violence delivered in snatches under his breath so as not to further antagonise the hijacker was not what I wanted to hear.

Thirty minutes out of Lucknow, the Fokker F–27 aircraft with about fifty people on board tilted gently in the air and turned back. An hour and a half later, we were still in the air, and Pandey was getting twitchy.

'Why are you not returning?' he shouted at a stewardess, his face riven with anger. 'I warn you to put this plane down.'

In the skies over northern India our lives were in the hands of a young man with hair-trigger emotions. On the ground at Lucknow airport, fire trucks, ambulances and commandos were assembling for a showdown. When the emergency services were ready, the control tower at Lucknow gave the pilot the all-clear for landing. As we began our descent I saw the lights of the city twinkling in the dark winter's night, and promised myself not to allow the hijacker to get us airborne again, no matter what my friend across the aisle thought about it. The hijacker too was improvising, and no sooner had we landed around 7.30 p.m., than he made his next demand. Still clutching his bombs, he went to the cockpit and began negotiating with the authorities, demanding that the BJP leader, Mr Vajpayee, who was also the MP from Lucknow and the only person to whom the hijacker was willing to surrender, be brought to the plane. In the hours that followed there was little to do but sit and wait. The hijacker would return to the cabin occasionally, keeping an eye on us, before disappearing again. As time passed I became increasingly pessimistic about the prospects for a peaceful resolution of the crisis. An even more ominous threat than the hijacker loomed — being 'rescued' by Indian commandos, which seemed to me far more likely to hasten our demise. For two hours I waited to hear the gunshots that would signal the end of the crisis, wondering how long the standoff would last. Finally, close to nine-thirty that night, the front hatch of the plane slid open and I saw the hijacker peering out into the darkness with an expression of incredulity. Mr Vajpayee had come to accept his surrender and assure him he would not be harmed.

'Is it Atal-ji?' he asked the stewards, and when they confirmed that it was, he turned to the rest of us, raising his fists in the air and revealing two screwed-up balls of paper — his 'bombs' — which he then hurled at us in triumph before leaving the plane, and heading off to prison.

The following morning the *Times of India*'s front page headline read 'Bomb Threat on Patna–Delhi flight; Passengers Freed at Lucknow — Hijacker Surrenders to Vajpayee'. The story quoted the BJP party president, Dr Murli Manohar Joshi, condemning the hijacking by a 'so-called' BJP activist, calling it a 'conspiracy' to tarnish the image of the party and the RSS, which he said would never support such an act.[4]

★ ★ ★

One of the most grotesque buildings in India stands on the main road that skirts the northern walls of Old Delhi, an area known as Tis Hazari. An Urdu term, it means a warrior in command of 30,000 horsemen, an apparent reference to the number of cavalry garrisoned there in days of yore. Today, it could refer to the number of rickshaws, trucks, buses, cabs, metro rail carriages and people that squeeze past on that sclerotic byway off India's Grand Trunk Road, honking their horns, crossing lanes and narrowly avoiding countless calamities as they run their amazing race every waking hour of every day. Overlooking it all, glum and grey, riddled with concrete cancer and stained by the phlegm of ages, stands the grotesque edifice of the Tis Hazari courthouse, the epitome of architectural awfulness shrouded in thick clouds of smog in winter and besieged year-round by half the touts and pleaders in India.

Six weeks after our visit to Neemrana, Janaki and I found ourselves entering the betel-stained corridors of the courthouse, bumped and jostled as we made our way to Room 137(c) and a sign that read, 'S.K. Malhotra, Addl. Distt. Magistrate (West)'. Around us swirled scores of black-cloaked advocates with white neckbands, khaki-clad police officers, under-trials in shackles, and the glue that holds them all together — the chai-wallahs. Absolutely everyone was there, except S.K. Malhotra, despite the fact that we had rather important business to transact with him. It wasn't the first of our problems.

In times of war or instability, people live fast or not at all, and the hijacking had only added to our sense of marital urgency. Just as Janaki had predicted, normalcy had returned in the wake of the demolition and riots. Some inner bearing seemed to ensure that India, however deep its wounds, was unable to maintain the rage for more than a few days or weeks. My own doubts faded away with the riots, more a case of the usual cold feet than any serious reservations. The alternative of slipping into aging bachelorhood seemed even more ridiculous than this race to the registry office. So what if we were to fail? At least we'd given it a chance, and by seizing the moment would not suffer years of regret over a missed opportunity.

So at 2 p.m. on Saturday, the fourth of February, we arrived at Tis Hazari to take our vows. But the clock or calendar hold no terrors for Indian bureaucrats and magistrates, and forty minutes after the agreed time we were still roaming the bustling corridors looking for S.K. Malhotra, and wondering how to produce various documents that had been demanded by other officials at the last moment. In every betel-juice stained corner and stairwell, convicts, cops and lawyers huddled in clouds of sour-smelling *bidi* smoke. Janaki's brother, Siddhartha — who as his father's only son got all the tough assignments — was hovering around, dressed, like me, in a suit and tie, uncertain whether to weep or murder someone, probably me.

'Disgusting place, *yaar* [mate]!' he said, his pinched nose recoiling at the all-pervasive stench of stale urine. And it was.

My plan for a no-fuss registry office wedding was teetering on the brink of disaster — just as Abba had predicted. With desperation beginning to take hold, I installed Janaki and our witnesses in a relatively quiet room and went off to try and sort out the problems of the missing magistrate and allegedly missing documents. In our rush to wed, no member of my family had been able to reach Delhi. It hadn't bothered me before, but now I felt bereft of hope and totally alone. A vision of a different wedding — planned over months with loved ones present, perhaps even a white horse and seven steps around the fire — taunted me. In room after room I found scores of people crammed like sardines, accusers and defenders, and bored dyspeptic judges. People were begging to be heard and lodging objections, lost souls in the madding crowd of India. Clerks bawled out names and instructions to beetle-browed scribes, who tossed dusty files between them like *chapattis*, tying and untying the cotton drawstrings, and scrawling in dog-eared registers, or clacking away at old manual typewriters, hoarding information like the *wazirs* of a paper empire. Did anyone know of an S.K. Malhotra and his whereabouts? He was 'out of station' or 'must be coming' they told me, but no two informants concurred. Increasingly frantic, I began showing my documents to bystanders, hoping somebody would help me. Finally, a conscientious Bengali clerk spared a precious moment of his time to inspect the file. Concluding that everything was in order, he informed me that S.K. Malhotra had nothing to do with our case. The concerned magistrate was actually a woman who was not sitting in Room 137(c), but in a different chamber.

'You best hurry up and reach that place,' said my beautiful Bengali. 'Otherwise you may be late for your own wedding.'

Pushing through the crowds, I hurried back, expecting to find Janaki justifiably upset. Instead, she was sitting calmly on a bench beneath a ceiling fan festooned in black cobwebs and a charred light fitting blackened by overloads. Looking lovely in a *churidar kameez* topped with a Kashmiri *jamawar* shawl and some antique jewellery her mother had given her, she was chatting gaily with the best man, Derek Brown of the *Guardian*, and our other witnesses. Relief washed over me, for I saw at that moment what a very, very lucky man I was.

But there was no time to waste. The room was found, the magistrate placated and at twenty minutes past three, under oath and duly attested, we were married in the eyes of India, amid a volley of kisses, hugs and shaking hands, and emerged from the grotty hellhole of Tis Hazari into what had turned out to be a beautiful day. The traffic on Boulevard Road seemed somehow lighter, the sun sunnier, and I only half-jokingly suggested that we should walk the short distance back to the Civil Lines.

'Are you mad?' my bride barked at me, delivering her first spousal insult, as she arranged herself carefully in the back seat of the car. With everyone else making a beeline for their vehicles and chilled champagne awaiting us at Commissioner's Lane, I followed her orders and joined the motorcade.

At Number Three, the compound gates swung open to reveal the assembled staff of the household beaming with smiles and hands clasped in namastes, waiting to felicitate us; and beyond them, Janaki's parents waiting with open arms. Neither of us, I am sure, had ever in our lives felt so relieved. Neither war, nor civil disorder, nor famine nor plague are as uniquely terrifying as getting married. Suddenly I knew why all those horse-borne grooms and their brides looked so miserable. But it passes.

It would take several more days to secure the full blessings of the state, the church and Janaki's extended family. But by the time we had exchanged rings, emptied the crates of champagne and cut the cake, and I had given her a *zarbuft* shawl I'd bought in Varanasi, we were ready to return alone to where it all began, at Neemrana. It had been twelve weeks from meeting to marriage, punctuated by India's worst period of civil disorder since independence. Life had seemed like a river in spate, at times almost drowning us. But when we collapsed onto the bed in 'Krishna Mahal', we knew that we had made it, perhaps just in time. Secure in the battlements of our new fortress, we peered out through the curvaceous arches of our balcony, saw a burnt orange desert moon, and knew that destiny was truly written in the stars.

* * *

A few months later, we departed India for a new life in Vietnam, where I'd been offered a two-year posting. Maya, being adventurous at heart, was all for it but Abba's reaction suggested a fear that he might never see his daughter again. His health had been in a slow state of deterioration since he'd been diagnosed with diabetes in his thirties. Janaki clung tenaciously to my promise that we would visit annually.

Three years later, towards the end of 1996, Abba suffered a heart attack. Rushing to Delhi, Janaki found him in frail health, his prognosis uncertain. In Vietnam she had worked as a correspondent with several American news organisations, and back in Delhi found that her services were also in demand in an expanding media market. The respected magazine editor Vinod Mehta had offered her a job on his new venture, *Outlook*. Would I, she asked, consider returning to India?

After ten years and two foreign postings, going it alone as a freelancer in India without the backing of a big organisation seemed like suicide, but I was ready for a new challenge. By early 1997 we were back in Delhi, sharing a four-room apartment with Abba and Maya in the Civil Lines, while the old bungalow underwent major extensions to accommodate our return to Number Three.

Part Three

9

Inhaling the Mahatma

You may kill me. That will not hurt me.
                                    Gandhi[1]

India had just turned fifty and was experiencing a serious midlife crisis. For all but five years since independence, the country had been ruled by the Congress, a remarkable achievement for any political party in a democracy. Sooner or later, however, its accumulated betrayals and failures would tell. The Narasimha Rao government's economic reforms had pleased economists but not the rural masses. In 1996, with voters turning in droves towards parties appealing to caste and religion, the Congress was defeated at the polls. For the first time, a rival political party won more seats than Congress in parliament, and that party was the Hindu nationalist BJP, anathema to all that Gandhi and Nehru had stood for. Yet it had not won an outright majority, and an unstable coalition of minor parties filled the breach in Congress rule until India could make up its mind. As the fiftieth anniversary of freedom approached, the eminent author and journalist Khushwant Singh boldly declared what many felt, but few dared say — that India had been happier under the Raj.[2]

Such a verdict, while understandable, concealed the fact that Indians were better off ruling themselves. Before independence in the late 1940s, only 20 per cent of Indians could read or write.

Famines were a common occurrence and women on average bore seven children.[3] An Indian born in 1950 could expect to live a mere thirty-two years. By the end of the twentieth century, that had doubled to sixty-five years, and two out of every three people were literate.[4] Improved agricultural methods had doubled food production, and although the population had trebled from about 360 million in 1951 to over a billion by the end of the 1990s, per capita incomes had kept pace. In short, there were many more people and most of them were better off. Nehru's interventionist strategy to provide basic education, food and health care to the masses had paid off, laying the foundation on which the growth-orientated policies of the 1990s could hope to succeed. But a free people's expectations, once raised, are difficult to satisfy.

Each January, India marks the adoption of its 1950 democratic Constitution with a military parade. Just back in Delhi, Janaki and I donned our best clothes and went along. As we watched ballistic missiles named after Aryan gods and Hindu warriors like Agni and Prithvi roll down Rajpath, it was clear that the Mahatma's vision of India as a loose confederation of self-sustaining villages was no longer on the agenda. What India wanted to be was rich and powerful, with a strong army and prosperous economy.

Over lunch at the Imperial Hotel after the parade, Janaki and I discussed plans for our new life together in India. This time she had the job and I was going it alone, without the cushioning of a long-established office and reliable staff. We had no car, let alone a driver, and would cook for ourselves, using the cook's salary to buy food. Living cheek by jowl with Janaki's parents, but determined to pay our own way, we both had to find and write stories.

Amid the gloomy introspection leading up to Republic Day I'd noticed a bizarre item in one of the local newspapers. Descendants of Mahatma Gandhi had won a court battle for possession of an urn containing his ashes, which had been locked in a bank vault for almost half a century. A long-delayed ceremony was being held to immerse the ashes at the confluence of the Ganga and Yamuna rivers, and allow the father of the nation — all of him — to rest in peace. Attracted by the sheer oddity of the event, I bought a train ticket to Allahabad, reaching the city in time to attend the ceremony.

On 31 January 1948, the body of the greatest Indian of the twentieth century, Mohandas Karamchand Gandhi, was committed to a sandalwood funeral pyre on the banks of the Yamuna River in Delhi. After Gandhi's pyre on Raj Ghat was reduced to cold ashes, relatives had sifted carefully through the cinders, removing one of the three spent bullets that had killed him, and shovelling his ashen remains into urns for distribution to far-flung parts of the country. According to Hindu tradition, the ashes would be immersed in the rivers and seas of India. Gandhi's chosen successor and independent India's first prime minister, Pandit Jawaharlal Nehru (the 'pandit' signifying a high-caste Hindu Brahmin), had taken one urn to his home town of Allahabad and immersed the contents at the sangam. Another urn was sent to Orissa, a balmy state fronting the Bay of Bengal, where it sat in a bank vault in the state capital, Cuttack, undisturbed and unimmersed, for almost fifty years.

The precise reason why the remains of the father of the nation had not properly been disposed of was a mystery. According to one theory, they'd been ensnared in a power struggle. One of the ministers in Nehru's Cabinet who'd taken them to Orissa wanted them to be immersed in the Bay of Bengal, near the temple town of Puri, but Nabha Krishna Chatterjee, the state's chief minister at the time, had objected, pointing out that Gandhi-ji had refused to visit the town because its famous Jagannath Temple would not allow entry to Untouchables. Before the feuding politicians could settle the argument, however, they lost power or moved on. In 1956 the state capital shifted from Cuttack to Bhubaneshwar, and the lonely urn was left behind, first in the chief minister's old office, and then in a bank vault. Forty-four years later a bank official told a newspaper reporter about the ashes, and the reporter's subsequent story caught the eye of 36-year-old Tushar Gandhi, the Mahatma's great-grandson. Tushar Gandhi did what any self-respecting Indian does when confronted by injustice: he filed a court case, and even employed his great ancestor's weapon of choice, the hunger strike, to ensure proper disposal of the remains. The case went all the way to the Supreme Court of India, which in November 1996 rejected Tushar's application to take the ashes on a yatra across northern India but granted him permission to immerse them in the Ganga according to the Mahatma's philosophy, in the simplest manner possible, and with an official of the Orissa High Court present.

The night before the immersion was due to take place, a wooden box containing the copper urn arrived at Allahabad Junction railway station after a nineteen-hour journey from Puri, and was greeted by large crowds. Across eastern India that cold January of 1997, the Purushottam Express had carried the ashes, accompanied by Tushar, who was born in 1960 and had never met the Mahatma. At station after station along the route, the train was waylaid by onlookers curious to get a glimpse of the holy box containing the holy urn containing the holy ashes of the holy body of the great soul of India, delaying its arrival at Allahabad by several hours. As the train finally trundled into its destination, chants of 'Mahatma Gandhi zindabad' (Long Live Mahatma Gandhi) and '*Jab tak suraj, chand rahega, Gandhi tera naam rahega*' (As long as the sun and moon remain, so will Gandhi's name) rent the air. Railway officials had obtained old recordings of the Mahatma's favourite *bhajans*, or hymns, which issued from a public address system normally reserved for arrival and departure announcements. Tushar, a rotund man of bear-like countenance, with dark loose-locked hair and a bushy beard, emerged from a second-class carriage with the garlanded box borne aloft. Security men quickly bundled him into an official vehicle, which took him to the city's Circuit House, home to visiting bureaucrats and VVIPs (Very, Very Important Persons).

In a country where politicians trade heavily on ancestry and symbols, the immersion had provoked a jaundiced response from commentators, who suspected Tushar Gandhi of using the occasion to launch a political career of his own. The Congress Party had lost office the previous year, and the present government in Delhi had stayed away from the ceremony, denying it the sanction of the Indian state. As the grandson of the Mahatma's second son, Manilal, Tushar was little known, although his father ran a small Gandhian non-violence centre in the United States. He called the immersion 'a very sacred duty'[5] and denied any cunning scheme to plunge into politics. One year later, Tushar would stand for election to the national parliament and lose.

In the grounds of the Circuit House, reclining in a sea of white cotton under an expansive *pandal*, or tent, Congressmen, Gandhians and mourners sat cross-legged in front of the box containing the urn, and sang hymns late into the night. The presence of people from all of India's main faiths could have been a moving tribute had it happened spontaneously. Alas, they had been assembled as if by quota in the dead symbolism of secular orthodoxy.

Next morning, taking a boat from the riverbank, I headed out towards the sangam. In the distance I could see Tushar, who bore no resemblance to his famous forebear, surrounded by the official party on the tented pontoon that was decorated in the orange, green and white colours of the Congress, and India. A second pontoon floated nearby, from which the tripods of press photographers sprouted like a forest. Clambering aboard it, I saw Tushar and his wife and young children greeting Romesh Bhandari, the Congress governor of India's most populous state, as well as the state Congress Party chief Jitendra Prasad and Allahabad mayor Rita Joshi. Tushar had removed the soccer-ball sized urn from its box and was exposing it like a relic before the people around him, who jostled to press it to their foreheads in a gesture of homage. This final darshan completed, he handed the vessel to a *panda*, or Brahmin who assists in Hindu rituals, who removed the seal and began pouring milk and water into the urn, adding turmeric, saffron, red *gulal* powder and various fruits. Brown-husked coconuts were broken and their liquid contents added to the brew, while their shells were cast into the river and oil lamps were lit. The pandas chanted Sanskrit shlokas and stirred the cocktail of death and rebirth by gently rocking the container. Mixing done, Tushar knelt at the edge of the pontoon, held the urn over the water and upended it.

As Tushar Gandhi lifted the urn containing his illustrious ancestor's ashes, I saw a cormorant plunge headlong into the river, emerging with its beak fastened on a flapping fish. Bending to pick up my camera, I lost my balance and had to flap my arms like wings to regain it. For a moment I stared straight into the water and knew I did not want to fall in there. We were a long way from the shore, and even a strong swimmer would have difficulty negotiating the shifting currents at the meeting point of the two big rivers. I was not a Hindu and had no wish to be anything more than a witness, certainly not a participant, in the immersion ritual. After this brief scare, I got the camera and knelt down in a space between the television tripods and trained my lens on Tushar, who was also kneeling, engulfed in a forest of arms and hands reaching out to touch the urn. As the container tilted, the weird cocktail of liquids the priest had poured into it began to trickle out, followed by ... nothing.

No ashes. No Mahatma.

For what seemed like an eternity, the upturned vessel kept everyone hanging in suspense. Where had Bapu gone? What had become of his mortal remains? The VVIPs looked concerned. Tushar gave the urn a shake.

Then it fell. Not just a cascade — a torrent congealed into an avalanche — ashes spewing forth towards the water. The faces of concern turned to smiles, and a few people began applauding. All watched in awe as the horn of ashen plenty gushed with funerary abundance, Tushar and the panda gave it a few more shoves to ensure that all the contents were acquitted. Having defied their efforts to turn him into sludge, the Mahatma made his final journey as a fine, flowing powder.

Through the viewfinder of my camera I noticed two men standing in the river, observing proceedings and wearing baseball caps with official passes pinned to their pullovers. They were not walking on water, but knee deep in the middle of the sangam, indicating that the river at this spot was actually extremely shallow. At the same time, a strange mist had formed on the water, surrounding the two men in skirts of fog. Either the light breeze was catching the ashes as they fell, or the cascade had clotted on the surface of the water, preventing all of the ash dissolving properly. The fine dust now billowed up into the air. The Mahatma was escaping, Houdini-like, in a final act of Gandhian resistance, taking to the air rather than taking a holy dip. The dignitaries looked on helplessly, some covering their mouths and noses with their shawls. I heard somebody cough and saw Tushar and the panda reaching down to mix the ash in the water by hand. Clicking away with my camera, I didn't realise that the amorphous cloud was creeping closer to me, pushed along by wayward zephyrs.

The first thing I noticed was a strange, metallic taste in my mouth. Then, a peppery sensation infiltrated my nose, like that preceding a sneeze. Suddenly, shockingly, I realised that I was *inhaling* the Mahatma.

The mortuary mushroom cloud passed over the pontoons and floated back up the Ganga. On the boat ride back to the shoreline I silently pondered what had happened. The ceremony had coincided with the annual Magh Mela, a smaller version of the Kumbh Mela bathing festival, when millions of pilgrims flock to Allahabad from all over India. From mid-river, the pilgrims looked like ants, crowding a flat horizon. But as we came closer, individual figures were discernible; a man bathing a baby, another with his hands clasped in prayer. Yet my thoughts were preoccupied with the stale scrapings — powdered burnt hair and skin fifty years old — that had penetrated my being. At that very moment, Gandhi was dissolving into my bloodstream. I remembered the Indians who fifty years earlier had followed the funeral boat carrying one batch of remains out into the Arabian Sea off Bombay, desperate to catch a speck of his ashes. Now I'd gotten a lungful.

Hours later, back at the hotel, the taste of the Mahatma lingered. The preternatural encounter would become, for me, a symbol of my new life in India, unmediated by an expatriate comfort zone. Real, and often surreal, a strange and accidental communion. But it also represented the passing of Gandhi's vision, its decline into an empty language of symbols and 'isms'.

By deifying the Mahatma, they had finally buried him.

10

Diary of a Munshi

It was only after Janaki and I had married that Abba had handed me a bound photocopy of the family history, taken from a book held at the India Office Library in London. *A Short Account of the Life and Family of Rai Jeewan Lal Bahadur, Late Honorary Magistrate, Delhi, with Extracts from his Diary relating to the time of Mutiny, 1857* had been compiled in the nineteenth century by the magistrate's son. Much more than a typical genealogy, it was a sprawling tale of war, rebellion, shifting alliances and the struggle for survival that is India.

According to the family legends passed down by Brahmin priests, the Bahadurs of the Civil Lines traced their descent from a single common ancestor belonging to the Mathur Kayasths, or scribe caste. This ancestor, whom they called Andhi Bharat, was the son of a blind woman from the village of Kukraj, somewhere in the Rajasthan Desert. In a devastating war with a neighbouring kingdom, the entire family had been put to death. Only the blind woman, who was pregnant at the time, was spared. Wandering alone she was taken under the protection of a Hindu priest who was travelling to Narnaul, an ancient trading post and now a prosperous provincial town 40 kilometres from Neemrana. With the onset of her labour pains as they journeyed, and wishing to conceal her condition, the woman sent the priest off in search of water, and gave birth alone in the desert, hiding the child some distance away. Returning with the water the purohit found the mother in distress and urged her to reveal where she had put the child. Reaching the spot he found the baby lying on the sandy ground. Standing over it, with its wings raised to protect the infant from the sun, was a *cheel*, or hawk. Ever since, the cheel has been worshipped as the Mathur Kayasth clan's deity, and Narnaul is called the *thamba*, or place of halt, where Andhi Bharat grew to manhood and re-established a family line that had so narrowly — as if by divine intervention — avoided extinction.

Although the truth behind the myth is unlikely ever to be verified, by the seventeenth century Andhi Bharat's descendants were beginning to appear in the historical record. They had not merely survived, but had grown to become a powerful Narnaul family with links to the Mughal emperors of Delhi. In the 1600s, a member of the family, Raja Raghunath, had travelled to the then new city of Shahjahanabad, now Old Delhi, to serve in the court of the Emperor Shah Jahan. The raja would rise to great renown as the senior-most Hindu official in the Mughal court. His mastery of Persian, in which all Mughal documents since Akbar's time were recorded, propelled his brilliant career as a *munshi*, a kind of scribe–accountant in the *diwani*, or revenue collection department of the administration. Although the author of the *Short Account*, Lala Maharaja Lal, claims the raja as a direct ancestor, other accounts refer to him as Raja Rughunath Khatri, suggesting he might have been of a different or mixed caste.

The munshis — usually of the Kayasth and Khatri castes — were what historian Sanjay Subrahmanyam calls the 'Persianized Hindu scribal class', men of high learning and versatile intelligence whose knowledge of history, law, languages, statecraft, poetry and book-keeping took them to the far corners of the empire, and who in the process developed a personal code of honour and devotion to those they served. One of the earliest, Chandrabhan 'Brahman', summed up the versatility required in the trade in a letter to his son:

> Scribes who know accountancy as well are rare. A man who knows how to write good prose as well as accountancy is a bright light even among lights. Besides, a munshi should be discreet and virtuous.[1]

Raja Raghunath must have been an exceptionally adept and upright munshi, because a compendium of the Mughal nobility, the Ma'asir ul-Umara, records that in the twenty-third year of Shah Jahan's reign he was awarded the title of Rai, or Chief, and given a golden quill case called the *qalamdan*, whose holders enjoyed direct access to the emperor. Three years later he was promoted to the post of custodian of the royal records, and three years after that, in 1657, upon the death of Sa'ad-Allah Khan who was regarded as one of the greatest men of the age, became *diwan ala*, effectively prime minister. It was a time that marked the high point of Mughal architecture, with the completion of perhaps the most divine structure ever built by human hands, the Taj Mahal at Agra. But it was also a time of great turmoil, with wars against the Persians and Marathas. Raja Raghunath's career was interrupted when Shah Jahan was arrested and imprisoned by one of his sons, Aurangzeb, triggering a war of the succession with the crown prince, Dara Shikoh.

The etiquette among Mughal bureaucrats was to remain neutral in such cases.[2] But on 20 June 1658, two days after the surrender of Agra Fort made Aurangzeb's victory clear, Raja Raghunath and other high nobles and officers of the state presented themselves at the fort to offer their services, and the raja resumed office serving as one of the Mughal ruler's principal advisers.[3] As the raja's other main responsibility was the collection of tribute from the various vassal states that were subordinate to the Mughals, a force of 2500 *sawars*, or cavalrymen, was placed at his disposal. The hand that held the pen now also wielded a mighty sword. He continued to discharge his duties until 1663, when, in the sixth year of Aurangzeb's reign, 'the ministers of destiny folded the documents of his life'.[4]

By the time the British came on the scene, the descendants of Raja Raghunath were still a wealthy and influential family living in the walled city of Delhi. The Kayasths' place in the Hindu caste system had never been clearly defined; it was assumed that they ranked somewhere between Brahmins and the Vaishyas, or producer caste. But their proximity to Muslim royalty over centuries had rubbed off on them. Although they continued to observe Hindu practices and rituals, they were steeped in Persian language and culture, enjoying a diet rich in meat and wine, and confining their women in purdah (seclusion). While none of the raja's descendants had reached his lofty heights of public office — official posts were not hereditary in Mughal times — they were still employed as senior bureaucrats at royal courts in Delhi, Hyderabad and several smaller kingdoms.

But as the Mughal Empire went into a slow decline, life in Delhi became less predictable, most violently evinced in the Persian warlord Nadir Shah's sacking of Delhi in 1739. As the Mughals ceded more and more ground to the British East India Company and its soldiers, the Kayasths sensed the direction in which things were moving. They began studying English and soon would be acting as go-betweens for the British in their dealings with the Mughals. Girdhari Lal (1770–1844) served as munshi to Sir David Ochterlony and Sir Charles Metcalfe when they were the British residents to the Mughal court at Delhi. His son Jeewan Lal followed him into the service as administrator of the various pensions paid by the British to the king's family. As a result, Jeewan was in daily contact with the Red Fort for years, and was given the title of Bahadur, a Mughal term meaning brave, by the British who bestowed it as a reward on loyal supporters and subjects. As one British official wrote:

A very highly educated, most courteous, pleasant man. His opinion was taken in connection with every matter relating to the court at Delhi, the princes, the swarms of applications for compassionate allowances, rewards, compensation for losses.[5]

In 1857, when the last Mughal emperor Bahadur Shah threw in his lot with a popular rebellion against the British, the position of the Kayasth munshis became delicate once more. Indian sepoys serving with the British forces rebelled suddenly after rumours spread that the bullets they were issued had been greased with pig and cattle fat. The revulsion at such cultural insensitivity, combined with longstanding resentment against British high-handedness, forged unprecedented if short-lived Hindu–Muslim unity and a determination to oust the white overlords. The Hindu scribe Jeewan Lal, then aged fifty-one, was forced into an invidious choice between Muslim and Christian overlords. He chose to be 'loyal to his salt', siding with the British who were his employers. In the four months that the rebels were in control of Delhi, with British forces encamped on the Ridge, he remained in the walled city, harassed by looters and threatened by elements of the court, who rightly suspected him of feeding intelligence to the British. But Jeewan Lal's house was a veritable fortress, constructed with stones salvaged from the ruins of Feroze Shah's fourteenth-century capital. Secure in his bastion, he sent a message to Sir John Metcalfe (nephew of Sir Charles) and other senior British officials asking for orders and offering sanctuary in his home to any Englishman who might need it. He also engaged two Brahmins among others as spies to report on the rebels' doings. Throughout the ordeal, he kept a diary.

12th May, 1857 — Two Mooglee Telungas [rebel sepoys] came to my house, and commenced disturbance. Dhunna Kahar paid them four rupees and made them go away ... Two other Telungas entered my house, and took away my goods, *viz*, floor carpets, pillows, books, one box containing cash and jewels and shawls, &c., value about 2,000 rupees ...[6]

On 19 May, a stranger approached the house dressed in the robes of a Hindu ascetic, 'only his eyes were blue,' noted Jeewan Lal, clearly struck by this feature, highly unusual among the people of the subcontinent. Despite greeting his host with the words *Jai Sita Ram-ji ki* (Hail Sita and Ram), and being fluent in Sanskrit and Urdu, the stranger turned out to be an Englishman in disguise, carrying important letters to be delivered to regional chieftains urging them to join forces with the British. After two hours in conversation, the mysterious messenger stole away into the galis of the walled city. Travellers on all roads leading into and out of Delhi were being thoroughly searched by the rebels, and anyone found aiding the British faced certain death. Despite the risks, Jeewan Lal passed on the messages, and the support of the chiefs he contacted played an important part in the subjugation of the Uprising, known to the British as the Mutiny and to modern historians as the Indian Rebellion of 1857.

Underlying Jeewan Lal's loyalty was a hard-headed calculation that the Uprising would fail. It was, he told an emissary of the Raja of Ballabgarh, 'a cloud of steam'. The rebel faction within the Mughal court continued to pressure him, sending hundreds of men armed with sabres to sack his home and demolish parts of it. Ambitious nobles handed him papers forcing him to sign over property he held in Chandni Chowk, the main street of the Old City. On 4 August 1857, Sir John Metcalfe sent Jeewan Lal a message that the British were receiving reinforcements from Punjab and would soon conquer Delhi.

'The delight this news produced in our hearts was like the new life which a timely shower gives to a garden,' Jeewan Lal wrote in his diary.

On 7 August a detachment of Mughal troops stormed his home, arrested him and held a dagger to his throat, declaring 'This is the man that sends news to the English!'

As Jeewan Lal wrote in his diary, 'We poor Mutsuddis [writers] were threatened so far that guns being placed over our shoulders were fired.'

After being detained for a day while the rebels argued over his fate, he was eventually released, but only after being relieved of more of his possessions. On 13 September, Sir John and the British detachment encamped on the high ground on the Ridge overlooking Delhi received a letter from Jeewan Lal reporting that the rebels were increasingly disheartened and 'beginning to flee'. That night, the British launched their assault to retake the walled city.

Sir John Metcalfe would later write of the munshi that:

No more trustworthy or loyal native servant has the British government ever had, and no more trustworthy or reliable source of information could be obtained than the record he has left behind of the summer of 1857.[7]

In the aftermath of the Uprising, the British hung the rebels from trees and seriously considered demolishing the city's main mosque, the Jama Masjid. Instead, they occupied it, much like American troops occupy Saddam Hussein's palace in Baghdad today. The last Mughal king, Bahadur Shah, was exiled to Rangoon by the British, who assumed sovereignty over all India. Refusing offers of financial reward from the grateful new overlords, the loyal munshi retired on a monthly pension of twenty-eight rupees, devoting his energies to such social reform causes as the education of women. Despite stiff opposition from families in the deeply conservative walled city, he helped open the Indraprastha School near the Friday Mosque, the first girls school in Delhi, and later threw his weight behind campaigns to reduce crippling wedding dowries. He was also a vigorous advocate of immunisation and of general income tax as a tool of development.

His activism was recognised with the award of several titles, bestowed by the British viceroy, Lord Lytton. In retirement, he helped several British writers to complete their accounts of the Uprising and histories of northern India. Carr Stephen acknowledged that without Jeewan Lal's help, his *Archaeology and Monumental Remains of Delhi* would never have been written.[8] Upon his death in April 1884, the *Civil and Military Gazette*, as quoted in *The Statesman*, wrote that 'In him, we have lost perhaps the best informed student of Indian history in northern India'. He died, according to his daughter-in-law, uttering the words 'Ram, Ram, Ram'.

Out of self interest, fear, or merely the old munshi code of loyalty, the Rai Bahadur had sided with the Europeans against their mutinous sepoys. In a sense, that put him on the wrong side of history, but history is a creature of hindsight and is often selectively rewritten. Perhaps in Jeewan Lal's mind the Christian British were preferable to a continuation of Muslim rule; he doesn't say. All that his diaries reveal is a staunch loyalty to his masters and a certitude that the Uprising would fail. Also, the very reforms he championed, and which the British supported, would ensure that the Raj was shorter lived than the Mughal empire. The spread of literacy and modern political, legal and business ideas energised the new Indian nationalist movement, which in less than a century would force the British to leave.

Ironically, universal education also put paid to the Mathur Kayaths' livelihood as niche providers of language and financial services to government. Ever the modernists, they sent their sons to England to study law, and established the Kayasth Mercantile Banking Company at Delhi, the first in a series of successful financial ventures. Janaki's great-grandfather Raj Narain — who, like the Nehrus, attended Cambridge — became one of India's most successful barristers. With his earnings, in 1902 the family purchased a plot of land just north of the city walls. It was overgrown and still littered with cannonballs from the Uprising, but there he built the whitewashed bungalow at Number Three Commissioner's Lane where his great-granddaughter Janaki would grow up.

The Bahadurs wore their remarkable heritage lightly. Janaki had not even mentioned it to me.

11

Three Commissioner's Lane

For almost 400 years, the Mathur Kayasths had been living within a five-kilometre radius of the walled city of Delhi. If not exactly immoveable, they were certainly steadfast in the face of India's turbulent history. From the Mughal war of succession in the 1660s, to the 1857 Uprising and Partition in 1947 — when Abba was given a gun and told to fire on miscreants — they had survived and sometimes prospered. In 1948, as a young man, Abba had joined the throng on Raj Ghat watching Gandhi's cremation, and as a student of St Stephen's College his classmates had included a young Punjabi called Zia ul-Haq, who went on the become the military ruler of Pakistan. There was barely an inch of ground in the neighbourhood that didn't bear the imprint of the Bahadur family's past, from the Red Fort where their ancestors had served, to the Yamuna River where Abba and his siblings enjoyed swimming as children. Now an outsider's name — mine — squeezed onto the plate on the gatepost at Three Commissioner's Lane in the Bahadur-dominated Civil Lines.

Now in his seventies, and having made a good recovery from what he pointedly referred to as his 'so-called heart attack', Abba had resumed the meticulous work routine that had served him well for forty years. Every day, six days a week, he would attend the offices of The Instalment Supply Limited, dressed in a tailored business suit, white shirt and narrow dark tie. Around noon he would walk across to the Imperial Hotel, where a select group of fellow businessmen who became known as the 'Coffee Club' would swap business and political gossip, which they found useful in navigating the shark-infested waters of Indian capitalism. Returning to the office, his lunch — hot from Maya's kitchen — would be delivered in a stainless-steel quadruple-deck tiffin box by one of the drivers. After lunch he would take a nap, sitting up in his chair in the lunch room, before resuming work in the afternoon. A great dancer and socialiser in his youth, he now enjoyed his evenings at home, with a coffee, snack and a good book in the hours between his return from work and the regulation two pegs of Scotch before dinner at ten.

I had never heard him raise his voice, his displeasure shown only in a concentrated frown that drew his hawk-like eyes rather too close to his nose. Otherwise, he was generally resigned or amused, with a mischievous smile never far from his lips. The frequent arrival of baskets of fruit and other gifts at Number Three testified to the respect and affection in which he was held by business associates, family and friends. He was the Banyan tree under which the family sheltered and struck new roots.

Abba's 'so-called heart attack' had been the trigger for many changes at Number Three. A long-delayed partition of the one-acre block between him and his siblings was to take place, along with major extensions to the old bungalow in order to create separate accommodation for the future needs of his three children and their families. Towards the end of 1997, having lived for most of the year in temporary accommodation elsewhere, parents, children, in-laws and servants trooped back to the high-walled compound on the corner of Commissioner's Lane and Maharaja Lal Lane. The quarters allotted to Janaki and myself were more like a spacious new home. Her cousin Yasmeen Tayebbhai, an architect by profession, had given us six airy rooms, most of them overlooking a small private garden.

We filled the bookshelves and threw down some cheap rugs and kilims, hung framed Madhubani prints from Bihar, Raj-period lithographs and some striking abstract canvases painted by Yasmeen's husband, Ajay Desai, and furnished the place with walnut desks from Kashmir and teak sidetables from Kerala.

In addition to the tribe of cooks, sweepers, drivers, maids, gatemen and gardeners already employed by the family, we engaged the sweeper's sister, Sushila, as our housekeeper. The diminutive widow, who could not write a word of Hindi nor speak a word of English and whose deep fatalism was enlivened by a bright, chuckling laugh, soon made herself indispensable. But that was where the servant raj ended. For transport we relied on Lovely Singh's taxi stand, and we bought a washing machine instead of employing a dhobi.

Within weeks I had established a small office, and my initial forays as a freelancer led to a contract to represent the *Sydney Morning Herald* and *The Age* in the region. With no office staff, I placed an advertisement on a noticeboard at the nearby Delhi University and found Sanjay Jha, a passionate and persistent law student from Bihar, who did the work of three people in half the time. Intensely interested in politics, economics, social trends, media and countless other issues, Sanjay embodied the incredible drive of his generation, the first in post-independence India to realise that reliance on the state is a poor substitute for individual initiative. He'd arrive on his scooter, stylish in tight-fitting jeans and wrap-around sunglasses, mobile phone welded to his ear, and fluent in several languages, all of them used within a single sentence sometimes. He was up to date with all the latest gadgets and advice on how to get a faster Internet connection, and had an insatiable hunger for the minutiae of Indian public life and global issues. Where others might resent a request to research some complex aspect of the national budget, Sanjay would seize on it with an almost terrifying intensity.

'You have ignited my mind, boss,' he would tell me, producing chapter and verse on the issue, along with a raft of people to interview and all the necessary travel arrangements within hours. His relentless energy made me feel old by comparison, but his support eased my transition from New Delhi expat to Old Delhi local.

'Face it, boss, you're no longer a *gora* [white person]. You are half-Indian now,' he would tell me, and indeed that was how both Indians and foreigners increasingly began to treat me. My Hindi had improved, although I was still far from fluent and lacking in confidence. Hari Lal's visits had resumed, although less frequently than before because the Civil Lines was some distance from his usual haunts in the diplomatic enclave. My former foreign correspondent colleagues had almost all moved on, replaced by a new generation who wrote much the same stories as their predecessors, and made me realise that the normal three-year stint in India was barely enough time to scratch the surface. Enthralled by the sensations that a billion-strong democracy can generate, most of us had missed the less spectacular, but much more important story — the one about India's remarkable progress and resilience.

The Bahadurs at Three Commissioner's Lane were not political people but, like the munshis of old, they were affected by political upheavals and had their views.

Maya's Brahmo background made Hindu nationalism anathema to her, but Abba was more worried by the Congress's populist socialism, which he believed had caused incalculable losses to the country.

'We Indians are very clever people, but in all the wrong ways,' he would say, twisting his hand to indicate a general slipperiness. 'So many teachers at government schools don't show up for work because they're moonlighting in other jobs. They only come to collect their salaries. Then these bureaucrats are also killing this country, and politicians only want to make money.'

Indians of Abba and Maya's class and generation had been inspired by Gandhi's Freedom Struggle, but disappointed by the outcome. As a young woman, Maya had participated in a 'Quit India' procession from Indraprastha College to the Ram Lilas grounds near Mori Gate.

'Independence was just a big hoo-haa,' she'd say, complaining of declining standards of decency.

'When I was young, we used to walk up and down the streets in Daryaganj at night. The servants would come with us and we'd feel completely safe. Now, the streets are full of *goondas*, you know, thugs. Before independence, if I saw anyone on the road doing something wrong, say, ill-treating an animal, I would stop and tell them, "Hey, don't do that. You're hurting that animal." But after independence if I said that, they'd say, "Who are you to tell me anything?" They thought that because India was free, so nobody could tell them what to do.'

Like me, Maya had come to the Civil Lines as an outsider. Her father's Brahmo passion for setting up English Medium schools had given her a peripatetic upbringing that included stints in Abbottabad, Dehra Dun, Karachi and Delhi. Although her family were not wealthy, at nineteen she had won a scholarship to study in the United States. Returning to Delhi in 1953, she had thought to carry on her family's involvement in education, but discussions soon turned to finding a suitable match for her. The names of several eligible young men from top families had already been entertained. Then, through a college friend, she met the stylish and charming Krishen Bans and they began seeing one another — dancing at the Roshanara Club and going to English language movies at the Ritz Cinema in Kashmere Gate.

It had always puzzled me slightly why the Bahadurs had acquiesced in their daughter's desire for a quick wedding. One day, as we chatted in her reading area, Maya let slip the answer. She and Abba had done exactly the same thing. They hadn't even had an engagement. 'Abba was going to a wedding in Hyderabad and he wanted me to come along with him. And I said, "We can't just go like this!" So we got married and went. All my Brahmo friends said, "You have to go to the courts" — because Hindu marriage in those days was just a ceremony, no paperwork — but we did it the Kayasths' way. This *pandit* married us off. I don't even have a marriage certificate.'

Compared to the Brahmos, even the cosmopolitan Kayasths seemed traditional. It was only two generations since Abba's grandfather Raj Narain had led the clan out of the walled city, ordered the women to remove their *naths* — nose rings large enough to fit over their heads — and started the practice of eating at tables and chairs in the British style, instead of cross-legged on the floor. In those days, the family system in which the eldest male made all important decisions and women lived in a Hindu form of purdah still prevailed. Though they shunned some traditions, the Bahadurs had no desire to ignore the annual Hindu festivals such as Holi and Diwali, in fact, they revelled in them. One of Abba's cousins, Om Lata Bahadur, had even written a bestselling book on the meaning and celebration of these festivals which sustained community life in the Civil Lines as they did in communities all over India.

Like everyone else at Number Three, Maya was a voracious reader and could always be found dressed in one of her many saris, ensconced in an easy chair in her bedroom, and surrounded by a clutter of tea trays, reading glasses, tissue boxes and massive piles of books, newspapers and magazines. While Abba dissected the Indian press with a forensic eye for political nuance, his wife preferred *National Geographic* and the *New Yorker*. Her carefully catalogued bac issues of magazines filled numerous book cases, all fitted with glass doors to protect them from Delhi's incipient dust, providing a treasured link with another world.

In the quiet lanes of the Civil Lines the day was ushered in by the paper-wallah, who delivered the newspapers. Then came the *subzi-* wallah, around whose vegetable cart the entire domestic staff of the compound would gather to hear the neighbourhood's gossip. Finally, the shrill cry of '*kabar-reee*' from the beyond the high walls would announce the arrival of the *kabari*-wallah, front man for the world's most efficient waste-paper and glass recycling system. Night and day, the call of the *muezzin* from the mosque on Alipore Road marked the five daily prayers of the Muslims, adding another thread to the complex tapestry of our lives. Few Muslims lived in the Civil Lines, and the discordant muezzin could provide a rude awakening at six in the morning, but the Hindu Kayasths would have felt uneasy should the minaret ever fall silent. Even the insistent urgings of the muezzin, however, could not wake the listless chowkidars — our supposed guards — who dozed day and night in their gatehouses. Deserted on summer days, the somnolent streets named after the ancestors only really stirred in the early evening, when sari-clad *ayahs* would emerge, pushing babies in strollers or chatting over fences, and hump-backed cows foraged in the garbage pile at the end of Maharaja Lal Lane.

Atop the jungle-covered ridge line not far away stood several stone towers shaped like bastions and cathedral spires where, in the summer of 1857, British forces had regrouped after being expelled by rebels from the walled city. Etched on the base of the Mutiny Memorial, erected in 1870, are the names of 2613 red-coated soldiers who stayed loyal to the British and paid the ultimate price. A hundred metres from our front gate was Qudsia Bagh, the garden in which the British set up their gun batteries for the final and successful assault on the rebels. In another country, the area between Delhi University and Kashmere Gate would be a treasured memorial park. In India, it was slowly disappearing under blocks of flats and flyovers.

Older Delhi-wallahs like Abba could recall childhood trips by horse-drawn tonga to picnics at Lal Kot in the days when people were still permitted to climb to the top of the Qutub Minar, a thirteenth-century Islamic tower on the southern outskirts of Delhi — and *shikar* expeditions to Mehrauli to bag partridge, blackbuck and chinkara, or Indian gazelle. The Muslim separatist insurgency in Kashmir had put paid to his trout-fishing holidays and people no longer hunted around the metropolis that Delhi had become. My brother-in-law Siddhartha's weekend golf game was the norm nowadays.

Indian families have a place for everyone and put everyone in their place. My early difficulties with the nomenclature of an Indian joint family meant I followed Janaki's lead in the protocols of address. Her brother became my Dada (elder brother), and her father became my Abba. Nobody seemed to mind if I failed to add the right *Bhua*, *Mashi*, *Bhaiya*, or *Didi*. The rest of the family went by their initials. Sister-in-law Tarini was T; aunties Lalit, Kamal, Madhur and Veena were L, K, M and V; and in the tribe of cousins, Yasmeen was Yas, Sakina was Mittoo, Mehreen was Mehr, Rohit was Rohi and Meera was Chubby. Only cousin Zia retained her actual name. My early uncertainty about the amount of sledging that went on at the dining table was soon allayed. Janaki was very close to her mother, with whom she could discuss anything. Her relationship with her dad, by contrast, was a kind of extended comedy hour. The one person who really had her measure was her elder brother. One withering look from Siddhartha and she'd be lost for words.

One morning, brushing my teeth, I saw in the bathroom mirror something that froze the toothbrush in my mouth. Over my shoulder two very hairy hands and equally hairy feet were clambering along the parapet just outside the bathroom window. They belonged to a rhesus macaque, the first of many monkeys who would make their presence felt in our home. Families of up to twenty of them would gambol in single file along the boundary walls, or engage in raucous domestic disputes in the trees, making the foliage shiver and sending squirrels sprinting for cover. They drifted down from the Ridge, a jungle now but once the hunting park of the fourteenth-century Central Asian Feroze Shah, who once ruled Delhi. An elusive golden brown mongoose was also occasionally seen, slinking nimbly along the drain grate on the southern edge of the property, and it was not uncommon when opening the curtains in the morning to find a peacock and his brood admiring their own reflections in the window.

It felt good to share our refuge with these creatures, whose days in the city were so obviously numbered. As the old bungalows were pulled down and replaced by apartment blocks, the greenery in our compound was becoming a rarity. A profusion of fan palms, frangipani, towering trees and soft groundcover plants made an oasis just a stone's throw from the walled city. Red-cheeked bulbuls and green parrots hung upside down in mango, neem and gulmohar trees, while black butterflies hovered in the ferns. All year round, large hawks, or cheels, would perch on the rooftop water tanks that provided a commanding view of the enclave, their long high-pitched whistles a constant reminder of their role as the Bahadurs' tutelary deity.

The king of our urban jungle was Rama Sri, another widower, who'd been the *mali*, or gardener, at Number Three for at least thirty years. A humble but dignified man, his namaste was delivered with tightly clasped hands and a nod that was more of a quick bow. He glided rather than walked, stepping lightly in bare feet with his wiry frame draped in a *banyian* (singlet). His unseen presence could be signalled by a whiff of sour bidi smoke from the garden, or the metallic clack of the heavy iron mower, or the scratching sound of leaves being swept off the lawn as he moved about taking cuttings, watering plants, or planting winter vegetables.

Emerging from his rudimentary quarters at the rear of the bungalow, he'd appear unannounced at the kitchen door, offering a cane basketful of fresh *mouli* and lettuce — *salard*, he called it — or politely asking if he could use the telephone to sort out some personal matter. Unaccustomed to the new touch phones, he would pick out the numbers on the keypad carefully, one button at a time, cradling the receiver as if the slightest pressure might break it. While Sushila and the other staff at Number Three might get the occasional hurry-up from me, Rama Sri had an almost mystic quality that inspired awe. His only vice that I knew of, apart from his bidis, was throwing stones at the peacocks to drive them off his vegetable patch. Once or twice a year, he would return to his village somewhere in the Himalayan foothills to check that his small parcel of land there was being used productively, and see that his married daughters were living happily. Once, when I thanked him for some small service, he replied in Hindi, 'So long as I'm alive, I will be doing this only.' His garden dharma personified the dignity of labour one encounters so often in India, and reminded me of my own father, who embodied many of the same sturdy virtues.

By early June, when the air became clammy with humidity and newspapers taunted their readers with reports of far-off rain, Rama Sri would scan the skies for signs of the monsoon. Then, in late June or early July, when the waiting became unbearable and our hopes for a good drenching were fading, the yowl of a peacock or a gust of wind, or a low rumble of thunder and a change in the light, would alert us to its arrival. The sky would darken, illuminated by fluorescent flashes that silhouetted the trees. The wind would start to buffet the bamboo *chik* screens that hung across the verandas. Birds would fall silent, the temperature would drop, and it would begin to rain, large, fat drops at first, and then a torrent. The rain would drum on the broad-leafed bamboo fronds that bent beneath its touch, and all you could hear would be rolling thunderballs hurled by an angry god in a heavenly bowling alley. Gradually the tumult would ebb. Steam would rise with a faintly rancid smell, and the gurgle of trickling water would be heard from all corners of the garden. Venturing outside you might find that a potato tree or other plants had fallen, and that the earth — bone dry a few hours earlier — was damp and fecund, with white blossoms knocked off branches and strewn across the lawn. The geckos grew fat on mosquitoes, and washed clothes could take weeks to dry. All through to September, the monsoon cast its blessings and plagues on northern India, bringing relief from the heat, but also devastating floods and outbreaks of viral fever.

As the seasons shifted, so too did our diet. Early summer brought the first mangoes, starting with the prized Alphonso and followed by the Langra, the Dushheri, and finally the Chausa, by the time the monsoon started. Because mobile refrigerated food storage was still rare, the arrival of apples and cherries from Kashmir, fresh tamarind, custard apples and melons, along with indigenous fruits like *ber, falsa, jamun* and *chikoos*, was as good a guide to the season as the calendar. The old mango tree in the compound, the fruit of which never seemed to ripen, provided a tangy base for *achar*, or pickle, and all fruits were considered tastier to the Indian palate if served with a sprinkle of salt and pepper. Along with unfamiliar fruits, the dining table at Civil Lines boasted an array of vegetables that were new to me: the knobbly-skinned *kareila*, or bitter gourd; green *parhwal* pods with their creamy pulp and edible seeds; *bhindi* finely chopped and deep fried until its was crunchy. The small, spherical squash called *tinda* were stuffed with onion and *masalas*, and *dal* was served with a *tarka* of cumin seeds and dried red chillies fried in ghee.

The centuries of Mughal rule had also given the Kayasths, like most people in northern India, a taste for meat. We got our mutton — which in Delhi means goat — from a Muslim butcher, Mirajuddin & Sons in Khan Market, where the meat-wallahs sat cross-legged on a raised wooden platform dissecting the various cuts, gripping their knives with their toes! Maya's version of mutton *ishtoo*, cooked on the bone with whole black cardamom pods and eaten with marrow spoons, was a lunch favourite; it was served with paper-thin *romali roti* or heavy *sheermal* flatbread brought warm from bakers in the walled city. Replete after a dessert of *gajar ka halwa*, a rich, sweet mixture of grated carrots, milk and *kheer*, we would be packed off for our afternoon snooze, an essential part of a busy life in Delhi.

The Bahadurs had perfected the art of living in a hostile environment, improvising where necessary to cope with Delhi's crumbling infrastructure. With the potable water supply restricted to a few hours a day and the electricity supply unreliable, water had to be pumped into the rooftop tanks whenever it was available. Petrol generators and banks of car batteries were used to provide light and power during the frequent blackouts. In summer you didn't need electricity to have a warm shower; the tap water ran boiling hot, and we kept the geysers switched off to create small reservoirs of cool water. In our quiet quarter of Old Delhi, a city that wears its dysfunction like a threadbare but familiar jacket, time-worn traditions lingered. But beyond the compound walls, new upheavals were brewing.

By the mid-1990s, more Indians were voting BJP than for any other party, and the Hindu nationalists had emerged as the only national alternative to the Congress. At the same time, a surge in support for regional parties elevated them to the role of kingmakers in an increasingly competitive political environment. Regional pride was manifested in the country's biggest cities reverting to their pre-colonial names. In 1996, Madras — capital of the southern state of Tamil Nadu — reverted to Chennai, and Bombay followed, abandoning its Portuguese name in favour of Mumbai, derived from an important local deity, Mumba Devi. Calcutta became Kolkata. Of the four major metros, only New Delhi survived because the traditional name of Dilli referred to the walled city, not the new capital built in the twentieth century to house the administration. For the new regional parties, the nuances of caste, language and religion provided a more useful currency than the big ideas, such as secularism and nationalism, of the two national parties. They would happily sell their support to the highest bidder in exchange for a ministry. With the Congress in disarray after its defeat, and the coalition that replaced it tottering, the Hindu nationalists could sense that their moment was coming. In late 1997, after only one year in power, the coalition government of Prime Minister Inder Kumar Gujral' fell and fresh elections were called. The nationalists geared up for a final decisive push towards power.

The prospect of the saffron forces of Hindu nationalism ruling India got mixed reviews at Number Three. Maya was horrified by the mere thought of it.

'They'll never get my vote, with their Ram and mandir mischief. It's ridiculous! You can't run a country on slogans,' she said.

Janaki — although less partisan than her mother — was also troubled by the BJP's record of stirring up communal hatred. She'd inherited her father's disdain for the Nehru clan's corruption and cult of personality, but also shared her mother's revulsion when it came to religious chauvinism. One morning, reading the newspaper at the breakfast table, she reacted with uncharacteristic vehemence to the news that the BJP party president, Lal Krishna Advani, was launching another of his cross-country yatras in a truck decorated to resemble Rama's chariot.

'It's so pathetic, browbeating millions of poor Muslims. What have they done to deserve this?' she said. 'There must be fifty mosques built on top of old temples in this country. Should we demolish all of them? Why not build a future, instead of digging up the past like this?'

Abba's position was different. As a businessman, he'd never liked the left, and had been drifting away from Congress since Mrs Gandhi nationalised the banks and suspended democratic freedoms by declaring a state of emergency in the 1970s. Although impressed by the Rao government's economic reforms, he disliked the Gandhi family political cult, which still bore heavily on the Congress. Like many middle-class Indians he was socially liberal, but had moved towards the BJP by default, without necessarily embracing their more sectarian policies, which, in any case, he saw as political window dressing, likely to be abandoned in the event that they should form a government.

In my early days as a correspondent I would have rushed to judge him as a closet fanatic. Having personally witnessed the extremity of some Hindu nationalists, I certainly found his opinions confronting. But everything and everyone around Krishen Bans testified to his decency, so instead of making snap judgements, I swallowed my arrogance and listened to him. In the process I learnt that the nationalist support base included two very different constituencies: *banias* (traders and businessmen) fed up with Congress socialism, and a smaller hard core of chauvinist fanatics. Often in the early evenings, when Abba enjoyed a snack of *pakoras* and coffee, we would sit together discussing the situation in the country. He was always curious about my travels and the top politicians I'd been meeting. Equally absorbing to me were the snippets of news and gossip that he shared, and which always provided a balance to the breathless coverage in the newspapers. Life in the Civil Lines cured me of our Western tendency to prescribe what others should think and feel, to define the limits of reason and justice, and to lecture rather than listen.

12

Cow Belt Cowboy

I am a worshipper of the cow.
Gandhi[1]

The Aryans were cowherds, heavily dependent on their stock
for survival. They drank cow's milk and cow's urine, still
considered a tonic, and used cow dung as fuel for cooking and
fertiliser for their crops. The distinctive humped zebu breed — the
world's oldest domesticated cow, which originated in India — is
mentioned in the *Rig Veda*, and its image occurs frequently on seals
found in sites associated with the Indus Valley civilisation. Because
the cow was so essential to life, Aryans were reluctant to kill any,
but would partake of the beef if the animal died of natural causes.
Respect for cows came before respect for people. While a human
being could be brutally killed, a cow must be protected. As early
Hindus absorbed influences from peace-loving folk like the Jains
and Buddhists, they extended their respect for the cow's life to all
life, with Brahmins adopting a vegetarian diet. They composed
odes to cows, not unlike the pastoral poets of England in a more
bucolic time than today, and believed that merely to touch one was
sufficient to banish all one's sins. To be bovine was to be divine.
One of their gods, Krishna, was a cowherd who made love to
milkmaids. Another, Shiva, chose the bull Nandi as his mount.

Like the wholesome people of rural America described by H.L. Mencken, they went to sleep with the cows and woke up with the cows. Every day they waited for the cows to come home. Cows are to Hindus what apple pie is to Americans: something inalienably good. The cow — not the dog — is India's best friend. Spend even a brief period of time in the country and you will more likely than not find yourself infected to some degree by its contagious passion for these quadruped ruminants. The cow's maternal concern for its calves might strike you as touching, and its hypnotic contentment as wise. A set of drooping ears flicking away the flies, or big, long-lashed cow eyes, might even strike you as attractive.

For centuries, cow slaughter has been the focus of many protests, and cows are often in the news. The Muslim taste for beef caused so much disquiet that the first Mughal emperor, Babur, advised his son and heir, Humayun, not to mess with the cows because nobody who did would ever be able to rule the Hindus. The cow, he told his son, is like their mother. The British, who ignored Babur's wise advice, ruled more briefly than their predecessors. During the Freedom Struggle against British rule, one of the movement's leader's, Lokmanya Tilak, spoke the immortal words 'Kill me, but spare the cow'. When freedom came it was, of course, fitting that India's new Constitution should include a clause dealing with four-legged friends. Article 48 of the directive principles requires the states of the Indian Union to prohibit cow slaughter.

India today has more than 200 million cows, one for every five people and one-fifth of the world's cow population. Indian cows produce more milk than anywhere else, and the most milk in India is produced in Uttar Pradesh. When Indians speak of the Cow Belt, they are not referring to a narrow strip of leather useful in holding up people's skirts and trousers. They are talking about the broad shoulders of India, the wide stretch of land between the Himalaya and Vindya mountains, the spine of which is the Ganga and the heart of which is UP. In peninsular India, where people lived closer to the sea, fish always provided a valuable adjunct to people's diets. But in the northern plains, crisscrossed by invaders and frequently caught up in war, the cow was their staple.

Alas, nowadays the term 'Cow Belt' is often used derisively to denote all that is crude and backward in Indian society, a lawless place full of vulgar people where literacy is low, birth rates high, economic growth virtually nonexistent, and whose politics resemble a stockyard sale. UP — home to the Ganga, the Kumbh Mela, five former prime ministers and the Taj Mahal — had, by the 1990s, become the butt of jokes. Its politicians were no longer the patrician Congressmen of an earlier era, but betel-nut-chewing, cow-milking Yadavs and Singhs, whose earthy vernacular and yokel antics appealed to large sections of the community. With their brazen mouths brimful of *supari* (betel) juice, Cow Belt politicians in UP, Bihar, Madhya Pradesh and Rajasthan win votes by declaring their love for cows and securing funds to establish cow research and protection units. Much of this type of bidding is no more significant than the dust raised by cows as they return to their shelters in the evening; but it wins hearts and minds of rural folk, even though the same politicians have failed so miserably to promote growth and reduce corruption. Compared to the great metropolises of other states, UP's cities are stunted, none with a population greater than three million people, despite there being 170 million people in the state. The state is a very large farm, and the biggest source of cheap migrant labour for the rest of India.[2]

The Cow Belt was also the setting for India's version of China's Cultural Revolution. The Ayodhya temple movement had struck a chord mainly with high-caste but poor young men in the Hindi-speaking heartland, while the caste politics unleashed by V.P. Singh also spread like wildfire. In early 1998, with another election under way, I left the comfort of Delhi for the Cow Belt, to see how the other half lived, find out how they intended to vote, and look up an old acquaintance who probably would not remember me, but who in his own small way reflected the mood of the times.

East of National Highway 28, between Allahabad and Lucknow, lies a cluster of five villages known as Saraiya Maafi, where men lounge on string cots smoking hookahs, while their tattooed women queue for water at steel handpumps. There is no running water and no electricity; householders rely on 12-volt batteries that regularly need to be carted 5 kilometres to be recharged. Nor is there a single telephone; the nearest place with a landline is 19 kilometres away, and villagers rely on a wireless loop line in case of emergencies. Most people are farmers, tilling the land by day and sheltering in mud-brick huts under terracotta roofs at night, soothed by country-made liquor. They get two crops a year, three in a good year, mainly wheat, rice, chickpeas, peanuts, lentils and sugar cane. There's enough to eat. In fact, the food is delicious. But the land owns them, not the other way around, and caste and lack of economic opportunities mean there isn't much social mobility. Politics is dominated by the land-owning Yadav castes, and the once respected Brahmins are poor. White faces are rarely seen there, evoking intense curiosity on the rare occasions they appear. Very few Indian villagers have ever travelled by plane, but the man I went to Saraiya Maafi to see had once flown, which was how we'd met.

Satish Chandra Pandey was free on conditional bail, restricted to his village as India's glacially slow legal system made a show of dealing with his case, which involved the hijacking of a passenger plane with forty-eight people on board as it flew over northern India in January 1993. The last time I'd seen Pandey was the moment of his surrender, when he threw his fake paper bombs at me and the other passengers on the plane he'd hijacked. He'd been led away by police and spent four years in prison before being granted bail. I'd gotten married, left India and had now returned on his trail.

Dressed in a jacket and tie to make a strong impression, I found my way to his house to be told that he wasn't home. Soon, however, a family member dispatched to the fields to find him returned with good news. Satish-sahib was coming. While we waited, I caught up with the family's history, as told by his younger brother Girish.

Like many high-caste Brahmins, the Pandeys were not particularly well off, owning eight *bighas* — about 5 hectares — of land which they'd tilled for three generations. Satish and Girish had attended missionary schools up until the twelfth class, although Satish had repeated a year after a scandal in which he and three other boys had reported an illicit relationship between two teachers, then refused to apologise for raising the matter. Entry to convent schools had been facilitated by their father's service in the Indian Army as a *subedar*, or junior commissioned officer and clerk in the Ordnance Department. His father's job had taken the family all over the country, even to New Delhi, which they remembered with great fondness, but also to Allahabad, Lucknow, Jabalpur and Nasik. Satish had aspired to be a Test fast bowler but had failed to realise that ambition. His wife died while giving birth, as did the child.

Satish had not even arrived at the house but already I felt I was getting to know him: the rootless upbringing, all those schools joined and left, including the convent school, with its whiff of corruption; the righteousness of a stubborn youth, and his unjust punishment; the vision of India, what it was and what it should be, seen from the capital; the high-status Brahmin heritage contrasting with the family's modest circumstances; the sense of discipline and duty instilled by a military father; the lost wife and child; even the unrealised ambition to be a cricketer. Then the bold assertion that got his name in the newspapers, followed by four years in jail, during which time his parents died. Finally, he'd ended up back here, bogged down in hours of backbreaking labour every day on the small family plot.

At last the man I had come to see walked into the earthen courtyard in front of the house. At twenty-five, Satish was small and imperfectly formed, barely reaching my shoulder and with a smile that from a certain angle looked more like a grimace. He wore Western clothes, rubber *chappals* and a white scarf around his neck, and was breathing heavily, as if he'd run in from the fields, which he had. A smudge of orange tilak in the centre of his dark brown forehead said Hindu. As he smiled and shook my hand, he resembled a game show guest, pleased by his sudden celebrity but uncertain about how brief it might be. He was looking around, checking whether the other villagers were seeing this — Satish Pandey giving darshan to a foreign visitor. And sure enough, a crowd was forming, although it mainly comprised children. Seeing that he did not recognise me, I decided not to tell him that I had been on board Flight IC 810. Instead, I told him the half-truth; that I was a correspondent covering the election campaign. I'd heard of his exploits on behalf of the temple movement and wanted to get his views on the political situation.

Relief flooded Satish's face and I saw a man who longed to be happy. Age-wise he could still pass for a teen, and his thick, neatly cut black hair shone with youthful vigour. But close up you could see the premature grey hairs — he was a worrier — and his teeth and lips bore bright orange supari stains. Calling for two chairs and a kitchen table to be brought out of the house, he offered me a seat in the straw-strewn courtyard where a large buffalo grazed. One of the children brought stainless-steel cups full of water and a plate of sweet *barfi*. Satish-ji, I said to him, tell me about the hijacking.

'I was ready to die,' Satish responded in Hindi with a headline writer's knack for getting your attention. 'Ready for the pilot to lose control, or for commandos to shoot me. In any case, I knew I didn't need to buy a return ticket. The night before leaving the village, I showed the family my air ticket. I said, "I have to go to Delhi."'

UP Brahmins have a history of boldness — the sepoy who triggered the Indian Rebellion of 1857 was Mangal Pandey — but Satish's defiance set me back on my heels. Having spent years thinking of him as an irresponsible fool, my subconscious had tricked me into expecting contrition, not pride. But this not-so-humble farmer retained his audacity, ego and grand ambitions.

Out of the Cow Belt came Satish Chandra Pandey, the Brahmin with a mission. Before setting out for the airport, and not wishing to waste money on expensive town food, he had packed his own tiffin. Without a car, and with no buses serving his village, he had asked his brother to give him a lift on his bicycle, and together they had pedalled the 19 kilometres to the nearest train station. Before boarding the Varun Express from Sultanpur to Lucknow, where he would board the plane, Satish told his brother, 'Make sure to get tomorrow morning's newspaper.' That night, back in the village, Girish tuned to BBC Radio's Hindi service just in time to catch its report of the events at Lucknow airport. Next morning, before the family had even had time to get a newspaper, police arrived at their home and began a thorough search of the premises.

Satish Pandey considered himself a Ram Bhakt, or devoted servant of Rama. In Hinduism, Bhakti is the name of a revolutionary tradition stretching back some 2000 years.[3] It democratised the faith by teaching that knowledge of the scriptures and ritual sacrifices are not essential for salvation. As in the words of John Lennon's 1960s anthem, all a *bhakt* needs is love, but in order to focus that ecstasy, new gods — manifestations of the unknowable Almighty — would be needed. Bhakti drove the development of cults surrounding avatars such as Rama and Krishna, and in the process created the popular Hinduism we know today, a spiritual hypermarket in which individuals choose the deities that most suit their own personalities and needs. As an alternative to the rigid laws of karma, which dictate that actions in this life determine one's lot in the next, Bhakti introduced divine grace. The gods can be fearsome, like Kali, or winsome, like Krishna, but they must, the bhakt believes, reciprocate genuine love and devotion.

For India's Hindu nationalists, this divine concept would become a tool for political mobilisation. As a teenager, Satish Pandey had been inspired by BJP leader Lal Krishna Advani's cross-country yatras demanding construction of a Rama temple at Ayodhya. But in

1992, when the kar sevaks succeeded in demolishing the mosque, they'd done it without Satish, much to his disappointment. While he was toiling on the family farm, history was passing him by. For him, the very survival of Hindu culture was at stake. Many countries were Christian, many were Muslim and Buddhist too, but only two countries — India and Nepal — were Hindu. If Hindu feelings such as antipathy towards cow slaughter were not respected here, where would they be respected? If monuments to Hindu humiliation were accepted in India, where could the Hindus call home? So, in the month after the demolition, with Hindu nationalist organisations banned and some of their leaders in detention, Satish decided that he must do something about it.

Hindu philosophy provides various insights into the battle between right and wrong. Gandhi's doctrine of Ahimsa, or non-violence, advocated a Christ-like self-sacrifice as the best response to evil. It turned out to be an effective strategy to end British colonial rule, but it might not have worked against Hitler, a reality the Mahatma himself understood. Although he tried to reconcile it, his view was also contradicted by his faith's most influential moral treatise, the *Bhagavad Gita*, or Song of God. In the *Gita*, the hero Arjuna's agony of indecision on the eve of battle against his predatory cousins parallels that of Christ in the Garden of Gethsemane. Lord Krishna speaks to the warrior about karma, the philosophical law that says he cannot escape action, nor the consequences of his actions; whether he chooses to fight or flee, people are going to die. But whereas Jesus resolves to sacrifice his own life, Arjuna resolves to fight others, and does so with the blessings of a god. In the hands of philosophers, the *Gita*, like the Bible, is a sublime statement on the human condition; the struggle between conviction and doubt, between action and passivity, between good and evil. At the moment of truth, man reluctantly embraces his dharma and a hero is born. But in the hands of a troubled nineteen year old, the holy book could be a licence to kill, a licence issued not by generals acting under the authority of elected leaders, but by his conscience. Nathuram Godse, the Mahatma's assassin, was no Arjuna; it's not known whether he acted on his own initiative or under orders, but he invoked the *Gita* to justify the murder, blaming Gandhi's non-violence for the Partition that cost up to a million lives. Just like Godse, my hijacker believed that India was the Hindu homeland and was under threat. Just like Godse, he believed that an extreme act — like taking fifty innocent people hostage and endangering their lives — was justified in a good cause. As the historian Stanley Wolpert has written, 'Karma Yoga has thus been used to justify the worst sort of antisocial behaviour, and to invest modern Indian violence with an aura of religious rationale.' We can't blame religion for our misinterpretations of it. Crimes of conscience will always be with us. Our only defence is the law.

Satish leant back in his chair, relaxed and comfortable now, answering questions with a broken smile and a knowing glance to his audience. It was unusual in an Indian village for an open-air chat like ours not to attract a larger crowd and, looking around at the small band of children, I wondered if adults were avoiding their famous neighbour. In order to get a sense of his standing in the village, I asked if he would mind showing me around. As we wandered the dirt lanes, he made a point of talking and smiling at other people, but their reactions were guarded. Either Satish and his views were unpopular, or people feared being seen to associate with him. He seemed uncomfortable, as if not wanting to strike the wrong person at this crucial moment in his interaction with the outside world.

Satish had paid a price for his decision to hijack a plane, perhaps not as high a price as he should have paid, but a price nonetheless. Despite the pro bono services of a star lawyer, arranged for him by friends in the movement, it had taken four years for him to obtain bail, and legal opinion was that the case would take twenty years to reach a conclusion. He was not permitted to leave the village except to report monthly to police in Lucknow. His father, Ram Kumar

Pandey, who had thrown himself into his son's defence, fighting all the way to the Allahabad High Court where the case was still stuck, had died while Satish was in prison, as had his mother, Maya Devi, who was only forty-six when she developed a fatal brain tumour. As the eldest son, Satish had inherited the responsibility of preserving and maintaining the family's lands, a difficult job in a lawless area where well-connected thugs often made it into positions of power.

Yet ultimately, Satish believed his hijacking had been a good investment in the future — his own and India's — and his confidence was not entirely misplaced. An analysis of 500 candidates published by *Outlook* magazine during the election campaign found that seventy-two had extensive criminal records. All had managed to have their convictions delayed or overturned by resort to influence peddling and legal stalling.

Returning to the courtyard after our walk around his village, Satish called for more sweets and water. I couldn't fault his hospitality. As an ordinary mortal, he must have experienced some fear prior to his bold act of hijacking, I imagined, but he denied ever feeling the slightest anxiety. When the former prime minister Narasimha Rao had vowed to rebuild the mosque, he simply 'flew into a rage' determined to attract the attention of the government.[4] He was confident that the party he supported, the BJP, would win the election, and fully expected that when they did, the charges against him under the *Terrorist and Disruptive Activities Act* would be dropped. Not only that, but they would establish a new Hindu *rashtra*, or nation, in which Hindu values, like cow protection, would have to be respected by Indians of all faiths.

Gradually, as he became accustomed to my presence, Satish became expansive, bordering on cocky. He said that his act of hijacking the aircraft had made him a significant person, a person whose commitment and bravery had been demonstrated in a concrete way that nobody could ever take away from him.

'What I did was noticed in high places,' he said.

Noticed, yes. But hadn't Mr Vajpayee publicly scolded him for his use of 'wrong methods'?

Satish smiled slyly and, in a sage tone that suggested I ought to know better, answered, 'Atal-ji has to talk like that. He's a politician. He doesn't need to promise to liberate other Hindu sites. People like me will take care of that.'

With that he got up to relieve himself, leaving me to consider the implications of his statement.

Napoleon once said that 'Glory is fleeting, but obscurity is forever'. For Satish, it seemed, one shot wasn't enough. He was biding his time, awaiting the call to more glory. He had found a way to stand out among India's teeming billion which required no wealth or skill, just audacity and determination. Worse for me, my visit seemed to have given him new hope and energy, the celebrity and attention he so deeply craved. He had spoken about 'doing something more for which I'll be remembered'.

Far from having seen the error of his ways, Satish clearly was prepared to act again. That phrase, 'people like me'. What sort of person was he? He denied belonging to any political party and said he had acted entirely alone in hijacking the plane. But obviously he considered himself as part of a movement, a movement with a clear distinction between the political leadership and the grassroots cadre that allowed its leaders to deny knowledge or approval of action by those lower down in the hierarchy.

When he returned to the courtyard, Satish was holding a folded piece of paper which he duly presented to me. It was his trump card, a letter typed in English on the official letterhead of the Leader of the Opposition in parliament, Atal Bihari Vajpayee. Dated 27 June 1996, three years after the hijacking, it was a personally signed letter of condolence to Satish on the death of his father.

'I share your grief,' Mr Vajpayee had written to the hijacker. 'I pray to the Lord for your father's soul and [to] give the family members the strength to bear this.'

I was stunned. Looking up from the letter in disbelief, I saw Satish nodding and smiling at me. He was right about the difference between a politician's public position and his private feelings, and I had been naive to imagine otherwise. Vajpayee's own colleagues in the nationalist leadership called him 'The Mask', the friendly face selling their hardline policies. And Satish Pandey may have been useful to them too. The nexus between mainstream politicians and the mob is one of Indian democracy's unhappy features. Vajpayee, Satish said, had helped him to secure the services of his celebrity lawyer, and another senior BJP leader, Brij Bhushan Sharan Singh, himself in jail at the time, had bribed the guards in order to spend time with Satish, who was not supposed to meet other prisoners. All of them, from top to bottom, were united in their cause, if not their tactics. Satish was desperate; Vajpayee was patient. Satish was a gambler; Vajpayee was cautious; Vajpayee had a vested interest in the comforts and privileges of power. Satish had nothing to lose. What united them was their allegiance to the loose confederation, or 'family', of Hindu nationalist organisations known as the Sangh Parivar.

Satish had made his point well. But I was holding a trump card of my own.

We had been chatting for two hours, most of it occupied with Satish's boasting, when I told him that I had come to Saraiya Maafi with a hidden purpose. In a sober tone, I explained that for years my plan had been brewing — five years, to be exact — ever since the fateful day of 22 January 1993 when, returning to New Delhi to be reunited with my fiancee and begin preparations for our wedding, I'd had the misfortune of being a passenger aboard a plane — a Fokker F–27, if memory served me correctly — that was hijacked en route from Lucknow. I told Satish about the terrible trauma the forty-eight passengers had suffered, as they considered their fate, of the confusion and upset that my own family had gone through when they learnt of what had happened, and how I'd always believed that one day I would catch up with the person who'd been responsible for the whole thing.

The revelation that he was sitting before one of his own victims drew a sharp intake of breath from the hijacker. His eyes darted left and right, vainly searching for support from among his audience of children and ruminants. 'But what did *I* do?' his helpless, innocent expression seemed to say. He was, I realised, fearful. Had I come alone? Was I armed with some form of weapon, legal or otherwise? Now Satish knew what it was to be ambushed. He might be sitting in the courtyard outside his own home, in his own village, in his own country but, suddenly, anything could happen to him. If I felt as strongly about honour as he did, a premeditated act of violent revenge was not out of the question. He could be a dead man.

Reaching into the pocket of my jacket, I produced a white handkerchief which I used to wipe the barfi crumbs off my fingers. Then I extended my hand towards the hijacker in friendship.

'*Koi baat nahin*,' I said to him. It doesn't matter.

I've never seen anyone look so relieved. The realisation that he was okay, that he would not suffer consequences released an audible gasp from the young farmer.

'You didn't think I wanted to take revenge, did you?' I said, ribbing him.

He laughed ruefully, apologising for any inconvenience to my family. He called for yet more sweets, the traditional gesture of felicitation, and as we ate them and the tension dissipated, he began to recover his former bravado.

Did he have any regrets?

'Never!' replied Satish. 'You know, the Hindu nation was threatened. And if the Hindu nation is threatened, I will do anything.'

But what about the law? Surely, in a democracy, it represented the collective view of the Indian people about the way citizens should conduct themselves, about right and wrong. Didn't he have a social responsibility to abide by it?

But Satish was dismissive, falling back on his circular ideology.

'When the law respects Hindu sentiment, then I will respect the law,' he said.

Religion, politics and law form an unholy trinity at times in India and elsewhere, and the question of who defines Hindu sentiment wasn't going to be worked out that afternoon. But six years after the demolition, this young farmer from the Cow Belt still burnt with a zeal to right ancient and contemporary wrongs. His anger, and that of people like him, would change India.

13

Explosion of Self-esteem

How is it then that I have become so evil and detestable?
Gandhi[1]

For Indians influenced by what became known as the Bengali Renaissance, English — not just the language, but the ideas of democracy and justice it articulated — promised a better future than did the vernacular for an ancient Asian civilisation. The British Empire had been an imposition: Indians were discriminated against in their own country, and economic activities that posed a threat to British industry, like milling cotton, were discouraged. Yet for many Indians, and particularly for the Brahmo leader Ram Mohan Roy, the arrival of the British had presented an historic opportunity to revive India's own greatness:

Far from desiring the expulsion of England from India, he [Ram Mohan Roy] wished her to be established there in such a way that her blood, her gold, and her thought would intermingle with the Indian, and not as a blood-sucking ghoul leaving her exhausted. He went so far as to wish his people to adopt English as their universal language, to make India Western socially and then to achieve independence and enlighten the rest of Asia.[2]

The ideas of the Bengali Renaissance triumphed in the Indian Freedom Struggle, quite ironic given that the principal enemies in that struggle were the British. India became a secular state with English the primary language of public and intellectual life. But by the early 1990s, a new sociological phenomenon had emerged in the cities of northern India — the middle-class politicised Hindu.

My first experience of these 'born again' Hindus came in my second year in New Delhi, after I had shifted to a new apartment in West End, a colony popular with retired army officers. The owner of my flat, who lived downstairs, was a retired general. Occasionally, the general would invite me downstairs for tea, and his anecdotes and recollections drawn from a remarkable life painted a vivid picture of Delhi in the decades immediately following independence. The business side of our relationship he left to his daughter, a stocky woman with a huge *bindi* spot between her large eyes, who insisted on sharing her strident political opinions with me at our very first meeting.

'The Muslims have to be brought down a peg or two, otherwise there will be chaos in this country,' she said, tossing a saffron-coloured dupatta over her shoulder and flicking back her jet-black mop of hair. 'If they think Pakistan can help them here, they've got a big surprise coming.'

The great Hindu thinkers of the nineteenth century were mature adults, capable of acknowledging that while Muslim rulers of India had flaws, they also had good points. Aurobindo Ghose described the Mughal Empire as 'great and magnificent', 'powerful and beneficent', full of 'genius and talent' and 'infinitely more liberal and tolerant in religion that any medieval or contemporary European kingdom or empire'.[3] India's Nobel prize-winning economist Amartya Sen noted in *The New York Review of Books*, 'If the Hindu middle classes in some parts of India have suddenly become more aware of alleged misdeeds of Muslim rulers in the past, it is not because new historical facts have just been discovered. It is because

Hindu activists have been trying to re-create a mythical past, mixing fact with fantasy.'[4]

Affluent, yet aggrieved, the New Hindus flaunted their beliefs the way fashion-conscious people brandish accessories, including claims that Jesus lived in Kashmir, that the Ka'ba in Mecca was originally a shrine to Shiva, that Homer's *Iliad* was copied from the *Ramayana*, and that the Taj Mahal — a jewel of Islamic architecture — was originally a Hindu temple. Educated at 'English-medium' schools and universities, their Hindi was awkward, but using and improving it became a political statement. The accoutrements of faith — raki strings on their wrists and bindi spots on their foreheads — became for them political statements, symbols of the new Hindu consciousness. Small things irritated them greatly, like the naming of a major boulevard in New Delhi after the Mughal emperor Aurangzeb, who died some three centuries earlier.

Their ageing poster boy — he was in his sixties by the time they discovered him — was Lal Krishna Advani. To his critics, Advani was 'a dangerous fascist willing to risk riots and flames to hold power', but to others, he was a 'gracious, personable, by turns funny and earnest, and not at all stuffy' political leader.[5] With the possible exception of the fascist label, it was all true. Accused by Pakistan of once having plotted to assassinate that country's independence leader, Mohammed Ali Jinnah, Advani was a high-caste Hindu educated in a Christian missionary school who, at the tender age of fourteen, joined the RSS, becoming head of the outfit's Karachi branch ten days before Partition. The Advani parents were refugees, resettling in India, where their son studied law, while rising through the ranks of the Hindu nationalist movement. An ascetic figure with a bottlebrush moustache and unfashionable spectacles, he'd spent decades in the political wilderness, which, combined with his refugee roots, forged in him a grim determination to achieve his goals. In the early 1990s he played the crucial hand in his lifelong political game, seizing the leadership of the Ayodhya temple movement and traversing tens of thousands of kilometres in a truck decorated to resemble Rama's chariot. As a campaigning tactic, it was a straight steal from Rajiv Gandhi's 'Roadshows', but with religious trappings. While usually careful to avoid language that might get him into trouble personally, police logging his progress concluded that wherever his yatra went, sectarian violence between Hindus and Muslims flared. In 1990, Advani's first yatra from Somnath to Ayodhya was blamed for triggering riots in which some 500 people were killed. The 'Pink City' of Jaipur reportedly 'ran red with blood', as the procession dubbed 'Chariots of Fire', for the amount of Muslim property torched by mobs along the route, passed by.[6] Insisting he had no regrets, Advani kept up his strident campaign, until the agitation culminated in 1992 with the kar sevaks demolishing the mosque before his eyes. Along with other leaders present on that day, he was charged by police with 'criminal conspiracy, intentional destruction and defiling of a place of worship, criminal trespass and intimidation of public servants on duty.'[7]

Not surprisingly, Advani was widely seen as a Muslim-baiter and hardliner, but the longer I watched him, the more I felt that his principal aim was attaining high public office. Not known for being particularly pious, religion was just one trick in his bag of gimmicks. A strict vegetarian with reserves of energy that belied his sixty-eight years, he didn't need an election to launch a campaign. In 1997 I'd joined him on a yatra to mark fifty years of independence. On that occasion he was playing the freedom fighter, travelling in a van decorated with nationalist icons, including Mahatma Gandhi, and calling on the crowds to join him in a three-point pledge — not to give or receive bribes, to put patriotic duty before self-interest, and, the ultimate irony, not discriminate on the basis of caste or creed. However his message was anything but Gandhian.

Huddled in the truck's air-conditioned cabin as we veered perilously close to Ayodhya, the BJP leader was in high spirits, despite a sore throat caused by his relentless speechifying at stops along the way. More people were voting BJP than ever before, partly due to the party's stand on Ayodhya, he felt, despite the fact that the agitation had occasionally gone out of control. As we'd both personally witnessed the demolition I thought to ask him how he'd felt on that day.

'It was the happiest day of my life,' he said, smiling, and I duly reported the comment for my newspaper, along with his prediction that India and Pakistan would one day be reunited, erasing the division created by Partition, which he described as 'one of the major traumatic events of my life'.

'We think in terms of a voluntary coming together of these two parts of undivided India,' he said, repeating that his party was committed to building a glorious Rama temple on the ruins of the 'disputed structure', and that India needed nuclear weapons, a decades-old demand of the Sangh Parivar.[8] In the very next breath he would tell you that the BJP was deeply committed to India's multi-ethnic character, which must be defended at all costs, and that Muslims had nothing to fear. Advani was a hard man to pin down. Some years later, appearing before a judge investigating the circumstances of the demolition, he testified that he'd 'seldom felt as dejected and downcast' as he did on 6 December 1992, prompting one of his political opponents to comment that 'L.K. Advani speaks in different tones at different times'.[9] Perhaps I'd misheard him, but he was smiling when he'd said it was a happy day.

Advani's agitation had been credited with the growth of the BJP's numbers in parliament, but its downside was that it scared most people, and the party had never managed to attract more than 20 per cent of the national vote. The BJP's solution to the problem was to promote its healing face, the 'Saffron Nehru', Atal Bihari Vajpayee. Another veteran, Vajpayee was a gentleman of the old school, an *éminence grise* more inclined to poetry than hardline ideology. A lifelong bachelor, he was a dab hand as a chef, liked a drink, and was an admirer of Nehru. In his youth he had dabbled in left-wing politics, but eventually found a home in the Sangh. An instinctive moderate, he was most at home in parliament, where the finer points of debate brought out the orator in him. While Advani would go to extremes to prove his Hindu-ness, the Brahmin Vajpayee was more comfortable in his skin, a reassuring figure, and not just for voters. His fellow Brahmins in the high-caste dominated Sangh Parivar never seriously challenged him as leader, and even political opponents like Narasimha Rao called him a personal friend. His greatest asset was an ability to reach out to people across the political divide; for example, he sincerely believed Muslims should be welcomed to join the nationalist movement. In Vajpayee, Hindu nationalism had developed a leader who could win friends and influence people, at least other politicians if not a majority of voters. They respectfully called him Atal-ji, and while Advani roused the rabble, Vajpayee was sewing up a broad coalition that might well catapult his party to power at the next elections.

He didn't have to wait long. In 1988, the BJP won the largest slice of the vote — 26 per cent — but this time its fourteen-party National Democratic Alliance, comprising turbaned Sikhs, Kashmiri Muslims and Tamil actors-turned-politicians, had the numbers to rule. The unlikely alliance — which reflected polyglot India, not the Cow Belt alone — would give the Hindu nationalists something they had always lacked: legitimacy. In return, they would pay a hefty price for power by declaring a moratorium on contentious issues, foremost among them, their promise to build the Rama temple at Ayodhya. Plans to remove the special status of Kashmir, which prevented outsiders buying land there, and to abolish Muslim personal law, under which polygamy was legal for men, were also jettisoned. But Vajpayee had one ace up his sleeve and, after an initial bluff, he played it.

On the eve of his swearing-in as the Indian prime minister, I went along to the 'press meet' at which Vajpayee would unveil his program. It was a warm, sunny day, and as I entered the garden of Atal-ji's bungalow, the large *shamiana* — a kind of tent erected for conferences and wedding parties — buzzed with media and politicians from all over India and the world. The BJP's election manifesto had promised to 'exercise the option to induct nuclear weapons' and I expected this issue to dominate the questioning. Although all India's main political parties supported the nuclear capability, and the bomb was already thought to be 'on the shelf', there was still nervousness about going public on it. Even Indira Gandhi, who'd conducted nuclear tests in 1974, had declared that India's nuclear capability was purely for peaceful purposes; in other words, that it was not a weapon for induction into the defence forces. What the BJP had proposed was a profound shift in policy, a break with decades of foreign policy based on Nehru's 'non-alignment' with great powers and the Mahatma's stated opposition to weapons of mass destruction. Yet none of the other reporters present seemed interested in raising the issue. Nobody wanted to make a bad impression on the prime minister-elect at his very first news conference, but it was inconceivable that the nuclear pledge not be the subject of a question. Reluctantly, I raised my hand and asked Mr Vajpayee when the new government would conduct a nuclear test.

'There is no time frame,' he replied, pausing as he often did to measure his words. 'We are keeping the option open, and if need be, that option will be exercised.'

In fact, as later became public, Vajpayee had already consulted India's nuclear scientists and was intent on delivering on his pledge. The Hindu nationalists saw nuclear weapons as symbols of power, an entry pass to status and credibility in international forums. They were also payback to China for its victory in the brief border war with India in 1962, and a sop to the Hindu nationalist grassroots who felt betrayed by the backtracking on Ayodhya. Instead of a grand Rama temple, they would be placated with an offering of fire.

A few weeks later, on the afternoon of 11 May 1998 — the Buddha's birthday — truckloads of Indian Army personnel were deployed to villages in western Rajasthan with orders to evacuate all residents from their homes. At 3.45 p.m., under a cloudless sky, a tremor suddenly jolted the ground beneath the feet of the evacuees, and large cracks appeared in their simple mud-brick homes. The impact was felt 100 kilometres away. Three nuclear devices including one hydrogen bomb, the world's most devastating weapon, had been placed in bomb shafts deep beneath the desert near the town of Pokhran, 550 kilometres southwest of New Delhi. Two days later, two miniaturised nuclear bombs designed to be dropped from aircraft or fired by artillery guns were detonated at the same site.

Neither the Indian Cabinet nor even the defence and external affairs ministers, whose portfolios were most directly affected, were consulted on the decision to test. Instead, the decision to make India a nuclear-weapons power was taken by a handful of senior ministers belonging to the RSS.[10] A member of a group of Western diplomats meeting External Affairs Minister Jaswant Singh that afternoon was present when the minister received a phone call telling him what had happened.

According to the diplomat, who asked not to be identified, Singh visibly stiffened and said, 'Sir! Yes sir! Is that right sir? No sir.'

'Then he brought us into a tight group around him, and said, "You won't believe this — India has just tested. Only five people knew. I have to go on TV tonight. This is dumb, dumb, dumb!"'

According to George Perkovich, an authority on the Indian nuclear program, 'a handful of politicians instigated by a handful of scientists with little experience in international affairs was pushing India across a portentous strategic threshold whose implications they did not fully appreciate'.[11] United States spy satellites, meanwhile, had failed to detect preparations for the tests.

Wild celebrations erupted across India in response to the big blasts. Newspapers called it an 'explosion of national esteem', and Hindu nationalist organisations carried sand from the test site to every corner of India, promising to build a temple to a new national goddess, Atomic Shakti (Strength). I could imagine all kinds of intelligent responses to a nuclear explosion, but cheering euphoria wasn't one of them. In an eerie fusion of politics, religion and science, Pakistan followed suit weeks later with its own series of tests, establishing a new, but more dangerous balance of terror. Public opinion polls showed support for nuclear weapons running at 90 per cent in both countries. The few voices of dissent — from the United Nations Security Council to the villagers around Pokhran demanding compensation for their houses — made little impression.

Beyond political calculations and Hindu nationalist pride, most Indians — certainly most educated Indians — welcomed the news because they believed that the global nuclear order was unjust. As Chandan Mitra wrote in the *Pioneer* newspaper:

For nearly 20 years, India has been slipping in its own eyes. Insurgency, terrorism, secessionism and mounting parochial sentiments have been eating into the vitals of the nation's resolve ... A country that cannot look itself in the eye, cannot hope to establish eye contact with any semblance of authority with others ... India, despite emerging as a model of democratic freedoms, is subjected to tirades in the name of human rights. Washington, the global supercop, turns a blind eye to Islamabad's shenanigans — first in Punjab and then Kashmir. The US also seeks unrelentingly to bamboozle India into signing a patently unequal CTBT [Comprehensive Test Ban Treaty] so that the nuclear haves can live in cosy comfort, subjecting the havenots to nuclear tyranny in perpetuity. Among the members of this elite club of nuclear haves is a country which went to war with India thirty-six years ago and continues to illegally occupy a vast amount of our territory. The mere exhibition of nuclear fire-power might not immediately alter these realities; nor will they change global military equations. But they will assertively establish that India refuses to accept pushover status forever; that, while it may be a soft state internally, an iron fist camouflages the velvet glove when it comes to dealing with external threats.[12]

India's ambitions would no longer be constrained by Gandhian homilies about non-violence and non-alignment. The Hindu nationalist era had started with a bang, a bold gambit that successfully masked the political weakness of the BJP government. At a summit of South Asian leaders held in Colombo in July that year, Vajpayee signalled that his moderate Hindu nationalism would set the tone and transcend the narrow politics of the Sangh Parivar:

> We [the South Asian nations] represent great civilizations, ancient yet vibrant and alive, and yet we are amongst the poorest in the world ... Enough of sterile ideology. Enough of hostile nationalism. Enough of conflict on the basis of religion and creed. Enough of poverty and backwardness. Let us grow rich together.[13]

But an act of singular violence would also define the first year of Vajpayee's rule.

Instead of confrontation with India's large and still politically influential Muslim community, the BJP's rise to power coincided with a shift towards confrontation with the much smaller Christian minority, who represented a mere 2.3 per cent of the population, but ran 20 per cent of primary schools, 25 per cent of orphan and widow care, and 30 per cent of all work with the handicapped, AIDS sufferers and lepers. It began suddenly, as if someone, somewhere had turned the violence switch to 'on'. Reports of attacks on Christian clergy and property, especially in the tribal districts of Orissa and Gujarat, started filling the newspapers. Human rights organisations monitoring the violence reported that the state apparatus in both places had either colluded with the perpetrators or been indifferent to the plight of the victims. Then, in January 1999, in the tribal belt of Orissa in eastern India, an Australian missionary called Graham Staines and his two young sons were attacked by a Hindu mob and burnt alive in their vehicle, during an annual Bible camp in the village of Manoharpur.

The leader of the mob was a Hindu nationalist. But the home minister in the new BJP-led government, Lal Krishna Advani, who was himself under investigation for inciting communal hatred, moved quickly to defend the Sangh Parivar organisations behind the anti-Christian campaign.

'I know these organisations,' Mr Advani said, 'and they are not criminals.'[14]

Part Four

14

Genesis in Oriya

'The Indian mind is enslaved,' said the doctor, a well-groomed man in a freshly laundered white shirt and neatly trimmed goatee, closing the file with an air of finality.

It had been a trying few weeks for the physician, arguing with contractors to fit out the surgeries properly, and assembling an entire medical staff from scratch with only weeks to go before the opening of the new hospital in Baripada, in northern Orissa on India's Bay of Bengal coast. It was the summer of 2004, and my yatra had taken me by plane from the bone-dry furnace of northern India to the slack monsoonal heat of Baripada, the town Graham Staines had called home. At the Mission House, one of the town's frequent blackouts had killed the bungalow's ceiling fans and, in the turgid air, small beads of sweat had begun forming on Dr Ravi Zakrias's forehead as he waded through the piles of paperwork needed to turn the Graham Staines Memorial Hospital into a reality. As he did so, he was letting off steam about what clearly was one of his pet hates — Hinduism.

'Our people live in constant fear of evil spirits. It's related to their belief system,' he said. 'From childhood, if I'm talking to you and a gecko cries, it means that whatever was said at that moment will come true. If a bell rings while I'm speaking, it has a different meaning. Some of these superstitions go back all the way to the Hindu scriptures. You can't separate Indian philosophy from the people's culture and habits. The Indian mind is enslaved by fear and superstition. It's enslaved by Hinduism.'

With the official opening of the hospital only days away, the building contractor wanted more money to clear last-minute hurdles, which no doubt the contractor himself had created intentionally. But Dr Zakrias's analysis was more than merely a product of frustration. It was a deep and abiding conviction.

'Look at the parts of India where there is more Christian influence, like the south,' the good doctor said, warming to his theme. 'People are better off. People's relationship with Christ changes them. They become calmer — less prone to drunkenness and violence.'

Five years earlier, I had sat with the widow Staines in this same room of the Mission House in Baripada in the first few hours after she learnt that her world had changed forever. I had attended the funeral, watching as the three coffins — the large one containing the charred remains of her husband, and two tiny others her sons — were carried out of the bungalow and taken to the cemetery. There, standing beside the graves with her daughter, Esther, Gladys had smiled with a surreal composure as she greeted hundreds of mourners from around Mayurbhanj district, a rock immoveable in a sea of tears. She was glad, she said, that God had allowed her sons 'to suffer for Jesus' sake'.[1]

'It pleased the Lord that my dear husband and children be burnt alive by communal militants.' Her one great desire was 'that each citizen of this country should establish a personal relationship with Jesus Christ who gave His life for their sins'.[2] It sounded so robotic, just like the mothers of Muslim suicide bombers who express pride in their dead children, and willingness to sacrifice their living ones. Either Gladys was in shock, or being strong for her daughter, or both.

No faith, I am sure, can make a mother insensitive to the death of her children; it can only give her the strength to cope with it.

Now, years later, as I sat chatting to Dr Zakrias and waiting for Mrs Staines, her one surviving child, Esther, tapped away at a computer, checking her email. Thirteen at the time of the killings, she had grown into a willowy young eighteen-year-old with a long blonde plait and a soft brogue acquired at a south Indian boarding school. Esther was preparing for university in Australia, a country she associated with elderly relatives and the occasional holiday. A few months earlier, on the fifth anniversary of her father's death, she had gone to the village of Manoharpur, five hours' drive through the jungle from Baripada, and placed a plaque on the wall of the prayer hall there. She was, she told me, 'kind of looking forward to a new start'. Lord knows, she deserved it.

The Staineses were moving on, scarred by tragedy but consoled by their faith. God had a plan for them — beyond their understanding perhaps, but all would be revealed in time. Gladys's dignity in the face of evil had touched India, making her its most famous Christian since Mother Teresa. In a true act of Christian charity, she had forgiven the murderers and found the strength to attend the trial at which Rabindra Kumar Pal, alias Dara Singh, and fourteen others were convicted of the murders. As he stood in the dock, Gladys had looked into Dara's eyes, but the murderer turned away. He was sentenced to death, but was appealing. Gladys, meanwhile, had thrown herself into fundraising for the hospital project amid an outpouring of public support.

'Gladys should remember she is not alone in her time of crisis, for millions of Indians are with her,' Abhay Mokashi, a columnist for the afternoon daily newspaper *Mid-day* had written, dismissing complaints by Hindu activists that Graham Staines had been converting tribals to Christianity by offering them inducements, which is a crime in Orissa. 'I do not know if Graham Staines [was] involved in religious conversions. One thing he definitely did — he converted leprosy patients into human beings, for the treatment meted out to them, even by their near and dear ones, was worse than that given to animals.'[3]

Buoyed by the support she received from Indians, the widow buried her grief in the quest to build the hospital, pestering the authorities on behalf of the project. The construction site on the spacious grounds of the Mission House now teemed with sari-clad women balancing loads of bricks on their heads, and men with limbs like taut rope clambering up and down bamboo ladders. It was almost finished, this monument to her husband's conviction that service to people is worship of God.

In January 1965, on his twenty-fourth birthday, Graham Staines arrived in Orissa to serve the poor and sick, and spread the gospel of Jesus. Born in Palmswood, Queensland, in 1941, to a devoutly Christian mother and an alcoholic father, Staines was accustomed to hardship and warm weather, but not to the culture shock of life in the tribal districts of eastern India, where the Evangelical Mission Society had been working since the late nineteenth century. At his first base at Rairangpur Mission, 55 kilometres from Baripada, his diaries recorded his impressions of an alien culture:

There was a dam being built about 80 km from our Mission House. The people believe that if there is human sacrifice the dam won't break. So, they kidnap somebody and bury him in concrete.[4]

Although Staines had quite obviously not witnessed the sacrifice in question, such things were not unheard of in India, providing the young missionary with a vivid sense of his environment and purpose. Since St Thomas the Apostle's legendary arrival on the Malabar Coast in 52 AD, India has been a place of allure for evangelical Christians. Although Thomas is said to have established seven Christian communities on the Malabar Coast in the area known today as Kerala, a greater impetus to Christianity's spread was the arrival of large numbers of European traders, journeymen and missionaries in the wake of Vasco da Gama's voyage to India in 1498.

India remembers da Gama's bloody vengeance on Hindus and Muslims who resisted his incursions, and the arrival of the Inquisition in the Portuguese enclave of Goa, where heretics were burnt at the stake. The British during their early years in India banned Christian missionary activities, not wishing to provoke confrontations that might jeopardise the East India Company's lucrative trade. But pressure from the churches to allow proselytising eventually prevailed, and from 1813, the gates were thrown open. School and church construction took off apace, funded by patrons in Europe.

In his autobiography, Mahatma Gandhi recalls his youth in coastal Gujarat where 'In those days Christian missionaries used to stand in a corner near the high school and hold forth, pouring abuse on Hindus and their gods.'[5] Gandhi's own Hindu faith grew stronger throughout his life, partly in response to the Christian presumption to exclusive truth, so alien to Hindu values.

Indian sensitivity to aggressive soul-saving was a contributing factor to the 1857 Rebellion against British rule. When, ninety years later, India won independence, its new laws protected freedom of religion, but not freedom to proselytise, with the Supreme Court ruling that converting people to one's own religion is not a fundamental right. Conversion by 'force, fraud or inducement' is unlawful, and conversions can be prevented by law if they threaten public order. Orissa, with its large tribal population, has its own special anti-conversion laws, but curiously, these do not apply to proselytising Hindus.[6]

By the 1990s, India had practically ceased issuing new missionary visas; only existing missionaries like Graham Staines could extend their stay. Ageing priests, brothers and nuns, some of whom had spent most of their lives in India and could not conceive of returning to their unfamiliar homelands, were literally a dying breed. They had, however, planted the seed of their faith, and the vast majority of India's clergy are now Indian by birth.

★ ★ ★

My arrival in Baripada coincided with the 2004 Jagannath Festival, when idols of Krishna are taken from the temples and hauled through the streets on huge wooden juggernauts by female devotees. Amid massive crowds, fourteen-wheel chariots, carved with images of Hindu gods, creaked and shuddered as they rolled heavily past roadside stalls doing a brisk trade in pilgrim accessories, such as coconuts, tulsi leaves and oil lamps. In the blazing tropical sun, a forest of arms, like the ones you see at pop concerts, threw rice and wheat towards the giant vehicles, and bandsmen pounded drums and blew conch shells. The missionaries could preach all they like, but the religion of the Brahmins was as resilient as ever and many thousands of pilgrims had flooded into Baripada from across northern Orissa for the festival.

Orissa was once home to one of India's great empires, the kingdom of Kalinga. In 261 BC, India's most famous religious conversion took place there, when the Hindu emperor Ashoka embraced Buddhism in repentance for the huge loss of life in his ruthless war to conquer the kingdom.[7] Despite Ashoka's conversion — perhaps because of it — Orissa remained a bastion of the faith, boasting more Hindu temples than 'the rest of Hindustan put together', according to the nineteenth-century scholar James Ferguson.[8]

Nowadays, northern Orissa is a tropical backwater of rutted roads. It is home to one of the four Hindu shankaracharyas, sometimes called popes, based in the seaside town of Puri, but also to a large population of animist tribals, whose worship of trees and rocks is sometimes mistaken for similar Hindu rituals. With no scheduled flights to or from Delhi, I'd flown to Ranchi in neighbouring Jharkhand state, and then embarked on a seven-hour bus journey. En route I'd seen tribal men armed with bows and arrows hunting by the roadside, and stopped briefly at a resettlement camp in which other tribals were being encouraged to abandon their nomadic huts made of twigs and leaves, and move into the camp's permanent concrete-block dwellings. Aboriginal culture in India is a civilisation on the cusp of extinction, and missionary Hindus, Christians and left-wing insurgents fighting the central government in tribal areas are conducting the last rites.

At the Mission House in Baripada, men in singlets were preparing lunch in the bungalow's courtyard under the spreading canopy of a mango tree, grinding garlic, ginger and mustard seed into a paste for fish curry and boiling rice in a huge brass *karai* over a wood fire. Another group of young men with Old Testament names such as Gideon and Solomon were wheeling a painted barrow into the courtyard, having just come from the festival. They'd gone there to proselytise, singing Christian hymns to the accompaniment of a battered harmonium that sat on the barrow, and to try to sell Christian literature. Picking up one of their books, I saw that it was designed for basic readers in a comic-book format. It was Genesis in Oriya, a language whose letters resemble melting light bulbs.

Into the courtyard strode Gladys Staines. She was an extraordinary figure of a woman, big-boned, pale and dressed in a sari, towering over the gaggle of short, dark men who struggled to keep pace, and with whom she conversed in a patois of Oriya and English. She'd been micro-managing the layout of cabinets in the hospital's wet areas, run off her feet which were shod in missionary sandals, the kind with a leather loop over the big toe. She vaguely remembered me from the funeral, but struggled to string sentences together in English, so absorbed had she become in her environment. The stresses involved in the hospital project were etched on the forehead of the 53-year-old daughter of a dairy farmer.

'This has been the biggest test of my life,' she said, using the word 'test' in the Christian sense; a test of faith, a trial set by God. 'Since Graham died I've been very, very busy. I've been under a lot of pressure, almost to breaking point, just hanging in at the moment, that's all.'

Like her late husband, Gladys Weatherhead came from provincial Queensland, where the sermons can still be fiery and interpretations of scripture literal. They'd met in this very room, he a Baptist pastor in his early forties, so absorbed in his work that he'd not had the time or opportunity to marry, and she a young nurse from a Brethren family, travelling as part of 'Operation Mobilisation', a Christian mission to Asia. They'd corresponded, leading to Graham's proposal and an Australian wedding, before returning to Orissa. She'd been living in India for more than twenty years.

Taking a seat on a bamboo settee, Gladys called for chai, removed her spectacles, and began cleaning them with a handkerchief. 'The hospital project was going really well until January, and then it stopped for a month because the contractor is trying to extract money from us. It's a terrible headache.'

The fact that her main headaches were with tradesmen put the problems with extremists in perspective. Violence against Christians had come off its peak, with Prime Minister Vajpayee pressing the Sangh Parivar to desist. In October 1999, I'd been sitting with an RSS senior leader, Kuppahalli Sudarshan, at the organisation's Delhi office when a call from Mr Vajpayee came through. For ten minutes the prime minister urged Sudarshan to call off agitations ahead of the planned visit of Pope John Paul II to India later that month. Sitting cross-legged and bare-chested in a dhoti and beads, the Kannadiga Brahmin and known hardliner, who'd attended his first RSS assembly at the age of nine, gave no guarantees, but the visit went ahead smoothly.[9] The Pope proceeded to India, where he issued a clarion call for the conversion of Asia, predicting it would be 'the land of bountiful harvest in the coming millennium'. Calling on missionaries to be humble, and to adopt Asian cultural idioms for their message, he nevertheless declared that 'in the end, it is martyrdom which reveals to the world the very essence of the Christian message'.[10]

The year before John Paul II's visit, the powerful Cardinal Joseph Ratzinger, with the Pope's approval, had issued a formal Vatican notification denouncing Indian Catholic priest Father Anthony de Mello, who had questioned whether direct faith in Christ was the only path to salvation.[11]

On the wall behind Mrs Staines, a portrait of her late husband and sons — a trio in kurta pajama — gazed down on us. An inspirational psalm inscribed on the wall clock read 'Wait on the Lord, and keep His way'. The 'way' of Baptist-orientated evangelicals is the Bible, which they believe is the only true source of knowledge about God. Looked upon as mavericks by the mainstream churches, they are conservative on social issues such as homosexuality and abortion, but radical in their rejection of centralised ecclesiastical authority.

Swami Vivekananda, one of Hinduism's great missionaries, once famously said that Hindus accept all religions as true. While the post-Vatican II Roman Catholic Church had embraced the 'rays of truth' in other religions, well-funded US-based Christian outreach mouthpieces such as *Mission Frontiers* had no qualms sowing hatred among their flock, describing Hindu civilisation as 'the most perverted, most monstrous, most implacable, demonic-invaded part of this planet'.[12] Some Protestant churches had tried to move with the times, but the Evangelicals stuck firm to the conviction that we are all damned by original sin unless we accept Jesus.

'We're certainly not liberal in religious matters,' replied Gladys, when I asked her about it. 'We follow what the scriptures teach.'

The Bible was the backbone of Graham Staines's life. Every morning at 5.30 he would wake at the Mission House in Baripada, read his Bible, and after a breakfast of wholemeal porridge, eggs and toast, depart for the mission's leprosy home in Baripada to begin his day's work. The home, which had been started by the Hindu Maharaja of Mayurbhanj, who later handed the institution over to the Evangelical Missionary Society, was located in a pleasant grove on the outskirts of town, where I found a neat, self-sustaining commune for some of India's most rejected people. At the morning prayer service, elderly women who'd been cured of leprosy greeted me with the stumps of their wrists clasped in humble namastes. In the guest book, an entry dated four days after the missionary's murder read 'Seeing the creative and imaginative vision here I feel we have lost a dear child of God'.

It was rapture in the service of the Lord that kept calling Graham Staines back repeatedly to the tribal villages of Mayurbhanj and Keonjhar districts of Orissa. Bogged down in administrative work in Baripada, he looked forward to his trips to the hill country, where he preached in tribal languages and was doubtless confirmed in his conviction that Christianity was the answer to India's needs. But his widow told me that in the final years of his life, Graham Staines had been working with an almost manic intensity. Far from winding down his commitments in anticipation of a comfortable retirement, Gladys said, he was 'doing the work of five people', like a man possessed, racing against time.

'He was definitely overworking in the last few years. He was constantly tired and his perceptions were clouded,' she said. 'He was very particular that everything be done properly and correctly. With him, everything was black and white. Nothing was grey.'

The jungle Bible camps were held in the cooler months when the temperatures became chilly in the hill country outside Baripada. The events attracted hundreds of people to the village of Manoharpur, 160 kilometres away on a rutted road through a verdant valley, where eight score Santhal families lived in rammed-earth homes with thatched roofs. In the remote tribal areas where nothing much happens, some people came out of mere curiosity, others with the desire to find meaning in their grinding lives. Many could not read the scriptures that Staines-*dada* had translated into their languages, but for those who could, they were a revelation. In a joint dispatch published in *Tidings* in April 1997, Staines and his wife expressed satisfaction with the Evangelical Mission Society's progress in Orissa. 'The first jungle camp in Ramchandrapur was a fruitful time and the Spirit of God worked among the people,' they wrote. 'About 100 attended and some were baptised at the camp.'

The program for the camps consisted of Bible readings, home science, slide shows and hymns. For Straines's two sons, Philip, aged ten, and Timothy, six — angelic boys who'd inherited their mother's Nordic complexion and knew their prayers and hymns by heart — the planned trip to Manoharpur in the winter of 1999 was a thrilling prospect. Older brother Philip was just back from boarding school in Ootacamund, 2000 kilometres away in Tamil Nadu, and he and his brother were particularly excited about sleeping in the jeep, a request their father was happy to grant, as it was the only place in Manoharpur guaranteed free of bed bugs. As they set out from Baripada, two days after Staines's fifty-eighth birthday, accompanied by an Australian friend Gil Venz, they were all in high spirits. But all was not well in the poor tribal animist communities of Keonjhar district, where some of India's poorest people had become pawns in an increasingly hard-fought struggle for their souls.

Life in the tribal villages of Orissa is rigorously Spartan. Most people survive on subsistence farming supplemented by traditional hunting. Social services are virtually non-existent, and the drinking of alcohol and the local toddy called *handia* blights many communities. Amid such poverty it doesn't take much to provoke jealousies and feuds, and religious conversions had proven to be deeply divisive. Christian converts tended to be more prosperous because they shunned alcohol. At the same time, their new, exclusive faith saw them reject ancient customs, such as leaving their lands fallow during certain festivals, bringing bad luck on their villagers, at least to superstitious minds. The Christians' withdrawal from important aspects of community life — fetes and *poojas* deemed idolatrous by their pastors — deepened the divide.

Into this volatile mix came Dara Singh, a young man from Etawah in Uttar Pradesh, described by police as 5 feet 6 inches in height, thin, with sunken eyes, a long nose, beard, and often seen carrying a towel over his shoulder. Dara belonged to the generation of Hindus radicalised by the Ayodhya temple movement. People who knew him described him as a party worker of the BJP who was active in election campaigns and in the activities of the nationalist movement's youth wing, the Bajrang Dal. In 1981 he'd drifted east to Orissa, settling in Keonjhar district where, between jobs, he talked big about the coming Hindu rashtra. At first his anger focused on the Muslims, in particular the truck drivers who transported cattle to the slaughterhouses of Kolkata, a business dominated by Muslims because Hindus consider cows as sacred. Opposition to cow slaughter is a folk tradition in many parts of India, and popular ballads extol the bravery of Hindus who risk their lives to save them from harm. But like Muslim extremists who desecrate the Koran by claiming that it justifies the murder of innocents, Dara Singh twisted the *Bhagavad Gita*'s spiritual call to arms to suit the same purpose. By distributing the livestock he liberated among the Santhal, Mahanta and Ho peoples of the area, Dara Singh gained popularity, as well as notoriety. The police knew of his activities — at least nine cases against him had been registered — but either due to sympathy for his views, or lack of interest, did not interfere with his Robin Hood-style crusade. In the tribal areas, word spread that if you wanted a problem fixed, you should call Dara Singh. Eventually, the competition for tribal souls between Christians and Hindus came to his attention, and drew him back to Manoharpur, a village where he had worked for several years in the grocery shop of a friend's family.

On 22 January, Graham Staines, his two sons and his friend Gil Venz drove into Manoharpur, a simple village where lanterns had not yet been replaced by electricity and hand pumps provided water. Staines knew of the undercurrent of violence that afflicted the area, and that his jungle camps were causing controversy. His dispatches, co-authored with his wife and published in *Tidings*, plot the gradual rise in religious tensions in the area.

Mayurbhanj
19 September 1997

The Ho believers in Thakurmunda still face persecution. From time to time the village people have beaten them up, broken their bicycles and not allowed them to worship in their own Church building. Three people came to Baripada to meet district officials and petition for justice. Pray that action will be taken to allow freedom to worship.

22 February 1998

We have just arrived home from the Baliposi camp a day early. Some people from a Hindu militant group who are persecuting the Christians came to the camp but were not able to disturb the meetings. On the last day the police came and told us to stop the meeting and leave, as they would not be able to protect us ... election-related requirements left no men to spare.

19 May 1998

There are many new believers in the Manoharpur Church and the work is growing. The devil is now finding opportunity to hinder the work of God. There is disagreement between the young people and the older men of the Church. A problem arose about the land on which the Church is built and the planned Vacation Bible School had to be cancelled.

19 May 1998

We have been told that a militant Hindu group plans to concentrate on Mayurbhanj and Keonjhar districts to turn Christians back to Hinduism.

19 June 1998

The Vacation Bible School that was to be held at Manoharpur was cancelled because of problems in the Church there.

21 August 1998

There are still divisions in the Church at Manoharpur.

19 December 1998

It is encouraging to hear of some improvement in the Church at Manoharpur and that they are preparing for the jungle camp.

This last dispatch, dated only a month before his death, reflected hope that the problems were on the mend, but it had been a tough year and a feud for control of the Manoharpur prayer hall had divided the congregation at a time when it was increasingly under threat. Graham Staines knew that resistance to his work was becoming more organised. He may even have heard the name of Dara Singh. Yet for reasons only he really knew, the missionary had decided to take his sons into the heart of darkness.

Dara Singh had his own crusade and it was diametrically opposed to the mission of Graham Staines. The two men had never met, but they were on a deadly collision course.

★ ★ ★

For most of its existence, Hinduism has contained no ritual for converting outsiders to its way of life. Aloof in their castes, the early Hindus wanted to exclude the animists around them, not include them. Only in the nineteenth century, with Christian missionaries making inroads into Hinduism's base, did the religious reformer Swami Dayanand Saraswati create a ceremony to baptise converts. Over a century later, in October 2005, an American Hindu convert was denied entry to the Lingaraj Temple, in the Orissa state capital of Bhubaneshwar, by priests who believed that only Indians could be Hindu. Even the most open-minded of faiths have their bigots.

At the Hotel Ambika, beneath a mural of Ganesh and his preferred 'vehicle' — the rat — the goggle-eyed Bengali receptionist Tapan had seized control of my movements. Mentioning to him that I wanted to get a feel for the countryside in which Staines had spent his final hours, he'd arranged for a succession of drivers to come to the hotel and negotiate terms for the hire of a jeep to Manoharpur. They came and went, talking in conspiratorial murmurs to Tapan, before declining the job. So rich were the pickings for taxi drivers in Baripada during the Jagannath Festival, Tapan told me, that drivers considered the idea of leaving town to be a form of lunacy.

'Over here nobody wants to take any risks,' he said, placing a paperweight on the flapping pages of the hotel register that were being turned by the ceiling fan. 'You see, sir, you may find a driver who speaks English and Oriya, but it is very rare to find one who speaks English and Santhal. This is the problem. In any case, all are busy with this festival. There is tremendous rush on their vehicles.'

While the search continued I did the rounds in Baripada, dropping in at the Mission House a few times between meetings with local police and reporters. A journalist on the local newspaper *Samaj*, Vijay Aggarwal, whose office was bedecked in portraits of Hindu deities, duly framed and garlanded, warned me that, five years after the Staines killings, missionary activities were still the focus of tensions in the tribal villages.

'Reports are pouring in of continuing conversions in remote pockets,' he said, like a reporter trying to sell his editor on a story. 'These sometimes lead to conflict followed by *tenshun*. In most rural areas, the tribals they are neglected by the state administration. They have no drinking water, no rations, and no *gow*-ernment privileges. They have no employment, medical or education facilities. Schools are far.'

When I pointed out to Aggarwal that the missionaries were providing the very education and health services that tribal people in remote areas needed, he stuck to the reporter's script of quoting what others say.

'It is alleged that some people coming from Christian countries convert by offering money and better living standards. If somebody has malaria, the Christian will give medicines and then try to convert. Those who are converted lead a better lifestyle and it becomes an eyesore for their neighbours, and leads to more *tenshun*.'

I knew for a fact that Graham Staines had made a point of charging for medicines in order to avoid this very allegation of using inducements to convert, but also to avoid creating an unsustainable dependency. By comparison, Dara Singh's gift to tribals of the cattle he had 'liberated' as they were being trucked to slaughterhouses was a clear case of inducement.

Mr Aggarwal left me in no doubt that some Hindus in Baripada, and even tribals in the villages, were deeply suspicious about the activities of Christian missionaries. But at the local police station, Inspector Dhiren Chandra Nanda told a different story. Informed that I would be visiting Manoharpur, Nanda pressed a buzzer under his desk and told the supari-chewing underling who answered it to bring the Staines file. The file, when it came, overflowed with hundreds of pages of documents, which Inspector Nanda scanned through oversized spectacles like a Brahmin perusing a holy text.

'There is no word in the dictionary sufficient to condemn the heinous act of Dara Singh,' he said, eyes tracking through the documents line by line. 'I was officer in charge in that area. I saw the boys. They were very lovely boys. The problem is, our legal system is so lengthy that it takes years together for pronouncing judgement, and as you know, justice delayed is justice denied.'

The killer was being transferred soon to Baripada in order to be present during one of the court cases against him. I'd heard that security in the town had been boosted because of fears that his supporters might try to liberate him from police custody. But Inspector Nanda advised me not to confuse a noisy minority with the silent majority.

'Dara Singh has totally lost his base,' he said. 'Nobody is supporting his action. Everybody in Manoharpur is condemning him, regardless of caste or religion.'

In fact, Dara Singh had plenty of sympathisers, and the party they voted for was in power in Delhi. He even had a fan club, the 'Dara Sena', whose leaders were demanding that Gladys leave India.

'People *will* want me out of the country,' Mrs Staines had replied when I'd asked her about the Hindu nationalists. 'Over the years things have changed as the situation has become more hostile ... While I'm here, I'm an enigma to them.'

The following morning, giving up on receptionist Tapan's complicated approach to hiring a taxi, I walked to the bus station and was able to engage Dilip, the first driver I met. As the narrow, winding road from Baripada tracked into the hills, it traversed forests of giant-leafed sal trees alive with birdsong. The termite mounds were almost the size of houses, and the bitumen was broken. Where the tarmac existed, it served as a drying platform for freshly harvested chilli and rice. In the cleared valleys, yoked buffalo churned the mud of paddy fields that produced three crops a year, and women in bareback saris suckled infants by the roadside, covering up when cars passed. Graham Staines, making his final journey towards Manoharpur on the same road, would have recognised the Garden of Eden. And like Eden, the garden was troubled, and the people worshipped snakes.

Halfway to Manoharpur, the open-sided jeep I'd hired in Baripada pulled up outside a low-slung barracks-like building with a sign that read 'Arul Doss Memorial Tribal Boys Hostel'. It had taken the police a year to apprehend Dara Singh, who'd been sheltered by sympathisers in the area, time enough for the Hindu militant to kill again. His next victim had been a Muslim trader, Sheikh Abdul

Rehman, who'd had both his hands chopped off before being burnt alive in Padiabeda village.[13] Then the 35-year-old Indian Catholic priest Father Arul Doss was killed at a prayer meeting in the village of Jamabani by assailants wielding bows and arrows.

Walking towards the boys hostel that bore the murdered priest's name, I could hear the sound of a harmonium and songs sung by children wafting across the fields. Inside, a fastidiously neat young priest in a starched white linen shirt and silver-rimmed spectacles looked anything but pleased to see me.

'We need to be cautious about people coming here,' said Father Joshi, casting anxious glances at my driver, Dilip, who was hanging around outside. 'This area is sensitive. They are looking at us with suspicious eyes.'

The mission Father Joshi was running took in children up to thirteen years of age whose homes were too remote for daily travel to school to be practical. Their families paid 125 rupees, or about $3 a month, for their food, lodging and education. The boys were mainly from tribal backgrounds, but a few from Hindu families also attended. The late Arul Doss had been based at the hostel at the time of his murder. Seated at the late priest's desk, beneath a calendar featuring an image of Mother Teresa, the new head of the mission occupied the chair of a dead man.

'I know it could be fatal,' he said, brow furrowed as he fumbled nervously with a stapler. 'It's not a religious problem. It's instigated by some people for private interests. But we cannot ignore it.'

The mission's response to the volatile issue of religious conversions was remarkable in itself — Christian scriptures were no longer taught in the school, not even to Christians. But in Baripada, rumours abounded that Father Doss had, in fact, been a rogue. Journalist Vijay Aggarwal had repeated a story I'd heard independently from several other people in the town.

'Arul Doss was sexually harassing. Local people have told us he was exploiting their girls. Who all are coming for religious work, they are making them pregnant and leaving them in precarious circumstances.'

When I asked Father Joshi about it he seemed genuinely shocked, and claimed it was the first he'd heard about it in the five months he'd been at the school.

'It's not the case in India. The family values are there,' he said, leading me to the classroom from where the music emanated. Half a dozen boys of various ages were practising for a theatrical performance aimed at raising awareness of AIDS, which would soon tour the tribal villages. The missionaries could teach reading, writing and arithmetic, they could run a dispensary and impart health awareness. But in India, Christianity was the religion that dare not speak its name, and Christian missionaries — even Indian-born ones — were an endangered species.

From the hostel, the road rose again, crossing the range to Thakurmunda, the main town in the area, before the final 10 kilometres to Manoharpur. Entering the village we found it difficult at first to locate anything resembling a centre to the hamlet. Efforts to obtain directions proved fruitless. Dilip tried his Oriya, I tried my Hindi, but all inquiries were rebuffed with cold silence.

'I think maybe we should leave this place,' said Dilip, looking as nervous as Father Joshi had been.

The way people turned their backs on us — the cold shoulder in a warm country — was doubly disconcerting, and unprecedented in my time in India. Yet so complete was their denial that I could not be sure whether it stemmed from fear or hatred. We were simply invisible and untouchable. Finally, after walking around for a quarter of an hour being shunned by everyone, a spry, silver-haired lady responded when we asked for directions to the place where Graham Staines was killed.

Lokmi Dey was in her eighties, she said. Not much more than a metre tall and wearing rubber chappals and an off-the-shoulder Orissa sari and red wrap skirt, she led us along the main street, past mute onlookers standing in huddles on their porches. Behind bamboo scaffolding, a high brick wall had been constructed across the front of the village's Christian prayer hall, where Staines's daughter, Esther, had six months earlier unveiled a plaque to her murdered father and brothers, on the fifth anniversary of their deaths. But far from protecting the church, the wall seemed purpose-built to hide from view Manoharpur's dirty little secret, a prison of faith in which the village's besieged Christians now prayed.

Muttering and shaking her head, Lokmi Dey wrung her simple bangles as she showed me the spot where the missionary and his sons had bedded down for the night. The boys had asked their father to place straw on the roof of the jeep, thinking it would insulate them from the cold night air of the hill country in winter. But a greater threat loomed in the darkness — a stalker and his helpers. In the neighbouring village of Dumuridiha, Dara Singh — who'd been told about the Christian camp by people from nearby villages and been asked to stop it — had gathered his supporters together on an open field. They lit a fire and shared a meal of flattened rice and *jaggery*, a Last Supper before arming themselves with the holy daggers called trishuls, the long staves called *lathis*, and medieval flaming torches. At a signal from spies already stationed in Manoharpur that the Staineses were asleep in their car, the vigilantes set off for the village. Just after midnight, Dara's tribal army stormed Manoharpur, screaming at the tops of their lungs as they raced towards their quarry. While some surrounded the jeep, others barred access to anyone who tried to intervene, turning villagers and Staines's friend Gil Venz back into their houses. As his cohorts beat on the car with their staves, Dara Singh and his men slashed its tyres, smashed the windows and began beating the missionary and his sons with their weapons. Surrounded by the mob and prevented from leaving the car, the pastor battled in vain to protect his sons, no doubt hoping that help would soon arrive. But such was the speed, planning and ferocity of the attack that there was no escape. Dara

Singh took the straw from the jeep's roof, scattered it under the car, and with one of the flaming torches ignited it. For thirty minutes the assailants stood beside the car watching the Australians being burnt alive. When dawn illuminated the charred wreckage, the three bodies were found huddled together, Graham Staines curled protectively over his sons. The attackers had long since fled, raising slogans of victory.

Five years later, and contrary to what the police inspector had said, Manoharpur still simmered with the resentments that flared so tragically on that night. Perturbed by the villagers' displeasure at our presence, Dilip began begging me to leave, and I realised that there was little point staying. I looked one last time at Orissa's Ground Zero, a dusty strip of road outside the prayer hall, scene of murder most foul, and imagined their screaming. Lokmi Dey stood beside me in the hot sun with an expression of impotence and sadness. Did she think the missionaries had conducted conversions with inducements?

'I think so,' she said, according to Dilip's nervy translation.

But it hadn't stopped her lending assistance to a despised outsider like me.

Bending low, I touched her feet and took my leave.

★ ★ ★

Gandhi once said 'My belief in the Hindu scriptures does not require me to accept every word and every verse as divinely inspired'. His message to missionaries was that they should avoid the sin of arrogant pride:

If you feel that India has a message to give to the world, that India's religions too are true and you come as fellow helpers and fellow seekers there is a place for you here. But if you come as preachers of the 'true gospel' to a people who are wandering in darkness, so far as I am concerned, you can have no place.[14]

In the thirty-four years that he lived in India, Graham Staines kept strictly to his faith. In some of his dispatches published in *Tidings* he displayed little grasp of the finer points of Hinduism, describing its old orthodoxy Sanatan Dharma as 'an animist sect' — akin to labelling Judaism as a primitive superstition. Perhaps he thought it had something to do with Satan. Clearly, nothing he had done justified his murder, and if the faiths of Dara Singh and Graham Staines were to be compared on the basis of their actions, there was no doubt which would win. The vast majority of Indians believed that Dara Singh's actions had brought shame on India and Hinduism. Only a handful of people interested in a political career saw a purpose in making him a hero. The tragedy, it seemed to me, was that people of strong faith couldn't see through such political manipulation and find the obvious common ground between them. The Baptist embrace of a direct, personal relationship with Jesus is not unlike the popular Hindu tradition of Bhakti. But neither Dara Singh nor Graham Staines would have known that.

Why did Graham Staines take his boys to Manoharpur, I kept wondering? Was it carelessness, or a bad call? Or had faith, perhaps even a desire to give his sons an early taste of missionary work, blinded him to the dangers? In the twelve months leading up to the Staines murders, more incidents of violence against Christians were recorded in India than in any year since independence. One month before the Staines killings, on Christmas Day, Hindu extremists had gone on a rampage in the Dangs tribal belt in the western state of Gujarat, attacking and burning churches, mission schools and shops owned by Christians. Thousands of Christian tribal community members in the region were also forced to undergo conversions to Hinduism.[15] In Orissa, too, there had been trouble, with at least thirty Hindu–Christian clashes the previous year, and more such incidents in the previous twelve years than in any other state in India.[16] In the authorised account of the murders, *Burnt Alive*, the pastor was portrayed as a man who'd 'decided to follow Christ no matter what the personal cost ... he knew that nothing significant was ever achieved without opposition'.[17] Gladys's remarks when I'd met her in Baripada about her husband's perceptions being 'clouded', and about how the obvious tensions in the tribal areas 'did not unduly worry him', hadn't struck me as anything unusual at the time. Now I wondered. Six feet under the red dirt of northern Orissa, these were questions he couldn't answer. But Gladys could.

'Graham had said that he would go to the camp by himself,' she told me when I rang her some time later, 'and I said "Philip" — that's the elder one — "Philip likes going with you". So Graham said, "Okay, but if I take Philip, I'll take Timothy as well, because they don't see much of each other."'

Not much evidence of a plot for world domination there. It hadn't even been his idea.

'I've had to think about that myself, also,' Gladys said. 'That was a decision we made.'

The inquiry ordered by the Vajpayee government into the murder was told that Staines harboured a 'deep hatred for other religions', but his widow denied the claim, which she said was based on a misunderstanding of her husband's refusal to eat *prasad* — food blessed under Hindu ritual. To do so, Mrs Staines said, would have been against the Bible's teachings. The inquiry produced the politically convenient finding that no organisation was involved in the murder, even though the Commission's own investigating team concluded that Dara Singh was a Sangh Parivar activist who had attended RSS rallies and campaigned for the BJP during elections the previous year.

The Evangelical Missionary Society had suggested that Gladys Staines return to Australia, possibly for good. She would be able, her superiors felt, to have a rest and get counselling, talk through issues and find out what God wanted her to do. It would mean leaving the Mission House, a sacred site to her, the only home she and Graham and the children had ever shared. In a few more days the hospital would be inaugurated, and the Bible camps in the tribal belt that had claimed the lives of the missionary and his two sons would continue, led by Indian pastors. Not surprisingly, Gladys saw all that had happened in biblical terms. In Baripada she had told me, 'The Bible says that in the last days, what is wrong will be right, and what is right will be wrong, and we're seeing that happen. Anyone who wants to do right is put down as having an ulterior motive. And anyone who wants to do wrong is fine.'

Hindus don't believe in Judgement Day; they believe in rebirth and revival.

Through it all, Gladys Staines had not wavered, but her most precious memories were not of a religious crusade, but of her days as a newlywed, sharing the joys and burdens of family life, and picnics beside waterfalls.

'You know, as the years have gone, it's been a deep sadness to me that this has happened. I miss my family terribly, and as the years go by, I miss them more.'

It was all over, the last days, not quite as prophesied.

15

Seven Cities of Delhi

Two years after the Staines murders, Janaki and I made the difficult decision to leave India. After five happy years in Civil Lines, it was not religious intolerance that led to our departure — much as that did become a hallmark of the Vajpayee government — more a prosaic need to revive links with my Australian family and homeland, or risk losing them forever. We moved into our cramped Sydney flat at first, then bought a house in the countryside, and both began working from home, contributing to various magazines and newspapers. Living in a village of 400 people in the Southern Highlands of New South Wales was Janaki's introduction to life in Australia, and she quickly made new friends in that intimate and supportive semi-rural community. We visited India frequently, sometimes together, but often alone, sometimes for work, and at other times to see the family.

When I returned on my yatra, six years after the nuclear summer of 1998, India was in the grip of an economic and cultural revolution of a kind not seen since independence. The rise of the Hindu right may have stirred a torrid debate about the country's future, but economic liberalisation was embraced by all who governed, even the communists in West Bengal. Forty billion

dollars in foreign investment had flowed in since Dr Manmohan Singh's first reformist budget in 1991, and consumerism was the new religion. McDonald's and Domino's had opened franchises in Kashmere Gate, and the idols of Indian gods and goddesses on sale in Khan Market were made in China. In the summer of 2004 I was struck by just how quickly 'timeless' India could change. New Delhi, once a dozy government town, wasn't just growing, it was proliferating, throwing off far-flung suburbs like sparks from a catherine-wheel, its population leaping from eight to fourteen million people since the early 1990s. Two hundred and fifty thousand immigrants arrived each year,[1] yet the capital still maintained the highest per capita income in India. The biggest impact was felt in urban areas like Gurgaon, on New Delhi's southern outskirts, where telephone call centres serving both domestic and international customers had sprung up, creating some 150,000 new jobs. The Indian middle class had more than trebled in size from 8 per cent of the population in 1981 to 25 per cent in 2001, spawning a new and not always pretty materialist culture.[2] Delhi's rising middle class had taken refuge in guarded, gated communities, wherein to escape the prying hands and eyes of the poor.[3] For me, there were two leitmotifs of the new prosperity; one was the flyover, great concrete arches that leapfrogged colonies and intersections like giants from another world. The other was the depilated executive reading his economic newspaper in the spacious back seat of his chauffeur-driven limousine, the cabin so deeply air-conditioned that beggars at traffic lights could cool their hands on the windows. At home, yoga programs on private cable TV stations and personal trainers helped urban Indian executives cope with stress. But there was no escape from the telephone. Mobile phone ownership had grown from zero to forty-five million in four years, and by 2008 was expected to pass 200 million handsets.[4] Broadcast media, once dominated by government, had become one of the country's most dynamic sectors, with scores of local and global channels offered by private operators at prices even the poor could afford.

New private schools and private hospitals where you paid by credit card were mushrooming across affluent South Delhi, where the idea of waiting for the government to do things was no longer in vogue. Property prices were soaring, and almost 200,000 new cars annually rolled onto roads, the trusty Ambassador now outnumbered by Japanese, Korean, European and American vehicles of more modern design.[5] There were still 260 million people earning less than a dollar a day. But in the decade to 2003, the number of Indians officially classed as poor fell from 40 to 26 per cent of the population.[6] Perhaps that was why the face of the Mahatma, mischievous as ever, beamed incongruously from the new one-thousand rupee notes.

At the National Gandhi Memorial and Library in Delhi, icons associated with the father of the nation gathered dust, including the walking stick he'd used on the Salt March to Dandi, and the blood-stained dhoti he was wearing when he was shot dead. Also on display was the funerary urn his great-grandson Tushar Gandhi had emptied into the sangam at Allahabad in 1997, showering me with ashes. I'd been corresponding with Tushar, who like older Gandhians was scandalised by the betrayal of his famous forebear's abstemious legacy.

'Bapu would have been utterly disappointed to see the direction India has taken,' he emailed me. 'Today's India has split into two parts — the urban, westernized, developed India of extreme wealth and modern development, and the impoverished, imperilled India of its backward, rural villages.' Certainly, Gandhi's aim of building an India in which 'there shall be no high class and low class of people; an India in which all communities shall live in perfect harmony' had never been further from reality. The people had turned back to older gods and goddesses like Laxmi, the goddess of wealth.

At the Civil Lines, the gardens of the old bungalows continued to be carved up to create new houses and apartment blocks, and on the vacant block adjacent to Number Three, a triple-storey, fence-to-fence McMansion had sprouted, casting shadows on our lawn. The previously occasional sound of a truck's horn on the Ring Road had now become a more or less continuous chorus. Lovely Singh was worried by the looming spectre of the Delhi Metro, an affordable hi-tech mass-transit rail system funded by Japanese concessional loans, which promised to liberate millions of motorists from traffic jams but also threatened the livelihoods of taxi and rickshaw-wallahs like him. The system had thirty stations already on line and almost 200 more planned, and it made the subways of New York and London look archaic. To everyone's surprise Delhi's Metro-wallahs lifted their game by not groping women or spitting supari juice. The Metro provided an alternative vision of an India in which government solved problems rather than causing them, and in which people of all classes and castes sat cheek by jowl, going about their business in relative comfort.

Civil Lines had its own underground station with escalators and wheelchair access, and the Ring Road gridlock we'd suffered for years on trips to New Delhi became a less frequent experience. But Lovely had an unlikely ally in Maya, who no longer seemed to believe in the possibility of positive change in India, and who declared defiantly, 'Metro retro. I *certainly* won't be travelling on it!' Holding the fort in our small corner of Civil Lines was our housekeeper Sushila, whose life had become easier but less interesting. We'd kept her on, our own small contribution in a country without a social security system, but there was less work to fill her days, and she kept beseeching us to return permanently. Standing just over a metre tall, the illiterate widow and grandmother, whose late husband's name was tattooed on her inner forearm, was the daughter of servants and knew no other trade. She would shuffle into the house in her sari and rubber chappals each morning, uttering an oath to Shiva, and return across the Yamuna River in the afternoons to the sprawling suburbs where she lived in a small flat with her son, daughter-in-law and their *baccha*, her cherished grandson.

For the previous six years, India had been ruled by Atal Bihari Vajpayee's Hindu nationalists, the first non-Congress government to complete a full term. Strengthened, rather than weakened by their diverse coalition, they had stared down sanctions imposed by Western governments in protest at the nuclear tests, and called the bluff of their opponents at home and abroad. The then US President, Bill Clinton, had visited New Delhi in the year 2000 and praised Mr Vajpayee as a visionary statesman, despite legions of American NGOs lining up to condemn the Sangh Parivar's 'war on minorities'. In Washington, India was now seen as an important balance to the growing economic and military power of China, and there was talk of a permanent seat on the UN Security Council and G8 (Group of Industrialised Nations). The once loud chorus of condemnation of India for attacks on Muslims and Christians in Kashmir and elsewhere had diminished to hardly a peep. Vajpayee's coalition was getting plaudits, not brickbats, for producing success rather than excess. Instead of demolishing things, they were building them.

On a sprawling site on the east bank of the Yamuna, protected from the threat of flooding by massive earthworks, a monument to assertive Hindu identity politics had arisen. In New Delhi's crowded ensemble of magnificent ruins, most of them the legacy of Muslim rulers, there are few conspicuous examples of Hindu architectural splendour. Some say this is because the early Hindus inhabited thatch and bamboo structures, others that Muslim conquerors demolished the great Hindu temples that pre-dated their arrival. Francis Wacziarg, one of the saviours of Neemrana, had his own theory. 'Hindus are great builders,' he once told me, 'but until now they have not been so good at maintenance.'

Now the finishing touches were being put on the largest Hindu monument ever constructed on the plains of Indraprastha. Built at a cost of $40 million, Akshardham was more than a mandir: it was a Hindu theme park, including water features, boat rides, an IMAX cinema and 20,000 idols. The Delhi Development Authority had bulldozed the slum tenement homes of 140,000 poor people, and changed the course of the river to enable its construction.

History was being written in reinforced concrete and slabs of marble, and Akshardham was a monument to its brute physicality and mythic inspiration. History was also being rewritten, not always well. The fatuous delusions of Hindu nationalist 'histories' — that Hinduism was the root of all the world's religions, and that only Muslim rulers of India were guilty of demolitions and pogroms — were no longer restricted to the schools run by saffron organisations. The Indian Council of Historical Research was now stacked with nationalist fellow travellers, the beginning of a 'Long March' through the country's institutions armed with what the *Times of India* called 'a religious approach based on falsification and fabrication of evidence', or what one columnist called 'The Hindus Did Everything (But the Muslims Stole the Credit)' school of history.[7]

The crusade for a Rama temple in Ayodhya, which had fuelled their entire movement, remained unfulfilled, but now institutions of state were hard at work looking for evidence that an earlier temple existed beneath the rubble of Babur's Mosque. In August 2003, the Archaeological Survey of India (ASI) had been ordered to undertake excavations at the site. The Allahabad High Court had instructed the government's archaeologists to be especially careful not to disturb the Rama idol in the makeshift shrine erected by Hindu extremists in 1992, apparently fearing any such action could inflame the thousands of Hindus who now performed darshan there every day. Amid dark murmurings from secular historians that the ASI had been politicised under the Vajpayee government, the excavation proceeded. Eventually the ASI produced a 574-page report in two weighty volumes which was supposed to be for the court's eyes only, but copies of which had ended up on archaeologists' desks all over Delhi.

In the plush oasis of the Qutub Institutional Area on the arid southern outskirts of Delhi, a scientist who'd lent his reputation to the cause of the Ayodhya temple movement was claiming victory in his struggle to establish the veracity of the claim, and had invited me to his office to review the findings. Driving towards Qutub with Lovely, we passed the stone remains of at least seven former capital cities that had once stood on the plain. New Delhi was the eighth, but all around it massive conglomerate bastions and finely carved facades in stone stretched for mile after mile, preserved and well tended in some parts, built over and occupied by squatters and grazing cows elsewhere.

Among the oldest carved stones in the entire city is a tapered column of polished limestone that stands overlooking the ring road and evokes more than 2000 years of Indian history. The pillar is one of a series of columns erected 250 years before the birth of Christ at multiple sites by order of the Emperor Ashoka. Their purpose was to pronounce imperial edicts urging Ashoka's subjects to be considerate towards slaves, respect teachers and parents, and be generous and kind towards all living beings. Over a thousand years later, in 1353, the Turkic Muslim ruler Feroze Shah Tughlaq ordered that two of the pillars — one located at Topra in Haryana, and the other near Meerut east of Delhi — be brought to the capital to add lustre to his sultanate. The Topra pillar, measuring 13 metres in length and weighing 50 tonnes, was toppled from its plinth onto a deep bed of silk cotton, then wrapped in reeds and animal skins, and loaded onto a barge that floated it down the Yamuna. In Delhi it was offloaded by thousands of men, who hauled it to Feroze Shah's *kotla*, or fortified palace, where a stone platform was painstakingly constructed in a series of steps that raised the pillar to its present elevation. The second pillar was installed in the shah's hunting park on the Ridge, where it overlooks the walled city. For almost 700 years the two columns have been recognisable landmarks on the Delhi plain, their moral precepts etched in ancient Brahmi script and still visible close up, despite over 2000 years of weather.

The road took us past beggar hutments and the rocky outcrops of Jawaharlal Nehru University, a kind of academic oasis shimmering in the heat on the city's outskirts, to the Indian Archaeological Society, where Dr Swarajya Prakash Gupta awaited me. A driveway lined with pot plants led to a neat two-storey building swathed in bougainvillea, where Dr Gupta's spotless office revealed a scientist's love of order, files stacked neatly in pine veneer cupboards. On his desk was a copy of the ASI's spiral-bound report — thick as a phone book — entitled *Ayodhya 2002–03*.

'Have you seen this?' Dr Gupta said, eyes bulging behind huge owl-like spectacles, as he pointed to the report. 'The Archaeological Survey of India has concluded that the so-called Babri Mosque at Ayodhya was erected directly on top of a pre-existing Hindu temple. In front of that temple there was a big hall of around eighty-four pillars. The remains of some fifty pillar bases have been found. It is for anybody to see it. We've been vindicated. You will take tea?'

With his wiry, nut-brown frame, clad in the short-sleeved bush shirt of an outdoors man, and sporting a utilitarian watch with a black leather strap on his wrist, Dr Gupta looked like he'd just returned from a dig in some sunny far-off spot. His face was a jumble of features — flat nose, crooked teeth, silver hair on a balding dome — all galvanised by passionate excitement. Like many Indian men of his age, he did not bother to trim the hairs in his ears and thick black tufts sprouted from both sides of his head.

He'd been fossicking around the Ayodhya site for some fifteen years, claiming to have found sixteen black stone pillars and the remains of a burnt brick wall in the early 1990s. A few days after the demolition he'd rushed to Ayodhya to inspect two stone tablets unearthed by the kar sevaks bearing inscriptions which stated that a pre-existing temple on the site was dedicated to 'the Lord who humbled Bali and defeated Ravana', in other words, Rama.[8] Within a week he had vouched for their authenticity, describing them as having 'tremendous historical value.'[9] Now he was convinced that India's highest archaeological authority had confirmed his earlier finding. Radiocarbon technology dated the earliest ruins to the tenth century, plus or minus a century, and signs of human occupation of the area stretched back to 1000 BC.

'There are many examples of stone sculptures bearing images of Hindu gods and goddesses under that hill. Nearly seventy of them,' Dr Gupta said. 'Swastikas also. The Hindu cross symbol. Just like the Nazis'.'

Realising the unfortunate parallel, he paused for a moment and then added, 'Of course, they changed our Hindu swastika. Nazis made it the other way round.'

Just then his mobile phone rang loudly to the tune of 'Home on the Range', and he snatched it from the desk in front of him.

'Hullo? *Ha, bolo* Nandan (Yes, speak Nandan).'

It was Sangh Parivar headquarters in Delhi calling. The RSS supreme leader, K.S. Sudarshan, wanted to see him and he would be advised of the time and venue shortly. A visible straightening of the digger's spine suggested an honour bestowed.

Earlier in his career Dr Gupta had been a leading light in India's archaeological firmament. During Indira Gandhi's time he had personally selected the bronzes that decorated the prime ministerial residence; and as director of the Allahabad Museum he had escorted Sonia Gandhi and her children on guided tours of India's magnificent art heritage. He'd done pioneering work in Russia and Central Asia, had studied at the Sorbonne in Paris and the University of London, taught at Harvard, and had written a book on the roots of Indian art that was standard reading for Indian students. But wisely or otherwise, Dr Gupta had bought into India's most searing controversy. He'd been drawn into gladiatorial contests in archaeological journals and the mainstream media, trading vicious rhetorical blows with his enemies, who were 'all Muslims and Marxists', in India's version of the history wars.

'I've been criticised by everyone who is not an archaeologist. They decry Hindu tradition and that makes them scholars?' he exclaimed in a shrill, histrionic tone. 'If my findings support the Sangh Parivar, it's not my fault. At the age of seventy-three, I have no axe to grind. I'm an excavator, and I have one leg hanging in the grave.'

Groping under his desk for what I gathered was a button, he triggered a hallway chime that sounded like birdsong. Moments later a young *peon* of mute — almost downtrodden — humility, the kind who serves in many Indian homes and offices, appeared carrying the tea. Dismissing him with a perfunctory nod, Dr Gupta continued.

'What they, the ASI, have said is that it was a large Hindu temple of the medieval North Indian style. It has a *shikhara*, you know, that spire. The presiding deity was Vishnu. Now there are many emanations of Vishnu, but we know it is Rama because the inscription found there refers to the god who killed the ten-headed demon. That is, the demon of Lanka — Ravana. The inscription mentions Vishnu, then it zeroes in on Ram.'

The inscription to which Dr Gupta referred had been found in the rubble after Babur's Mosque had fallen, carved in Sanskrit on a one-metre by half-metre broken stone tablet. Given the history of fabrications by temple adherents ever since the Rama idols 'miraculously' first appeared inside the mosque, I asked whether forgery could be ruled out. In archaeology, the context in which material is unearthed is crucially important, and other Indian archaeologists I'd spoken to regarded this particular find as highly suspect, 'discovered' as it had been by members of a mob in the process of committing a criminal act. If they were willing to break the law to break the mosque, surely other misdeeds were not beyond them? But Dr Gupta took exception to the question, and suddenly I realised he was shouting at me.

'What? You think everyone has been cheating?' he erupted, waving his hands and arms about like a dislocated human windmill. 'Epigraphy is a science, I'll have you know. If anyone can forge it we will give five *lakh* rupees! They were not archaeologists who destroyed the so-called mosque, but they did recover hundreds of items of archaeological significance. The organisers were announcing that anything of significance should be kept. These are very wrong questions you are asking.'

My questions, I was sure, were entirely legitimate, and of concern to other Indian archaeologists, but the sheer stridency of Dr Gupta's outburst made me pause. Looking slightly self-conscious, he drew the bulky ASI report towards him, and peering down his nose, began turning the pages.

The drive to demolish mosques built on top of temples, of which there were said to be hundreds, struck many Indians, such as the liberal journalist Praful Bidwai, as opening a can of worms that was better left closed.

Should this country go on a spree of bloodletting and razing of monuments regarded as examples of history's 'wrongs' — in the way the Taliban destroyed the Bamiyan Buddhas? Can the vandalism of the past justify revenge-driven vandalism today? The ethical answer must be a resounding no.[10]

When I asked Dr Gupta about such views, his reply was laced with sarcasm. 'You see, this is all the leftist propaganda literature that you've been reading. See, I will tell you — all religions in the world are based on one principle: you can either take it or leave it. Can a human being be born out of a virgin mother? Take it or leave it! It's a question of the belief of millions of Christians. There's no question of scientifically proving it.

'Take the case of Islam. It is said that at Jerusalem where the Al-Aqsa Mosque is standing — I was in Israel, so I know it — that Mohammed-sahib one day thought that he should also go to heaven and see those beautiful girls which he is promising to every one of his disciples. So in the early hours of the day, he takes a horse with wings, goes to heaven, spends some time with those heavenly, beautiful girls, then comes down, and where the horse touched the ground, that became sacred to the Muslims, and they built the mosque called Al-Aqsa. Believe it, or leave it! Whether Rama was born in Ayodhya or not is a question of the belief of millions of Hindus. Who are you to judge? You are not Indian. You are not Hindu.'

It didn't take much to tread on Dr Gupta's corns, and I wondered frankly whether his scientific research could ever be reconciled with his theological opinions. When I asked whether, as a Hindu, he personally believed that Rama's *janmasthan*, or birthplace, was directly under the mosque, he erupted a second time.

'Again you are harping on this thing. I'm not here to answer your personal questions,' he snapped, abrupt and affronted. 'As a Hindu, yes, I believe the tradition. But my findings are those of an art historian, a digger who himself has dug the site before demolition. I'm not an activist.'

Suddenly equable again, Dr Gupta began pointing out pictures of the Ayodhya mound featured in the report, many of which I recognised.

'You see here. This is a cross-section dug within 10 feet of the makeshift temple that was erected after the demolition. The entire area was done, divided into trenches, as it would be done anywhere in the world. I have lived and worked in thirty-five countries by now and I can tell you, no archaeologists in the world could do a better job than this team has done. Five months is a very limited time for a 40-foot dig, but they have done a first-class job.

'See all the Hindu images on these pillars, the celestial semi-goddesses who are always dancing or making music or playing with balls? They have all been defaced. See the peacocks and the sacred water pitchers? Can anyone say this was not a Hindu temple? This is about 30 feet down. Absolutely scientific.'

In his quieter moments, Dr Gupta's love for his work shone through with a passion that bordered on melancholy, and I felt torn between empathy for his plight and concern that the line between faith and science should not be blurred. Other respected Indian historians, like Nayanjot Lahiri, paid due respect to Gupta's achievements, especially earlier in his career, but simply couldn't understand his willingness to advise the Sangh Parivar.

'Who would want to write history for goons?' Nayanjot asked when I met her to discuss the issue. Her response to Gupta reflected the view among many of her colleagues that the nationalists were not merely challenging versions of history, but the very existence of history as a scientific discipline capable of discerning fact from fiction, and truth from myth.

When a country's history becomes politicised, as it had in India and elsewhere, the national conversation that sustains a healthy society congeals into recriminations. History becomes a contact sport in a political Coliseum. Character assassination replaces academic debate, and the protagonists retreat into their sects, emerging only to lob missiles to the delight of a sensation-addled media. History wars are civil wars without the gunpowder. Yet for all his turbulence, Dr Gupta was at least challenging conventional wisdom, a healthy if lonely thing to do in any discipline. Where would we be without alternative histories?

The Archaeological Survey of India had found beneath Babur's Mosque evidence of several previous structures built over the centuries, including a 50-metre-long wall and fifty exposed pillar bases. It described distinctive features 'associated with the temples of north India'.[11]

But the unfortunate truth that a true believer like Dr Gupta couldn't face was that the ASI dig had turned up no conclusive evidence that a Rama temple had existed beneath Babur's Mosque, and certainly nothing to confirm that the spot was Rama's birthplace, and until some credible authority did, the claims would remain highly contentious. Given Ayodhya's multi-religious history, the scrolling floral designs gracing the buried architecture could have been Jain or Buddhist, or belonged to a Shiva temple. How the buildings had been destroyed, whether by man or nature, and if by man then by whom and why, was unclear.

★ ★ ★

It was only a few minutes' drive from Dr Gupta's office to Lal Kot, the Red Citadel, where the remains of cities built by Hindu rulers dating back to the eighth century can be seen. In the twelfth century one of them, the Rajput Hindu Prithviraj Chauhan, seized Lal Kot and had massive ramparts with thirteen gates constructed around it. The Chauhans' defeat in 1192 by the Afghan warlord Muhammad of Ghor, made possible by in-fighting among Hindu kingdoms at the time, marked a watershed in Indian history. For another eight centuries no Hindu ruler would occupy the throne of Delhi. The new Muslim overlords built India's first mosque, the Qu'watt-ul-Islam or Might of Islam, near Lal Kot, and the victory tower adjacent to it known as the Qutub Minar.

The Qutub complex is one of India's best preserved historical monuments, a place of green lawns and impressive ruins. From a distance, the 80-metre-high Qutub looks like the brick kiln chimneys you see all over the Indian countryside, a tapered stack slightly bulbous in the middle. From the elaborate minaret, intricately ornamented in red and cream sandstone, the muezzins called the faithful to prayer in an Indian Islamic state. Close up, the divinely inspired ribbed tower resembles a mighty quiver of arrows clasped in ornate bands. It is decorated with inscriptions in curling calligraphy, its girth ringed by four projecting star-pointed balconies. To build the mosque, the first Muslim rulers of Delhi demolished some two dozen Hindu and Jain temples in and around the site, and used their finely carved pillars to erect a house of prayer for Allah's believers. The roof of the Might of Islam's cloister is supported by dozens of square stone columns 4.5 metres high, carved with images of graceful Hindu *apsaras*, their faces and breasts smashed by Muslim iconoclasts.

At the northern gate to the mosque I paused to take it all in. Groups of French and Japanese tourists were milling around between the carefully preserved ruins and well-tended gardens, holding their brochures over their eyes to reduce the glare, as myna birds warred over food scraps. For over a century, the Archaeological Survey of India had been maintaining the mosque, buttressing the mortar at weak points and carefully cleaning the fluted stone to expose its finer details. At the base of the mosque walls, a dry trench, perhaps a moat in olden times, had been swept meticulously clean, exposing a significant detail. Cemented into the wall at the base of a staircase was a small stone tablet markedly different from the other bricks surrounding it. Carved in relief on its face was an unmistakeable figure with the head of an elephant. It was Ganesh, the remover of obstacles, patron of literature and education, son of Shiva and Parvati, one of the most beloved gods in the Hindu pantheon. Time had worn down his features, but the outline of his trunk was clearly visible. In fact, there was only one difficulty any Hindu might have had in recognising the image — it was upside down, as it had been for 800 years.

Like most Indophiles, I had collected my share of Ganeshas, including one in antique ivory depicting him reclining in a canoe, his much-rubbed pot belly as polished and prosperous as that of a Chinese Buddha. Especially popular with children, it was Ganesh that all Hindus prayed to at the beginning of any enterprise. The Hindu labourers pressganged into demolishing their own temples and building the mosque would have whispered their devotion to him at the start of every day, and would not knowingly or willingly have installed the idol in this disrespectful way. The likelihood was that they were forced to do so, as a deliberate humiliation and dishonour to their gods.

Historians reward the ruthless, reserving a place in posterity for their brutal acts, while the humble rarely find room in the history books. Intellectually, I appreciated the need to preserve the Might of Islam, regardless of its morally dubious provenance. Fashions, even moral fashions, change, but the blunt facts of history are immortal. Yet standing in the shadow of the Qu'watt-ul-Islam, I found myself, for the first time, sharing the anger of the nationalists, some of whom had been laying siege to Lal Kot of late, demanding the right to worship the Ganesh stone and other Hindu elements within the complex.[12] Had it been within my power, I would gladly have wrung the necks of those early Muslims who covered their barbarism in the accommodating skirts of religion.

Moving inside I wandered among the defaced Hindu columns of the 'mosque', wondering if I might have more in common with Dr Gupta than I realised, when I noticed a young Indian man studying the structure. He was tall and wiry and wore a neatly pressed chartreuse-coloured shirt and denim jeans. He was not loitering with intent to bother, as so many young Indian men do in such places, but had come alone and seemed genuinely curious about the monuments. Having spent years in India being sidled up to by pests, it was my turn to do the sidling. What was his religion, I wondered?

And what did he make of the beheaded stone *apsaras*, or angels, hovering over the finely carved corbels?

The young man was not from Delhi, but had come to the capital to work and study. He belonged to a Hindu family, and had the fresh-faced well-groomed looks of a sports star. When I approached him and said hello, he flashed a shy smile and chatted with an almost military politeness about his life and family. It was exciting to be living in the capital, he said, mixing with other young people from all over India and having access to his country's major institutions, from libraries and universities to museums, galleries and parliaments. Whenever he had spare time he would take off to places like Qutub Minar to enrich his knowledge and experience of India's history and heritage.

'Basically, I like the carved stones and sculptures. I'm proud, sir, that in India, such monuments are still preserved. They are not diminishing,' he said.

But did he not know the history, I asked? At first, perhaps, discretion got the better of him. But after a moment's hesitation, he answered the question.

'Actually, I *do* know the history of this place, sir. Of course, it bothers me,' he said. 'As a Hindu I am against what they did. Such beautiful sculptures should not be damaged.'

It seemed a rather mild reaction — I'd felt anger and I wasn't even a Hindu. But the young man seemed to be processing his emotions through the cool deliberation of intellect. Then he continued, somewhat sheepishly.

'You are thinking that perhaps because I am Hindu, I will want to bring down this structure, and build a temple or something of that kind on top of it.'

It had crossed my mind.

But the young man, who was as much a Hindu as the strident Dr Gupta, saw things differently.

'Of course, I am sad that these things were done, sir. Yes, Hindus have the power to demolish all these monuments now if we wish it so. But we should also learn from the past, nah? So why demolish? What we have we should keep. That way we will certainly know the true history of India.'

16

Virtual Reality

Deep Singh was a young man in a hurry who worked in a call centre in Gurgaon, the new El Dorado rising in what recently had been mustard fields on the border between Haryana and the National Capital Territory of Delhi. In the forecourt of New Delhi's Regal Cinema, where we'd agreed to meet, his tall frame, clad in a sporty spray jacket and jeans, towered over the milling crowds. From the cinema, the traditional meeting place for New Delhi-wallahs, we made our way through the midday crush — made worse by excavations and diversions for the new Delhi Metro station — and headed for a nearby McDonald's Family Restaurant, home of the Aloo Tikki Burger and the Maharaja Mac.

With his groovy sideburns and well-cut hair, Deep embodied the collegiate style popular with well-heeled teenagers of the cosmopolitan capital. To old Delhi-wallahs, Haryana was the boondocks, full of yokels; but to young, smart, middle-class kids from the provinces — like Deep — the glass towers, shopping malls and multiplex cinemas of Gurgaon were the acme of modernity. The son of a *subedar*, or mid-ranking officer, in the Indian Army, he came from a village in deepest UP, and believed in the Indian dream of freedom, family and riches. His generation of urban youth were India's most optimistic since the Freedom Struggle, the first with unrestricted access to the Internet, global television and global brands. They had a school textbook knowledge of Gandhi, but had barely experienced the rule of the Nehru-Gandhi dynasty. Socialism, with its trade unions and disdain for religion and celebrities, struck them as odd. Why would anyone ban Coca-Cola, as one Indian government had in the 1970s, or question the value of spiritual faith? Nuclear weapons, like a good cricket team, were for them sources of pride. But if you asked them about politics they would hesitate, sounding slightly vague, before lamenting the generalised corruption that plagued the nation they referred to as 'My India'. Their priorities were a good social life and attaining jobs in an intensely competitive market. 'Trendy clothes, trendier lifestyles, modern mindsets, tech-savvy homes, nuclear families, cell phone addiction, internet surfing, fast food, fast cars, fast life,' wrote one columnist, summing up their options.[1]

The new, more globally influential Indian seemed like a child of capitalism, but was actually a product of Nehru's government-led investment in education, agriculture and health care. They were children of social democracy delivered by capitalist midwives and they were in a majority. Half the population of India is under twenty-five. Had he been born in China, Deep might have been working in a factory. Instead, he was in services, which accounted for over half the economy in a country that had leapfrogged the industrial age.

India's transformation from Licence Raj to Info-Tech Las Vegas began with Y2K, the anticipated collapse of global computer networks that technicians feared would not handle the date change at the end of the millennium. To reduce the massive cost of finding a solution, American companies outsourced the work to low-cost IT centres in southern India around Bangalore. The year 2000 meltdown never eventuated, but it hastened the birth of the Indian software industry. Liberalised world trade and investment laws, combined with improved IT and telecoms, saw labour transformed from a national to a global commodity, in which low-cost countries with large pools of skilled workers, like China and India, held a competitive edge. For what it cost a global accounting firm to employ a single American junior accountant, it could employ four Indian accountants with the same level of skills.[2] By 2005, India was the world's largest provider of offshore services, controlling 44 per cent of the market, and, according to one study, stood to attract up to fifteen million jobs currently done in the West.[3] People whose jobs were transferred were described as having been 'Bangalored'.

While China had become the world's factory, India was becoming its back office. Global corporations, such as American Express, General Electric, British Airways, Citigroup, Hewlett-Packard, HSBC and H&R Block had led the charge to relocate customer care, medical transcription, data entry, credit-card billing, insurance-claims processing, legal research, map digitisation, radiology analysis, graphics, airline ticketing, animation, biotechnology, private tutoring, tax returns, actuarial work and financial analysis to India. While outsourced services varied in standard, they resulted in average cost savings to the companies of 40 per cent per employee position transferred. A report published by McKinsey found that in 2002 alone, General Electric had saved $340 million by outsourcing to India.[4] Another study warned, 'It is likely that globalisation will sweep through the formerly cosseted ranks of service workers. The relocation of services offshore and especially to India has the potential to reorganize the global economy.'[5] India's huge population, for so long seen as a handicap, began to be seen as an asset. The education system was turning out 250,000 skilled engineers a year, a resource some compared in value to Middle Eastern oil reserves.[6]

Another resource capped for decades and now finally released was Indian enterprise. As analyst Joydeep Mukherji observed:

Perhaps the most important long-term impact of IT success is cultural; Indians are seeing that it is possible to get rich based on talent and not on connections and corruption. IT is making the capitalist pursuit of wealth a legitimate enterprise in a country that once disdained it.[7]

As an Indian call-centre employee, Deep was part of an economic revolution that global analysts were calling 'the biggest watershed in global affairs since the birth of the modern national state system'[8] and he knew it. He could reel off dozens of fascinating facts about Business Process Outsourcing (BPO), the wonder of the age. Most call-centre workers were aged between twenty and forty, he told me. Almost half of them were women. After undergoing a 45-day training program in computer literacy and the different dialects of English commonly spoken in the West, the new call-centre staffer joined a company which never closed, organised on three eight-hour shifts around the clock. The monthly salary of about 10,000 rupees or $25 a month was twice what a teacher in a government school earned, but without the security of a job for life. In his organisation, there were both domestic call centres, where Hindi was the main language, and international call centres where English dominated. Staff members were assigned to either 'inbound' or 'outbound' desks. Inbound was when a customer called in needing help. Outbound was when the call-centre staff made unsolicited calls to members of the public, trying to sell them stuff. The workplace was caste free, theoretically, with a 'Don't ask, Don't tell' policy, but educated upper castes got most of the jobs.

Queuing for our meal, I noticed one of the young Indian McDonald's staffers pouring French fries from a paper sack into wire baskets and lowering them into a vat of boiling oil. He set the empty sack down briefly near the counter, close enough for me to read 'Produce of USA. Keep Frozen.' printed in English on the outside. Somehow in a world of global corporations it made sense for American farmers to grow potatoes, and McDonald's to process, freeze and ship them to India, where they presumably sold them at a loss in order to generate brand loyalty and market share.

As we squeezed uncomfortably onto our tiny seats, juggling our trays and straining to be heard over the din, it struck me that call-centre customer service was the equivalent of fast food — a nicely packaged homogenous confection that rarely delivered on its promise. In cities all over the world, householders were growing increasingly impatient at being called at home by Indian marketing employees asking for 'just one minute' of their time. With their low levels of trade union membership, call centres had been described as the 'Roman slave ships' of the twenty-first century, or modern work places with nineteenth-century labour rights. All communications between employees were taped in some form and randomly checked by management in the name of quality control. Mistakes led to warnings, and warnings on three consecutive days could lead to dismissal. Staff members' moods were monitored for cheerfulness. Some workers had difficulty coping with the intense pressure to perform, reporting symptoms such as nausea, insomnia, chronic fatigue, depression and stress, due to odd hours and the 'emotional labour' of being nice to rude customers.[9] By coincidence, I happened to be one of the customers Deep's telephone company 'cared' for, and had recently found that their assurance of nationwide coverage fell far short of the reality. It was somewhat disconcerting now to realise that the anonymous flak catcher who'd borne the brunt of my ire could have been Deep himself.

Nobody had told Deep that he was a 'cyber coolie', the demeaning term used by critics of the industry to describe call-centre workers. To his Team Leader he was a Customer Care Executive, a team member with potential also to become a Team Leader. His enthusiasm and commitment to his company reminded me of the Indian Pizza Hut staff I'd heard about who, when their American CEO arrived to tour to the Taj Mahal, formed a choir outside the seventeenth-century monument so that his arrival was enhanced by their stirring rendition of the Pizza Hut company song.

Deep was working in a modern, hi-tech environment, earning a better than average salary. More than that, the job came with a ready-made group of young friends, and one free meal a day. He considered his 48-hour, six-day working week as a form of free language training which might help him get a better job down the line, and treated it as part-time job to fund his studies and extra-curricula activities. At twenty-four he was a committed student, undertaking two degrees. On the wall of his one-room flat, which cost him 1000 rupees or about $22 per month, he'd placed a chart of English words he was trying to remember. His social life consisted mainly of cruising with friends at the new shopping complexes sprouting on the capital's outskirts.[10] All of which would have been sufficient had it not been for the thing he wanted most — to make it in Bollywood.

Celluloid dreams meant more to Deep Singh than cyber reality.

'There are only two types of person in this world,' he told me, an old head on young shoulders. 'Those who want money, and those who want name. Name and fame are what attracts me. Even my work at the call centre can prepare me. It is a kind of acting.'

He had the look, that clean-cut boy-next-door lock-up-your-daughters charm of a Shah Rukh Khan. There was only one cloud on the horizon of his bright future. His father opposed the idea.

'I showed him all my newspaper clippings from amateur theatre productions I've performed in, the certificates I've received. I've told him that I also have a good job. But still he is not satisfied. He only knows government service. But in my India of today there are many other opportunities. I can dream of stardom, but he cannot. That's the main problem.'

★ ★ ★

Maya could not conceal her disappointment. One of the family's adopted sons, the abstract painter Ajay Desai, had invited us to the opening of an exhibition of his work at New Delhi's *Nature Morte* gallery. Unsure what to wear I'd opted for the white cotton kurta pajama I normally wore only at home, topped with a black sleeveless vest. The moment she saw me, preparing to leave at the sound of Lovely Singh's horn, Maya's lips pursed and her nostrils flared in an expression of visceral distaste. Either I'd stepped in something foul on the way over, or it had something to do with my clothes.

'What is it?' I asked, taken aback. 'Is it the vest?'

'Noooo,' she said in a long, high-pitched moan that dropped an octave as it persisted. 'No, no. But ... you've joined the kutta brigade!'

Dog brigade? I really must have stepped in something.

'No, no,' Maya kept on. Her overacting was the limit. 'Not *kutta*. *Kurta*. You've joined the kurta brigade!'

Now I was the one who was disappointed. For a start, I hadn't joined any brigade. In fact, from an early age I'd committed myself to *not* joining brigades. Not dog brigades, not shirt brigades. When other boys joined scouts, or cadets, or the Boy's Brigade, I'd fled to the church and become an altar boy, dressing up in capes and vestments and serving wine to ageing bachelors with similarly appalling taste in clothes. In high school, when membership of the football team was the definer of inclusion, I'd fled to the beach, and the surfer's solitary karma. I was not a *joiner*.

'What brigade is that again, Maya?' I asked.

'You knowww,' she said, still elongating her vowels like one recently bereaved. Then her demeanour changed abruptly, and she turned coy and embarrassed. 'Like those jhola-wallahs with their shoulder bags and sandals. It's too ...'

'Go on. Spit it out.'

'Too *desi*.'

I couldn't believe my ears. Too Indian.

In most places, people want you to fit in, but in India, they prefer you to be different. Some deep well of enchantment or self-loathing has made them like this. They're like an immune system that welcomes viruses. To be *phoren* is divine, but to be desi is dismal. How Gandhi sold them on his *swadeshi* self-reliance line is an inexplicable miracle. Rule India? They'd much rather someone else do all the work. How else could the country have been ruled by outsiders for so many centuries? Like me, most Indians are not great team players. Every four years when the Olympic Games roll around, the sport they do best in is recrimination; blaming each other for why India wins fewer medals than Ethiopia. On the cricket field, when an opposing batsman skies the ball, the catch will go begging as the Indians settle the protocols regarding whose catch it is and translate the decision into the appropriate vernacular. They literally don't speak the same languages, don't eat the same foods, and don't worship the same gods. They are strangers to themselves, and yet they are a nation, and quite often win cricket matches with acts of sheer individual brilliance against better organised teams. This is the Great Indian Conundrum.

My kurta pajama made Maya's skin crawl because I looked too much like a local. Her dismay must have been building up over some time. My process of cultural assimilation had been slow, but what I had accepted went deep and personal. In the beginning, India struck me as the world's weirdest country. Then one day, to my great surprise, I woke up feeling absolutely at home there. Small superstitions or words, particular festivals and customs, had permeated my being as if by osmosis; a roll of the head to indicate agreement; touching the feet of a guru; or invoking the name of Rama instead of Jesus for a change. It no longer struck me as strange to bow before a Hindu idol in respect, or pray with Sikhs like Lovely Singh in a gurdwara. In the West, we may accept greater numbers of foreigners as migrants and refugees, but in our hearts we expect them to be like us. In India, you can speak Hindi badly and no one will be offended, because it is not considered unusual among Indians to speak Hindi badly themselves.

Marriage — I had found — was a major plus when it came to being accepted. The news that I was 'married to an Indian lady' — as my passport recorded — would transform complete strangers into brothers, uncles and aunties wherever I went. Nobody in India expects you to give up your own identity in order to be Indian except the government — which has not embraced the concept of dual citizenship — and a few hippies who never left Goa or Rishikesh. Even the extreme Hindu nationalist ideologue Veer Savarkar accepted that marriage to a Hindu was a virtual certificate of nationality, something 'which really fuses, and is universally admitted to do so, two beings into one'.[11] Although their violent deeds sometimes belied it, the nationalists believed that India's unity, openness and tolerance was principally a product of Hinduism, and I shared that belief with them.

At *Nature Morte* Delhi's art crowd was enthusiastically partying, and Ajay was revelling in early sales of his colourful contemporary canvases. He was an intense and erudite Gujarati, whose vast knowledge and voluble nature sustained many great conversations. As an artist married to an architect — Janaki's cousin Yasmeen Tayebbhai — we'd been talking recently about India's absorption of influences, from the Mughals to the British, and how it had moulded the Indian identity in strange and wonderful ways.

'The Brits were using anything and everything, taking elements from anywhere and everywhere,' Ajay had said, revelling in the eclectic dynamic. 'Colonial architecture incorporates a lot of Indian elements. They wanted a hybrid and they were conscious of their place in the continuum of this country, just like the Mughals.'

Not all Hindus regard the Mughal and British empires as having been entirely negative periods for India. Yasmeen had lent me a standard text at the Delhi School of Architecture, Satish Grover's *Buddhist and Hindu Architecture in India*, which actually praised the Muslim conquests for introducing something new as an alternative to orthodox Brahminical architecture:

Another of the seemingly endless and periodic invasions of India — this time that of the Muslims — finally and mercifully called a halt to the humdrum activity of throwing concentric walls and *mandapas* of florid columns around the ancient temples of southern India ... the invaders tapped the Indian builders' resources in giving a new lease of life to architecture in India, by building great and glorious mosques, palaces and tombs ...[12]

India's greatest building, perhaps the world's, is the Taj Mahal at Agra, and whatever a few Hindu supremacists may think, the building is quintessentially Islamic. India sometimes brought out the best in its conquerors.

A few days after Ajay's opening, I'd met him at the National Gallery of Modern Art, opposite India Gate in New Delhi. He was waiting, arms casually crossed as he perused the prints on sale in the cavernous foyer of the building. A compulsive and prolific worker, he resembled a human paintbrush, with his bristling moustache and tousled hair, flipping through a book on the work of K.G. Subramanyam, whom he'd studied under at art school in Baroda before moving to Delhi. Subramanyam had been a student of Nandalal Bose who, along with Gaganendranath and Abanindranath Tagore, was considered one of the fathers of modern Indian art.

In 1947, India awoke in freedom to find that, despite an artistic heritage stretching back 7000 years, it did not possess a single major art gallery in its capital. The donation of a grand domed palace by the Maharaja of Jaipur in 1954 gave it one. Next, they had to decide what to put into it. What they chose reflected the Indian pathology of outside influence, and the ongoing debate about how properly to deal with it.

Before the arrival of European explorers, traders, missionaries, and colonists in the sixteenth century, India artists worked mainly in temples and princely courts or in folk art traditions. Styles of painting and sculpture varied widely in different parts of the country, from the Persian-influenced miniatures of the Rajput and Mughal courts, to the sensuous stone and bronze sculptures that lavishly decorated Hindu temples, and the animist aesthetic of tribal cultural traditions. But the rise of British power would trigger revolutionary changes in

Indian tradition. The British East India Company, formed by royal charter in 1600, was a trading company whose primary aim was to return a profit to its investors, not impose British political or religious institutions upon India. The journeymen of 'John Company', as the firm was known, wanted mementos of their adventures in exotic lands. The 'Company School' of art was the initial response of Indian artists to their wealthy new patrons.

Having been hard at work preparing canvases for his just-concluded exhibition, Ajay was in expansive mood. We climbed the grand staircase inside the NGMA that led to the gallery featuring a few surviving examples of Company Art, and as we entered the gallery, he was stopped in his tracks by a sixteenth-century portrait of an itinerant entertainer by an unknown Indian artist, titled simply *Juggler.*

'You see, this fellow is juggling more than just those balls,' said Ajay, marvelling at the small portrait in oils. 'He's juggling an *entire* shift in perspective.'

There was a tortured feel to the juggler, a tension so palpable you feared the subject might spill the balls and scatter them across the gallery's floor. It reminded me of the way the early European artists in Australia fumbled to represent their unfamiliar environment. But in *Juggler* the anonymous artist was struggling with a new way of seeing the world — the single vanishing point perspective of European realism. The images of deities that had always been popular in India held no charms for most Europeans of the time. They wanted scenes from nature and the bazaar, and realistic portraits of themselves, sometimes in native costume. In 1790, the first British art school was founded at Poona and others followed, teaching the new methods.

In Indian art traditions, portraiture was reserved exclusively for the gods. Like ancient Greece — and unlike ancient Rome — Indian rulers and patrons deferred to deities. It wasn't that artists were incapable of naturalistic portraits and scenes — the frescoes that cover the cave walls at Ajanta and Ellora prove that they could paint realistic images — it was that art served a higher purpose than vanity; it was a language of symbols available only to the culturally literate.

A Rajasthani court scene hanging nearby gave Ajay a reference point. The colours were vivid and the subjects sketched in relatively few, bold lines. A single painting was partitioned into discrete windows that framed a variety of different activities all going on inside the royal palace.

'See, this Rajasthani fellow is showing you what's happening inside the building, but in the same painting he also shows you what's happening *behind* the building,' said Ajay, with the small chuckle. 'The perspective is lifted so you can wander around in that space, look behind that tree, and so on. But this simply wasn't realistic enough for most Europeans at that time.'

Before the British, the Muslim Mughals had introduced the emperor portrait, ironic given Islam's traditional aversion to figurative art. Later, British artists including James Baillie Fraser (1783–1856) and Thomas Daniell (1769–1837) introduced European techniques of perspective to Indian landscapes, struggling bravely to convey the alien textures of Indian life to a foreign audience.

'I mean, look at this. John Constable could have made this sketch — and here — a miniature painter trying to paint like Titian,' said Ajay pointing to several examples on the NGMA's walls. 'This is an Indian artist painting the kind of thing that an Englishman coming here would want to take back home. To the new patrons this may have seemed like progress, but something gets lost along the way.'

What had been lost, or at least misplaced, were indigenous art traditions that reflected Indian ways of seeing the world.

The late nineteenth century was a time of political and social ferment in India. The first uprising against the British in 1857 had collapsed, but the search for an Indian consensus to challenge colonial rule was intensifying. Hindu social reformers jostled with orthodox Brahmins and secular modernisers. Indian artists, too, began to reflect the growing nationalist sensibility in the country. In doing so, they unconsciously paid homage to the ideals of their oppressors. Previously, the role of the Indian court artist had been to reflect the glory of the ruler, the temple sculptor to reflect the glory of god, and the folk artist to communicate the cultural knowledge of the tribe. The erotic temple decorations at Khajuraho and Konark reflect the Hindu belief that even sexual indulgence can lead to enlightenment, if pursued in a true spirit. Muslim iconoclasm and Victorian priggishness posed a challenge to that sensibility, and the idea of the artist as an agent of change and social critic, which began percolating through Indian art circles in the nineteenth century, was something entirely novel.

'The entire history of Indian modern art is one long agony of how to deal with the external. Generations of Indian artists have fretted whether they were too Indian, too British, not global enough, too global,' said Ajay, leading me in to the next gallery on the upper level.

Rounding a bend, we came face to face with a large oil painting of Saraswati, the Hindu goddess of knowledge, by the nineteenth-century artist Raja Ravi Varma. In my travels in southern India I'd managed to pick up a number of antique prints based on the work of this scion of minor royalty of Travancore in today's Kerala. A century after his death, a new market for Varma's work was emerging among the expanding Hindu-dominated middle class, and a sheaf of his oleographs discovered in a cluttered bric-a-brac store in the backstreets of Hyderabad in southern India and priced at a thousand rupees apiece was a rare find. Among the prints were several images of Hindu gods, some clothed in faux jewellery and sequined apparel. But my favourite was a naturalistic portrait of a single-masted sailing boat shooting the rippling surface of the Ganga. At the tiller sat a smiling, low-caste boatman, and seated in the middle was an upright Rama with Sita draped in a crimson sari, and standing behind them with his quiver of arrows, brother Lakshman keeping a watchful eye on the mighty river. As a painting it was only competent, yet by drawing on the profound love of the personalised god that is the hallmark of the Bhakti tradition, Varma had produced a deeply moving work of art. The brothers looked like boys, slender and bare-chested with their hair piled up high on their heads in beehives, as they headed undaunted towards their exile. I'd seen that lightness of concern repeatedly in Indian faces, whether marching to war in the mountains of Kashmir, or clinging to the roofs of trains and buses. These gods under sail could have been any ordinary Indian family out for a Sunday boat ride, and Varma had used the techniques and perspective of European naturalism to portray them. But to understand what was going on, you needed to understand Hinduism.

In the late nineteenth century, with the heady atmosphere of freedom beckoning, Varma and his brother toured India in search of images with national appeal. It was during this trip, according to one biographer, that Varma decided that all his heroines would wear saris — as opposed to the *salwar kameez* of the Muslims. His decision helped popularise the graceful garment, and broaden the brothers' market.[13]

In 1894, returning from a second tour, Varma's national vision blossomed. Simplifying his line, he made the leap from the easel to the printing press, establishing the Ravi Varma Pictures Depot at Malvali near Bombay. While Varma and his brother still laboured with the brush, their emotionally charged images of the gods could now reach a massive audience through the medium of the oleograph. By varnishing and impressing an ordinary colour lithograph with a canvas grain, the new European technique gave prints the appearance of oil paintings. Synthesising Western naturalism and technology with ancient Indian religious and literary heroes, Ravi Varma became India's first national artist, but also engaged a highly lucrative commercial proposition. Business houses soon realised the potential of his images to 'sanctify' their products and began featuring them in the free calendars they distributed at the beginning of every year, and the Congress Party adapted some of his techniques for their agitprop.

'Colonialism took us backwards in some ways, but it also shook things up,' said Ajay, as we made our way downstairs. 'It challenged our *complacency*.'

It was a generous statement, one that reflected the growing self-belief of Indian artists. They had better things to do than bang on about the damage done by the Mughals and the British, and happily acknowledged the role of individual Britons like E.B. Havell, the principal of Calcutta's School of Art at the turn of the twentieth century, who championed such Bengal school artists as Abanindranath Tagore and Nandalal Bose. These two artists looked to India's indigenous art traditions, such as Rajasthani and Pahari miniatures and the Kalighat vernacular art sold as souvenirs to pilgrims at the Kalighat temple in Calcutta, for the way forward to a truly Indian modernity. For the rest of the twentieth century, Indian artists would struggle to find the right balance between past and present, universal and particular, and indigenous and foreign. Some artists and writers, such as the Nobel laureate Rabrindranath Tagore, looked east, visiting Japan and immersing themselves in different Asian traditions, while others like Amrita Shergill spent time in Europe. They knew of Picasso and Cezanne, but were just as interested in Tantric symbolism or, as in Ajay's case, pure abstraction. There was a nation to paint, a world even, and space in which to paint it in the postmodern period.

Downstairs at the NGMA, the pictures were arrestingly contemporary. There was 1997's *Riot* by Sudhir Patwardhan, depicting a red double-decker bus on fire in Bombay and a child being put to the sword, and Jyoti Bhatt's *Reminiscent Images*, which featured the Indian tricolour limp at half-mast on a Hindu trident.

17

The Temple of Justice

My firm opinion is that the lawyers have enslaved India.
Gandhi (a lawyer)[1]

Since the days of Rama the idea of justice — seeking it and
getting it — has been a principal preoccupation of the Indian
people. They are a patient people, which is just as well because when
it comes to justice, they have to be.

According to a popular legend, India holds the record for the
most protracted law suit ever adjudicated — a dispute over control
of a Hindu temple in Pune that went to court in AD 1205 and was
finally concluded in 1966. Frivolous litigation was a national sport.
A man in West Bengal was suing the winner of the Nobel Prize for
Economics, Amartya Sen, for daring to call himself a Nobel Prize
winner. Sen's claim to the prize was unimpeachable yet, for reasons
known only to His Honour, a judge was prepared to hear the
complainant.[2] Twelve years after the riots at Ayodhya, not a single
individual had been convicted by a court for their role in the
demolition, which had defied the explicit orders of the India's
highest court. If justice delayed is justice denied, then India had set
the benchmark in denial. A former chief justice of the Supreme
Court, Justice R.C. Lahoti, put the problem in a nutshell: 'There is
too much law, and too little justice,' he wrote.[3]

At a conference of High Court judges held in Delhi in 2004, pendency — the huge overhang of unresolved cases — was the main topic of discussion; that and who was filling what judicial appointment and where. Attending the meeting out of curiosity, I had met a senior official from the country's busiest and — except perhaps for the Supreme Court — most esteemed judicial bench, the Allahabad High Court. Omkhar Nath Khandelwal, a suave middle-aged man with silver hair, was a former district judge of Varanasi and now registrar at Allahabad. Rather than explain the gridlock affecting the court in theoretical terms, he thought a day or two in Allahabad would make the issue crystal clear to me. I might even get to meet a few of the venerable judges. Since my first visit to Allahabad for the ceremonial immersion of Gandhi's ashes, I'd had fond memories of the so-called 'Oxford of the East', a treasure house of Indian culture, fine arts and humanities, with deep roots dating back thousands of years to the *Ramayana*.

Arriving on the overnight train from New Delhi, I was greeted by newspaper headlines describing anarchy in Allahabad. The normally staid columns of the city's newspapers were brimming with indignation provoked by the construction of a culvert on Kutchery Road, and an indefinite strike by *safai karamcharis* — street sweepers — now in its fifth day. The *Hindustan Times'* correspondent breathlessly reported 'Cars, scooters, cycles, rickshaws crisscrossing from all directions ... Also cattle, dogs and pigs wrestling to get in and out as if they had some important errand to attend to', while the strike had left 2000 cubic tonnes of uncollected garbage on the roadsides, giving citizens 'no option other than to inhale decomposed material and polluted air'.[4] That sounded familiar, but it was hard to reconcile the stories with what, by Indian standards, remained a neat, somewhat somnolent university town of well-stocked bookshops and diminutive Premier Padmini cars driven by black-cloaked *vakils* (advocates).

At Anand Bhavan (Blissful Manor), an architectural folly and ancestral home of the Nehrus, now a museum, I inspected rooms where the Mahatma would often be found sitting cross-legged and bare-chested, spinning cotton into *khadi*. Like his host, the rich lawyer Motilal Nehru, and Nehru's son Jawaharlal, Gandhi was a lawyer, who decided that the overthrow of British rule could not be accomplished by litigation. Such was the force of his commitment and charisma that he managed to persuade both Nehrus into following his example. The spot where they burnt their Savile Row suits on a bonfire in the garden of Anand Bhavan is now marked by a memorial. Anand Bhavan was donated to the nation by Motilal's granddaughter, Indira Gandhi, when she was prime minister in 1970. Inside, the public could marvel at Motilal's silver toiletry bottles and wicker palanquin, Jawaharlal's tennis racquets and a copy of the Harrow school register from his years there, and old photographs of Gandhi-ji and of Rajiv Gandhi as a child.

The care lavished on the Nehrus' old mansion contrasted starkly with the neglect shown to the many superior buildings that graced Allahabad's boulevards. Cathedrals, colleges and courts — towers in stone with domes dusted in aquamarine tiles — recalled more ambitious times, when British empire builders could afford to let their imaginations run wild. Arresting examples include the Allahabad Museum, a repository of mind-boggling antiquity; the Mughal emperor Akbar's imposing sixteenth-century fort overlooking the sangam, now under the control of the Indian Army; the magnificent Indo-Saracenic style university; and St Joseph's College and Cathedral on Tashkent Road.

The decline of Allahabad, a city of a million people with no direct air service to the capital 1000 kilometres away, was emblematic of Uttar Pradesh as a whole. By the early 1990s, a man born in India's most populous state could expect to live twenty years less than one born in Kerala. The majority of people in UP had not completed primary school and only one in four women could read or write. Studies by the Nobel Prize-winning economist Amartya Sen and his colleague Jean Drèze found that entrenched social conservatism undisturbed by a moribund bureaucracy was to blame for the state's poor performance. In one department, however, Allahabad had flourished: more court cases were filed in this single city than in any other jurisdiction in India, or indeed, Asia.

Six hundred years before Christ, suspected criminals in northern India faced an extremely elaborate judicial process in which the suspect deposed before seven officials in turn before his case was decided. The later Mughal empire Qazi system imposed a local form of Islamic law. But in the century after the Mughal emperor Aurangzeb granted trading concessions to the British East India Company, India became a minefield of overlapping legal jurisdictions, including those of the Portuguese colonies and princely States. In British India, the King's Courts, constituted under the authority of the British Crown, and the Company Courts, dedicated mainly to resolving commercial matters, shared the caseload. It was only after the 1857 Rebellion, when London formally incorporated its Indian possessions into the British Empire, that legal reform took place with the issue of Letters Patent by Queen Victoria for the establishment of resident courts at Calcutta, Madras and Bombay. Eight years later, in 1869, Allahabad became the principal court of the North-West Provinces, and in 1919 shifted to the colossal edifice of fawn-coloured sandstone set under an expansive dome that it occupies today.

The massive colonial-period Allahabad High Court squats behind iron palisades like an Indian Hagia Sophia without minarets, an edifice designed to inspire awe. Arriving at the courthouse, I was greeted by a banner advertising a 'Mega seminar — Law as a Career'. Walking through a quartered garden of lawns and potted bougainvilleas, I entered a cavernous hall hung with a massive crystal chandelier that resembled the lobby of a grand but rather shabby hotel. In 1975, history was made here when the Honourable J.M.L. Sinha found the empress of Indian politics, Indira Gandhi, guilty of electoral malpractice and banned her from contesting elections for a period of six years. Ever since, Allahabad has enjoyed a special place in the Indian psyche. Horse-hair wigs and ermine-collared robes are still worn on ceremonial occasions, and marble honour rolls and oil-painted portraits of judges preserve a tradition of dignity that elsewhere has long since disappeared from Indian public life.

Despite his kind invitation, and several telephone calls alerting him to my impending arrival, Mr Khandelwal seemed taken aback to see me when I entered his office, a room of cave-like gloom with an unfathomably high ceiling illuminated only by a downcast desk lamp. In his reticence I sensed a collision between formal politeness and a crowded schedule. Dressed in a grey woollen jacket with a thin black tie and the gold clips of a twin pen set peeping over the pocket of his jacket, he rose slightly in his chair, strained to smile and pointed me to one of eight chairs ranged around his expansive glass-topped desk. The desk was stacked high with piles of green cardboard files festooned with tabs and stickers, and a grand bank of telephones occupied the return. Reaching under the desk he pressed a buzzer, and a liveried attendant appeared from behind some drapes wearing a red-and-white turban with a gold fringe and carrying a tea service.

'You do one thing,' Khandelwal told me, untying his first bundle of files for the day. 'Have some tea, while I arrange for somebody to take you on a tour of the court building. Would there be anything else you would be needing?'

I'd been hoping to talk to a judge or two, somebody who could enlighten me regarding the current state of pendency. But, reminded of this, Khandelwal — whom I'd been told would soon be elevated to the bench himself — winced perceptibly and said 'Judges will be a problem. But let us see what may be possible.'

Indians apply themselves to the law with unparalleled commitment. Lodging a criminal case is easy, requiring only a visit to the local police *thana* to lodge a First Information Report detailing the alleged crime and suspected perpetrator, which the police are then duty-bound to investigate. Because lodging a civil case is also cheap and easy, frivolous litigation floods the courts. On average it takes ten years for a court case to be completed. In October 2004, for example, the Delhi High Court ordered that a 55-year-old bank clerk who'd been sacked thirty years earlier be reinstated. Padam Chand Gupta's entire working life had been spent fighting against his dismissal from the Syndicate Bank in 1974 for allegedly misappropriating funds. Gupta had been invited to resume work just five years short of retirement.[5] The outcomes of other cases redefined the term anticlimax; two property cheats waited twenty-eight years to hear a Delhi judge pronounce them guilty, then soften the blow by suspending their two-year jail term.[6] Anyone given a life sentence could expect to serve the bulk of their sentence before their appeal was concluded. Not surprisingly, most people confronted by arrest on such charges abscond if bailed. Around 70 per cent of people in detention had been convicted of no crime, but were merely awaiting trial. Some blamed an oversupply of lawyers for the burgeoning caseload, others a shortage of courts. One advocate I'd met even blamed the Hindu gods, believing that the mythological intrigues played out in the religious epics set a bad example. In India, there is a tendency to mythologise entrenched problems, as is apparent in the school of thought that sees a malfunctioning judiciary as a success, a tribute to Indian democracy.

'This is what makes India such a wonder, such a contested place,' a magistrate who'd helped me through the legalities of the marriage process once told me. 'Indians have not retreated into themselves yet. They're still fully engaged in the battle of life. We like this environment of *tamasha* [fuss]. Everyone must have their rights. Everyone is fighting to be heard.'

★ ★ ★

Before leaving New Delhi, I'd consulted one of India's top lawyers, Ram Jethmalani. The newspapers that week had been full of legal sensations — inquiries initiated or dropped by the Central Bureau of Investigations under political pressure, state witnesses suborned and turned hostile, even corruption among judges.

'That's dirty politics for you,' said Mr Jethmalani. 'Some powerful person is interested in prosecuting and he gets the better of the police. Half these cases should never have been started, and the other half is incompetently investigated. Then there's the pressure to stop proper investigations. Delhi runs on connections — police, politicians, lawyers — everyone has connections. Mr X will call his friend, who is a senior bureaucrat, and complain that the Municipal Corporation of Delhi people are hell-bent on harassing him. "Who is the officer concerned?" his friend will ask, and then call the officer and say, "*Arre*, don't trouble him."

'In any case, you cannot improve character by law. The legal system can play some part in improving character, but basically you need character to run a legal system. This is the paradox. In the days of the Freedom Struggle, our leaders went to jail and became heroes. They always pleaded guilty. That's the difference! They defied the law because they believed that it was unjust, and they were prepared to bear the consequences. Today, our leaders play the martyr.'

According to Jethmalani, India required five times the number of courts that it currently had. Through sheer bureaucratic inertia, almost one in five judicial posts was vacant. Public interest litigation, another name for class actions, had made the law more accessible than ever. But getting a result and getting out of court had never been more difficult.

'But really judges are to blame,' said Mr Jethmalani, 'in the sense that when you have so much of delay in disposal of cases you create opportunities for interference in the judicial process. Even the victims of crime lose interest in getting justice.'

Now, sipping my tea in the registrar's office in Allahabad, I noticed in the higher reaches of the room an honour roll that recorded the names and tenures of all the court's registrars, from 1868 when the first, William Tyrell, occupied the post, all the way to Mr Khandelwal, who'd taken charge in 2002. In the lower reaches of the room, dark, flashing movements at the periphery of my vision suggested a small mammal picking up biscuit crumbs. Chik screens in the open doorways kept out the flies, and a constant stream of underlings and visitors came and went from the office, pausing behind a modesty screen until summoned. Looking down on it all, half asleep, was the Mahatma, who'd held firm views about the legal profession and who, as a lawyer, knew what he was talking about.

'The profession teaches immorality,' he wrote in a booklet called 'Hind Swaraj', considered to be the most coherent exposition of his world view.

It is exposed to temptation from which few are saved ... The lawyers, therefore, will, as a rule, advance quarrels instead of repressing them. Moreover, men take up that profession, not in order to help others out of their miseries, but to enrich themselves ... It is within my knowledge that they are glad when men have disputes. Petty pleaders actually manufacture them. Their touts, like so many leeches, suck the blood of the poor people. Lawyers are men who have little to do. Lazy people, in order to indulge in luxuries, take up such professions ... It is lawyers who have discovered that theirs is an honourable profession. They frame laws as they frame their own praises. They decide what fees they will charge and they put on so much side that poor people almost consider them to be heaven-born. Why do they want more fees than common labourers? Why are their requirements greater? ... If pleaders were to abandon their profession, and consider it just as degrading as prostitution, English rule would break up in a day. They have been instrumental in having the charge laid against us that we love quarrels and courts as fish love water. What I have said with reference to the pleaders necessarily applies to the judge; they are first cousins; and the one gives strength to the other.[7]

Perhaps all the years he and Nehru spent in British jails (over a decade in the case of Nehru) had left him bitter?

At the Allahabad courthouse, told that I had come to investigate the vexed issue of pendency, one of my fellow guests — an amiable former judge of Kanpur — shared his thoughts loudly, as if fishing for the registrar's approval.

'UP is one-fifth of India. We have a population of fifteen *crore*, so naturally our High Court must be the largest. If we had one judge per ten lakh of people, it would make 150 judges. Actually, we have only half that number. Then there is the litigious nature of our people. Once poverty is there, persons become very conscious of what is their right. Then, you have political instability this last twenty years, and where there is political instability, people challenge the laws. The pendency never decreases. We have 200 new or amended laws passed by parliaments in this country every year! All these new laws are being manufactured and challenged. We need new courts if we are to be implementing all these laws. We have a backlog of twenty-odd years. Criminal appeals decided by district judges in 1981 are only now reaching this court on appeal. Then there is population growth. Every year India adds another twenty million people. What to do?'

A large sculpture of the elephant-headed Ganesh, similar to one I'd seen in the home of Ram Jethmalani, stood in the corner of the room, the Hindu 'remover of obstacles' obviously much in vogue in the varicose legal system. Khandelwal, meanwhile, had continued juggling telephones and files, trying to find a judge with the courage to meet me, and anyone willing to discuss the sensitive issue of pendency. Every few minutes more bulging files would be delivered to his desk, personnel issues mounting even more rapidly than court cases. The files spilled across to the conference table and were climbing the walls, threatening to swamp him. The cause list for that day alone ran to 214 pages. *Chandra Deo Pandey vs Basu Deo Pandey* — presumably a land dispute between brothers — was in its thirtieth year. One of the parties to the case of *Kundan Lai vs Anil Kumar* had died, presumably unsatisfied.

While I was reading the list, a young man had sidled up to me, apparently on Khandelwal's orders. Shanta Nand was a judgement writer who'd been assigned to lead my tour of the courts. From the registry Shanta took me along dimly lit corridors to the court's museum, which held replicas of famous documents, including a judgement written in Hindi by the great populariser of the *Ramayana*, Tulsidas. There were nineteenth-century plaints on stamp paper issued by the East India Company, and *firmans* written by Akbar, Jahangir and Shah Jahan. Through the red-carpeted Judge's Library, where the wigs conferred under portraits of their predecessors, we strolled through Acting Chief Justice Markandi Katju's private chambers, which were cooled by a bank of four air-conditioners and fitted with His Honour's own bed, to which he sometimes retired during lunch. Although well qualified for the position, an accident of birth meant Justice Katju could not formally be appointed as chief justice. When I asked where Katju had been born, Shanta replied, 'In Uttar Pradesh.'

'But we're in Uttar Pradesh,' I said, perplexed.

'Correct!' replied Shanta. 'In 1994, the Supreme Court decided no judge can become chief justice in his own state.'

It was all in the interests of neutrality, of course, but like their British predecessors, India's High Court judges might not even speak the vernacular of their appointed jurisdictions. They were strangers in a very strange legal land.

The Chief Justice's court was a vast auditorium teeming with black cloaks flapping under no fewer than twenty ceiling fans. There were at least a hundred advocates seated, and another hundred standing along the side of the room, and I thought for a moment that we'd found the 'Law as a Career' seminar. The entire scene resembled a painting by a Flemish old master. Of the fifty-two courtrooms in the complex, this was the largest, and presiding over proceedings was the Acting Chief Justice himself, a frown between his bushy eyebrows as he dictated an order barely audible over the hum of conversation. Engraved in large letters in English on the timber facing of the bench were the words 'Truth Always Triumphs'.

Returning to the registry, I found Mr Khandelwal, this time transformed from harried bureaucrat into charming host, his desk surrounded by a phalanx of advocates representing the local Bar Association. The lawyers had requested the meeting ostensibly to demand faster service of notices, but instead the wily registrar was serving them tea and sharing jokes amid an atmosphere of mutual back scratching. Everyone knew the various Bar Associations were among the most vigorous opponents of legal reform in the country.[8]

'In the law, you are like the god,' one of the advocates was telling him, raising gales of laughter all around. They resembled a cast of characters from a medieval guild, some wearing thick bifocals, others with vermilion tilak daubed on their brows, and one quite cross-eyed.

Drinking the registrar's tea and nibbling his biscuits was clearly a chance to hobnob with the registrar and get noticed. Khandelwal, for his part, was displaying a chameleon-like quality that probably explained his stellar progress through the galaxy of Indian law. He was waggling his head amiably, teasing and laughing, but the moment they left amid florid expressions of thanks and praise, his face resumed its immoveable set, as he addressed himself to the latest dumbwaiter-load of files. Interrupted by a telephone call, he sat up straight in his chair, concurring with the caller, and looked at me before putting down the phone.

'I'm afraid the judges are too busy to meet you today. Perhaps another time,' he said. It was a bit of a blow and I tried to suppress the thought that the Acting Chief Justice was probably sleeping in his cot as we spoke. 'But you wanted to discuss pendency,' he continued. 'And you are in luck. The relevant person is prepared to meet you, only there should be no quoting by name.'

In the office of the Registrar (Inspection), it was 1965, the year India and Pakistan fought their second war for control of Kashmir. Each Tuesday, at the Allahabad High Court, they turned back the clock, devoting the entire day to the hearing of old cases. 'The oldest case is 1965,' said the official who dared not speak his name, a dapper man in a navy jacket and dotty tie, as a clock ticked rather too loudly on the wall. 'Slowly we are moving forward to the present.'

How slowly, I wondered? Producing a weighty register which apparently contained the pendency figure for the state's courts, he began flipping the pages, occasionally touching his thumb to his tongue. The Registrar (Inspection) cleared his throat, measuring his words before speaking.

'On the thirtieth of June 2004,' he said, 'seven hundred and seventeen thousand, seven hundred and four cases were pending in this court, including the Lucknow Bench. Between first January and thirtieth June this year, the High Court disposed of seventy-six thousand, four hundred and three cases. But seventy-nine thousand, nine hundred and sixty-one new cases were instituted.'

They were going backwards, and that didn't even include the district subcourts where another million or so cases awaited a hearing.

I'd had my day in court, and returning to Khandelwal's office, found him busily granting requests for transfers and dictating correspondence to a stenographer, while continuing to turn over page after page in his files, like a reading machine.

'You must have heard about the all-out efforts being made to reduce pendency,' he said, chirpy between dictating letters. 'So much of labour they are putting in!'

In an effort to rein in runaway pendency, officers of the court were grouping cases with similar points of law and types of relief at issue, and thereby curtailing unnecessary argument. There was discussion of eliminating anachronistic laws left over from the colonial period, and simplifying consumer protection, land acquisition, accident claims and family court matters. Conciliation and arbitration were to be encouraged, as well as an amnesty on the payment of exemplary fines. Government was the biggest litigator in the country, and notoriously reluctant to settle. But if they agreed, there could also be new courts and fast-track tribunals sitting three shifts a day, like factories. The number of permissible adjournments and appearances could be limited. Judges could be performance-tested, like athletes, and held to targets of timeliness. Already, judges were remaining in their chambers until eight o'clock at night just to clear cases. At this rate the backlog of litigation would be cleared by, well . . . never.

Perhaps they were doing India a favour, collecting all its squabbles, petty and profound, and storing them in their cave, like nuclear waste, slowly degrading with a half-life of a million of years.

★ ★ ★

It was an enormous relief to escape the claustrophobic confines of the courthouse, where the calendar was stuck at 1965, and emerge into a sunny afternoon. The traffic 'chaos' reported in the press consisted of little more than a few camels hauling cartloads of hay. Enjoying the fresh hay-scented air, I decided to head down to the Ganga.

The meeting point of India's two most revered rivers is marked by a Mughal-period fort and some makeshift structures of timber and thatch that get washed away occasionally when the rivers change course. From beyond the distant banks a fluky wind carried a herdsman's cry, temple music and the call of a muezzin. Having rested a while on the bank, I climbed down to the shore and clambered aboard one of the skiffs that takes pilgrims to the sangam, where they make their humble offerings to the river gods. Pushing off with a great oath, the boatman navigated a path between pot-bellied men deep in prayer and women in saris waist-deep in water. Ahead of the boat, where the waters whorled and eddied, other boats had been lashed together and anchored as a mid-river mooring for pilgrims who wanted to bathe there. On the decks, junior Brahmins with top-knots broke coconuts and chanted Sanskrit prayers, as pilgrims collected Ganga jal in plastic soft-drink bottles.

The holy pandas were rough types, whose demands for money for spiritual services rendered could get quite menacing. Knowing their scams, I lingered there for a while, teasing them by refusing to pay for a blessing.

The reverence of Hindus for the place they call Prayag, the 'place of sacrifice', stretches back beyond recorded time. The Mughals renamed the nearby city Allahabad, but the word never replaced the Hindu name for the sacred zone. Akbar the Great (1556–1605), who built the fort and married several Rajput Hindu princesses, was an open-minded seeker of spiritual truths, who convened a council of scholars to hold open debates on the merits of Hinduism, Christianity, Judaism, Buddhism, Zoroastrianism and Islam without fear or prejudice. It was a very Indian thing to do, but the emperor was criticised by the Muslim clergy. Undeterred, and perhaps motivated as much by vanity as piety, he founded a short-lived syncretic religion called Din-e Illahi (Divine Faith), with himself as its spiritual head. Some believe Allahabad is, in fact, a mistranslation of Illahiabad. But the faith failed to convert even the emperor's own sons, and both Hinduism and Islam survived his challenge.

Once every twelve years, Prayag becomes the venue for the largest gathering of human beings in the history of mankind. The Maha Kumbh Mela, which means Great Festival of the Nectar Pot, last took place in January 2001, when over thirty million Hindus formed a congregation visible from space. The festival recalls a mythical sky battle between gods and demons for control of an urn containing *amrit*, the nectar of immortality.

According to legend, drops of it spilled at four places, most importantly at Prayag. Every twelve years, a new city rises on these sandbanks, more orderly and law abiding than any other city or institution in India — certainly better run than the courts — challenging the idea that the secular is always more practical than the religious. Hindu priests devise horoscopes, dispense Ayurvedic medicines, and preach endlessly in a kind of spiritual Olympics.

Then, at the end of the month, the city vanishes, as if erased in a gigantic conjurer's trick, its population dispersed across the broad expanse of India. I had attended the Kumbh that year, arriving on the eve of the most auspicious bathing day. Taking a dip, however, was the furthest thing from my mind. I'd come to watch, not to worship or catch typhoid in the Ganga, and there was plenty to see.

Stumbling around in the pre-dawn darkness on the western bank of the Ganga the following morning, I had spotted a naked, ash-smeared sadhu brandishing a trident and sitting astride a stocky white horse. As I got closer, I saw that he was held up at a police barricade, awaiting permission to proceed onto one of the barrages erected to convey pilgrims across the shifting sandbanks to the sangam. There were so many people but no apparent focus, and I felt I must be miles from where I should be.

Just as I was about to move on, a young man in flowing saffron robes accompanying the sadhu challenged me, saying 'No photos!' But when I showed him that I was not carrying a camera, his tone changed instantly to sincerely friendly. The young Swami Vedanta was connected in some way to the Nirvani sect of Naga sadhus, religious ascetics who took vows of chastity and poverty, burning their clothes and wandering India naked for the rest of their lives. They'd been given the honour of bathing first on the most auspicious day by the religious committee overseeing the Kumbh. Vedanta himself had been living in a cave in the Himalayas near Gangotri for three years, although an influential friend had ensured he was provided with every convenience, including a cave phone. He was also well travelled, rattling off the names of various places he'd visited in Australia.

As we were chatting, a tremor of anticipation suddenly moved through the crowd near us, and I saw police clearing a path and the naked horseman easing his mount forward.

'Are you coming?' cried Swami Vedanta, excitedly, leading the way to the sangam, which was still cloaked in night somewhere in the distance.

Wandering lost amid tens of millions of people, I had accidentally stumbled upon the head of the main procession of the Kumbh. With the friendly swami beckoning me to join him, I hastened to catch up, and walked the entire length of the procession a few steps behind the naked sadhu, as he led the largest human congregation in history in Hinduism's most revered ritual. Along the route, foreign tourists and Indian pilgrims stared awestruck at the holy white man — me — so obviously eminent as to be chosen for this unique honour.

Nearing the bathing spot the procession halted as police made last-minute arrangements to ensure an orderly march to the water. Just then, Swami Vedanta — who had objected to photography when we first met — produced a small camera from beneath his robes, and asked if I would take his photograph with the naked sadhu and his horse. Happy to oblige, I took the camera and shot a few frames. But no sooner had I returned the Swami's camera than a policeman, alerted by the flash, threw me out of the parade. By the time I reached the riverbank, when the barricades were dropped soon after sunrise, the Nagas had completed their bath and departed, and I never saw Swami Vedanta again.

The sadhus had charged into the water, dancing and whooping like children, followed by tens of millions of ordinary Hindus who waded in more cautiously. Submerged in their common identity, they washed away their sins in a joyful and infectious spirit. It all looked like so much fun that for the first time in my life I envied them their vivacious faith. Stranded on the sidelines by myself, I scooped up a handful of water and dabbed it on my forehead.

Strange things seemed to happen at Prayag, mystical things that challenged both professional objectivity and spiritual scepticism.

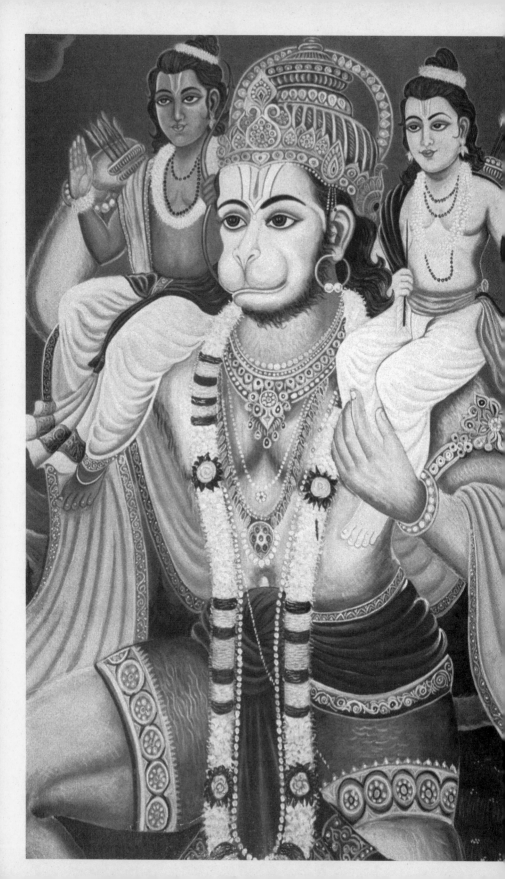

18

Return of the Hero

Deep Singh was going home. For seven months he had not seen his family, as he chased the dream in the call centres and shopping malls of Gurgaon and New Delhi. He would return to his village of Gopiganj bearing gifts — and I was going with him. He was cashed up and dressed up, hair cut and sideburns shaved, as we sat together on the bus at Lucknow waiting to get under way.

I'd arrived that morning by bus from Allahabad, having stopped en route at Saraiya Maafi to see if my hijacker friend was home. He wasn't, and I was miffed when his brother Girish informed me that Satish Chandra Pandey was now living in a hotel in the city I'd just left. Girish was cagey when I asked what Satish was doing there, but others in the village were under the impression that the hijacker was working for the re-election of the local BJP member of parliament, Dr Murli Manohar Joshi, who held a senior portfolio in the Vajpayee government. If true, it would not have been unprecedented in the lawless politics of the Cow Belt. The Congress Party had endorsed as its candidate in Sultanpur another hijacker, Devendra Pandey (no relation), who, with his brother Bolnath, had seized control of a plane in the 1970s. The people had elected him and he'd become a bigwig in the party's state organisation.[1]

Before departing Allahabad I'd purchased a copy of *Starteller* magazine, a popular astrological monthly whose advertisements thoroughly complemented its articles. A Chennai-based firm was offering 'energised gems' guaranteed to solve such problems as being overlooked for promotion and childless marriage. Not having children in India is considered a tragedy, and well-meaning strangers constantly questioned me about my tragic, childless state.

'*Bhagwan ki merzi hai,*' I'd tell them, glancing skywards with a resigned expression. It's the Will of God.

Starteller's resident astrologer was reporting Saturn in the second house of Gemini, and warning that the memorial erected on the site of Rajiv Gandhi's assassination in southern Indian had been designed with incorrect *vaastu* alignment, making it inauspicious. The advice to the authorities was to erect a hospital in the southwestern corner of the site to remedy negative cosmic consequences. This method of propitiating the gods was clearly the magazine's stock in trade. My horoscope was grim. Not only would I suffer a financial crunch, but friends and even relatives might ditch me. There would be quarrels within the family and misunderstandings with my spouse. Nor was there any point in buying next month's edition of *Starteller*. 'For another 2½ years troubles will continue,' the seers foresaw, with a professional precision that also provided specific remedies. In order to avoid the full brunt of planetary fury I simply needed to worship the Hindu monkey-god, Lord Hanuman, apply yoghurt to my forehead and feed snakes with milk.

However, in my darkest hours, I would not be alone. Those born in Aries could expect relatives and friends to 'turn inimical' and could be attacked by their pets. 'A sense of fear may always prevail,' the magazine warned. Businessmen would suffer heavy losses and be deceived by partners unless they fed buffalo with millet and donated four bottles of wine to a temple and avoided green clothes. Cancerians were set for disease, and mental agony would be 'the order of the day'. They needed to 'feed monkeys with jaggery'. Leos would be subject to injuries resulting in knee fractures, and tax raids. 'Life will be in turmoil,' they were told, but if they wished they could water pipal trees daily and put turmeric on their faces. Librans would be subject to black magic and a 'fear complex' (reading *Starteller* alone could give you that). Most likely they would lose their memories and fail in love affairs. For career women, 'Even with hard work, job satisfaction may be a mirage'. The solution was not to quit, but to 'Feed sweet biscuits to crows.' Scorpios generally would be okay, but should ensure that the lights were switched off at all times in the rear rooms of their homes. For Sagittarians, however, 'Home front will turn into a war front ... Financial problems will throttle you'. The only solution for them would be to pour eight quarter-litre bottles of alcohol into a river. Capricorns should hold onto their alcohol; haunted by miseries on many fronts, they would need it. Betrayal by colleagues, inquiries and punishments were 'in the offing ... Health problems may add fuel to the fire'. Unmarrieds were warned against 'falling prey to the advances of the cunning youth', but the cunning youth could be avoided by donating 3.4 kilograms of sugar to a widow, who — if she also happened to be a Capricorn — might find it useful should she too fall prey to the cunning youth.

We were rolling forward, with the bus driver unleashing his standard-issue Bhangra cassette, played at peak distortion with lung-busting tabla and bass accompanied by a boisterous Punjabi chorus. I wanted to warn Deep about the dangers he'd be facing as a Leo, but the loud music and wild swerving motion of the bus had somehow put him to sleep, his well-coiffed head slumped on my shoulder. He'd been telling me what an exhausting year he'd been having, and how he missed his mother, whom he hadn't seen for seven months.

Beyond the limits of the Grand Trunk Road, a patchwork of maize and cornfields blanketed the countryside, and dark green mango trees and cropped fields flew past as the driver sounded his trumpeting horn. I caught a whiff of cow dung on the breeze, and realised that I kind of liked UP, and the lightness and freedom that you sometimes experience travelling rough in India. Some three hours after leaving Lucknow, the bus reached the outskirts of Faizabad, and the turnoff to Deep's village of Gopiganj.

Past fields of sugar cane and lentils, the unpaved lane took us to the Singh residence — a single-storey brick bungalow with a spacious roof terrace shaded by mango trees and banana palms — where Deep's family rushed to embrace him. Brothers, cousins and his mother greeted him like a returning hero, which, in a way, he was. His father was not home, not even in India, but serving with an Indian peacekeeping force in Ethiopia. The *subedar* had survived Rajiv Gandhi's doomed Sri Lankan deployment, and it struck me how even in the most anonymous village in India, decisions taken in New Delhi could be matters of life and death. Keeping his distance as I entered the house was Deep's grandfather, who'd once been the village *pradhan*, or head man, and active in the freedom movement too.

'He hates white people,' said Deep, smiling incongruously when I asked what was up with the old man.

Anyone who could hold a grudge that long — Granddad must have been in his nineties — deserved respect, and I cherished the old man's animus as a living link with India's momentous history. Deep was distributing his gifts — gadgets, crackers and Archies greeting cards — a one-man demonstration of trickle-down economics in action as he soaked up the affection the recipients showered on him.

'I love my village,' he said, 'if not to live, then at least to visit here. There is so much greenery, and the unity of the people is something special. New Delhi is so fast, and there is no friendship between neighbours.'

Of the 285 million Indians who inhabit cities, most come from villages like Gopiganj, lured away from their rural homes in search of opportunity, or driven away by caste and religious prejudice. Some find urban anonymity preferable to the jealousies and feuds of the village; others lose their way, cut off from the roots that sustain them. At least three million migrants who'd come to Delhi from the countryside in recent years had ended up in slums, earning as little as 1000 rupees a month, or about $22,[2] straining at rickshaw pedals, or sleeping under flyovers. Others, like Deep, celebrated both worlds, and moved between them. It occurred to me at one point that he was like the reverse image of another army son from the Cow Belt, Satish Chandra Pandey, my hijacker — only taller, better looking and less inclined to blame the world for his problems. He was the good seed, and for his sake and India's I sincerely hoped that his dreams would come true.

After settling in, Deep took me on a tour of the area, tailed by his cousin Munoo. It was a mixed community of Rajput Hindus, lower castes and Muslims, numbering some 250 people, most of whom worked the land and spoke the Awadhi dialect of Hindi. The neighbouring village of Birbalpur, situated on the national highway to Lucknow was where the real power lay. It was a mainly upper caste settlement which was home to the current *pradhan*. When I asked people in Gopiganj what they thought of their elected representative, more than one replied, 'He eats money.'

When I asked Deep if anything had changed in the village since he'd left, he pointed to a call centre of a different kind — an STD/IDD telephone booth.

'You cannot say any more that we villagers live in ancient times. This is a modern village now,' he said, elated. But there was more to Deep's homecoming happiness than family or phone booths. The call-centre work was starting to bug him.

'It's very stressful. The moment you finish one call, another one comes to you,' he said. 'If you're working on the outbound desk, you have to make at least 250 calls in your shift, and speak continuously for eight hours. At the end of the day they de-brief you, and put you under pressure if you haven't made any sales. Some weeks you might not have sold anything.'

Coming from such a positive young man, Deep's lament seemed doubly serious. 'Some people are good at it,' he continued. 'They're the ones who make Team Leader. Then they only handle problem customers.' He'd left one call centre and joined another, and had abandoned his correspondence course in aeronautical engineering because of lack of time. Yet without a degree of some kind he might have no alternative but to keep wearing that telephone headset.

Then there was the abuse — targeted as well as spontaneous — that call-centre employees were under strict orders to ignore. While most householders would just hang up on intrusive calls from the centres, some organised enemies of Business Process Outsourcing (BPO) were deliberately calling outsourced customer service desks, aiming to demoralise staff with sexual taunts and racist slurs.

'I made one woman cry and promise to quit her job in 60 seconds. You can do it too!' boasted one such manly vigilante. 'Often they give me a "courtesy laugh" as if I were joking and ask how they can help me . . . I've been doing this about 20 minutes a day. It's great fun.' Instead of allowing their staff to hang up on their tormentors, the call centres were offering them yoga classes and stress management training.[3]

The relentless strain and insecurity of call centres were giving Deep nightmares. 'I dreamt that aliens were attacking India. There was a big *kund*, you know, like a pond, and the aliens dropped an atomic bomb in it,' he said, looking around as if people might think he was crazy. 'I was running to rescue my family, and we all took shelter under a tree. There was a big building there, 100 storeys tall, like the World Trade Center, and one of the alien space ships used a giant magnet to pick up the whole building. It was such an incredible dream that when I woke up I wrote down all the details. It could make a film.'

Deep wasn't alone in his cyber-trauma. Chetan Bhagat had written a novel, *One Night @ the Call Centre*, in which an agent in Gurgaon tries to make team leader in order to win back his girlfriend, but is sabotaged by his manager.

The good news for Deep was that his hopes of making it to Bollywood had received a modest boost. He'd been getting part-time work as an actor with the Ministry for Information and Broadcasting, earning the casual artistes' rate of 125 rupees per day plus 400 rupees per show. He now spoke knowledgeably about 'face work' and 'body work', in the parlance of his craft, and was in rehearsal for an Independence Day gig to be staged in front of the President of India. In the past year he'd watched eighty-five English and US movies, which he had studied for acting technique and colloquial expressions. His father still didn't approve, and there'd been more problems on the home front over his marriage plans. Finding a bride was a major challenge for Indian young men, given the country's cultural preference for male children which had produced 35 million fewer women than men.[4] As a Rajput Hindu boy from an army family, Deep had been receiving overtures from similar families keen to forge an alliance. And not just one or two — seven young women had been introduced. He even liked one of them.

'I talked to her for half an hour. In looks, she was fifty-fifty. Unfortunately, she was not educated, but the main thing is that she should be Rajput.'

'So, what happened?' I asked, angling for an invitation to the wedding.

'Nothing,' said Deep.

'You rejected her?'

'No, I liked her. *He* rejected her.'

'Who did?'

'My father.'

When a young man can't even choose his own bride, it's little wonder that some of them go round demolishing mosques and hijacking aeroplanes.

Deep, of course, was philosophical about it. There would be other girls, maybe a sixty-forty, or even a seventy-thirty. Or maybe, if he really got lucky, filmstar Aishwarya Rai would show up in the village and lure his father away.

With one eye on Bollywood, and the other on pleasing his parents and paying the rent, Deep had a compromise that would keep everyone happy, including himself. He would do an MBA to achieve financial security, but keep up the acting work in order to become, if not the next Shah Rukh Khan, then at least a full-time professional artiste in the Hindi language.

'In India, we have three societies — the poor, the rich and the middle,' he said, preparing me for another one of his maxims. 'The poor know they will never be rich. They don't have to think about these things. The rich, of course, will always have their silver spoons, and they also need not to worry. But we middle people, we could easily become poor; or if we work hard, or get lucky, maybe could get rich. Whatever we do, we must struggle. Always we must fight and fight and fight.'

★ ★ ★

From Gopiganj it wasn't far to Faizabad, the former capital of the princely state of Awadh (Oudh), and from Faizabad just a few kilometres more to the old Hindu temple town of Ayodhya. When I told Deep Singh I wanted to go there he bridled uncharacteristically.

'There are so many other holy places in India — Mathura, Haridwar, Varanasi, Puri. But Ayodhya is famous only for bitterness,' he said, and he was right, of course. Ayodhya wasn't just the name of a scruffy old town on the Sarayu River; it was a byword for hatred, violence and chauvinism. But like one of those weepy veterans who insist on revisiting old battlefields, I needed to see Rama's old capital at least once more before I died.

On 28 March 1528, the first Mughal emperor, Babur, paused on the banks of the Sarayu near Ayodhya on his victorious march through India. A descendant of both Genghis Khan and Timur the Lame, he had come a long way since first crossing the Indus into Hindustan in 1519, on a whim, as recorded in his memoir, the *Baburnama*:

> ...nothing to count had fallen into the soldiers' hands during the three or four months we had been leading this army. Now that Bhira, the borderland of Hindustan was so near, I thought something might fall into our men's hands if, riding light, we went suddenly into it.[5]

Three days after arriving in Hindustan, Babur's men were cutting off heads, and what subsequently fell into their hands was one of the richest empires in history, despite the fact that the country was not to their leader's taste:

> Hindustan is a country of few charms. Its people have no good looks; of social intercourse, paying and receiving visits there is none; of genius and capacity none; of manners none; in handicraft and work there is no form or symmetry, method or quality; there are no good horses, no good dogs, no grapes, muskmelons or first rate fruits, no ice or cold water, no good bread or cooked food in the *bazaars*, no hot-baths, no colleges, no candles, torches or candlesticks.[6]

Babur's pride was outstripped only by his ignorance. As he rested by the Sarayu, some 10 kilometres from Ayodhya, he was once more confronted by the defects of Hindustan. His forces were facing the usual resistance by pagan Hindus egged on by their Afghan overlords, and he'd picked up an ear infection, only the latest in a series of illnesses he'd suffered during the military campaign. Still, his illustrious achievements on the battlefield no one could deny, and just the previous year he had assumed the title of ghazi, or victor in a holy war, even though the bulk of the Indian resistance was led by the descendants of Muslim rulers who'd reached India centuries before him. At Ayodhya, as elsewhere, Babur's men 'drove the enemy like sheep before them', capturing some Afghans whose heads they 'cut off and sent in', at which point the town's ruler 'flung himself into the jungle and escaped'.

By 2 April 1528, Babur was feeling sufficiently improved to head out for a spot of hunting. What happened next, his diaries do not tell us. One of the most controversial episodes in Indian history disappears in a five-month hole in Babur's account. Historians speculate the diaries were destroyed in a storm. Two years later, Babur would be dead. I had visited his tomb in Kabul, where the wars that were his forte were still raging. His descendants would rule India for 300 years. In Ayodhya, a small inscription carved in Persian on a modest mosque recorded his legacy:

> *By the command of the Emperor Babur,*
> *whose justice is an edifice reaching up*
> *to the very height of the heavens,*
> *The good-hearted Mir Baqi*
> *built this alighting-place of angels;*
> Bavad khair baqi!
> *May this goodness last for ever!*

Baqi Tashkindi (Mir Baqi) was the *hakim* or military commander and chief administrator of the area, which under the Mughals would be known as Awadh. He did not mention if anything was standing on or under the site prior to construction of the mosque. He used some black stone pillars carved with images such as the lotus, the water pitcher, scrolling vines and the figure of a woman, which appear to have come from an earlier building, but exactly what type of building it was is not clear. Fifty years after the mosque was completed, perhaps the greatest Rama devotee in history came to live in Ayodhya. In 1575, the poet Goswami Tulsidas, author of the most popular version of the *Ramayana*, settled in the temple town to pen his *Ramcharitamanas* (The Lake That is the Story of Rama), which would make its hero one of the most popular gods in India. Nowhere in his extensive writings does Tulsidas mention that a Rama temple existed on the site of Babur's Mosque. But Tulsidas was living in a country ruled by Babur's sons and grandsons. Even his silence is ambiguous, and the European travellers who followed him to the town in later centuries, like the Austrian Jesuit priest Joseph Tieffenthaler, merely reported rumour and gossip they picked up secondhand from locals. With no conclusive evidence either way, rumour prospered, fuelled by mischief, misunderstanding, litigation, wishful thinking and hatred, in the centuries that followed.

In Faizabad, founded in 1700 by a Muslim *nawab* and now the centre of the district administration, officials had grown accustomed to their city's troublesome twin-town. The commissioner, Arun Kumar Sinha, was a beaver-like Hindu man with a bristling moustache trim as the hedge outside his British-period bungalow. As the court-appointed receiver of the disputed site at Ayodhya, which had been compulsorily acquired by the government, he would visit it once a week to ensure that everything was in order.

'Do you pray there?' I asked.

'Not while I am on duty,' the Commissioner said, slightly evasive, when we met at his office. I'd known he was on duty because the large red light outside, like some sacred host in a bureaucratic tabernacle, was glowing. A little prodding revealed that several years before taking up his post, he had in fact visited the site in a personal capacity, and taken darshan of the idols installed in the tented temple erected by the kar sevaks on the ruins of the mosque.

'It's an emotional issue — emotion is the key to understanding this country,' he told me.

But Ayodhya wasn't just an emotional issue; it had legal, political and religious dimensions. India's courts had long recognised the Hindu rite of Pranapratishtha — endowing with breath — by which idols — *murtis* — are animated, literally given life. In law, a properly sanctified murti has the same legal rights as any other citizen of the republic. It can own property and sue or be sued in a court of law. It can vote, although perhaps fortunately in this case, voting in India is not compulsory. With the Hindu nationalists in power, prosecutions relating to the demolition made little progress. Lal Krishna Advani — one of the accused — was the home minister, in charge of the country's Central Bureau of Investigation.[7] In May 2003, ten years after it brought charges against him and seven years after a court found he had a case to answer, the CBI decided there was insufficient evidence to proceed against him. The courts instead had ordered the Archaeological Survey of India to determine whether an earlier structure existed beneath the mosque. In the meantime, police had garrisoned the site. The chief police official in Faizabad was a clean-cut, super-efficient young senior superintendent of police. When I dropped in on him, Binod K. Singh was bawling at a junior officer for some small breach of duty, his muscly forearms and braid-festooned shoulders exuding authority.

'We've got fifteen companies of Police Armed Constabulary, and five companies of Central Reserve Police out there. That's about 2000 men deployed in and around the site,' he said. 'The current concern is not mass gatherings — pilgrimage is regulated and we stop mobs miles from that place these days. The worry is a suicide strike by Muslim militant groups looking to stir up trouble. We sweep the site for explosives every morning and evening.'

It was costing the government more than $1 million a month to provide security for the idols. On the positive side, said Superintendent Singh, a decided change in the atmosphere between Hindus and Muslims in the twin towns of Faizabad and Ayodhya had been noted.

'During recent festivals, I personally have seen Muslims showering the Hindu participants with flowers, as they passed the main mosque of Faizabad,' he said, obviously moved by the gesture.

I'd heard about this nostalgic movement for reconciliation between the two communities from other informants. In 2003 one of the chief priests of Ayodhya, the Mahant of the Hanuman Gari temple, a short walk from the disputed site, had invited local Muslim leaders to celebrate Roza Iftar, the breaking of the Ramadan fast, at his residence adjacent to the temple. There he had presented them with new garments for the year ahead and served sweet jalebis and invited their imam to lead prayers to Allah. I wanted to meet this remarkable priest.

From Faizabad to Ayodhya I took a ride in a jumbo rickshaw, seated opposite a Muslim woman in full chador. We played complicated eye games, taking turns to look and not look, until we both got bored and watched the driver sounding his horn, which involved holding two naked, sparking wires together with his fingers. The bazaar that led to the Fort of the Monkey God was lined with sweet shops and stalls selling religious paraphernalia; but there were few other businesses functioning apart from those serving the needs of pilgrims. The development and growth of a town of 50,000 people remained hostage to the permanent threat of religious violence. In the newspapers it was just a headline, but here in the narrow lanes of Ayodhya, the consequences of politics were starkly apparent.

The Hanuman Gari was a fortress of pink stone built on a steep hill in the centre of the town. A small lane at the base led around to a clean and airy room where Mahant Gyandas awaited. As the president of the All India Akhara Parishad, Gyandas had the unenviable task of trying to organise the country's most anarchic and individualistic group of citizens — the 650,000-strong community of sadhus, or wandering Hindu ascetics. He had recently overseen arrangements for their participation in a *kumbh mela* (bathing festival) at Ujjain, at which the sadhus typically took centre stage as militant, and often naked, defenders of the faith. Gyandas was also a much-feared wrestler, who had chosen physical discipline rather than devotion or knowledge of the Vedas, as his preferred path. What better way to attain enlightenment and merit than slapping a headlock on your opponent?

Seated on a raised wooden *takht* in the shade of an open veranda, the bearlike priest had shoulders round as boulders, and nipples that disappeared under fleshy manboobs. He was clothed, mercifully, in precisely three items of apparel: a skimpy piece of red cloth that wrapped his torso from his shoulder blades to his knees; a piece of string worn over his right shoulder; and a simple steel ring on one finger. His right ear looked to have been chewed at some point, but it had healed, and he sported a Sanskrit tattoo on his right bicep that read 'Om' in Devanagari script. Behind him, stood two uniformed police officers cradling submachine guns but there appeared to be no imminent threat to his life. Indeed, his skin glowed with health, his closely trimmed silver hair and beard shone likewise, and he emitted a fetching scent of sandalwood. A soothing harmonium played somewhere in the background.

On 6 December 1992, as Ayodhya approached its dark noon, the head priest of the Hanuman temple had been seated on this same takht. As Muslim homes came under attack, his residence had begun to fill with Muslim families frightened for their lives in a town seized by the mob. It was, unconsciously, the repayment of an old debt. The fortress of the faith that towered above us, catching rays of the afternoon sun, was donated to Ayodhya's Hindus in the nineteenth century by a Muslim nawab.

The *mahant* thought that a new mosque and temple should be built side by side to bury the conflict and open a new era of friendship between Hindus and Muslims. He wanted the traditional *parikrama*, or circular pilgrimage held annually around Ayodhya, to be thrown open to Indians of all faiths. Gandhian goodwill was back in style in Ayodhya, but those who preferred confrontation were still active, with one Sangh Parivar organisation planning to commemorate 6 December as 'Valour Day'. When I mentioned this, Gyandas's sunny expression changed to an expression of outrage.

'They exploit in the name of Hindus,' he said, referring to the Hindu organisation in question, the Vishwa Hindu Parishad. 'They exploit in the name of Rama. For them, it's a business. They are swindlers of money and property, grabbers and snatchers, blackmailers and thieves. Thugs! A religious mafia! Dharmic mafia! Hindus don't kill people without reason. This Sangh Parivar, they are not Hindus. They have no mercy in their hearts. They are demons disguised as Hindus. They are anti-India. Only during elections do they take the name of Rama. They are separatists, terrorists. That idiot Ashok Singhal [leader of the Sangh Parivar] has come to me twenty times trying to win my support, and twenty times I have said to his face, "You and your anti-socials have been looting our Lord. You looted Hinduism on that day." We banned him from the inner circle at Ujjain. I told the District Magistrate, if Ashok Singhal interferes, there will be turmoil among the sadhus and saints.'

When I glanced at the guards, wide smiles had parted their lips. Gyandas was looking at the various other petitioners waiting to see him, nodding as if encouraging people to join him in lambasting the nationalists. As I left his compound, he called out after me, 'Don't forget what I told you. Remember, they are thugs and hoodlums!'

From the Hanuman Gari, the narrow lanes which tracked uphill towards the disputed site were lined with stalls selling provocative DVDs of the demolition, complete with triumphalist voiceovers. Nearing Manas Bhavan, the former guesthouse now taken over by security officials, the shops and houses of a normal town gave way to the architecture of a besieged state, steel staked fences and lookout towers, barbed wire and sandbagged police posts, over which monkeys clambered and warred. The macaques ruled large parts of the town, scooping prasad into their mouths with mechanical efficiency, one grain at a time, or just licking it off the pavement directly.

The guards on duty alerted the local intelligence people to my arrival, and the intelligence people wanted to see my passport and asked the usual questions. The site was open to the public for seven hours a day, and as I stood waiting to be cleared, a family of pilgrims including a cute little girl dressed as if for a birthday party in tassels and bows passed by. Access to the site was via a series of mesh-enclosed walkways, cages really, and it took me a while to get my bearings and realise that I was entering through the same alleyway that Natasha Singh and I had used on the day of the demolition. It was a sad recollection. Although Natasha had survived the mob she had died the following year in a helicopter crash in Afghanistan. Now I felt her presence once more here in Ayodhya. Following the steel grate corridor I caught glimpses of the familiar no-man's land between Manas Bhavan and the mosque, except that the mosque was no longer there, bulldozed into a mound, garrisoned and covered in fireproof yellow plastic sheeting.

The whole area looked smaller than I remembered — a common trick of memory — and much of the rubble and bricks remained where they had fallen twelve years before. Parts of the earth had been divided into trenches by the Archaeological Survey, avoiding several Muslim graves that had survived the demolition, others having been dug up by the Hindus. The walkway zigzagged a few times, then finally led onto the rubble in front of the small tented shrine perched atop the ruins of the mosque. The paramilitary police on duty had turned into *pujaris*, assisting the pandit to hand out prasad to the pilgrim family that had passed me earlier. Another family in front of me had brought their newborn baby to present before the idols. All this was touching, but also ineffably sad, that one person's sacredness could so easily be another's profanity.

The first family had taken darshan of the idols and were moving off when suddenly the air was shot through with squeals and screams of the most alarming kind. A few metres ahead of us, a large male monkey had penetrated the caged walkway and was attacking the little girl I'd seen entering the site, scratching and snatching at a bag she was carrying, obviously believing that it contained food. The little girl was beside herself with terror, and too panicked to realise that she should let go of the bag. Before her father could rescue her, the hairy animal got what it wanted and nimbly escaped through the hole it had entered by, leaving the little girl tearfully gulping for breath.

On the long walk out, surrounded by the ghastly architecture of state failure — the cages and barbed wire, tarpaulins and trenches — I had to remind myself that the idols had been inside the mosque for over fifty years. In a bizarre way, the status quo had been maintained — except that the mosque was missing.

When I telephoned police superintendent Binod K. Singh to ask about the police-cum-pujaris, he was apologetic. 'Ideally they should not do it, but the duty there is very monotonous. It's not a popular posting. We rotate people through as often as possible to minimise contamination. But you know, all of them are Hindu or Sikh, and every day you have pilgrims coming, long queues forming and so on, and the police will just try to expedite things. The large-heartedness is there. After all, a mandir is a mandir. It's a question of faith.'

Finding my way to the back of the fortified area for a second look towards dusk, I caught sight of the neem trees under which I'd seen the terrified police huddling in 1992. It was bathed now in a surreal orange light. Much of the open ground inside the barricades had turned to jungle, and monkeys leapt with superb athleticism from lamp-post to lamp-post. As darkness fell on Ayodhya, and the police settled in with their lanterns for another long night of duty, peacocks mewed, dogs barked, and children played by the open sewers of paupers' homes, a stone's throw from Rama's 'birthplace'.

At the Trivedi Guest House, where I'd taken a room, the proprietor was a former civil servant, homeopath and self-declared saint who ran a temple and a pharmacy, as well as a lodge. Dr Shyam Narain Dubey was the Hindu holy man from central casting, with a long silver beard, a moustache that flapped as he spoke, and a philosophy that spanned both the profound and the ridiculous. He claimed to have met Subhash Chandra Bose, the Indian independence leader who had fought on the side of Japan in World War II, after Bose's mysterious disappearance in an alleged plane crash.

'He did not die. When I met him in Nepal, he was 101 years old. He was an old sadhu,' said Dubey, who also claimed to have provided political advice to the Gandhi family. 'I met Mrs Gandhi twice. I was a saint at that time.'

Saintliness in the Hindu tradition is a lifestyle, not just a title. It's entirely possible to live as a saint for years, then go and do something different. Not all ex-saints fall, as in the Christian tradition. Some just soul change, downshifting to less onerous occupations.

The downstairs dispensary of Dr Dubey's guesthouse had shelves bulging with tinctures and expectorants, tonics and complexes, dilutions and gripe mixture. A former education superintendent of Faizabad, Dubey had the sadhu market wrapped up. Wandering ascetics wobbled into his store day and night, calling him Maharaj, and getting discounts on their medicines. Dubey himself had spent years meditating on the sandy banks of the Sarayu, and spent much of the 1990s raising funds for his crowning achievement, the Sita Ram Nam ashram, temple and dairy farm built near the river, where the name of Ayodhya's most famous couple was chanted without rest, twenty-four hours a day, seven days a week, fifty-two weeks a year.

On my first night in Ayodhya, Dr Dubey had kindly invited me to sample his *kitchri*, a relatively bland concoction of dal and rice prescribed for sick people. Kitchri had a reputation as bachelor food, as Dubey had been a widower for forty years, his kitchri was divine.

'This is the food of saints,' he said, opening his gummy mouth wide for me to peer in. 'Only one tooth, see. I am eighty-five. It is a very young age.'

In the dim light of the dispensary, which doubled as a parlour room, my host interrogated me in a rasping, loud-hailer voice. 'For what you have come to Ayodhya?' he asked, suddenly wary within his silver hair ball.

'I want the truth about what happened here in 1992,' I said, somewhat grandiloquently. But Dubey was unfazed. Immediately, he reached under his desk, which served as our dining table, and produced a sheaf of his handwritten writings on Truth.

'Troot-th is a difficult area. It is old, but seems new,' he opined sagely. 'All souls are equal from an ant to an elephant. Troot-th is always pious. Always good. But it is complex. A good man is not what he wears — robes of saffron, a beard. He *may* be good, or it may just be a way of making MUN-NEEE! We need *inner* prosperity.'

Very early the next morning I was woken by what I thought was the sound of someone being murdered by strangulation. It was coming from downstairs, and rushing to the balcony, I saw Dubey leaning over a bucket next to a tap engaged in a profoundly disturbing exercise in retching, hacking, yowling and primordial screaming.

'Are you all right, doctor?' I called down to him, receiving in reply a backward wave of his arm.

'I am clearing my body of impurities,' he said, eventually turning his beatific smurf face to look up at me. 'Would you like to join me?'

Oddly enough, I would have. Making ugly faces and screaming is a time-honoured and efficacious yogic start to the day, improving muscle tone and relaxing the face and neck.

'Maybe tomorrow,' I said, returning to bed. By the time I emerged for breakfast, Dubey was sitting on his front porch wearing a saffron-coloured dhoti and smock, nicely paired with a pair of brown suede Hush Puppies. He'd already swept the road outside the shop and made a small bonfire with the sweepings, which now smouldered acridly while he methodically cut an apple into slices to eat equally methodically, while watching the traffic pass and the fire smoulder. When I complimented him on his dhoti, he replied, 'It is the colour of the sunrise,' before launching into more free philosophy and advice.

'In the city there is no calm or peace. Everyone is busy in money matters. You want money matters? Here in India? No! You will never get it. Worldly affairs are clouding your mind, so you cannot see God. You are full of cheatings from your native place. Purge them all. Make yourself empty. Open your mind, light will flood in.'

From Dr Dubey's guesthouse it was a short walk to the palace of the ancestral Raja of Ayodhya, Bimalendra Mohan Pratap Mishra. The palatial complex was slowly decaying, the once graceful approach now marred by the presence of a petrol station which had opened just outside the gates. Inside it was the usual collection of dreary stuffed lions, captured in the moment of their final roar, dim oil portraits of ancestors, and dusty chandeliers. As I arrived at the palace, the raja, an elegant middle-aged man dressed in an emerald-green kurta and white pajama pants, was farewelling a family of South African Hindus who'd called to see him out of little more than curiosity, from what I could gather. India had managed the decline of its princes, from feudal rulers in their own right to living tourist attractions, with an ancient grace. A raja might no longer have a kingdom, but people from all walks of life would still fall at his feet, revelling in deference with an enthusiasm that made it seem decidedly pleasurable. Indian gods never quite die. There will always be someone who still believes in them.

I had heard that the raja had offered a large piece of land in the town for the construction of the adjacent temple and mosque complex Mahant Gyandas had spoken about. He'd also given refuge to terrified Muslims on Demolition Day.

'It was the crime of the century, like the Bamiyan Buddhas. Different religion, different monument, but same destruction,' he said, when I asked him about that day. 'We defiled their god, and said, "If your god is so great and powerful, why is he not helping you now in your hour of distress?" That is the way of the barbarian. I'm sure you know that, traditionally, the flower sellers at Hindu temples in Ayodhya were Muslims. We were able to save some of them, but we could not save the masjid. One hundred and forty thousand paramilitary troops were around this town, and they did nothing.'

India's composite culture is much older and more supple than its democracy. The poet Kabir was a Muslim who declared, 'Kabir is the child of Allah and of Rama. He is my Guru. He is my Pir', and the Bollywood cinema is a melting pot that mirrors India's ethnic and religious diversity.[8] The ancestral Raja of Ayodhya remained aloof from politics, confining himself to cultural pursuits, such as organising music and literary festivals in the town.

His offer of land to resolve the dispute was not just a noble gesture; his palace was doomed to crumble to dust if he couldn't find an income stream to fund its expensive upkeep, and turning it into a hotel was the obvious answer. He spoke passionately about the beauty and historical significance of Ayodhya, its architecture and multi-religious history and fame all over Asia. But until peace returned, few tourists would come.

Political violence involving religion is usually portrayed as medieval recrudescence. In India, however, the problem seemed to have a more modern pathology. Elected politicians are willing to sacrifice social cohesion in return for votes, reviving ancient caste divisions and religious enmities in the process. Ayodhya had occasionally suffered from outbreaks of violence between different religious groups; but the more recent violence is largely imported. The people left to heal a wounded community are the 'medievals' — priests and rajas. The modern, rather than the medieval, is the main force driving communal violence in India today.

Walking the streets of the old town that afternoon, I began to see Ayodhya's potential. Centuries of religious patronage had produced some architectural follies deserving of preservation, foremost among them Raj Sadan, the raja's palace. I met pilgrims from Japan and

Korea, and could envisage newly wealthy Chinese boosting religious tourism to sites associated with the Buddha, who is said to have spent fourteen rainy seasons in Ayodhya. In the fifth century AD, the Chinese pilgrim Faxian had visited, reporting that at least a hundred Buddhist monasteries were functioning. The whole town could be a religious and historical theme park.

Lifted by these hopes, I rounded a bend and came face to face with the past. It was the blue-walled lane where, on 6 December 1992, I'd become entangled with the mob. Once more I smelt their sweat and the burning shame of raising my fist with a 'Jai Sri Ram', just to save my own neck. Twelve years later it still stung. But the lanes were calm and quiet now, with their small shops and shrines, and I decided that I liked Ayodhya, however scruffy and problematic it might be. Rama's compassion — *maryada* — had returned to the town and the healing had started, although a few crusaders remained.

In the warren of ashrams, monasteries, temples and *dharamsalas*, I came upon a vacant lot that was being used to store hundreds of tonnes of elaborately carved stone pillars intended eventually to be used to construct the new Rama temple. The Hindu nationalists had done a good job mobilising support and donations for the cause, to which the magnificent architectural beams and members here attested. They even had a huge model made out of plastic and lit up with bulbs showing what the temple of triumph would look like. A panda sat beside the model tying *rakhi* strings on the wrists of anyone who made a donation. The practice of *raksha sutra*, or amulet protection, was at least 3000 years old, and could be traced back to the Vedic scriptures in which Lord Indra's sister ties a sacred thread on his wrist to keep him from harm in his war with the *rakshasas*, or demons. Despite the dubious destination of the money I paid for one — I was literally incapable of resisting them — and wore the roseate silk bracelet until it broke over a year later.

A short distance away, I found the house of a man I'd been looking for, Satendra Das, the Mukhya Archak, or chief priest, who'd spent over a decade tending to the idols now being worshipped under armed guard on the ruins of the mosque. The odd-eyed priest lived in a rundown compound, in a single room crowded with books and images of the gods. His beard was long and silvery, like Dubey's, but even when he smiled his face was sad, as if weary with the burden of knowledge. Someone had tried to cheer him up, placing on his bed a heart-shaped cushion embroidered with the words 'Have a Nice Day' in English; or perhaps he'd bought it himself. At sixty-five, he led a team of four pujaris who tended to the needs of the living idol of Rama now installed in the makeshift temple. Early each morning just after sunrise he would enter the disputed site through the duty gate, and watch over his assistants as they gave the deity a change of clothes and performed the first two ceremonies of the day, returning to his home around nine.

'This is a very sacred duty. I feel that the idol is him, Rama. He is alive and I go to meet him every day,' the pujari said, reclining on a bolster on the floor, as small mice made darting runs across the room in defiance of the industrial-sized rat trap sitting empty beside the bed. It was a catch-and-release trap, the kind that allows Hindus to free the captured mouse — or even rat — without harming any of God's creatures.

On 6 December 1992, after the riot began and the two side domes had already fallen, Satendra Das had entered the mosque. In March that year, he had been appointed as priest to the idols installed under the central dome of the Babri Masjid. Now, with that dome about to collapse at any moment, he was ready to lay down his own life for that of a god.

'I felt bad. I thought, "This building is a temple. It's a temple that is being broken. I was afraid the roof would fall on me. The kar sevaks were looting whatever they could find inside. There were some donation boxes. They looted them, and some jewellery and utensils that were kept there. It was kar seva of the looters".' The pujari laughed a laugh that was even sadder than his smile.

Inside the crumbling mosque he had found the idols on their platform, and roped in some volunteers to remove them to safety. 'The altar was heavy. It took four or five persons to lift and carry it out. We took it some distance away, and placed it under a neem tree, where it was kept under guard. The last dome collapsed a short time later. Several people died when it fell on them. It could have fallen on Rama.'

Das clenched his teeth momentarily, one eye glaring at the open doorway.

'You know, it wasn't only that building they demolished on that day,' he said. 'The Ram Chabutra, that small shrine donated by a Mughal king to the Hindus for their worship, was also destroyed. It was still standing after the mosque had gone, but that night some VHP leaders came and incited the kar sevaks to demolish it also. That was a historic mistake on the part of the VHP [World Hindu Council]. About a dozen temples were demolished by them, some before December the sixth. Sumitra Bhavan, Lomas Bhavan, Qatar Mundup, Sakshi Gopal and Bade Hanuman Temple. Sita ki Rasoi [Sita's Kitchen] is intact, but it is in a bad condition. There were many places where different people believed that Rama was born. But the VHP said there should be only one janmasthan:'

Hinduism, the world's most evolved belief system, had always been too catholic for those who dreamt of Hindu unity. But the pujari was ultimately optimistic.

'The time is not far off when this problem will be resolved,' he said, hope flooding his eyes as he announced a prophecy. 'It will happen in my lifetime.'

On my way back to the guesthouse, I stopped to purchase a garland and some sweets for Dr Dubey, whose eccentricities had endeared him to me. Accepting the gifts on my return, the good doctor held them first to his forehead, then presented them to his small altar to obtain the god's blessing and handed them back to me. Over another of his fine kitchri dinners that night, he spoke more about the good works under way at his temple by the river, and we agreed to visit it the following morning.

The Sarayu east of Ayodhya is flanked by wide expanses of sand, gravel and *kasehri* grass that ripples in the breeze. Dubey and I made our way towards his temple, past cows that grazed to the hollow clank of their own bells. At the Sita Ram Nam ashram, the penitents prepared breakfast in a kitchen where none but Brahmins could enter. There was nowhere to sit, so Dubey and I squatted on the driveway and waited until a midget sadhu less than a metre tall brought our *nashta*, spicy vegetarian *mouli*, and *lokhi pakora* served on the leaves of a palash tree. They watched us eat, sadhus in all shapes and sizes above and below the waist, hair in buns and dreadlocks, faces smeared with streaks of sandalwood, the original hippies respected as pillars of society by those who wore trousers. Wandering the earth in search of truth and rejecting the slow death of conventional wisdom, they embodied India's enduring freedom.

After breakfast, Dubey showed me the pilgrims' quarters, the cow sheds and vegetable gardens and a small shrine to his own guru, who had 'left his body'. The whole time we'd been there, the nagging chant of '*Sitaram Sitaram Sitaram-ji, Sitaram Sitaram Sitaram*' had been drifting across the ashram from a tall tower in the middle of the settlement. Broadcast on a crackling public-address system, I assumed it was a tape recording, but when I asked about it, Dubey claimed the continuous chanting, which had been going for eight years now, was always performed live. I didn't believe it.

'Can I go up and see for myself?' I asked.

'No, you may not,' said Dubey. 'As Gandhi-ji said, you must DARE to believe!'

We'd walked a few hundred metres back towards the road when doubt immobilised me.

'Dubey-ji,' I said to him. 'Please don't be offended, and try to understand. I must see to believe.'

And with a grimace and a flick of his hirsute head, he waved me away and told me to do what I must.

Climbing the tower, the insistent drone of the chanting grew louder in my ears, and I wondered what sort of Heath Robinson contraption the old rogue had set up there. The staircase zigzagged its way up to an open terrace with a fine view of the river and fields. A small shrine about the size of a bathroom, offset slightly to obscure the sanctum, stood to one side. Venturing closer, I wondered how Dubey would take to being exposed as a faker. Would he kick me out of the guesthouse, or lodge a case of trespass against me at the local police thana and bog me down in eternal litigation in this life and the next? Like Arjuna on the battlefield, I hesitated for a moment. If I turned back now I could still take his word for it, and avoid embarrassing him. But to retreat was never really an option. To doubt was my dharma.

Rounding the entrance to the shrine, I came upon four men of different ages seated in a semi-circle and professionally miked, playing finger cymbals, tabla and harmonium, and happily chanting the name of Rama and his bride.

Part Five

19

An Inner Voice

I am an Indian.
Gandhi (Sonia)[1]

The New Delhi telephone book — now available on CD — is replete with Gandhis. There's a Gandhi Cycle Store, a Gandhi Photostat, Gandhi Exports, Gandhi Bookhouse, Gandhi Properties, Gandhi Electric Company, Gandhi Glass House and the Gandhi Scientific Company. There are Manjeet Gandhis, Manoj Gandhis, Madan Lal Gandhis and Mahendra Gandhis. No Mahatma Gandhis, alas, but twelve Rajivs, forty Sanjays and even three Sonias. The Sonia Gandhi who would stand like Boudicca against the saffron hordes of Hindu nationalism is not listed. But a low profile can be deceptive.

Sonia had inherited India's most famous surname at the tender age of twenty-one, when she married Rajiv in a civil ceremony conducted in the garden of Indira Gandhi's residence in February 1968. Born Sonia Maino, to a Roman Catholic Italian family, her early ambition had been to become a flight attendant with Alitalia. At Cambridge, where she'd met Rajiv, she'd worked as an au pair while studying languages. Her transition from Italian bride to Indian figurehead was a bittersweet journey.

'In those days I had a vague idea that India existed somewhere in the world with its snakes, elephants and jungles, but exactly where it was and what it was really all about, I was not sure,' she would later write.[2] At first Sonia disliked Indian food. 'My palate would not accept the unfamiliar pungent flavours of Indian cooking,' she once recalled.[3] Nor did she like the clothes, preferring skirts and jeans initially. This posed no particular problem because Rajiv, who was soon to join Indian Airlines as a pilot, had no political ambitions. Sonia could adjust to her new home in her own time. She eased into the Gandhi family as the *bahu*, or daughter-in-law, and was put in charge of the kitchen, while her husband flew aeroplanes and her mother-in-law ran the country. Soon, with the birth of a son, Rahul, and a daughter, Priyanka, she was raising a young family. The family photos from the 1970s depict a blissful existence of domestic intimacies, high culture, and family holidays in the Maldives and other exotic locations.

The death in June 1980 of Rajiv's younger brother — and Indira's heir apparent — Sanjay Gandhi, marked a tragic and defining moment in independent India's history, and in the enchanted life of its First Family. Rajiv became the heir who was expected to enter parliament and succeed his mother. Four years later, when Indira was shot dead by her own bodyguards, the Congress Party turned to Rajiv to become prime minister.

'I begged him not to let them do this,' Sonia later recalled. 'I pleaded with him, with others around him, too. He would be killed as well. He held my hands, hugged me, tried to soothe my desperation. He had no choice, he said. He would be killed anyway.'[4]

Six years later Rajiv followed his mother to the funerary mounds along the Yamuna. Despite the Congress Party's appeal to her to take on the leadership, Sonia the widow retreated into mourning. The Nehru-Gandhi dynasty teetered on the brink of extinction. But India is a patient country where the call of duty is insistent. At first, Sonia confined her public activities to honouring the memory of her late husband's family. Foreign dignitaries visiting India would make formal pilgrimages to her residence at 10 Janpath in New Delhi, a kind of diplomatic darshan confirming Sonia's status as a living deity. Congress Party leaders also beat a path to her door, keen to embroil her in their factional squabbles and whispering campaigns against the new leader, Narasimha Rao. Frustrated by slow progress in the investigation into Rajiv's murder, Sonia lent them an ear, which they eagerly filled with gossip about Rao's alleged ambition to politically marginalise the family and portraying his failure to protect Babur's Mosque as a betrayal of the party's secular traditions.[5] When Rao's government was voted out of office in 1996, Sonia was drawn into the vacuum. A section of the Congress leadership convinced her that the party would be decimated at the next elections without the magic of the Gandhi name.

In mid-1997, she joined the Congress Party. At the All India Congress Committee in Calcutta in August, I witnessed her stage-managed political debut amid the carnival atmosphere of a political convention. Entering the Netaji Indoor Stadium, she headed for the seats reserved for foreign observers, knowing full well that the 10,000 ecstatic delegates would demand that she join the party leadership on stage. Once there, dressed in a simple lemon-coloured sari, she acceded once again, this time to calls for a speech. Stepping up to the podium, she slipped a piece of paper from the folds of her sari, on which was a prepared speech in Hindi, written not in the traditional Devanagari script, with which Sonia was not yet comfortable, but transcribed phonetically into the Roman alphabet. In it, she chastised the 112-year-old party for 'drifting away from the people'. Then, in January the following year, she travelled to Sriperumbudur, the town in southern Tamil Nadu where Rajiv had been killed, and declared, 'I stand here today on the soil made sacred by the blood of my husband who died a martyr to the cause of the nation's unity and integrity.'

From the outset, Sonia cast her decision to enter politics in terms that echoed the Indian epic sagas of great battles between good and evil. Neither communism, nor foreign influence, nor caste politics were her principal adversaries; the enemy was Hindu nationalism. In her first statement upon assuming the leadership, Sonia declared that 'the principles on which our great nation was founded are today under threat'. As a member of the Nehru-Gandhi family she had an obligation to stop the rot:

> I have photographs of my husband and my mother-in-law in my office. And each time I walked past those photographs, I felt that I wasn't responding to my duty, the duty to this family and to the country. I felt I was being cowardly to just sit and watch things deteriorate in the Congress for which my mother-in-law and the whole family lived and died. So, at that point I took the decision.[6]

In a rare interview with Shekhar Gupta, editor-in-chief of the *Indian Express*, Sonia revealed that the demolition of Babur's Mosque in Ayodhya had moved her to tears. She apologised on behalf of the party for the fact that it had occurred on the Congress's watch, and pledged that 'Such a thing won't be repeated'. Addressing a rally in Mumbai in February 1998, Sonia told her audience:

> The Congress has given you leaders like Gandhi, Nehru, Sardar Patel, Lokmanya Tilak, Maulana Azad, Indira Gandhi ... and the BJP has given you Nathuram Godse ... When the fire of communal violence was burning up your homes, the people who set it ablaze were sitting peacefully inside their homes ... I am the wife of Rajiv Gandhi. His ideals are what I have imbibed, they will be my ideals as long as I am alive! ... And if need be, I will lay down my life for this country![7]

As Prem Panicker, a journalist covering the speech for the Rediff on the Net website, commented, 'Maybe someday, Bollywood will make a movie out of this. And film critics will, in their reviews, dismiss the plotline as totally unrealistic.'[8]

The background to Sonia's unlikely rise was somewhat more prosaic. The vote-winning Gandhi name and rival ambitions of lower order Congressmen had given her the leadership on a platter, and political power was essential if she was to protect her family. Rival politicians, including some in Congress, were always threatening to use the lingering Bofors corruption scandal to drive the Gandhis out of politics. Opponents made great play of the Bofors case's Italian connection, a businessman called Ottavio Quattrocchi, who'd been implicated as a middle man in the alleged payment of kickbacks to Rajiv for sanctioning defence contracts. Quattrocchi had left India under a cloud of suspicion, having been a regular guest at Rajiv and Sonia's home. In India, where no court case ever really dies and ministers can pressure police to re-open old investigations, political clout is insurance against unwelcome legal harassment. The family, Sonia may have concluded, was vulnerable unless it resumed control of the party.

In March 1998, less than a year after becoming a member of the Congress, she toppled its president, Sitaram Kesri, in a party room coup. The decision to enter politics cost her a friend — the first friend she'd made on arriving in Indian thirty years before — the Bollywood film actor Amitabh Bachchan, who thought the move a tragic miscalculation, which would bring an avalanche of hostility down on Sonia's head. She ignored the actor's advice, and ever since they have taken pains to avoid one another.

Sonia's foreign origins had been an issue even in Rajiv's time. A wife with a foreign passport, his enemies said, might also have foreign loyalties, and could leak India's secrets to foreign powers. Although Rajiv's place in Indian history was secure, even he — like Rama — could not afford to ignore public sentiment. In 1983, soon after he entered politics, Sonia became an Indian citizen. Now, as leader in her own right, her foreign origins were once again an issue. To the nationalists she was 'Signora Sonia', and the Sangh Parivar delighted in taunting the Congress over her Italian-Christian heritage with catchy slogans like 'Congress party ka ek hi raasta, bolo Italian khao pasta' (The Congress party has only one road: speak Italian and eat pasta). Just as

Sonia refused to acknowledge the political legitimacy of the Hindu nationalists, so they refused to accept her as an Indian, and their targeting of Christians seemed tailor-made to kill two birds with one stone. Mr Vajpayee's response to the threat posed by Sonia was pithy. 'Democracy does not need a dynasty,' he said. 'India is larger than a family.'[9] But many voters disagreed; at least a quarter of them still voted Congress, and Sonia's rallies attracted huge crowds. In Bellary in southern India, I'd watched in disbelief as she drove through the town in an open jeep amid mass adulation. What shocked me was not the crowd's response, but her willingness to expose herself to the same danger that claimed the life of her husband. When I told her so, her response was, 'I prefer this sort of campaigning. I listen to the advice of my security officers, and don't go beyond what they allow me to do.'[10] She was known to watch old campaign footage of Indira Gandhi to hone her electioneering skills.

In 1999 Sonia entered parliament from her husband's old seat of Amethi. The party failed to win the election that year, but her performance was judged satisfactory for a first outing. Throughout the year she had taken a hard line against Hindu communalism, replacing the Congress Orissa chief minister J.B. Patnaik, on whose watch the Staines murders took place, clearly unafraid of being seen to defend Christian interests. In the years since Rajiv's death she had not remarried, completing the transition from the *videshi* (foreign) bride, who had refused to accept her husband's dharma, to the desi widow, who had assumed his political mantle. Like her late mother-in-law she wore simple cotton saris and minimal jewellery, wearing her hair in a modest bun like a peasant widow, complete with a suitably severe expression. Physically and psychologically she had toughened, and grown more comfortable in the vernacular. At the 2001 Kumbh Mela she had taken a dip in the Ganga — somehow managing to do it in private amidst the gargantuan crowds.

Politically, she accepted that, after years in the wilderness, the Congress was unlikely to win a majority in its own right and needed to tie up deals with regional powerbrokers, including former enemies. Behind the scenes, she was being schooled in her party's history and culture, and her speech writer knew which notes to hit — concern for the poor, the family tradition of sacrifice, and secularism. Sonia's progress was so seamlessly moulded that she soon seemed as much a part of the Indian political tradition as her desi predecessors. The time was not far off when voters would need to confront the real possibility that the next prime minister of India would be a woman born in Italy.

★ ★ ★

Gujarat is an arid state on India's west coast that has given the country many precious things. It produced Mahatma Gandhi, whose ashram on the banks of the Sabarmati River is a national monument. Gujarat is home to some of India's most enterprising business people, as well as the country's largest private industrial conglomerate, Reliance Industries. Sharing a border with Pakistan, the state produces 60 per cent of the world's cut-and-polished diamonds,[11] and its ship-breaking yard at Alang is the world's largest. Gujarat is a stronghold of one of the world's oldest religions, Jainism, and boasts significant physical remains of the Indus Valley civilisation. The Gujarat coastline is dotted with former Portuguese enclaves, such as Daman and Diu, and at Saurashtra is graced by the beautiful and historic Somnath Temple, restored almost a thousand years after it was sacked by a Muslim warlord. Gujarat has produced some of India's most accomplished modern artists, and its furniture and handicrafts — from jewellery to mirror work, embroideries and Patola tie-dyed silk textiles — are prized. The state is home to some fifty million people as well as the endangered Asiatic lion, of which only 300 or so survive in the forest of Gir.

Unfortunately, Gujarat also has a history of communal violence. Despite being one of India's richest states, the heavily populated crescent along which are situated the cities of Ahmedabad, Vadodara and Surat has witnessed hundreds of violent incidents between Hindus and Muslims over the past forty years. Gujarat is also home to a powerful criminal underworld which prospers by smuggling and bootlegging in a border state where prohibition is in force. By the mid-1990s, the BJP had become the dominant political force there, and used its power to stack the administration with RSS members. These ranged from members of police advisory committees to some 20,000 teachers recruited to serve in villages across the state.[12]

To the Sangh Parivar, Gujarat was a 'Hindutva laboratory', and in February 2002, the laboratory was poised to conduct a ghastly experiment. On the morning of 27 February 2002, the Sabarmati Express from Ayodhya to Ahmedabad pulled into Godhra railway station, nearing the end of a long and eventful journey. The train was carrying a group of Hindu nationalists returning home from the latest agitation in Ayodhya demanding that a Rama temple be built on the ruins of Babur's Mosque. Along the route, they had reportedly clashed with fellow passengers, throwing a young Muslim man off the train while it was still moving, after he objected to their behaviour. At Godhra station, an altercation occurred between kar sevaks and Muslim vendors. As the train departed the station at around 7.48 a.m., its emergency cord was pulled and it slowed to a halt. As it did so, the driver noticed a mob near the rail line pelting one of the carriages with stones. Then a fire was observed coming from carriage S-6, and when the flames died down, fifty-eight people were found dead, all of them Hindus.[13]

Five months before the incident, a Sangh Parivar activist, Narendra Modi, a hardcore RSS political organiser, had taken over as chief minister of the state.[14] Modi and his supporters seized on the Godhra tragedy, claiming that the fire on board the train was a premeditated terrorist attack, rather than a spontaneous clash that went out of control. The following day, Gujarat witnessed scenes of savagery that shocked the world. As Luke Harding reported in the *Guardian*, elements within the majority Hindu community 'went on the rampage — burning, killing and raping more than 2000 of their Muslim neighbours. Mr Modi's administration and police force were complicit in the carnage.'[15] Testimonies collected by the Citizens' Initiative (a coalition of over twenty-five non-government organisations) and submitted to the National Human Rights Commission catalogued the gang-rapes of Muslim women and girls, and claims that at localities such as Naroda Patia near Ahmedabad, the mainly Hindu police force sided with the mobs. One resident of the Ahmedabad neighbourhood testified that eight out of eleven members of her family were killed on 28 February, two after being raped:

> The mob caught hold of my husband and hit him on his head twice with the sword. They threw petrol in his eyes and then burned him. My sister-in-law was stripped and raped. She had a three-month-old baby in her lap. They threw petrol on her and the child from her lap was thrown in the fire. My brother-in-law was hit in the head with the sword and he died on the spot. His six-year-old daughter was also hit with the sword and thrown in the fire. My mother-in-law had with her the grandson who was four years of age and he was burnt too ... All this ended at 2.30 a.m. The ambulance came on the scene and I sat in it along with the bodies of my husband and children ... The police were on the spot but helping the mob. We fell at their feet but they said they were ordered from above [not to help] ...[16]

As Gujarat was engulfed in terror, some 90,000 people — mainly Muslims — fled their homes, taking shelter in temporary camps for the displaced, but Prime Minister Vajpayee — his saffron hem on show — issued equivocal statements on the violence. Other Sangh Parivar leaders went so far as to claim that the Gujarat 'experiment' in raising Hindu consciousness had been successful, and would be repeated all over the country.[17] Mr Modi organised a 'Hindu Pride' yatra and moved to hold snap elections in the polarised atmosphere.

When the elections were held, the mostly Hindu electorate gave Modi a thumping two-thirds majority.

'The man who has presided over a successful pogrom has used it as an electoral strategy,' observed the author and journalist Ramachandra Guha. 'What has happened in Gujarat is original in the sophistication and completeness of its articulation.'[18] Even with a successful government in New Delhi and the prospect of re-election to a second term, the nationalist movement seemed unable to divorce itself from the exigencies of mob violence. As Pratap Bhanu Mehta put it in the *Indian Express*, 'there are moments where Hindu nationalism needs the violent polarizing energies of Hindu communalism'.[19]

In the summer of 2004, Atal Bihari Vajpayee became the first non-Congress prime minister to complete a full five-year term, and buoyed by a surging economy and the success of his efforts to raise India's standing abroad, Mr Vajpayee was running for a renewed mandate. The BJP's slogan was 'India Shining', an assertion of its confidence that Indians felt as good about the country's performance as the government did.

The 'Saffron Nehru' had worked persistently to bring peace with Pakistan but, when his efforts failed, won a brief and popular border war with India's old rival. He'd defied the world by testing nuclear weapons and then welcomed foreign presidents and businesses to engage with India on its own terms. Only a reclusive Italian-born widow stood between Vajpayee and victory. Sonia Gandhi's riposte to 'India Shining' was '*Congress ka haath, ghareebon ke saat*' (Congress's hand will be with the poor), and she had wheeled out her secret weapon: Brand Gandhi. Like horses from an elite stable prepared for the richest race, the fair skinned, Kashmiri-descended political Brahmins were once again being paraded before the starter. Glamour girl Priyanka Gandhi — the great-granddaughter of India's first prime minister, Pandit Nehru, and not a candidate herself — had been mobbed at rally after rally. Her equally handsome brother, Rahul, was running hard in the family's pocket borough of Amethi. And

Sonia Gandhi was contesting the neighbouring seat of Rae Bareli, once held by her mother-in-law. It was politics at its most familial.

For months, politicians had been initiating 'mass contact campaigns' and *padyatras*, craving forgiveness from people they would rarely see outside election time. Pundits noted a 'healthy silence on religion', rather, candidates were embracing the new materialistic concerns of voters with slogans such as '*bijli, sadak, pani*' (electricity, roads, water). Voting was being staggered over several days to allow security forces to be moved to 'sensitive' parts of the country, and many of Delhi's fifteen million residents had stocked up on basic commodities, in particular alcohol, the sale of which had been restricted lest voters get too jolly. There were 600 million voters, making it the biggest free election in a single nation in history, and election spending of 116 billion rupees ($2.6 billion) was twice the national health budget.[20] The polls had already produced riotous assemblies, significant poster art and, during one nationalist campaign meeting in Lucknow where free saris where given away, a stampede in which twenty-one women had died. The saris had each been worth less than a dollar.[21]

The Hindu nationalist stalwart Lal Krishna Advani was back on the road, exhibiting his chameleon-like qualities and political expediency to a new generation of correspondents. In a piece for *Time*, mischievously titled 'Lie Another Day', Alex Perry reported:

> When I got down at a rally about 30 km from Ayodhya, Advani gave an impressive display of such expediency. After assuring me for half an hour that economic development was the BJP priority, he took the stage and bellowed: 'We will build a Ram temple in Ayodhya. India will be Ram's kingdom once more . . .'[22]

On the second Monday in May, voting in the final round of the fourteenth national elections since independence got under way in scorching temperatures across northern India. From early morning, candidates flocked to mandirs, mosques, gurdwaras and other places of worship in search of divine guidance.

At Civil Lines, the Bahadurs of Number Three Commissioner's Lane voted early to beat the heat, after which Abba was to be found back home reclining on one of the beds in Maya's room, the marble floor still chilled from the previous night's air-conditioning. Since retiring as managing director of The Instalment Supply Limited a few years earlier, his mornings had become more leisurely, and he was often to be found relaxing like this, chatting with his wife as she sat in her easy chair, resting her bad knee and surrounded by her newspapers, books, spectacles and pill bottles.

'It was pitiable,' Maya declared, disgusted and outraged by the state of the booths where they'd voted that morning. 'The whole place was stinking. Dirt and dust everywhere, and the desks and chairs were broken.'

Abba agreed with her. 'You got a whiff from the toilet as you cast your vote,' he said, making a face. But when it came to the desired outcome of the election process, the consensus between them collapsed.

'I'm not going to let those saffron-clad hypocrites tells me how to live my life,' declared Maya about the BJP. 'I'll never vote for a party that uses religion as a weapon.'

'They're not all like that,' Abba said, correcting her. 'Hot heads are there, but the economy is booming. Vajpayee is not a fundamentalist.'

However, Maya had made up her mind. 'I don't want those idiots coming back.'

'Then who will come?' Abba asked, a crafty question calculated to set her back on her heels. But Maya was having none of his reasoning.

'I don't care,' she said, point-blank. 'I don't need any more of their Hindutva rubbish. I would never vote for a party that is anti-Muslim.'

'BJP is not anti-Muslim,' Abba protested. 'They want Muslim votes. One or two people may be mad, but Congress has ten mad people.'

'So what happened in Gujarat? Tell me?' Maya demanded. 'Why did they go around burning churches and mosques?'

Abba's mouth tightened and his head drew back, as it did whenever the conversation turned to subjects he found disagreeable. 'These things normally are sparked by something,' he said.

'So, you kill 2000 Muslims? Is that what you're saying? You're justifying Godhra?' Maya said, her eyes bulging in an impossibly wide glare.

'Not justify,' Abba replied, frowning ever more deeply. 'There was a massacre of Hindus on a train. People react. They get blood in their eye.'

'Uff!' said Maya, exasperated. 'These guys with orange bandanas! They don't represent Hindus, and they don't represent India.'

'Don't write that,' Abba told me, seeing me taking notes, as I sometimes did when the conversation got interesting. Then, trying to stump his wife, added, 'So who represents India?'

'The Congress!' said Maya.

Abba's head rolled back again.

'That was in Nehru's time,' he said. 'Mrs Gandhi finished everything.'

But the mention of Indira Gandhi served only to bring a beatific smile of nostalgia to Maya's face. 'Mrs Gandhi was so cultured. So well read,' she said.

Then, just as suddenly, her euphoria clouded over. 'These new politicians are so uncouth. They're illiterate! They represent the rabble. They're not the sort of people who should be running the country.'

'Ridiculous,' Abba objected, staging a walkout.

Then, turning on the threshold of his bedroom with a resigned expression and holding his hands behind his back, he looked at me pointedly and said, 'As you can see, our votes cancelled each other out.'

That morning before coming to work, our housekeeper Sushila also had voted. The hardships of life had made her a deeply fatalistic woman, who believed that she was paying for the sins of a previous life. Her fifty years had taken a toll on her health and happiness. She'd lost most of her children through illnesses and accidents, and lived in fear of losing her remaining son and grandson. This simple woman's fierce devotion to her family moved me deeply. Sometimes, as she did the ironing or dusted in another room, I would hear her softly weeping over some sad memory. She had one consolation — a nondescript flat in a distant suburb doled out under a poverty alleviation scheme implemented in Indira Gandhi's time. Like Maya, Sushila was a big fan of the Congress.

Beaming with pleasure, as she arrived late for work that morning, the diminutive widow showed me her fingernail, on which an election official had daubed indelible ink to prevent multiple voting. 'I did it! I succeeded!' the proud set of her mouth seemed to say, and her eyes sparkled in delight. Sonia Gandhi's life might be a world away from Sushila's, but she had at least expressed an interest in the lot of the poor. Unable to read the ballot paper, Sushila had voted for the hand — the symbol of the Congress. And she had backed the winner.

From nowhere, Sonia Gandhi emerged to grab the prize, and the BJP slumped to a humiliating defeat, rejected by poor farmers in Andhra Pradesh and voters in Gujarat, who only a year earlier had backed it. After all the heat and noise of big issues like nationalism and secularism, local issues emerged as the deciders, and pundits who'd questioned Sonia's abilities were left wiping egg off their faces. Just a year before the polls, the *Financial Times'* Edward Luce had written 'Sonia Gandhi's Congress is experiencing difficulties, possibly terminal ... Is this really the person to take on Hindutva and defeat it?'[23]

Even in saffron strongholds such as Varanasi, Mathura and Ayodhya, the BJP's reign was over, its 'India Shining' campaign clearly a figment if its own imagination. Voters had dumped twenty-six serving ministers, including the external affairs minister, Yashwant Sinha, and the Hindu nationalist ideologue Murli Manohar Joshi. Hardline Hindu nationalists blamed the party's decision to moderate its platform in the interests of forming a coalition government for the defeat, but the broader consensus was that it had not addressed the bread-and-butter issues of the majority who lived in villages, and whose poverty rarely allowed them to feel good about anything. The campaign against the Nehru-Gandhi dynasty flopped; Sonia and her son Rahul had both won their seats, and everything pointed to the lady from Orbassano becoming prime minister.

Concluded analyst Pratap Bhanu Mehta: 'Many Hindus found their manhood and have decided to move on ... The BJP as a right-of-centre political party has a future only if it can articulate a Hindu nationalism without Hindu communalism.'[24] To others the identity politics of the 1990s had finally been dislodged by an issue that everyone could relate to — living standards.[25]

The following week, parliament's Central Hall was abuzz with the excited chatter of more than 200 members of the rejuvenated Congress Party. Power was once again within their grasp. As Sonia Gandhi rose to speak, the cavernous room fell silent in anticipation of her claim to the prime ministership. Instead, she said, she had heard a voice, like the inner voice Mahatma Gandhi spoke of.

'Today, that voice tells me I must humbly decline this post,' she said in halting, Italian-accented English. Sonia's oath of renunciation was greeted by gasps and moans from her disbelieving supporters. Tearful, panic-stricken MPs surged towards the podium, remonstrating with her not to abandon them. For three and a half hours — all broadcast live on national television — they begged, cajoled, bargained and even threatened her. Seated in the first row, directly facing her, son, Rahul and daughter, Priyanka, held her gaze. Sonia listened patiently, as crestfallen party colleagues begged her to reconsider. Outside the family home a former Congress MP, driven insane by his leader's abdication, brandished a pistol and threatened to kill himself before being disarmed by police. Hundreds of party workers lay down on the scorching pavements outside the compound, while others wrote protest letters in their own blood. Around the corner at the Congress Party's headquarters, enraged cadre smashed windows and thumped the car of the eminent economist and Narasimha Rao's finance minister, Dr Manmohan Singh, whom Sonia had hand-picked to assume the prime minister's *gaddi* (seat). But their protests were in vain. Sonia was unmoved.

'What happened on May 18 was an emotionally charged clash between irresistible desperation and immovable resolution,' wrote journalist Prabhu Chawla in *India Today*. 'What a story it has been, the story of Sonia.'[26]

As the message sank in, those close to Sonia, like the economist and party member Jairam Ramesh, felt themselves to be in the presence of greatness.

'A long line of renunciates have dotted India right from the days of Gautama Buddha to Mahatma Gandhi,' Ramesh said, 'and Sonia Gandhi has now joined that pantheon.'[27]

Like the political royalty that she was, the new Mrs Gandhi would rule from behind the scenes, enjoying the privileges of power without many of the pitfalls. The new government would be reliant on communist support to remain in power. Its longevity could not be assured, and it would be unwise to stake Sonia's new standing on an unstable government. Sonia's renunciation of power, far from being a saintly act, was a choice based on political calculations. Having decided she didn't want the chair herself, Sonia used her prerogative to rebuild bridges with a community that the Congress Party had once sorely abused. By appointing Dr Singh as the first Sikh ever to hold the prime ministership of India, she won back some of the Sikh support her party had alienated by failing to stem the 1984 Delhi riots. By declining the nation's top job she also shattered the Hindu nationalists' hopes of a quick return to power on the back of a campaign against her foreign origins.

For one of Sonia's supporters, the joy of victory was cruelly brief. A few days after the outcome, Sushila telephoned to say that she would not be coming to work. Her son, one of only two of her surviving children, had died suddenly of some mysterious illness. He had felt headaches, had been taken to hospital but was dead within hours. Overworked and underpaid, doctors at the public hospital to which he'd been taken didn't even bother to fully explain the death to the mother — illiterate and poor, she could not even be expected to comprehend, they probably reasoned. '*Bokhar*' was all she could tell me — fever.

Sushila had helped change the government but lost her only son. And nobody, not me, nor even the prime minister of India could do anything to change her cruel fate.

'*Meray haath mai likha hai* (It is written in my hand),' she said.

DARJEELING
ASSAM
NILGIRI
TEA
ASSAM
TEA
TEA
NILGIRI
TEA
DARJEELING
TEA
TEA
DARJEELING
TEA

20

The Prince and the Pauper

The Ramrajya of my dream ensures the rights alike of prince and pauper.
Gandhi[1]

In an Indian revolution, nothing seems to change — but everything is different. In the weeks and months that followed Sonia Gandhi's triumph, an orchestrated cult of personality reminiscent of a Stalinist dictatorship descended on the capital. After an interregnum of fifteen years, New Delhi was once again Gandhi Land.

Statues were being unveiled and flyovers named to honour fallen political warriors, the iconography and anniversaries of their births and deaths bombarding you at every turn. Massive images of Pandit Nehru, Indira Gandhi and Rajiv Gandhi towered over the capital's boulevards, and herds of uncomprehending but suitably frenzied school children assembled to hail the visionary Congress leaders, whose achievements were extolled in bulging newspaper supplements. The party's most accomplished propagandist, S.S. Prakasan, had outdone himself yet again, plastering the approaches to the All India Congress Committee's annual convention at Talkatora Stadium with posters that cried, 'Our pride is Mother India. Our guide is Mother Sonia.' The political resolution passed by the conference was an homage to the widow, whom it said had chosen party over power, service over a position, work over the fruits of success, and struggle ahead of comfort. 'In Indian ethos such sacrifice and self-denial is the tradition of ascetics.'[2]

But while Sonia was the undisputed empress, all eyes in the stadium were on the dynasty's heir apparent, 34-year-old Rahul Gandhi. Rahul's sudden emergence into the spotlight had caught the Indian political establishment off guard. For years, they'd considered his younger sister, the handsome and electrifying Priyanka, to be the more likely candidate. But now that he had arrived, no one was complaining. For Congress, the more Gandhis in politics the better. As one senior Congressman, Salman Khurshid, put it, 'They [the Nehru-Gandhis] win elections. I mean, in a democracy what more do you need? They win elections, they win handsomely and we believe we get more votes when they come to our constituency. So why shouldn't we support them?'[3] If Rahul made it to the top, he would be the fourth consecutive generation of his family to serve as prime minister, surely a democratic record. The benches in the Fourteenth Lok Sabha were crammed with the scions of other political families as well — Scindias, Dikshits, Pilots, Abdullahs, Deoras, and several Singhs. With Rahul entering parliament and Priyanka having produced a son, the charismatic but ill-starred Nehru-Gandhis could be part of India's future well into the twenty-first century; an enduring, elected monarchy. Harder to understand, perhaps, was why a young man with life at his feet would choose to follow his father and grandmother into a job that had led to both of them being assassinated.

Like his father, Rahul had studied abroad without great distinction. He'd taken a course in financial securities in Boston, dabbled in business administration and dated foreign girls. Suman Dubey, Rajiv's close friend and media adviser, had known Rahul since he was a boy. What sort of person was Rahul, I asked him, when I dropped by his office on Sikandra Road.

'Oh, he's a very sensible young man,' said Suman, melting with affection at the mention of his name. 'Like his father, he studies things in great detail. Like his father, he has a wicked sense of humour. He's very likeable. A very loveable chap — I can say that because he's so young. And the daughter too. She's like a firecracker. A *pataki*, if you know the Hindi.'

But why this fatalistic procession to the samadhis on Raj Ghat, and ritualising of death as heroic politics?

Suman grimaced ever so slightly, momentarily torn between his conflicting roles as close family friend and astute observer of the Indian political scene.

'If I could put it coarsely,' he said, tentatively, 'there's a family business. But let me put it less coarsely: there's a tradition. How can Rahul step away from that tradition? He'd have to be turning his back on a lot. It's a clarion call. And what can he do? He'd be marked everywhere as Rajiv and Sonia's son. Can he run a hotel? Can he go and do a job as a journalist, go out reporting, or accounting, or managing in this country? I'm sure Tony Blair's son will do what he wants. But here, it's very hard for Rahul.'

'The personal is political?' I asked.

'When it involves five generations of the family? Yes,' Suman replied.

The monsoon session of the Lok Sabha was under way, and I'd decided to attend to see the new political prince in action. India's temple to democracy is built on a grand scale, in the shape of the Colosseum, a place of gladiatorial contests. During sittings the streets leading to parliament are the scene of almost daily confrontations between police and demonstrators, who come from across India to vent their anger at legislators. In 2002 armed Kashmiri Muslim militants had stormed the building, leaving fourteen people dead and the neo-classical sandstone colonnades pockmarked by bullets. The attack — the objective of which appeared to be the murder of the entire elected leadership of India — brought India and Pakistan to the brink of a nuclear war, only four years after they'd flexed their nuclear muscles.

Inside its monumental portals, parliament is cool all year round, and its walls are graced by one of India's most ambitious artworks. The Lok Sabha murals, fifty-eight of them completed so far, each measuring 1.5 by 3.6 metres (5 by 12 feet), form a conspectus of India's collective memory since the days of the Indus Valley civilisation. Conceived in 1951, and progressively installed in the poorly lit circular outer corridor of the building, the murals teem with ethnic and religious diversity, a panoply of ideas and faiths spanning millennia. Shiva meditates, and Rama is crowned king of Ayodhya amid a storm of pounding drummers and writhing maidens; Buddha turns the wheel of dharma, while the early Buddhist missionaries fan out to bring enlightenment to East Asia, and Chinese pilgrim explorers like Xuanzang (Hsuan Tsang) head west to explore India; Feroze Shah, resplendent in Turkish-style helmet, oversees his slave army as they raise Ashoka's edict pillar onto its plinth; and the Muslim Mughal emperors are depicted as Indian-born rulers who revived and increased India's greatness. Great Hindu warriors such as Shivaji and the Rani of Jhansi, a Hindu woman who led an army as well as any man to confront the might of the British Empire, take their place in the pantheon, along with religious reformers like the Sikhs' Guru Nanak, and the Hindus' Swami Dayanand Saraswati. Then, as the timeline reaches the twentieth century, Gandhi strides forth with his walking stick headed for the salt shores of Dandi, while Subhash Chandra Bose, no less a patriot, repudiates non-violent resistance by siding with the Japanese against Britain in World War II. Then victory, the Indian tricolour is raised on the ramparts of the Red Fort and a new era for India begins. An inscription quoting Kalidasa reads: 'a prosperous state is heaven on earth'. Sadly, some of the paintings, all executed in tempera on Masonite board, are in a poor state of repair, affected by damp and darkened by accumulated dust and pollution.

Seated alone on a middle bench to the right of the speaker, Rahul Gandhi rubbed his square, stocky face and stifled a yawn.

He'd been up early attending a ceremony at Vir Bhumi to mark the sixtieth anniversary of his late father's birth. In white kurta pajama he looked the very model of a modern Congressman, a tad contemporary perhaps, with stylish spectacles and a decent haircut. Donning the antique headsets which provide simultaneous translations of MPs speaking in vernacular languages, he was soon chuckling, as the speaker attempted to contain a fracas arising from questions put to the government during 'Zero Hour'.

'Don't get angry. Pleeease don't get angry. Only Speaker can get angry!' the Speaker was saying. Now and then, a more senior colleague would flop down on the bench beside Rahul to mentor or amuse, or simply to be seen with the rising star of the Congress. He'd just won a five-year term with a 300,000 vote margin, so he didn't need their advice on that score. Other young scions of other political families, however talented, had to take a back seat — literally a few rows back — in deference to the first among equals. Like their fathers, they would seek to ingratiate themselves with the presiding deity, and if that failed, defect or rebel. The Cabinet was full of men who'd come crawling back after daring to challenge the dynasty.

My hopes of seeing the dynamic new prince of the Congress in action that day were, however, dashed. Four months since his election to parliament, Rahul Gandhi was yet to make his maiden speech, and I left the Lok Sabha that day without hearing him utter a word.

★ ★ ★

The exploitation of religion for political purposes had suffered a mighty blow, but caste politics of the kind unleashed by V.P. Singh remained a potent force. Without a centralised leadership structure like the Sangh Parivar, it had spread like a virus, infecting professional politicians who'd once prided themselves on their secularism, but would now spout any rhetoric in order to survive.

On the fourteenth floor of New Delhi's swank Taj Mansingh Hotel, high above the gridlock and politics of the capital, the man who best represented the new dynamic was holding court before a steady procession of scribes, emissaries and celebrities. Amar Singh was no respecter of dynasty or ideology. To him, Congress and the BJP were two peas in a pod, both Brahmin-dominated institutions of a dying political establishment. If he had religious beliefs, he didn't volunteer them, and the socialist label of his Samajwadi Party was just that, a label, providing a veneer of conviction to the new *dalals*, or power-brokers, who since 2003 had ruled Uttar Pradesh, population 170 million.

In the VIP lounge dubbed 'The Chambers', where soft lighting, soothing music, oriental rugs and a well-stocked bar calmed the capital's stressed-out executives, Amar Singh was making things happen, using what he called his 'connectivity', that unique ability to reconcile competing interests. The right word from Amar-ji, and the Reliance Group might agree to set up an industrial plant in your city. The right waggle from that top-heavy head, and a Bollywood starlet might leap from your giant birthday cake. But sitting cross-legged on a sofa, massaging his stockinged feet, he couldn't quite organise his dinner.

'Sorry sir,' the white-gloved waiter was saying, 'Chilli chicken will not be possible. Would you like to have *mast* chicken in continental style, or fried chicken?'

Amar Singh frowned and drew back his head to eyeball the man, his fierce glare and wispy moustache recalling a Central Asian warlord.

'*Arre, arpke pas kuch aur?*' he responded, asking what else they had.

'Chicken *tikka*?' said the servant, beginning to perspire noticeably. There was no caste solidarity when it came to dinner, not here on the executive floor.

'Ha [Yes]. Chicken tikka,' said Amar Singh finally, dismissing the waiter.

A former low-ranking student politician in the Congress, he'd found his niche by backing an ambitious provincial caste leader,

Mulayam Singh Yadav. The Yadavs were a numerically strong middle caste of farmers who owned their own land. Together with Muslims, who feared the BJP and distrusted the Congress, Yadavs formed the Samajwadi Party's support base in rural UP. Rustic interlopers on the national scene, Mulayam and Amar Singh didn't have much of a foreign policy, but their instinctive feel for the barnyard politics of the Cow Belt had won them several elections in India's most populous state, and Amar Singh was the power behind the throne. He could sew up deals that were prettier than the beautifully embroidered border of his kurta pajama, and then leverage the profits to forge new alliances. No one knew exactly where Amar-ji drew the line between private and public, government and business, or business and pleasure, but everyone made a packet. His political opponents believed Amar could have a man killed between the main course and dessert, and not get indigestion, but if he was guilty of anything, they had no evidence. He was an artful juggler disguised as a struggler.

'I have great admiration and respect for the people who are without pedigree,' he told me, patting down his comb-over and cupping one of his multiple chins as if weighing a goitre. 'As a child, I was not given the best of education, and even today I feel handicapped. Whatever little English I know, I have imbibed this knowledge by reading newspapers. When I first came to Delhi, people who now recognise me used to look through. They found me nobody. And even today large section of class thinks I am not from their clan. I am uncouth! I am rash! I am too blunt! But I have made my own space on ground, and in the sky as well.'

He grabbed a handful of salty namkeen snack mixture from the table in front of him and threw it through the gap between his two front teeth. Amar's family hailed from Azamgarh, a poor district in eastern UP, but in the nineteenth century had migrated to Calcutta, where his great-grandfather Ranjit Singh found work as a cook. The son of the cook became a successful lawyer, and invested in a hardware store, which he fully expected his own son to take over when the time came. But that son, Amar Singh, was not interested in hardware; his passion was politics.

'That was hugely rejected by my father,' he told me, never ceasing to munch, the yellow namkeen mixture coating his tongue. 'He totally choked my finances and patronage and support. He said, "If you want to lead your life your own way, then you should earn your own dough. Otherwise, if you want my support and patronage, then you will have to do what I want." I owe my success to him because he is the one who threw me on the road.'

It said a lot about Amar Singh's character that he considered being thrown out of his father's house a blessing. It set the stage for an unequal, and in his mind, heroic struggle — one befitting a Thakur (Kshatriya) caste man. With his spreading paunch, oily complexion and chubby cheeks, he didn't look too fit to me; even if he was chairman of the parliamentary committee on health. But when it came to survival, he was the fittest. He might wear sandals with socks, and shake his knee compulsively as spoke, but Amar Singh *mattered*. One of India's richest men, K.K. Birla, had noticed his unique talents when he was still in Calcutta, and put him on the board of his Hindustan group. Now, the boy from eastern UP owned a hydro plant in Karnataka and a chemical factory somewhere else.

When Australia's richest man, the late Kerry Packer, had decided to invest hundreds of millions of dollars in Indian media ventures, Amar Singh smoothed his path. Packer lost a fortune, but in Singh's view, they bonded.

'He introduced me to Nicole Kidman and took me to your girly bar areas in Sydney, what do you call it — Kings'a Cross? . . . Women he loves. In fact, his only regret was that he couldn't enjoy them more. And I agree with him. Power and women are the best things in life.'

It was hardcore gossip, but I had to wonder why he was telling me this? There was an edge to the anecdote, Amar Singh sending coded signals and talking in riddles.

One thing was certain: Amar Singh was a socialist of the champagne variety. At forty-eight, he had a big house in Greater Kailash II in ritzy South Delhi, stacked with *objets d'art*, and a state-provided MP's bungalow in Lutyens's Delhi which had undergone extensive and controversial renovations. He had Montblanc pens and Cartier eyeglasses, Rolex watches and a Lexus SUV. Yet, he insisted on calling himself a 'humble servant of the people'. Most of his 'people' could live for a year on what he spent in a day. But then, as Amar Singh liked to point out, 'Even Gandhian simplicity was an elaborate affair'.[4]

He'd roped in more tycoons than a cowherd rounds up heifers — Ambanis, Godrejs and Roys — all dying to do their dough in the Indian economy's version of a swamp. Reliance had pledged $2 billion for the power sector, and the Sahara Group $4 billion in housing. Critics cried 'crony capitalism!' — which sounded like a good idea to most people — and the party went on.

The way Amar Singh saw it, business interests needed love. 'We want to give them a sense of security, dignity and the assurance that they will get returns for their investment. Isn't this what a healthy economy is all about?' he asked. Nobody in Uttar Pradesh knew the answer.

There was only one cloud on Amar Singh's expansive horizon, as far as I could make out. It loomed over him like a pair of initials penned by a skywriter — R.G.

No member of the Gandhi family had been prime minister for fifteen years, and if Amar Singh had his way, none would ever again. 'I will DESTROY him!' he said, when I mentioned Rahul Gandhi, trying to act tough, but sounding more like a desi Dr Evil. The Congress Party's great wheatish hope had been trash-talking the Samajwadis, blaming them for UP's corruption and poor governance. Rahul was working the villages in his new patch of Amethi, trying to rebuild the Congress Party's base.

'He is a junior chap. He is a baccha [child],' said Amar Singh. 'He is saying a lot of things about us, claiming there is no law and order in UP, and so on, and insulting my leader, Mulayam Singh, who was a friend of his father. If Sonia declares that Rahul is the heir apparent and is going to succeed to the prime minister's chair, then I will address him differently. But let it be articulated. Once it is declared formally, that he's the crown prince of the country, I will keep my mouth shut. I will say, "He is a great guy. He's the reincarnation of Lord Buddha."'

What Amar Singh particularly disliked was the amount of column inches Rahul was generating in the country's print media.

'In the middle page of some elitist English newspaper, a two-line-thin corner space will be given to us. But Rahul Gandhi! Whatever *he* does — whether he flies a plane, or takes holiday with his girlfriend in Kerala — everything is a big news. And it has to be splashed in a MAJOR way. So this is the advantage you start with if you have got the pedigree. I don't resent Rahul for this. But I envy him!'

Amar Singh ran a meaty hand in a long slow sweeping motion back over his head. His eyes looked like microdots in his humungous glasses, but it gave him a sage-like look, the blind diviner of political fortunes.

'My fiercely independent nature may be the reason for lack of cordial relations between me and Madam, because between Crown and subject there has to be a code of conduct. There is an element of feudalism in them, because they are constant rulers. And I admit that I constantly flop that conduct. Pauper should have the mindset to take any sort of atrocities and insults from the king. But he should not have any right to raise his voice.'

'Deadly!' said an acolyte sitting on a bench seat opposite, and then I started to get it. This archly expressed victimhood was a lethal weapon in the street fight of Indian politics. To be aggrieved was to be heard. To be wounded was to find sympathisers. To fight the lonely struggle for justice and dignity was to be loved. To win was to be worshipped. Above all, to make people laugh was greatly appreciated, and to be a rogue was to be secretly respected. As he burped and groused and gnawed on his chicken tikkas, shamelessly posing as a martyr, Amar Singh personified the temper of the world's largest democracy, which had duly rewarded him. To the well-born rich he flaunted his crude nature. To the low-born poor he flaunted his *jingchak* style — Hindi for flashy and trashy — swanning around all the best parties with models on his arm, even though he had a wife somewhere. He'd even stolen Sonia's friend Amitabh Bachchan, whose friendship with the Samajwadi leader had given the party an infusion of glamour. Being noticed was more important to Amar Singh than being liked or admired, and by defying all the pieties and known laws of political gravity he'd struck a chord somewhere deep in the Indian psyche. He could squat here on the sofas in the executive club of the Taj Hotel picking his toenails if he liked, and they would all kow-tow to him because he didn't just wield power: he *was* power.

'I am in business the way that sugar is in the tea,' he confided, pushing his recalcitrant spectacles back up his nose. 'I just want to make money so that I can sustain my lifestyle in a nice, orderly, graceful style. I am not guided in money-making by greed. I am guided by need, and once my need is fulfilled I have devoted my time to politics.'

When I told Amar Singh that some people thought India had gone to the dogs because of his style of politics, he at first affected a thoughtful demeanour. 'I am aware of that perception,' he began, the soul of reason. 'No, it is not completely wrong.'

Then the fury of a Genghis Khan burst forth, a firestorm of class anger. 'They are the drawing-room gossip-mongerers and self-obeisant hooters!' he declared. 'Have they ever felt the scorch heat of the sun? Have they? Have they lived in a house where there is no latrine? Where you have to get up in the morning and go to the field to shit? I have done all that, so it makes me DIFFERENT! *I* can talk about poverty. *I* can talk about the scarcity. *I* can talk about the malnutrition,' he said, popping another tikka in his mouth.

India's experiment with democracy is surely the most interesting and important ever conducted; if democracy can work in India, it can work anywhere. In just sixty years, the ballot box, for all its failings, has devolved power in a society ruled for millennia by rajas, in the process becoming a powerful force for modernising a poor, illiterate and deeply traditional society. Caste and religious politics will inevitably play a role, along with the conceits of politicians, but their influence has repeatedly been moderated by the wisdom of ordinary citizens. The new leaders are not visionaries like Gandhi and Nehru, but dalals like Amar Singh, brokers who can mobilise constituencies and forge alliances. They love to think they own the car, but in India, the man you see driving the limo is usually a chauffeur. Amar Singh mattered most not because of what he achieved, but what he represented and what he prevented. For ordinary voters, he was someone like them, only more so, someone like them who had made it. He spoke the vernacular and focused on local — not regional or national, and definitely not global issues. What he prevented was the return of a dominant Congress. Once the grand old party's main stronghold, UP had been carved up and shared among political newcomers and pygmies. The lower castes had fled to the Bahujan Samaj Party (BSP), the Brahmins to the BJP and the Muslims to the Samajwadis, leaving Rahul Gandhi a flea-bitten inheritance. Amar Singh and people like him were the baccha's worst nightmare.

Amar Singh had recently been questioned by the Central Bureau of Investigations — the Central Bureau of Intimidation, he called it — as part of a corruption investigation

'I know it for sure that former IB [Intelligence Bureau] chief and former cop Narayanan, who is working in PM's office, is deputed to find something against me, so that I can be kneeled down. Maybe while I am talking to you I am under surveillance. Some Big Daddy is watching,' he said.

I don't think he was being paranoid. His name, Amar, might mean immortal, but there was a reckless quality about him that might just bring him undone. Among his enemies was Sonia Gandhi, recently named by *Forbes* magazine as the world's third most powerful woman. (US National Security Adviser Condoleezza Rice and Chinese Vice Premier Wu Yi were considered to be more powerful.)[5] The Samajwadis had blocked her attempt to form a government in 1999, forcing the Congress to wait five long years for another chance, during which the Hindu nationalists finally threw off their pariah tag. But Amar Singh was unconcerned.

'In politics, where enemies are enemies and friends are jealous, and with democracy now, there is no more feudalistic way,' he said, looking like the frog that had swallowed the mosquito. 'They cannot get me suppressed by an elephant, like good old royalty used to do. They cannot behead me because they do not like my face and voice. So, they have to put up with me. Any person with self-esteem and self-dignity cannot remain in Congress. I will smother them to dust. I will destroy the feudalistic Nehru-Gandhi family.'

★ ★ ★

'In ninety-one, my father died. I remember I pretty much decided that I was going to do something. So, on the train, when I was taking my father — his ashes — to Allahabad, I already had an idea. I didn't vacillate, actually. I just felt that my father was doing a job which he didn't complete, and I felt a certain amount of responsibility towards the people who believed in him.'

It had taken Rahul Gandhi thirteen years to make this journey, and there was still far to go. I had watched him that day in 1991, circling his father's body on the funeral pyre, dazed but composed in that surreal window through which life passes — to where, nobody knows. Ever since then, he'd carried the burden of an oath taken at the age of twenty. The memories of that terrible summer never faded, not for a second, not even for someone like me, who'd met Rajiv only briefly in those last frenetic weeks of his life. Some deaths never leave you, and now I was back again, driving the rural backblocks of northern India, this time with his son.

At first sight you would not necessarily have picked him for an Indian. He had his parents' fair skin and good looks; dark eyes with long lashes and dimpled cheeks on which his dark, fine-grained stubble looked almost elegant, and his smile held a hint of shyness. At thirty-four, with tightly-curled brown hair and neat sideburns, he looked younger than his father had at the same age; Rajiv was already married with two children and a bald patch. When I'd met Rajiv he had been prime minister once and wanted a second term. Rahul was a freshman. But in other ways they were almost identical; the mild manners and gentle, self-deprecating humour were there, and of course, the wardrobe. Like his father had right up to the night he died, Rahul wore white cotton kurta pajama and running shoes. He was more like a reincarnation than a son. How far would those runners take him, I wondered, and to what destination?

Rahul's mother and father had both held this seat of Amethi, which we now drove through. For his age, he was modestly affluent by Indian standards, with just over $100,000 in bank deposits, land, and shares in companies such as Intel and Ericsson. He also owned an 83 per cent share in a Mumbai-based engineering firm, Backops Services. But this was Rahul's true inheritance, a baked-earth road raised above a paddy field somewhere near Jais, between the Ganges and the Yamuna, the heart of Uttar Pradesh. Even poets had called it a godforsaken wasteland, but that was before science made seed more bountiful, and the Nehru-Gandhi family had lavished the villages with hand pumps and hospitals, even free trips to see doctors in Delhi for those in particular need. Now, as the local MP, Rahul was visiting the area every month, trying above all to wean his subjects off the dependence his own family had encouraged in them. He was accompanied by a family friend, Manoj Mattoo, and by Kishori Lal Sharma, a dumpy, mustachioed man who acted as a kind of pro-consul for the dynasty in its pocket borough. Manoj was a former pilot who shared the Nehrus' Kashmiri ancestry. He looked worn-out in a raffish manner, a middle-aged man in slacks and open-necked shirt with designer spectacles and a trimmed salt-and-pepper beard, and he reminded me slightly of Suman Dubey. When I asked Manoj if he was a member of the party, he said, 'No, thank God.'

Rahul wasn't giving interviews in Delhi, and in Amethi he had trained the local scribes well, talking to them outside the guesthouse at the beginning of his day, and then making his desire to be left alone for the rest of it clear. The Congress Party organisation was being kept at arm's length from his travel arrangements because, in Rahul's own words, 'when the party people get involved, there is a distortion'. 'Distortion' was code for paying people to attend meetings, discouraging them from speaking frankly and turning his every move into a publicity stunt. If Congress had a say he would be shown only approved projects and meet only people who'd been vetted. The young prince wanted no Potemkin-ised villages in Amethi; at least not before he'd had a chance to see the real thing. When a villager complained that their efforts to get the road resurfaced had gotten nowhere, Rahul had responded, 'You failed at first because you went through the Congress organisation.'

I had arrived unannounced the previous night in the town of Amethi, having driven from Lucknow. The poverty along National Highway 56 from Lucknow to Amethi was picturesque, mountains of green bananas swaying on the backs of trucks, and rickshaw-wallahs pedalling improvised school 'buses', small tin contraptions crammed full of children. Men squatted under hand pumps, washing their clothes without disrobing, and girls carried head-loads of grass in bulging jute bags. The paddy fields blazed with morning lotus in bloom and the roadside dhaba where I stopped for breakfast did a roaring trade in masala chickpeas with chopped onions, coriander leaves and lemon juice, served in leaf bowls. Beyond Jagdishpur, the roads crumbled and shrank to barely a car's width, and gangs of men broke stones in the hot sun all day to repair them. At one point, local youths with lathis blocked the road demanding a 'toll' to fund what they claimed would be future road works. I paid them, although I doubted a single rupee would end up in bitumen.

The town of Amethi itself, like most towns in Uttar Pradesh, was a utilitarian scrabble of concrete shops and narrow streets gridlocked by livestock and tractors. On the outskirts, a clutch of mouldy structures in an unkempt compound comprised the palace of the former Maharaja Sanjay Singh who, like many ex-feudals, had kept himself afloat by playing a deft hand in local politics. He'd won on a BJP ticket in 1998, and then lost to Sonia Gandhi the following year, before she handed the seat to her son, one form of feudal politics replacing another. Since independence, Amethi had only once voted against the Gandhis, when Sanjay Gandhi, Rajiv's brother, was defeated after the Emergency in 1977. A sprawling hospital complex in Munshiganj, not far from Amethi, memorialises Sanjay, and Rahul was staying at an adjoining guesthouse. When I called at the spotless, air-conditioned bungalow decorated with freshly cut flowers and garlanded busts and portraits of Sanjay and Rajiv, I found he was already out on tour, and would not be back until evening. Satisfied with having tracked him down, I left a note and went in search of a hotel.

Returning that evening, I found the compound besieged by thousands of people who had come from near and far, unannounced like me, hoping for darshan with Rahul-ji. Police had secured the perimeter fence and were setting up metal detectors to scan people. No amount of talking or card flashing could persuade them to let me in. Night fell and the blazing light and humming air-conditioners of the compound mocked the streets of Munshiganj, plunged in darkness as they were by one of the frequent power cuts. The amount of electricity produced in the state was 20 to 30 per cent lower than it had been in 1989, a testament to its moribund economy. The air was hot and full of bugs. Finally, in response to a note I'd sent in, Manoj Mattoo came to the gate.

'Your note says that you travelled with Rahul's father, is that correct?' he asked me. I said it was. 'Well, Rahul says that if you would like to come back tomorrow, say around 9 a.m., we will see what we can do.'

Next morning, I was led to a jeep, one in a line of vehicles outside the guesthouse, and told to get in. A few minutes later another jeep, this one driven by Manoj with Rahul in the front passenger seat, rolled out of the driveway, and then we were off on a madcap pursuit behind Rahul through the surrounding countryside. For half an hour the convoy sped through towns and hamlets, along raised levee banks and village roads, until eventually stopping near a cluster of brick-and-thatch houses surrounded by inundated rice fields. I saw a man running towards us from the head of the convoy, a messenger as it turned out, sent to fetch me. Walking to the head of the convoy, I found Rahul leaning against his jeep, completely alone except for a boisterous group of very young children whom he was bribing with sweets. Sweet supplies exhausted, he showed them the empty packet and they tore off to fight over the distributed booty. With nobody else around to introduce us, he held out his hand.

'I'm Rahul,' he said, smiling manfully, about as relaxed as it is possible to be in the presence of a stranger.

Manoj, a kind of chaperone and distant cousin who accompanied Rahul on his tours of the constituency, had gone into the hamlet to ask directions. When he returned to the car, flanked by a taut-framed bodyguard — who, I'd have thought, should have stayed with Rahul — we all piled into Rahul's jeep and set off again, the vehicle bucking and bouncing across the *kutcha* roads raised above a sea of bright green paddy fields.

Sitting beside me in the back seat, Sharma-ji, the family agent, struggled to read from a clipboard detailing a handwritten program for the day. In front, Rahul chatted amiably with Manoj who, although much senior in years, insisted on calling him 'Sir!'. Perhaps it was a legacy of his air-force background. When he chose to differ with Rahul — which he did often enough — it was by mildly and respectfully placing facts or arguments at the younger man's disposal.

All this he did with the particular grace of a Kashmiri Brahmin. The Nehrus never missed an opportunity to keep the Kashmir connection alive, spiking their conversations with Kashmiri words and trusting sensitive positions to fellow pandits. This tenuous link seemed to provide them with a sense of identity in their isolated world. Rahul's Jack Russell terrier was named *pidi*, Kashmiri for tiny.

Seven in ten Indians still live on the land, with some 650 million people dependent on agriculture for their livelihoods. There are 115 million farm households with an average holding of 1.4 hectares. India has achieved food security, but rural incomes are falling behind. More farmers should be switching to cash crops, but infrastructure and market mechanisms are inadequate to connect them to customers.[6]

There were no call centres or 'cyber coolies' on this campus; the women wore *naths* (large nose rings), and the naked children were covered in flies and talismans. All it took was a jeep and some petrol, a couple of trusted advisers and a little time to complete Rahul's political apprenticeship here in the Cow Belt. There was no bluster or wild threats like Amar Singh's; just a quiet, self-effacing young man working on his future.

'We're drawing-room politicians, just a little less drawing-room than others,' he said, rolling up his sleeves, revealing a colourful rakhi string on his wrist that could only have been tied on by Priyanka.

'When we go to some villages, they tell us, "Jawaharlal Nehru stayed here for several days." If we really wanted to know people's problems, we'd come and live here for six months. But we have to strike a balance.'

It was a job — a family business, Suman had called it — and Rahul ran it with the relaxed efficiency of an American corporate type. We all drank from the same bottle of Kinley water — produced in India by Coca-Cola — and affectionate sledging was encouraged.

'I hope Kishori has done his homework,' Manoj said at one point, winking at Rahul, when the phlegmatic, betel-chewing organiser became manic in his page-turning and note-taking.

Our first stop was a village clinic where the doctors were expecting us, but the media had been kept away. As Rahul stepped out of the jeep an elderly woman with rotten teeth threw herself at his feet.

'Nahin, nahin [no, no], Aunty,' he said, helping her up. The woman was followed by a woebegone man with diabetes, and another with arthritis. In the small six-room clinic a portrait of Mahatma Gandhi with a befuddled expression stared down from the wall over steel bed bases lacking sheets. Whatever patronage this place had had in the past, there wasn't much to show for it. Shadowing Rahul at a short distance, Sharma-ji scribbled furiously to record names and ailments, handing out chits to present at the Munshiganj hospital, or if necessary, Rahul would arrange treatment in Delhi under his 'MP's quota'. At one point Rahul comforted one particularly emotional old man by putting an arm over his shoulder. I'd seen Rajiv do exactly the same thing. When I mentioned this, Rahul replied, 'I'm not a patch on him.' The words seemed to catch in his throat, the emotions still raw even after all these years.

Our next stop was a village school, where the famous neta's arrival sent children stampeding to their places in assembly. Blackboards were fixed to the exterior walls of the buildings, with tuition done in the open, within sight of the emerald-green rice fields and brown mud levees. On hand-held slates each child had written a few letters in the Devanagari script, which Rahul inspected approvingly. The young boys wanted to be him; the young girls wanted to marry him. He was good with children despite not yet having any of his own, and was keen on a plan to introduce coaching centres in all villages in the area to improve the standard of primary education.

We hadn't been there long when Mattoo-sahib, in his laconic way, called time and we moved on to Hardhon, Matia Dumal, Varra and Kapasi, villages where the roads were so narrow that the jeep could not enter and we proceeded on foot. The people spoke Awadhi, an old form of Hindi, and babies with eyes rimmed in dark *kajal* to ward off misfortune hung from every young woman's hip. On one occasion, a knot of elderly women mistook me for Rahul, and had to be prised off my feet before falling at his.

The villagers considered themselves to be part of his family — he was the third generation of the Gandhi family to represent them — but the relationship also had elements of a cargo cult. The villages wanted stuff, above all, a short cut through the bureaucratic jungle to provide them with better water supplies, more reliable electricity and jobs. In every village they peppered him with demands for phone lines and ration cards. Those who could think of nothing more asked for things they already had, desperate not to waste the opportunity afforded by his presence. What they wanted most were more hand pumps to reduce the time and effort women spent carrying water. Pumps somehow had a way of always ending up outside the home of a Brahmin, who would forbid Dalits to use them. According to Mattoo, there were already 47,000 hand pumps in the Amethi constituency, more than enough to provide for people's needs, even if half of them were broken. Some villages were waterlogged they had so many pumps.

In the Hindi movie based on R.K. Narayan's novel *The Guide*, villagers praise a shonky swami who has brought them good luck.

'A school! A hospital! And now, now a post office! Swami-ji, you have turned this village into a heaven!'

This was more or less Rahul's performance benchmark. The easiest thing to do — the things most Indian politicians do — would have been to use his MP quota and give them more hand pumps. But here, Rahul's background in financial services collided with the demands of his largely illiterate constituents. Why not try rainwater harvesting and storage tanks, he suggested. One big overhead tank would serve the whole village cluster. It would cost five to seven rupees per family per month.

In the stifling heat, the men of the village sat in their loincloths on the shady side of buildings, listening sceptically to the young man's new-fangled ideas. For now at least, they were with him, the women more so.

'He is our baccha, and we will never leave him. The Gandhis are like our own family,' one elderly lady enthused, pointing a bony finger at me and adding, 'If the Congress sent *you* we would elect you!'

Driving between the villages in the air-conditioned jeep, Rahul was encouraged by the reception his new ideas had met with.

'If we can get five villages behind water harvesting it could take off. The villagers themselves can run it. They'll decide whether it's profit or loss,' he said, the returned expatriate in him all fired up by a vision of what India could be. Instead of waiting for regular electricity supplies, he thought, generators running on bio-diesel could be a smart alternative.

With an intellectual commitment to the poor, he was doing his best to connect with them. But they might as well have been Martians for all he shared in common with them. His father had had the same problem, a leader schooled in English in a country where less than four in a hundred people were fluent in that language. But Rahul didn't just speak English; he spoke corporate jargon, and even thought in it. 'Part of my job is to think about how to make people accountable; how to measure people effectively,' he told me. It was difficult to imagine these villages somehow connecting to the IT revolution in a major way. They struggled to get credit, and often couldn't pay back their loans when they did get it. Above all, the inexorable subdivision of their plots from one generation to the next was making farms uneconomic. But with his technocratic ideas, Rahul was confident that India would soon be a player on the world stage.

'India being a big country, it needs a massive push to start it rolling, but once it starts to roll, it takes a massive push to stop it. If you look thirty to fifty years ahead, which is where one should look, I'm pretty certain India will be one of the top five powers. The issue is whether we'll be among the top three or not ... That will make a big difference to how we impact poverty. Equally important is how we'll behave in that position. So, will we be a complete bully, or will we be a power that is more accepting?'

Unlike Amar Singh, Rahul had one eye on the village and the other on the world. But in the end, it all came back to the family. In the car, he grilled me for recollections of his father, even small details. It was all doubly relevant now that he'd gone into politics, all the things his father could never tell him. No amount of mentoring could ever replace a father, especially when the family put so little trust in the party. Then there was the issue of security. The closer he got to power, the more stringent the security cordon around him would become. He was racing against time on that front, soaking up this field experience while his minders would still let him. And having lost his father and grandmother to assassins, what faith could he have in shadows?

That very morning as we'd left the guesthouse, his security detail had been overwhelmed by a crowd of media and petitioners who had surrounded the jeep. He'd rolled down the window of his car and spoken to the crowd for perhaps ten minutes, as a plainclothes officer from his Special Protection Force detail stood awkward and tense beside the car door, providing a suggestion of security where none really existed. Rajiv's bodyguard, Pradip Kumar, used to do the same, and paid for it with his life. But as Rahul had already told me, his father's murder was the very reason he'd joined politics rather than avoiding it.

'I didn't think one should just get into politics for the sake of getting into politics. So I had a sense of working abroad to get an understanding of how things work ... But it took me thirteen years to feel I had a sufficient understanding of things, whereby I could actually, maybe help people, as opposed to being confused and bungling about.'

For more than a decade, Indians had wondered about Sonia's political motivations and intentions. Her initial rejection of a political career was understandable enough, but as she drifted ever closer to direct involvement, speculation about her reasoning became a national sport. Why would a mother who had lost her husband to politics willingly risk putting her children through more possible heartbreak? Talking to Rahul, the reason seemed pretty obvious: she was keeping the seat warm for him. When I asked if Sonia had known of his intention to complete his father's work, Rahul confirmed it.

'My mum was aware of my intentions,' he said, casually revealing one of India's best kept political secrets.

Our last stop before lunch was the bazaar at Sanjay Gandhi Nagar, a town named after Rahul's late uncle, where Rahul had agreed to the local Congress organisation's request to address a public meeting. Local by-elections were looming and the meeting attracted several hundred people, mainly curious young men who gawked at the famous Gandhi as he squatted in their midst on a dusty area of open ground behind the main street, waiting for him to impress them. But no surprises were in store. His speech sounded like a lecture on development and the boredom of the audience was palpable.

Had he given them the oratory of a Vajpayee or the trash-talk of an Amar Singh — anything at all to bring some skerrick of amusement to this boring town, he might have won them. Instead, he was just himself, a well-meaning, well-bred urban Indian. When he finished, the crowded pressed in on him with a banal curiosity, and he had difficulty extracting himself, shaking hands as he went. The local party bosses hated this habit of hand-shaking, a precedent they had no interest in following. A simple namaste of clasped hands would do, but Rahul couldn't break a habit entrenched during years in Europe and America. As we drove out of town, he seemed withdrawn, I thought due to his inability to connect with his audience. But a few kilometres along the road he turned to Manoj and said, 'I shook hands with a man back there. He had some kind of skin problem. Do you think I should wash my hands?'

Pulling off the road, the two of them got down from the jeep and opened the rear hatch. Rifling through the luggage, Manoj produced a bottle of disinfectant, a bowl and a bottle of mineral water, with which Rahul decontaminated himself.

Talk of lunch lightened the mood. Back in the car, Rahul produced bags of popcorn, which he passed around and ate, lamenting that he really should try harder to lose weight. At a predetermined spot along the road, Manoj turned onto a narrow trail which rounded a hillock, bringing us to a clearing dotted with some spreading muah trees. There, he dropped Sharma-ji and the bodyguard, where an advance squad of Special Protection Group officers had already taken up a position.

'This looks like the best picnic spot so far,' said Rahul with an almost childish sense of fun, proceeding to a small clearing on a finger of land bound by a low stone wall. Beyond the wall, white egrets waded in an emerald sea of paddy. Inside it, Rahul crouched, undid the cord of his pajama pants, and relieved himself, while Manoj laid out a simple lunch of cheese sandwiches, rolled paranthas, toffees and fruit juices on the bonnet of the car.

'You shouldn't be eating paranthas with that stomach of yours,' Rahul kidded him when he returned, washing his hands again, this time just with bottled water. I realised that these small jokes were Rahul's way of breaching the invisible cage in which the Gandhi name imprisoned him. At least he was aware of it, and at least he was trying. A few days later Manoj would narrowly survive a massive heart attack.

Hungrily devouring his lunch, Rahul regaled us with anecdotes from his childhood, growing up in his grandmother's home at Number One Safdarjung Road in New Delhi, now a museum honouring Indira Gandhi, who'd been murdered in the garden. Tens of thousands of people passed through it every day.

'You remember Shyam Lal?' he asked Manoj. 'He's dead now but he impacted on me in a big way. He was an uneducated chap who started off at the lowest rank — not a sweeper, but right around there — a cleaner. But by the end, seven years later, he was running the whole prime minister's kitchen, the pantry and the house, everything on his own without any help. There's a person I learnt a bit from.'

It reminded me of the Civil Lines, and the affection Janaki had for the older servants, an odd relationship mediated through class, caste, and disparities in wealth, but a relationship all the same.

'I tell you what else I learnt,' said Rahul, in a rueful, but still affectionate tone. 'A couple of tight slaps from my father and my grandmother when I was small taught me a hell of a lot. You know, if you were rude to the servants, I mean, your head almost came off. That was the way we were brought up ... when we watch a football match we side for the losing team. Always, we side for the weaker person.'

He'd inherited so much from his father — the name, the job, the politics, even the hobbies, having followed in Rajiv's footsteps by obtaining a pilot's licence — that his life seemed dangerously like a repeat performance. Like both his mother and father he'd won election from the parliamentary constituency of Amethi. Like his father, he'd studied at Trinity College, Cambridge, although he'd done rather better, completing a Masters in philosophy. Like his father, he'd become romantically involved with a foreigner, in Rahul's case, a Venezuelan architect called Veronica, and the gossip rags (and even the more 'respectable' newspapers) were having a field day speculating about the depth of their love, and the absence of a wedding ring. This caused much rolling of eyes in private among Congress Party leaders, who'd agonised over Sonia's foreign origins for decades. Why couldn't these Gandhi boys be satisfied with nice desi girls? Now like his father too he was on a quest to salvage the family's honour. Most Congressmen believed the young prince would not only become a successful politician, but eventually a wise leader. 'He [Rahul] is going to be around for a pretty long time,' said Salman Khurshid, the state Congress Party chief. 'He is going to have a very major role in Indian politics ... He is not just a clone, he has got something more ... [He is] meticulous in his career planning and not in a hurry ... he wants to do something that is strong and sound and deep.'[7]

The story about the servant and the Gandhi family's devotion to the underdog seemed an uneasy fit with dynastic politics, so I asked him how he reconciled the two.

'You see, the thing about dynastic politics is, it's about brand recognition. You recognise somebody, but then that person has to deliver ... Someone like my great-grandfather, and his father ... I mean, they basically sacrificed everything they had for the freedom movement. They literally took all their belongings and burnt them, and their house became the headquarters of the Congress Party. In my grandmother's case, she imbibed a lot of values from my great-grandfather, but she did very big things for India's poor. And that was where the appeal for her came from.'

After lunch, we got back on the road; more villages, more chits. The Gandhi family's winning margin in Amethi was as large as ever, but UP as a whole hadn't given them a majority in twenty years. He knew he was in for the long haul. Rahul knew this was his dharma. He talked freely about a wide range of subjects, from power-hungry bureaucrats ('the biggest problem facing India'), to Hindu nationalism. He was spoiling for a fight with the nationalists.

'I come from a Hindu background. But I don't see the need to use my gods to mobilise people. This is the same whether it's Muslim fundamentalism or Hindu fundamentalism or right-wing Christian fundamentalism in the United States. It's just people who are bankrupt of ideas. You can sell these things to people once, and then after that people turn around and say, "Okay, so what did I get from this?" The BJP thinks that India can be ruled with a rigid ideology and they found out right now that it can't. When I heard about the demolition at Ayodhya, I really felt that the heart of India had been hurt. Literally I felt pain, not because you're hurting a group, but because you're striking at the core of what this country is. This country is built on inclusive foundations. Whoever wants to come can come and we'll adopt you. Hinduism is built on that. It absorbs ideas and concepts. So that's why when I heard about the demolition, I felt that it was wrong. My father would not have allowed that. No question of it. If any one of my family was in politics — I mean, just in politics, not even in power — at that time, it would not have happened.'

There it was again, the family instead of the party, the true keepers of the flame of Gandhi and Nehru's legacy. Yet, when the opportunity came, as one day it would, the Congress would offer him the crown. And although he protested whenever the question of the leadership was raised, I felt fairly confident he would accept it. For the moment, he was the spare in case anything happened to Sonia. Talk of him leading the party in the 2009 elections seemed premature, but Congress leaders such as Salman Khurshid were already saying the leadership was his when he wanted it. The only question was whether he would live that long. So I asked how he felt about the security problem. Not for the first time that day, his voice thickened with emotion. It was deep and dark, with a kind of simmering but restrained anger, one thing I'd never noticed in his father.

'Since I was fourteen, when my grandmother was killed, we've had this security issue. With my grandmother, and with my father,' he said, the words coming in clutches. 'I mean, I don't really care about it, frankly. I mean, that's the best way to put it. I couldn't care less. It's not something I worry about. In fact, my security people, they're friends of mine and all that, but I could do with fewer of them . . . You're gonna die anyway.'

21

Opera in the Dust

The iconic final journey for a Hindu is a pilgrimage to Varanasi, to die upon the banks of the Ganga. Not everyone makes it, but those who do believe their reward will be moksha, liberation from the eternal cycle of death and reincarnation. For at least 3000 years they have been coming to die in the city of Shiva, whose job is to destroy the world so that rebirth and renewal is possible. Imagine a rundown, deeply religious Paris, an old city of high culture, where people cremate their dead on the banks of the Seine, a baroque gem on a mystic river. Like all great cities, it has many names, including the oldest, Kashi (the luminous one), and Banaras, a mangled transliteration by the British, which nevertheless has its own charms. I'd lived in India for more than two years before I made the pilgrimage to one of the oldest continuously inhabited human settlements on earth, older than Babylon and Athens or, as Mark Twain put it, older than history, tradition and legend, and looking 'twice as old as all of them put together'. The spell of this truly eternal city, once cast, never leaves you, and after that first visit I returned repeatedly.

My time in India felt like a series of *asramas* — stages of life — first, as a young reporter confronting the ugly face of Indian injustice and political violence. Then, as a member of a Hindu household, soothed and reassured by the warmth and stability of family life. My yatra had provided me with an opportunity for reflection, a third *asrama*. Now the fourth and final stage, *sanyasa* — renunciation, or letting go — beckoned. In Ayodhya, I'd realised that Hindu nationalism has very little to do with the Hindu religion, just as Muslim extremism has not much in common with the Islamic struggle for self-improvement called *jihad*. Politicians may speak the language of faith, but that rarely makes them holy, and it's difficult to think of a confessional state that hasn't been constantly embroiled in conflict. Politicised religion may simply be a gimmick devised by politicians to gain power; it successfully taps into fears about a rapidly changing, integrating world. But politicians who go to war in the name of religion, or priests who deny their flocks the benefits of contraception or vaccination on dubious theological grounds, won't survive very long in the twenty-first century. Politics is about acquiring and exercising power in this world; religion is about being worthy of salvation in the next. Like oil and water, they do not mix well. At times of crisis, a political priest or divinely inspired politician may make a contribution; but in the day-to-day affairs of church and state they should stick to what they know best, and avoid muddying the waters.

In Varanasi, the waters are always muddy, yet spend a few days there and everything becomes clear. For my trip there I'd taken along several books on one of India's most revered saints, Sri Ramakrishna, including Christopher Isherwood's *Ramakrishna and His Disciples*. Sri Ramakrishna was a bhakt, an instinctive seeker who finds fulfilment in a direct personal relationship with God. Born in rural Bengal into a Brahmin family in 1836, he exhibited spiritual tendencies from an early age. As a six-year-old boy while walking in the fields one day, he saw a flock of snow-white cranes in flight, a startling image against a leaden monsoon sky. Struck down by ecstasy, he was never the same again. Throughout his life he would be blessed, or afflicted, with this singular capacity for experiencing overwhelming joy. Recognised from an early age as a spiritual phenomenon, he became a Hindu priest at the Dakshineswar Kali Temple near Calcutta. One day at the end of 1866, Ramakrishna happened to notice a Muslim absorbed in prayer and asked the man to explain to him the mysteries of Islam. As another of his devoted biographers, the French author and Nobel Prize winner Romain Rolland wrote:

> ...for several days the priest of Kali renounced and forgot his own Gods completely. He did not worship Them, he did not even think about Them. He lived outside the temple precincts, he repeated the name of Allah, he wore the robes of a Mussulman and was ready — imagine the sacrilege — to eat of forbidden food, even of the sacred animal, the cow!... Ramakrishna realised the Mussulman God.'[1]

Ramakrishna's potent Islamic experience did not, however, lead to a lasting renunciation of Hinduism. Instead, as Rolland put it, 'The river of Islam had led him back to the Ocean.'[2] The experience convinced him that the god the two faiths were striving to know was one and the same, the only difference being that while Islam laid claim to exclusive truth about the creator, Hinduism taught that the human mind could not conceive of God's precise nature. Years later, Ramakrishna became acquainted with the Bible, again with tumultuous consequences. A series of visions and profound experiences ensued, culminating in his embrace of Jesus. Again, his temple-going fell away, and he was filled with religious ecstasy, which again led him back to the universal God. He accepted the divinity of Christ, but no more or less than he accepted the divinity of Krishna or Buddha. In his quest for enlightenment, Ramakrishna hurled himself against barriers and taboos of all kinds. At one stage, he took to cross-dressing, wearing a sari in public and feminising his appearance, as Isherwood writes:

Ramakrishna asked Mathur for women's clothes. Mathur provided him with a beautiful and valuable sari from Banaras, a gauze scarf, a skirt and a bodice. To complete the transformation, Mathur brought him also a wig and a set of gold ornaments. Needless to say, Ramakrishna's latest *sadhana* caused a whole series of scandalous rumours ... Those who saw him were amazed at the transformation which seemed to take place; walk, speech, gestures, even the smallest actions were perfectly in character. Sometimes, Ramakrishna would go to the house in the Janbazar district which had belonged to Rani Rasmani and live there with the women of the family, as a woman.[3]

Isherwood, who was openly gay, disputes the view that Ramakrishna's gender play had anything to do with homosexuality. Hindus traditionally have been free to approach God in many different moods; as a child before a stern parent, or as a friend, or even as a lover. Both men and women approach Lord Krishna, the great romancer of the Hindu Pantheon, in the guise of his consort Radha, who outlasted all his other wives and lovers.

By 1874, the Bengali saint's spiritual self-education was more or less complete. He had, as he put it, plucked three beautiful fruits from the tree of Knowledge — Compassion, Devotion and Renunciation. His God-intoxicated life is a testament to spiritual wisdom. In his own words: 'You must try all beliefs and traverse all the different ways once ... The tank has several ghats ... Let each man follow his own path. If he sincerely and ardently wishes to know God, peace be unto him! He will surely realise Him.'[4] Eventually, Ramakrishna came to see God in everything and everyone, from the most pious holy man, to the hypocrite and the criminal. Even before his death in 1886 at the age of fifty, he was recognised as an incarnation of God, and the most revered saint of Bengal. The temple complex at Dakshineswar on the Ganga is today a place of pilgrimage for devoted followers from all over the world.

In 1868, Sri Ramakrishna travelled to Varanasi. It was an earthly encounter scripted in heaven, the world's bravest spirit confronted by the city of Shiva, wildest of all the Hindu gods with his three eyes, the moon ensnared in his matted dreadlocks, neck swathed in cobras and the River Ganga cascading from his head. Crossing the Ganga, Ramakrishna was plunged into euphoria by the awesome sight of the city's 'condensed mass of spirituality' strung out along a 5-kilometre stretch between the Varana and Asi river junctions. He believed he saw Shiva himself bending over the funeral pyres, granting moksha to the dead.[5]

★ ★ ★

At Asi Ghat, where the Ganga begins its triumphal procession past Varanasi, workers from the municipal corporation were hosing off the mud of ages, vast tonnes of it dumped during the monsoon when the river can rise 20 metres up the brown stone ghats, even inundating the lower floors of some houses and temples. It looked like fun, blasting away at mud mountains with high-pressure hoses powered by noisy generators, but my position on the elevated veranda of the Hotel Ganges View was just too good to abandon. All morning since before the workers had come, I'd been perched there, thinking river thoughts and watching India's spiritual life unfolding as it has done every morning for thousands of years. The smell of incense and cow dung drifted up from below, and the pavement teemed with pilgrims and beggars.

Some made offerings at an orange Shiva shrine at the base of a pipal tree while others venerated a highly decorated snaggle-horned 'wishing' cow that stood nearby, flapping its ears and swishing its tail to keep off the flies. The barbers did a roaring trade tonsuring the sin-laden hair of pilgrims preparing for their ritual ablutions. Those who'd decided to keep their hair — and who'd already bathed — combed it while peering intently into mirrors. Those coming out passed those going in, the partially disrobed of all ages clambering gingerly across the muddy bank towards the fast-moving current. Higher on the ghat, vendors sheltered under circular straw umbrellas, every day a new beginning in which very little changes.

The chai tray had just arrived when my host, Shashank, the son of an old Banarsi family who had turned their home into a guesthouse, appeared on the balcony with a welcome as warm as the morning sun. A man of generous spirit and girth, he had grown up in this house where he still lived with his statuesque silver-mantled mother and their beloved pooches. Bespectacled and mustachioed, with frizzy hair greying, Shashank cut an elegant figure in a perfectly laundered white kurta pajama. Originally from Bihar, his family had purchased a large tract of land at Asi Ghat, part of which was later donated for construction of the superb brownstone Pancharatna (Five Gems) Temple, dedicated to Rama, Krishna, Shiva, Vishnu and Durga, a few doors up from their home.

'What a beautiful morning, nah? I hope you slept well,' Shashank said, between giving directions to a couple of houseboys engaged in the task of moving some furniture.

If it felt awkward to share his ancestral home, still tastefully decorated with antiques and *objets d'art*, Shashank concealed it gracefully, and would often join us at the dinner table in reminiscing about the culture of old Banaras in a lilting, almost musical tone, while in the next breath cursing its overpopulation and corrupt governance. His family, who were related to the Maharaja of Varanasi's clan, had kept alive the city's tradition of patronising the arts, organising exhibitions and literary soirees; supporting the culture, rather than simply living off it.

'Have you seen the river? It hasn't been so low for a long time. By the time it reaches Banaras there's hardly enough water left in it for a puja,' he said, urging me to see for myself. So when I'd finished my tea, I did.

A century after Ramakrishna visited Varanasi it was still easy to understand his excited embrace of the city. It towers over the steeply raked western bank of the Ganga, where the river writhes northwards like a fat python. On its banks, dhobis slap wet laundry not far from cadavers roasting on funeral pyres, life's drudgery and death's drama played out on a common stage before a riveted public. All the actors are real people, and when you come to Varanasi, you join the cast.

Early in the dry season, the river level had dropped dramatically, exposing a silt bank about 50 metres offshore. To superstitious Banarsis like Shashank, the sight of the sandbar was a bad omen. But pilgrims paid no heed, engrossed in matters of the soul, like busy delegates to a spiritual convention that had been in permanent session since Shiva, the first sadhu, Lord of the Universe, Lord of the Beasts, Lord of the Penis, left his mountain hermitage with consort Parvati, daughter of the Himalayas, and settled in Kashi. The 'sacred zone' of the city, a capillary network of lanes enclosed in the *panchakroshi* — a kind of spiritual ring road formed by an ancient pilgrim's path — encompasses layers of history. In 528 BC Siddhartha Gautama preached his first sermon as the enlightened Buddha before an audience of five people at Deer Park, just outside it. A thousand years later, the low-caste poet-composer Kabir — the son of a poor Muslim weaver who challenged both the Vedas and the Koran and propagated his own mystic faith based on love — was a familiar figure on the ghats. Islamic invaders and Christian missionaries all dreamt of conquering Varanasi, but the bastion of Hinduism, India's true north, held firm.

Spellbound by the teeming life of the city, I was unaware that my visit coincided with a unique religious and theatrical event. In the weeks leading up to Dussehra, the Hindu festival marking Rama's victory in battle over the demon king of Lanka, productions of the Ram Lilas, or Deeds of Rama, are staged in towns and villages across India, but the most elaborate production takes place at Ramnagar, on the right bank of the Ganga, a short distance upstream from Varanasi. Sitting on the veranda one afternoon, I'd met one of the other guests, a young American choreographer, Alissa Mello, who'd come with the sole purpose of attending the entire cycle of thirty-one performances staged over a month at various open-air locations around the town. It was a kind of Indian Bayreuth, attended by over half a million people each year, and that night I crossed the river with Alissa to witness the spectacle. I was quite relieved when Alissa invited me to join her at that evening's performance.

In the early seventeenth century, Tulsidas's version of Rama's story spawned a hugely popular form of religious theatre. In 1830, the British 'Company School' artist James Princep sketched the event at Ramnagar, which has been staged annually on the site for around 200 years. Little has changed in form or substance in the years since his visit. As in Elizabethan England, women cannot be actors. Instead, boys play all the main roles, including the female parts. The choice of child actors lends a more iconic quality to their performance, and the tremulous delivery of their lines gives an added poignancy to India's great national drama.

It was approaching dusk when Alissa and I arrived in Ramnagar, a town dominated by a fort. Built in 1725, fifty years before the American Revolution, the fort was the ancestral home of a line of kings said to be Shiva's ambassadors on earth. A large crowd had assembled at Panchavati Crossing, normally busy with traffic, now a vast open air theatre. They were villagers from the hinterland mainly, many of them illiterate, drawn by the oral power of Rama's story and the prospect of a big night out. It was day seventeen of the cycle, when Rama learns that Sita has been abducted, and when India's humblest animals and people — a vulture, the monkeys and a low-caste woman — step forward willing to sacrifice their lives to rescue her. The price of admission suited the villagers' pockets — the event was free, and there must have been 20,000 people milling around, raising clouds of dust that hung suspended in the slanting rays of the afternoon sun. The crossing was only one of a number of sites dotted over a 12-square-kilometre area where performances took place during the month. Stages, tents and paper effigies of some of the characters had been erected, between which actors and audience would migrate.

It was a rare thing to see Indian villagers out and about in their finery for an evening of entertainment that did not involve a wedding. Tattooed village women wore flashy jewellery on their ears, noses, necks, wrists, ankles and toes — in fact every visible part of their anatomy — and one stately *kisan*, or farmer, cut a dashing figure in a dusty set of tails, carrying an antique cane with a highly polished brass grip in the shape of a duck. Another man, obviously educated, carried a battery-powered torch and a thick, dog-eared copy of Tulsidas's *Ramcharitamanas*, the text on which the evening's entertainment would be based. All night he would scrupulously follow the action to ensure no deviation from the original.

The Ram Lilas of Ramnagar was virtually a year-round enterprise. Sourcing materials for the sets begins in February, and in June fifty Brahmin boys vie for the key roles in the epic. Tall boys with fine features are preferred, but two qualifications are essential: their voices must be unbroken and they must have no facial hair. They can be inducted as young as eight, progressing through the lesser roles to play Rama. Vinay Kumar Vyas, the boy who was playing one of Rama's brothers, Shatrughna, that night, would be Rama the following year, becoming the fourth generation of his family to receive the honour. After cast selection, a handful of the boys are taken from their families and housed in a rundown dharamsala not far from the fort, where they undergo intensive training for three months. Every morning at five o'clock the boys begin learning their lines, while artisans all over town build sets and the directors plan the largest theatrical spectacle in India. The maharaja pays the boys a paltry fee of ten rupees plus food per day, and 2001 rupees at the end of the month, a total of less than two dollars a day. As soon as their voices break or hair appears on their upper lips, their services are no longer required. But their celebrity, while brief, is spectacular. To their adoring audiences, the boys do not simply play gods; they *are* gods.

As we stood waiting for the action to begin, the crowd near us suddenly parted, making way for a group of men bearing a palanquin on their shoulders. In it was Sita, or at least the boy who played her part, festooned with garlands, mirror-work armbands and a shoulder-length wig. Before the goddess, grown men and women were prostrating themselves in reverence, and although Sita had no role in that evening's episode, her presence was considered essential, if only to avoid disappointing those who'd come from far-off places and could only attend this one night of the cycle.

Just then the maharaja, who sponsors the entire event, made a dramatic entrance, seated in a swaying *howdah* high above the ground on the caparisoned back of one of his elephants. The pachyderm strode slowly but deliberately through the crowd, as the maharaja reclined on bolsters, dressed in rich vestments, jewellery and a cap.

Maharaja Anant Narain Singh was new in the job, having assumed the throne on the death of his father in the year 2000. He was a pale-skinned young man who'd not quite shed his baby fat, and whose shoulders were set in a permanent shrug. No longer vested with temporal powers, the maharajas survived on popular goodwill and respect for tradition, but everyone I spoke to in Varanasi gave the current incumbent low marks for charisma, effort and performance. Despite his unpopularity, the maharaja's arrival signalled that the show must begin.

As Rama and Lakshman entered the field of action, the crowd parted, forming a wave as people bent down to touch the divine brothers' feet. Drums pounded and cymbals clashed as the two young boys, wearing gold crowns and holding bows and arrows, took up their positions. Caked in make-up, they were so heavily costumed that their small faces were barely visible. They'd been training for months in order to master the declamatory, almost nagging style in which their lines must be delivered. Now the moment had come.

With great presence for a small boy, Rama paused and began to wail in a high-pitched grief-stricken voice that Sita — now disappeared from sight — had been kidnapped. There were no microphones, but his rhythmic cadence carried across the heads of the multitude, now crouched in pin-drop silence. The abduction of Sita was no distant tragedy; the horror and shame of it were intensely felt among the crowd, as if it had happened that same day to their own wives, mothers or sisters. The boy Rama's lament, half-recited, half-sung, recalled an animal's whimpering for a lost mate. Then, hoisted onto the shoulders of some men, he was carried the short distance to the next tableaux.

Leading me through the crowd with the confidence of a veteran, Alissa was bursting with a typically American enthusiasm for the pageant, all focused and verbalised. She had attended every performance so far, getting more excited with each one, and gleefully pointed out pockets of elderly men, the Ramayani sadhus, who spent their lives reciting the epic, or travelling to various productions of it. Following the Ramayanis, we made our way to the halting place where the next scene would be played out.

There stood Jatayu, an effigy of the old vulture who is one of the most beloved characters in the epic. Sita sees the ragged bird as she is carried off by Ravana but, fearing that Jatayu will be harmed if he tries to rescue her, instructs him instead to find Rama and tell him of her fate. But Jatayu is a proud old bird and he tries to talk sense to the arrogant Ravana, who only mocks him. As Sita fears, Jatayu — whose tattered plumage testifies to many battles — allows his chivalry to overcome his judgement and, instead of fleeing, engages the ten-headed demon king in mortal combat. But his claws and beak are no longer sharp, and Ravana lops off his wings and Jatayu falls to earth.

The audience knew what was coming, the tragic scene in which Rama finds the fallen vulture. The bird clings to life, saving its last breath until he can tell Rama what has happened to Sita. Rama rests his hand on Jatayu to ease the old bird's pain, begging him to pull through so that they can spend more time together. But Jatayu is halfway to heaven and replies, 'When will I get another chance to die in the lap of God?'

On the baked earth fairground in front of us, the boy Rama stood dwarfed beside a 2.5-metre-high effigy of Jatayu. 'If any sinner takes your name,' he declared in the tremulous voice of a child, 'he is SAVED!'

A wave of audible grief rippled across the crowd, a collective heart-wrenched gasp, as the setting sun tinted the high scattered clouds in rose. Taking a burning sheaf of grass, the boy Rama circled Jatayu, just as a Hindu son will circle his father's funeral pyre. Then, placing the torch to the straw-stuffed effigy, he stood back as it exploded into flame, covering his face against the intense heat which died down in minutes, leaving only a scatter of embers.

For the next few hours, Rama and his brother wandered the dusty maidan asking birds, animals, even insects, if anyone had seen his Sita. Everything in nature reminds him of her. When no one can enlighten him, he turns finally to the moon. The crowd is dumbstruck, terrified. They have come from their villages where Rama's kindness and heroism are legend, only to see him shattered. He weeps, a boy. Here and there a voice was raised. 'Don't worry, Rama, we support you', and then the scattered voices gathered into a chorus, and they were cheering for him, 'Jai Sri Ram', victory to Rama. It was the cry I'd heard of Ayodhya, redeemed here in piety. In his hour of crisis, God is saved by his people, and never looks back.

In the Tulsidas tradition of northern India, the relationship between man and God is uncommonly intimate. The Hindu Bhakts believe that even all-powerful gods have no defence against their people's devotion, no more than parents could ignore the pleas of their own children. On the unlit field, we continued to pick our way around by torchlight, treading in fresh cow pats and trying not to get crushed by the maharaja's elephant. The crowd moved calmly in an orderly fashion, although the maharaja's police guard could not resist beating a few poor souls with their lathis. Sometimes we took wrong turns and ended up far from the action, but at others found ourselves seated in the front row, within reach of the small gods.

Wandering among the crowds after sunset, Rama and his brother seek out a low-caste woman who has spent years in penance in a forest ashram. Shabari has grown old waiting for this moment, but embraces it with the joy of a young woman. She washes Rama's feet and gathers some fruits, tasting them before offering them to her Lord, who accepts everything the woman offers him, unmindful of caste prohibitions. When she asks him how she can better serve him, Rama replies, 'Dear lady, I recognise no other kinship except devotion. Whatever may be a man's caste, piety, wealth, power or abilities, if he lacks devotion he is worth less than a cloud without water.' Shabari points the brothers in the direction of the monkey king Sugreeva, whose simian army will be their strength in the final battle to free Sita and slay Ravana. There will be another cremation that night, as Shabari steps into the fire, her life's work complete. The final scene for the evening is the first meeting of Rama and Hanuman, a partnership that will usher in the long-delayed golden age of Ramrajya. As he did in order to win his bride, Rama seals his alliance with Sugreeva by passing a test with his bow, felling seven trees with a single arrow. Amid the cheers of the vast audience, the boy Rama and his brother are both lifted onto Hanuman's shoulders and carried from the field of faith.

Whether dumbstruck in reverence, or ecstatically roaring '*Raja Ram Chandra ki Jai*' (Glory of Raja Ram forever) as they did at the end of some scenes, I have never seen an audience so completely engrossed in a religious service or theatrical performance, their souls 'roused by passion and charmed by eloquence', as the philosopher David Hume once described the impact of great art.[6] In a noble myth lay rapture. On the final night, the royal family's elephants would be placed at the disposal of Rama, Sita and Lakshman. All three would ride to the fort to be met by a barefoot maharaja who, dressed like a commoner, would wash their feet, then watch them eat a great feast.

Tulsidas died on Asi Ghat in Varanasi in 1623 at the age of ninety-one. His ashes were scattered in the Ganges, but he still speaks to India and, to my surprise, he had also spoken to me. His evocation of Jatayu's sacrifice had brought tears to my eyes. In the Upanishads it is written that 'God, the maker of All, the great spirit ever seated in the hearts of creatures, is fashioned by the heart, the understanding and the will. They who know that become immortal.'[7]

Sometimes India is like a lover who insists on showing you their worst side, knowing that you will still love them. At Ayodhya, I had seen the worst things that religion can make men do; to be God-intoxicated can be quite lethal. Now I had felt its glory. My time in India had been full of darkness and light, my experiences contradictory. But on a dusty field on the east bank of the Ganges, a simple theatre of the heart had taught me the true meaning of Rama's story.

And understanding is the stairway to devotion.

22

Swimming in Varanasi

All places of pilgrimage he finds within himself.
Narsinh Mehta (1414–1479)[1]

At Tulsi Ghat, a short walk north of Asi Ghat, the stone steps rise steeply away from the Ganga, crowned by a small shrine to the monkey god Hanuman. Passing the shrine I paused to clasp my hands and bow my head before the idol.

India is contagiously spiritual. The Hindi word for journey — *yatra* — has religious overtones, and 'What is your religion?' is the fourth most commonly asked question, behind 'What is your good name?', 'Which country?' and 'Are you married?'. If you nominate a faith, however qualified, Indian friends won't miss bringing a gift on the appropriate day of that tradition. If you say you're an atheist almost nobody will believe you. One day you find you have purchased an idol of Ganesh — just because he's such a cute god — and installed it in your home. Next, you begin felicitating all your Indian friends on the occasion of their religious festivals, from Eid to Holi and Guru Nanak's birthday. India's spiritual promiscuity has seduced you. Like Sri Ramakrishna, you are happy to 'Bow down and worship where others kneel, for where so many have adored, the kind Lord must manifest Himself, for He is all mercy'.[2]

Veer Bhadra Mishra had been up since first light, saying his prayers and performing his ritual ablutions. Every morning he would open his window facing the river and whisper a few of Tulsidas's verses. Then, dressed only in a thin cotton dhoti, he would descend the ghat to the water's edge and ease his body waist-deep into the river. Taking a few drops of water in his palm, he would dab it on his forehead, then plunge beneath the surface several times until he was completely drenched. Standing with his hands clasped, facing the rising sun, he would recite the Gayatri Mantra, then take a small sip of the water and return to his home to complete his prayers.

Late that morning, I found him in his reception room seated on a takht which was covered in mattresses and bolsters, and which occupied half the room. In the other half, some sofas and chairs were arranged in a semicircle before the platform. With a rangy frame, silver hair and luxuriant moustache, Dr Mishra looked more like a character from a Western movie — perhaps an ageing gunslinger — than a Hindu holy man. His mouthful of unruly teeth was a testament to bad dentistry, and the crows' feet around his eyes told of many smiles. His shoulders were wrapped in a simple, undyed woollen shawl.

When Tulsidas died at Asi Ghat in 1623, his followers elected one among them to carry on the poet's Bhakti tradition of personal devotion to Rama. Dr Mishra was the current mahant — from the Sanskrit *maha*, meaning great — the manager of a temple established by the saint some four centuries earlier. When he was eleven, Veer Bhadra — which means 'gentle and brave', and was the name of Lord Shiva's assistant — received the *janeau*, or holy string of an orthodox Brahmin, to be worn looped over the left shoulder and under the right armpit for the rest of his life. When he was fourteen, the death of his father, Bankey Ram Mishra, propelled him into the role of spiritual and religious leader of the Sankat Mochan Temple, one of Varanasi's most popular and important mandirs.

Although well versed in the Hindu scriptures from an early age, he was the first member of his family to undertake a secular education. He majored in civil engineering, and with a passion for mathematics and science, completed his doctorate. Married with children, his extended family occupied a warren of buildings surmounting the terraced ghat named after Tulsidas, who is reputed to have lived at house number B2/16. There, a pair of wooden sandals said to have belonged to the saint-poet is kept in a small shrine, like Rama's sandals that occupied the throne of Ayodhya, waiting for the prince's return.

I had called ahead from Delhi, asking whether the mahant would be available to meet me in the weeks before Dussehra, but had fudged the purpose of my visit. Our previous contacts had been in connection with his long-running campaign to save the Ganga from the human and industrial waste that made bathing in the river, let alone drinking from it, a health hazard. He was himself just recovering from a bout of hepatitis, no doubt due to his daily contact with the water. He'd had polio as a child, and walked with a stilted gait, and his skin was dimpled with small scars, perhaps a skin disorder or a long-gone case of pox. His campaign to save the river had made him known all over the world, and had influenced Rajiv Gandhi to launch a national clean-up campaign. But that was twenty years ago, and the issue had long since fallen through the cracks of the bureaucracy. Still, Dr Mishra battled on, running a small institute dedicated to monitoring the state of the river, in addition to his job of managing one of the most important and respected temples in Varanasi.

At sixty-six, he was prone to complain that his life was no longer his own. Staff from his nearby office shuttled back and forth carrying a constant stream of faxes and messages.

'I will tell you a joke,' he said, a weary smile crinkling his eyes as it spread across his lips. 'A mahant is somebody who has sinned in his seven previous lives, and is given this job as a punishment.'

Behind him, through an east-facing window, the alluvial flats on the east bank of the Ganga stretched into the distance. Miles wide, they disappeared under water during the monsoon, re-emerging in the drier months leading into winter. It was a layered view that the window framed. Beyond the vast floodplain, unblemished by signs of human habitation, stood a distant line of trees, and beyond the trees, the sky. Four hundred years ago, Tulsidas himself had admired that view, the antithesis of the crowded, restive city where he spent his final years as a famous yet humble scribe in the service of the epics. My time in Varanasi would be spent at the feet of the mahant, searching his wisdom for answers to questions that were pressing on me, the airy view behind him becoming a kind of mandala, or object of contemplation. Which was more powerful, I began to wonder — the beauty and majesty of nature, or the simple window that framed the view?

Now, seated before him, pride and embarrassment competed to tie knots in my tongue. As a writer I'd had cause on several occasions to speak to him, but this was different. I was embarrassed about seeking spiritual guidance. All I knew was that I trusted him, unlike the legions of scheming pandas, purohits and pujaris whose gouging ways make life a misery for so many Hindus, and the clever, charismatic gurus who cast their spells on mystically inclined foreigners. Much as I loved Dr Dubey in Ayodhya, his *troot-th* and serial chanting just didn't satisfy me. I remembered Gandhi's famous quote — that you get the guru you deserve — and hoped I deserved a good one. Would the esteemed mahant help a humble pilgrim who wished to understand more about Hinduism?

As he mulled over my request, Dr Mishra's time-troubled frown gave way to a more concentrated, thoughtful expression.

'You do one thing,' he said, sighting me along his protuberant nose. 'I am busy here at certain times of the day. But if you come once in the morning, maybe around eleven o'clock, and then again in the evening, either here or at the temple, I will try to answer any questions you may have.'

In my lap, the fingers that had been tightly crossed released their grasp.

The following morning, as I prepared to leave the Hotel Ganges

View for my first meeting with the mahant, I found my host, Shashank, pacing the veranda with an expression of deep concern.

'It's the kutta,' he said, his normally equable features upset. 'Some malady is afflicting her.'

One of the guesthouse dogs had taken ill, and no sooner had Shashank revealed the fact than two of his helpers emerged from inside, carrying the animal in a towel and laying it on an antique marble-topped table. The poor dog was virtually comatose, breathing heavily with a tremor in one of its legs. Behind the boys came Shashank's mother, wearing the white sari of widow, and shaking her head sadly. Further along the veranda a man whom I assumed to be a vet was taking syringes and ampoules from a valise. Approaching the animal with a large syringe in hand, he dabbed its scrawny limb with a swab and gave it four deep jabs. The pet registered not even the mildest protest. Administering one last poke in the dog's butt, the vet packed up his things, reclaimed his shoes from the pile at the front door, and departed. Wishing Shashank and his mother the best of luck for the dog's speedy recovery, I followed the departing vet, and headed for Dr Mishra's residence.

Varanasi wears its crud with pride, all funky and familiar, a symbol of higher preoccupations. Evidence of hardship was everywhere — an Untouchable sweeper scratching away at piles of garbage with a feeble straw broom; a legless beggar dragging himself across the pavement. To live in India is to come to terms with these things, even as they shame and repulse you.

At the putative house of Tulsidas I found the mahant perched on his takht, perusing the morning newspapers. Interest rates were down, which meant income for temples and religious institutions, most of which lived off interest on fixed deposits, was also down. Given India's lack of an effective social-security system, that meant hardship for those who relied on charities. The rich lavished money on temple construction, but other charitable works lagged behind.

'We priests are not so smart as to buy and trade in shares,' the mahant said, suggesting with a sweep of his arm that I take the seat to his right. 'Anyway, that is a big distraction. These religious institutions can only survive in a congenial environment. Yet, if even *they* become commercial, there will be no truly spiritual institutions left.'

The previous day I had left him with the first of many questions. Hindu friends had told me that their faith was essentially amoral; a religion with no commandments, that whether an act was right or wrong simply depended on the circumstances. Even the gods killed and cheated didn't they?

The mahant folded one arm under the other and cupped his great jaw in his hand.

'Name any action,' he said, challenging me with a piercing stare. 'Imagine two men are killers. One killed to defend his family from harm, the other to rob somebody. One is innocent and the other is guilty. Why? Because the motive is different. Soldiers are also killing, yet we regard them as heroes. Why? Because in some situations, maybe it's justified. We say that any action can be either sinful or meritorious. It depends on its relation to place and time, the situation and the intention.'

He was right, of course. Crime *is* relative to time and place. Once it was legal to burn witches in America. Pillars of the community would light the bonfire, but no longer. Today it's a crime to drink alcohol in Saudi Arabia, but not in Australia, where it's almost a crime to drink anything else. I was about to mention child abuse as an unqualified evil, but hesitated when I remembered that the age of consent differs from place to place and time to time.

'You see, the problem with humanity is that we are prisoners of action,' said the mahant, breaking into a chain of melodious Sanskrit shlokas (verses), and then translating them. 'In Sanskrit we say karma *bandha* — the bonds of action. We have no choice but to act. So long as anyone is alive, he must draw the breath. That is an action, and all actions have consequences. You may swallow an insect, or pass on some deadly virus to the person next to you. So, we live in a world where we must act, and cannot avoid the consequences of those actions. This is the law of karma. Does it sound like an amoral philosophy? Whether you agree with reincarnation or not, the concept of reap whatever you may sow will be familiar to you.'

I had heard that to be Hindu you must be born a Hindu. Was it true? The mahant nodded, closing his eyes drowsily for a moment as he pulled his feet up under his thighs.

'Yes, it is true that some people believe that. But in our Hinduism, there are many different paths, all leading to the same destination. You can reach the Divine by *jnana*, karma or Bhakti. That is, by knowing the Vedas, or by actions contributing to good karma, or through meditation and physical austerities, or by devotion. The Bhakti path was the way of Jatayu.'

My ears pricked up at the mention of the noble bird.

'Tulsidas-ji says, "Who could be like Jatayu? That vulture was a very dirty bird, eating non-vegetarian flesh. Who could be lower than him?" Yet that bird attained the place in heaven that the *yogis* and *rishis* could not attain. He died in the lap of Lord Ram, and tears rolled down Ram's face as that bird left this world. Ram begged him not to go. He said, "You are like my father." When I read that story it raises the hairs on my skin. Tulsidas-ji said that bird did the impossible to free people from fear and terror. It is also said that all the Brahmins on earth are below Jatayu. Rama himself said, "There are nine kinds of devotion, and if a person has even one of these, then he is so dear to me." So if one becomes dear to God, then everything is solved. That is the path of Bhakti and it is open to all persons all over the world. There is no discrimination because once you are bhakt, your caste, your creed, your nation and way of life, nothing can be a barrier to you, and you must be accepted better than any other Hindu in society.'

By translating the *Ramayana* into Hindi, Tulsidas had broken the Brahmins' monopoly over the Hindu scriptures, all previously written in Sanskrit, which only they could read. It unleashed an efflorescence of devotion that revitalised the faith and gave it strength to survive the challenges of life under Muslim rule. The religion of idols and chanting and hymns that dominates northern India today is largely the fruit of Tulsidas's democratic Hinduism and his *Ramcharitamanas*, the only book in Hindi widely accepted as scripture. But what was the point of a Brahmin spending his life in the study of the Vedas, when a bhakt off the street could instantly obtain a higher status? The mahant simply smiled.

'It's not a competition,' he said. 'We say there are many different paths to suit many different personalities. The person who knows the Vedas will certainly be respected, even revered maybe. But the illiterate man also must have a chance. He may not be able to read the Vedas, but by his actions he may be regarded as equal or even superior to a Brahmin.'

Coming from a Brahmin, I found this egalitarian take on Hinduism intriguing. What about caste, the hereditary assigning of status to individual Hindus, locking them into a lifelong, unjust hierarchy?

'You will be knowing about the father of our nation, Gandhi-ji,' the mahant replied. 'He became a mahatma. It means *maha*, great, and *atman*, soul. Yet he was born into the caste of Vaishya, the traders. By his actions, he became a saint, higher in status to any Brahmin.'

Newspaper reports had elaborated on the case of the American Hindu convert who'd been barred from entering a temple in Orissa. Who was right? The grim priests or my mild mahant?

'Unfortunately it is not understood by everyone in India,' the mahant said. 'Let those fellows do what they are doing. It is certainly a prescribed way of worshipping. But, personally, I would be pained to be responsible for enforcing such restrictions. At my temple, yes, only Brahmins can perform the services, but anybody, Dalits, foreigners, even Muslims are welcome to bring their offerings, some food or flowers, and the pujaris will convey them to Lord Hanuman-ji for his blessings. If you like our practices and if you are drawn to this — if you love this — then you have all the right to follow the path. That vulture,

Jatayu, couldn't be a Brahmin, but he became more than a Brahmin. Gandhi-ji was a Vaishya, but became a mahatma. Even *you* can also bypass the Brahmins and go ahead of them.'

'But you said it's not a competition!' I shot back.

The mahant smiled a wide, toothy smile.

'You are right,' he said. 'It seems you are following my words so carefully, I should be more careful what I am telling you.'

★ ★ ★

Asia's — and India's — first Nobel laureate, Rabindranath Tagore, once said, 'Faith is the bird that feels the light and sings when the dawn is still dark.' Earlier that morning I had undertaken that essential rite of any visit to Banaras — the boat ride on the Ganga. It was a blue, translucent morning and I was crossing Anandamayee Ghat on foot when a boatman called Hiro made landfall and asked if I'd like a ride. The sun had not yet risen, but the sound of bhajans drifted across the water from the *dharmasalas* fronting the river, along with a suite of other sounds etched in a background of silence; the caw of a crow, the creak of the oar, the slaps and grunts of the laundrymen, and the distant clang of temple bells. The surface of the river whirled and eddied like molten silver, reflecting the white and orange lights of the temples. A single star, perhaps a planet, lingered in the sky. Hiro's paddles were oblong slats of timber painted blue and attached to bamboo poles. As he rowed, they left arcs of concentric rings on the surface of the water, erased by the subsequent stroke. We glided through an armada of small votive lamps fuelled by camphor oil and set adrift by pilgrims on the main bathing ghat, past palaces and guesthouses, before returning to Asi.

The dialogue with Dr Mishra had been proceeding well, interspersed with long walks through Varanasi's older quarters, and happy hours browsing the prodigiously well-stocked shelves at the Harmony Bookshop. There was a lot to cover in a religious tradition so broad that it embraced the world's first conscious atheists, the Charvak materialists, whose happy motto was 'While you live, live happily. Take loans and drink ghee', and who believed the soul died with the body. At the Internet cafe a few doors down from the guesthouse, I supplemented our sessions with research, Googling 'Tulsidas' and finding his nine kinds of devotion: to admire the saints; to love the stories of Rama; to serve Rama; to sing Rama's praises; to repeat the name of Rama; to practise virtue and control vice; to see God in the world; to be accepting and not find fault in others; and to be honest and transparent. Some of the nine I had no hope of achieving; but I'd always seen God in nature, and I loved the story of Rama.

Scrolling through the pages, it struck me as odd that I should come all this way to Varanasi and end up spiritually surfing the web. But if Indian banks could install automated teller machines that enable online offerings to be made at places of pilgrimage, and Catholic parishes in the United States could outsource the saying of masses for particular causes to India on cost grounds,[3] anything was possible. In the next cubicle, another one of my fellow guests at the Hotel Ganges View, a young American, was trying to book a train ticket through the new online reservation system of the Northern Railways, which, if it worked, threatened to destroy the ancient Indian art of queue-jumping. Like *shishyas* kneeling before their gurus, we were gathered in our cyber temple, submitting our inquiries and requests to the global guru of the age.

During my wanderings in the city I had met another Hindu priest, Vyas-ji, whose job was to administer the oath to pilgrims intending to undertake the Panchakroshi pilgrimage, a six-day, 80-kilometre walk along the perimeter of the 'sacred zone' of Kashi, west of the river. Vyas-ji's office was beside Kashi Vishwanath Temple, a shrine whose inner sanctum is off-limits to non-Hindus. I'd spent a day in a hired jeep driving the route of the pilgrimage, which traverses a wide range of landscapes, from rural idyll to the cantankerous Grand Trunk Road, and hadn't expected more that a few insights from the priest into the current popularity of the pilgrimage, which should be completed on foot. But before I could say no, he had led me to the altar where the blessings were given to those who had it. Kneeling before him as he intoned the Sanskrit mantras, I was given a handful of rice and told to discard a grain or two for every verse he uttered, so that by the end, no grain remained in my palm. It was customary at the end to give a small donation, and for once I was more than happy to oblige. Before leaving, I asked Vyas-ji — who apparently could give you quite a scolding on a bad day — for his advice on my quest. To be a Hindu, he said, I needed a guru and the guru must give me a mantra. Next morning at my session with the mahant, I asked him why he hadn't given me a mantra, and whether we needed to formalise his role as my guru.

'You don't need any mantra or guru,' Dr Mishra said, laughing. 'Tulsidas-ji's *Ramcharitamanas* says this, and it is the backbone of this religion in northern India.'

Surely there must be protocols and procedures one must undertake, awkward ceremonies to embarrass and humiliate the initiate? What did you need to do to qualify, I asked him.

'You must love God,' said the mahant.

'Which one?' I countered. 'There are 330 million of them.'

'Love at least one. More if you prefer,' he replied.

'Only Hindu gods?'

'At least one Hindu god you should love. But gods of other religions also, if you like.'

'Anything else?'

'*Nuth*-thing.'

When the clock struck one, as agreed, I left the mahant to his lunch and headed down the steep staircase to Tulsi Ghat, full of the excitement of a hurdle cleared. Not only would I not need to be reborn to embrace Hinduism, but I could keep all the bits and pieces of other faiths and philosophies I had found interesting and useful over the years. I could wear my own clothes, eat meat, and not even be very religious. Work could be a kind of worship. The quest for bliss — which had always left me cold — was optional. You could become a Hindu, remain a Christian, do your work, be yourself and not become a spiritual bore or chanting drone. It sounded like my kind of faith.

With the sun just about vertically overhead, the riverside concourse was almost completely deserted, as if all its bustling humanity had been scorched off. Stripped of the crowds, the city flaunted its grand towers and battlements, a fortress of Hinduism. But despite its reputation as a place of redemption, Varanasi has always been a commercial city as well — unlike in Christianity, having money was no bar *per se* to salvation. If anything, it indicated that a Hindu had observed the injunction to be productive in life's second asrama, or stage. Most of the great stone concourses and mansions fronting the river were constructed with donations given by maharajas and other wealthy patrons. Yet there was also room for small businesses, backpacker guesthouses and small shops selling precious stones with their signs pointedly written in English. On the ghats of Varanasi, torrid touting went hand in hand with piety, as hawkers and crooks buzzed around, beseeching tourists to follow them into the darkened alleyways, to silk shops and yoga centres, or to change money or buy drugs. I didn't trust any of them, and although I tried to maintain a breezy distance, occasionally I was provoked into anger by their incessant offers of goods and services.

But that afternoon, even the touts were having their lunch, and I took the rare opportunity to walk undisturbed along the riverfront, admiring its imposing architecture. Barriers were falling away, and I experienced a feeling of being at home in India, taking pleasure in what it is, rather than fussing constantly over what it should be. I envied the bathers' freedom as they prayed and frolicked in the river. Would I ever have the courage to join them?

Heading towards mid-town, I rounded a bend and came up against what must be the world's most grotesque building, the electric crematorium which perches above the ghats on weirdly tall columns, like a praying mantis of Black Death. The huge incinerator was built as a pollution-control measure, providing cheap cremations for poor families who could not afford firewood and who would otherwise dump the bodies of their loved ones directly into the Ganga. But because electricity supplies in the state of Uttar Pradesh had become so erratic, some people still resorted to dumping. The crematorium must have been out of commission when I passed, for several Untouchables were tending burning pyres directly in front of the useless eyesore. Across the river, groups of pilgrims could be seen performing their ablutions on the sandbanks, technically outside Varanasi's sacred zone, but unwilling to subject themselves any longer to the filth along the ghats.

Further on, I crossed the city's main ghat, a popular spot crowded with pilgrims, sightseers and signage, beyond which the buildings were blackened by wood smoke. At Manikarnika, the burning ghat, I came upon an array of fires smouldering in the open on rising ground, overlooked by a hollow-eyed mansion built by the Maharani of Indore. It looked like the end of time, which in a sense it was — the hands had fallen off the clock tower that overlooks the pyres. Kites and crows wheeled overhead, while beneath them, the incessant activity around the death pits carried on. It was a sombre place, yet somehow comforting, death no longer a stranger. Adding to the air of dissolution, the spires of Hindu temples that had collapsed into the river poked above the surface of water. Standing at the margins, the tourists stared, stunned into silence by the ruthless efficiency of the Untouchable *doms*, as they raked over the ash heaps, picking out the odd gold filling. It resembled a medieval scene in dark oils. According to Hindu philosophy, when the universe dies, it will die here.

As I stood there hypnotised by the rhythm of death, one of the young touts that infest the place walked up to me, waved his hands in my face and said in a forceful tone, 'No photos.' I wasn't carrying a camera. But before I could say so, he leant towards me with a worldly air and whispered, 'But if you like, I can help you.'

The invention of taboos in order to profit from them is as old as death. Finding fifty *paisa* — a coin of no value — in my pocket, I gave it to him, a calculated insult that provoked his anger. Bad karma was everywhere in this sacred but hellish place. It was time to move on.

Intending to cover the distance from the burning ghats to the railway bridge that marks the northern boundary of Varanasi, I wandered into a landscape of unbelievable squalor. Animal carcases rotted and men urinated on the open river bank, the stench so overwhelming that I gagged several times before retreating into the alleyways of the old city, unable to complete my journey. Fumbling for a path through the twisting alleys barely wide enough for a cow to pass, I made my way to the golden spires of Kashi Vishwanath, India's pre-eminent Shiva temple, and one of the few barred to non-Hindus. But again, it was claustrophobic, the filthy alleys teeming with more touts proffering dubious services, and a heavy police presence to prevent violence between Hindus and the Muslims who controlled the neighbouring Jnana Vapi Mosque. The triple-domed, powder-blue masjid was built on the ruins of the original Hindu temple destroyed by order of the Mughal emperor Aurangzeb in 1669. At the adjacent Well of Knowledge, said to be the home of the living Shiva, the holy site resembled an armed camp, the Indian state's solution to ancient grievances.

The optimism of the morning, engendered by Mahant-ji's capacious welcome to Hinduism, had all but evaporated in the midst of Varanasi's squalor. The violence just below the surface in this holiest of Shiva's temples was the last straw. If, as the Hindu nationalist ideologue Savarkar wrote, the real and most important test of a Hindu is to feel like one, to adopt its culture and regard the land as sacred, then I never felt less a Hindu.

★ ★ ★

My walk along the Ganges had revived my scepticism, and as I headed to meet Mahant-ji at the Sankat Mochan Temple that night, I wondered about the value of a philosophy that so easily accepted squalor and injustice, and endowed violence with religious sanction. Those arrows that Ram had been shooting at Ramnagar all month weren't floral bouquets, and Hanuman's cudgel was lethal. Nobody expects society to be perfect, but if religion simply legitimises vulgar existence, then what actual purpose can it serve? And anyway, since when did I need a guru? Maybe I'd been in India too long.

At least at night you don't see most of India's horrors. The streets of Varanasi were alive with light and celebration, as Hindus observed the festival of Navratri, the Nine Nights of the Goddess Durga, symbol of maternal protection, fertility and wrath. In the congested lanes of the old city, people were anointing their ledgers and motor vehicles, schoolbooks and food, believing in the certain success of any venture begun in these auspicious days. With many people fasting during the day, the city had acquired the nocturnal intensity of the Islamic heartlands during Ramadan, and large crowds thronged temples, hotels and restaurants after sunset.

At the entrance to Sankat Mochan Temple in the south of the city, I arrived to find the evening arti — an uproarious form of worship involving clanging bells, singing and the passing of the devotees' hands over flaming oil lamps — in full swing. Touching the ground in respect as I crossed the threshold, I joined the congregation as it circled the shrine of the monkey god Hanuman, whose idol — said to date from Tulsidas's time — resembled two eyes upside down in bowl of bright orange sorbet. A small ensemble of musicians drummed up a storm with clanging gongs and a nagging chorus of 'SITARAM, SITARAM, SITARAM-JI, SITARAM, SITARAM, SITARAM'. It reminded me of a Baptist church service I'd once attended in a converted cinema hall in New York, except here there was no preacher and no sermon. In most

Hindu temples, the worship is quieter, more personal, but this bright band of believers made an invigorating change. Nevertheless, I recoiled inwardly at the sight of a group of devotees, including young children, grovelling before the deity on the checkerboard marble floor. Extravagant outpouring of devotion wasn't my path.

Making my way to the mahant's office in an upstairs room in the temple complex, I found him in the unexpected role of pupil, singing scales in a croaky voice at the behest of a pot-bellied troll of a man with a Friar Tuck hairstyle, seated at a harmonium.

'Christopher! This is Pandit-ji, my music teacher. We won't be a minute, so please join us,' he said.

Sitting cross-legged on the floor, the mahant closed his eyes in a frown of concentration, struggling to master the complex scales of a bhajan composed by Tulsidas, but almost immediately broke into a fit of coughing. Recovering his composure, he heroically resumed his song in a wobbly voice that fell far short of the high notes. He was singing by the seat of his pants, as Pandit-ji's fingers anxiously dug the notes from the harmonium, uncertain whether his pupil would make it. Then, out of the blue, the wheezing jalopy of Dr Mishra's voice struck the right chord, producing an almost mystical harmony, uplifted by hands and fingers which opened and closed like a lotus flower at the beginning and end of the day. It had gone eleven when he wrapped up his lesson and turned his attention to me.

'Did you have good day?' he asked, returning to sit on the floor in front of me after bidding farewell to the pandit.

I had warned my friend and adviser to expect tough questioning, not a hostile interrogation. But what transpired had more in common with a courtroom grilling than a respectful student's humble inquiry. Was he a sympathiser of the Sangh Parivar, I wanted to know? Was he a high-caste Brahmin of the kind who could not bear to touch an Untouchable? And what about all the filth and squalor I'd seen that day, even in temples and along the banks of the sacred river?

One by one, the priest listened to my questions calmly, responding with thoughtful answers that neither apologised for Hinduism's failings, nor defended the excrescences that disfigure such an old faith.

'Ram is much more than a temple, so I will never agree that doing that demolition was the work of Ram,' he said, when I asked whether he shared the joy some Hindus had felt after Babur's Mosque was felled. 'Every day people are demolishing buildings, and nobody feels there is anything bad about it, but the demolition in Ayodhya was different. Many people were saddened by it. Ram's mission was to free people from fear and terror, not to subject them to it. After Ayodhya, pieces of the mosque were taken around the country, but nobody offered me a piece of rubble. They know me. There was nothing religious in that action. There are many other important things we need to do today. If that thing is on the agenda at all, it should be very low. We probably won't get time to do it.'

Walking around Varanasi, with its thousands of temples and smaller shrines, and even hundreds of mosques and Buddhist *viharas*, I had found myself wondering if India was simply too God-focused. Maya would have been proud of me. So, it turned out, was the mahant.

'I fully agree,' he said, surprising me. 'We don't need any more temples. We can't take care of the temples we already have! I would argue this before any association of Hindus.'

Sometimes in India, people are excessively willing to tell you what they think you want to hear, and to hold back on news that might displease you. You are hoping that the air-conditioner will be fixed before summer? It will be done — by the winter — but they don't tell you that. Gurus can dazzle you with eloquence while picking your spiritual pocket. But the mahant was not trying to be all things to all people. He believed that India *was* the promised land of the Hindus, a land that had at times been besieged by aggressive proselytising by other faiths.

'First Buddhism weakened Hinduism, then for hundreds of years attacks by Muslim emperors were unrelenting. They levied a special tax on Hindus, so many converted to Islam,' he said. 'Look at the names of our cities. From Ghaziabad to Ghazipur you will find that the maximum numbers of names have a Muslim origin.'

On the issue of caste too, the mahant was prepared to be politically incorrect. He was appalled at the way low-caste leaders were blaming Brahmins for everything. Their term of abuse for those who disagreed was *manuwadi* — followers of the ancient and anachronistic Laws of Manu, which advocated strict caste separation.

'Show me where the Law of Manu is being implemented in this country! It is a nonsense. They are exaggerating all this for political gain. Because they have numbers, you see, they believe any insult they can hurl is all right, that they can tell any lie and it will be true. Let me tell you, my friend, it's open season on Brahmins nowadays. The pandit with the big stomach is blamed as the root of all evil. But this secularism is just crushing our society ... I tell you, my dear, whatever is left of India is with the manuwadis. If *we* go, India will go. And if India goes, the axle of all religions will be lost. Then who will sustain the world?'

Then again, he accepted that the pandits should get their own house in order. The state of their sacred River Ganges showed the defects in their piety.

'I don't know how we are surviving. It's God's grace that this country is not slipping away,' he said in a sombre moment. 'We never lived in an urban society like this. We don't have infrastructure. We think the wind god will clean our lanes. Even if you give a Brahmin 5000 rupees a month, he will not clean the road or toilet. That's his conditioning. But I can show you people who have changed, and India is an adaptable society.'

The fight to save the river was to Dr Mishra what the Battle of Kurukshetra was to Arjuna, the reluctant warrior of the *Bhagavad Gita*: a struggle for life against death, and light against darkness. At various points along its course, levels of faecal coliforms caused by sewage and the disposal of human and animal carcases were toxic. Irrigation canals, including one just above Ramnagar were making things worse, siphoning off vast volumes of water from the river and reducing its flow. Yet as a Hindu priest, Dr Mishra still felt obliged to take his daily dip and ritual sip, even though his health had clearly suffered as a result of doing so. He still remembered the exact moment when he first came face to face with the tragic reality of the river's affliction.

'It must have been in the mid-1960s. I was bathing at Tulsi Ghat, and I saw human faeces — raw sewage — floating very near to where I was doing my prayers. That was very, very disturbing,' he said.

For almost forty years he'd been fighting against the pollution, setting up the Swatcha Ganga campaign which funded a laboratory in Varanasi that constantly monitored pollution in the river and studied ways of ameliorating it. They'd concluded that a series of oxidation ponds that could work without electricity was the best solution, but vested interests, including the foreign aid lobby, were pushing for more expensive, less effective technologies to be used. Despite the odds against him, the indefatigable mahant refused to surrender to despair.

'Not all of those people whom we describe as Hindus are fully conscious of their obligations to our Mother Ganga. They should know what is God, and in some cases change their habits. I am not a member of any party, but I realise now that any great work for the society, for nature, for culture, cannot be done effectively without involvement in politics. This will take a long time, but in twenty to thirty years I think the whole nation will be toned up, and the society will become sufficiently responsible to take care of the fresh water bodies and rivers. One thing I know. The water that flows past us here is different every day, but the river remains the Ganga. She is sacred and she is eternal, just like our Sanatan Dharma, our Hinduism.'

Every time I felt soothed by an answer given by the mahant, another vicious criticism popped into my mind. The devil had my tongue ... or was it a Christian doctor I'd met in Orissa who'd said that the Hindu mind was enslaved by superstition?

'Perhaps Hinduism itself is the problem,' I suggested rather blithely to the mahant. 'Christian countries don't seem to have quite the same difficulties when it comes to public sanitation.'

'They have different problems,' said the mahant, his reply unusually brusque.

I detected the faintest hint of a raised hackle. The temptation to tease it out was irresistible.

'Even here in India, I've met people who embraced Christianity because they believe Hinduism lacks an adequate moral foundation,' I said, aware that I might be pushing things.

'Well, I don't care,' objected the mahant, who was only human after all. 'I pity such people that they don't know what this religion has to offer to the world today.'

But wasn't there a problem of authority? If every Hindu could tailor their morality to suit themselves, without the need to abide by fixed, universal standards, wasn't it just a philosophy of licence? Nathuram Godse had cited the *Gita* in defence of his murder of Gandhi. But the mahant had heard enough of my questions for one night.

'Look, nothing is perfect on this planet,' he said. 'But if you compare all religions of the world, I think we should be very, very happy that we have one that is much more open, and has given a lot of latitude for our spiritual practices and the path we can tread. Hindus believe in wellbeing and happiness in this world, and salvation in the next. We do not discriminate against gay people, or colourful people. Anyone can be saved. Even the flies and the insects will get salvation. So, in our diversity, where there are twelve philosophies, four castes, regional practices and so many gods, all these diverse rays meet in Ganga. It is Ganga that provides the focal point. The name of Ram provides a focal point. Tulsidas-ji said these two things are the basis for us to live in the Kaliyug, the dark age when hypocrisy is rampant. The sinners and criminals may now be very strong, but there are two things on which we can rely — Ram's name and the river.'

'Anyway,' he added, smiling with the self-conscious smile of a man who knows that his temper has almost gotten the better of him. 'As I have already told you, it's not a competition. The path may be different, but the destination in the same.'

Among some Hindus, there is a saying *Ishwar ek hai*. God is one. It is not high theology, but expresses the common view that people of all faiths, regardless of their differences, are striving for union with the same creator. The source of this liberalism can be found in the earliest Hindu text, the 4000-year-old *Rig Veda*, which teaches that 'Truth is one. Sages call it by different names'. In the *Bhagavad Gita*, Krishna expresses much the same sentiment when he says:

Even those who in faith worship other gods,
because of their love they worship me,
although not in the right way.[4]

'Hindu thought believes in the evolution of our knowledge of God. We do not say that the crimson flowers are all the truth, and the green leaves are all false,' wrote independent India's first president, Radhakrishnan. 'The soul of man is complex in character and so is the environment. The reactions of an infinite soul to an infinite environment cannot be limited to this or that formula ... Not one of them gives the whole truth, though each of them is partially true.'

Over centuries, India's Christians and Muslims, too, had been influenced by India's syncretic traditions. Even the illiterate Mughal emperor Akbar was moved by this spirit of soul convergence.

It was after midnight when a feeble scratching at the door attracted the mahant's attention. It was a temple attendant reminding him that his driver was waiting. We walked together down the stairs and across the mandir's darkened courtyard and climbed into his jeep. It wasn't long before we reached Asi Ghat, where the road surrenders to the river, and where my hotel was situated. Turning in his seat, the mahant handed me a box of sweets that had been blessed before the idol of Hanuman by one of the pujaris.

'I hope I will be seeing you in the morning,' he said. 'You know, I don't get the opportunity to talk like this very often. We mahants are trapped as well.'

Climbing the stairs to the guesthouse entrance, I found the veranda plunged in darkness and the front door locked. Pressing the doorbell brought one of the houseboys stumbling to the door, rubbing the sleep from his eyes. When he unlocked the door and let me in, I handed him the sweets.

'From Mahant-ji,' I said.

The houseboy stared at the box, as if he'd been given a bar of gold. 'You met Mahant-ji?' he said, thunderstruck.

Next morning I sensed an undercurrent of reverence when one of the houseboys brought me my chai. From the veranda I could see beyond the steel-grey Ganga a cloud bank of Himalayan proportions, visibly expanding as if captured by time-lapse photography. It was as pristine as a snowfield on top with a dark underside, a monumental facade consisting of nothing but moist air. Someone was giving the temple bell at the small shrine attached to the hotel an unholy thrashing, driving away evil. On a nearby rooftop, a young Westerner was doing his yoga, or puja — it could have been either — as a monkey rappelled down the side of the building. The bluff, hollow sound of a conch shell could be heard in the distance, while in the foreground, a water pump puttered.

As I took my breakfast, Shashank bounded onto the veranda, his features illuminated by a big smile. When he saw me, he made a movement with his hand, a sweeping forearm ending with a loose upward flick of the hand that suggested a problem solved.

'How's your dog. Has she responded to the treatment?' I asked.

'She has expired,' Shashank said with a beatific smile that suggested congratulations were in order.

'Oh. I'm sorry to hear that,' I said

What do you do with a dead dog in Varanasi, I wondered. But I needn't have.

'Our driver has taken her to the other end of Banaras, near to the railway bridge,' Shashank said breezily. 'He will dispose of her there in the river.'

At least it was downstream; we wouldn't be seeing the poor animal again. All that remained was a smouldering stub of incense on the table where the dog had been treated, placed there to purify the area. The smoke streamed in thick ripples, a wavering ribbon that mesmerised as it unfolded and expanded, minutely sensitive and submissive to the slightest breath of wind.

On the ghat that morning, heading for my darshan with the mahant, I found the Ganges in resilient mood, the air fresh and pilgrims dunking joyously. At Asi Ghat, where the river enters the city, the water is much cleaner than in other parts of Varanasi. Quite often the snouts of Gangetic dolphins could be seen breaking the surface of the water, startling pilgrims in boats. But the most striking aspect of the river's flow was its speed. Its very name means 'that which goes' and it flew like a bird as it rushed impatiently toward the distant ocean.

My arrival at the top of Tulsi Ghat coincided with the loud clanging of a temple bell and the delivery of some food scraps for the resident monkeys. Sidling nervously past them, I entered the house said to have once been Tulsidas's own home, and found Mahant Mishra looking refreshed in a newly laundered kurta and with his shock of silver hair neatly combed. Wearing a pair of oversized spectacles, he was poring over a sacred text, tracking the lines with his index finger.

'So,' he inquired, 'have you decided whether to become Hindu?'

'I think I *am* a Hindu,' I replied, 'Always have been. No need to become one.'

'That's good, *vairry* good,' said the mahant, pushing up into a cross-legged position and calling for sweets, cashew nuts and the frothy instant coffee that was the speciality of the house. 'Gandhi-ji said there are as many religions as there are individuals. Actually, this word "Hindu" is very new. Tulsidas-ji did not use it in any of his books, nor did he use the word "Mussalman". There is no need of following any religion. I say follow your dharma. Then you will never go wrong.'

I was leaving the next morning, and had come to say goodbye.

'Well, I will miss our conversations,' said the mahant. 'No more questions for me?'

There was one thing. I'd been thinking about it again, walking towards his home. Would it be all right, did he think, from a health perspective if, just once, I took a holy dip in the Ganga?

Squaring his shoulders, Dr Mishra looked down his long nose at me.

'Well, there are stretches of the river that are clean by any standards. Go about 15 kilometres upstream from Varanasi and you'll find beautiful clear water there. In the city, midstream is much cleaner than the banks.'

He smoothed his dhoti and averted his gaze uncharacteristically. My disappointment must have shown.

'But if you mean should you bathe here, on the ghat?'

I nodded. That was exactly want I meant.

'Well,' said the mahant. 'You know that there are many people in the city having jaundice. Many people who are having diarrhoea of one kind or another. Some expert came from America and collected the data and his report is with us. He says there is direct proof that people are getting these diseases by using Ganga water.'

'But you use it,' I said.

'Yes, and last year I got hepatitis.'

'Just from dipping? Or sipping it?'

The mahant smiled, abashed for some reason.

'Ahhh, what should I do? Let us invent a word between drinking and not drinking.'

'Gargling?'

'Maybe,' he said. 'I'm supposed to drink it. It is a sin for me to hate or suspect this water. Can you feel my problem, how painful it is not to be able to answer your question?'

But the mahant's existential dilemma over whether to sip or drink could not be allowed to distract me.

'Should I or shouldn't I take a dip, here, at Tulsi Ghat?' I pressed him.

'You see,' he said, grimacing slightly. 'At Tulsi Ghat the water will be cleaner than at the other ghats downstream.'

I knew that and told him so.

'Okay, okay,' he said finally, waving me off. 'You take a dip. Nothing will happen. But it *is* a proven fact that if the water is polluted you can catch diseases. Are we going to do some experiment here? It's a proven fact.'

Bending to touch his feet as he stood in the doorway of Tulsi Bhavan, I hurried away.

★ ★ ★

If you could visit only one place in India and still hope to feel that you had known the country, that place would be Varanasi. Yet the longer I stayed, the more keenly did I feel the invisible barriers that separate the indigene from the outsider. The separation simmered within me, a process of reduction, boiling down to the singular dilemma: to dip or not to dip? That was the question.

All day I'd been agonising about it, even venturing onto the ghat in the late afternoon. If Banaras was the quintessential Hindu place, a holy dip in the Ganga was surely the quintessential Hindu act, a baptism and reconciliation combined. As I crept hesitantly across the slippery bank at Asi Ghat, I found myself thinking about Hari Lal, his prayers and dictums about kindness and languages, how a few words of Hindi could take you a long way in India. Was I in his prayers, I wondered. And what were the words — in any language — that would take me to the river? It was my last night in Varanasi, an opportunity that might never come again. I'd been reading the *Bhagavad Gita*, jewel in the crown of Indian philosophy, in which God urges the reluctant warrior Arjuna to overcome his doubts and fears:

> *For all things born, in truth, must die,*
> *and out of death, in truth, comes life.*
> *Face to face with what must be,*
> *cease thou from sorrow.*
> *Action is greater than inaction:*
> *Perform therefore thy task in life.*[5]

I was stepping gingerly towards the water when I saw a bundle of rags floating on the surface. It was a curious shape, resembling a broad-shouldered hunchback seen from behind, and the current was gently rotating it, until back became front, and I found myself staring into the hollow eyes of a grinning cadaver. How it mocked me, that corpse. Overwhelmed by revulsion, I scrambled to get away.

Back at the hotel, I took a long, long shower, then joined Alissa and some newfound friends of hers for a clandestine drink on the terrace. Alcohol was not permitted at Shashank's place in deference to its location within the sacred zone, but I needed an antidote after the shock earlier in the evening, and found the company of my fellow travellers deeply reassuring. The conversation buzzed with excitement as people recalled the incredible things they'd seen, smelt, tasted, heard and done in Shiva's city. The young American I'd met in the Internet place that morning proudly showed the railway tickets he'd purchased online, paid for by credit card and had delivered to the hotel that afternoon. We toasted his success. But when the conversation turned towards the squalid state of the river and its environs, I felt as if the Ganga was stalking me.

'How could anyone swim in that water? It's so obviously filthy,' said one of the guests.

'I know,' I responded, feigning outraged incomprehension.

Over dinner that night, Shashank's chronic lamentations about India's paradise lost, the corruption of politicians and the cultural bankruptcy of the nouveau riche were almost comforting, a familiar dirge.

'What to do?' he concluded, as always, shrugging his shoulders.

Later that night, alone in my room at the guesthouse, I opened my dog-eared copy of the *Bhagavad Gita*, and began reading again at the point where God assumes the *avatar* of Krishna, and gives Arjuna his roadmap to perfection in this life and the next:

The man whose love is the same for his enemies or his friends,
whose soul is the same in honour or disgrace,
who is beyond heat or cold or pleasure or pain,
who is free from the chain of attachments

Who is balanced in blame and in praise,
whose soul is silent,
who is happy with whatever he has,
whose home is not in this world,
and who has love — this man is dear to me

But even dearer to me are those who have faith and love
and who have me as their End Supreme;
those who hear my words of Truth,
and who come to the waters of Everlasting Life.[6]

When I awoke next morning, the sun was in my eyes and the *Gita* lay open on the bed. There was a slight chill in the air, and the staff and guests of the Hotel Ganges View had yet to stir; even the ghats were quite empty. Slipping on a thin cotton kurta pajama and a pair of sandals, I grabbed a towel and headed out onto the concourse.

Hindus may consider Varanasi the ideal place to achieve moksha, but not everyone goes there to die. At Tulsi Ghat, a sprinkling of bathers were enjoying a pristine morning, some deep in prayer, others lathering their bodies with soap and brushing their teeth with neem twigs. Around them, the river swirled and sparkled like liquid diamonds infused with the rising sun, and there were no dubious objects floating in the water. Sitting on my folded towel on the cold stone steps above the concourse, I tried to remember past watersheds. There was the obvious one, baptism, which I couldn't remember, and paddling into big seas on a surfboard as a youth off the coast of Australia, a joyous, terrifying experience. Once, in Europe, I'd waded into a river to sneak across a border between two countries, but my nerve failed and I'd retreated sheepishly to where I'd started. Taking a dip in the Ganga ranked with all of those, a religious experience, an extreme sport and a dare I'd given myself. But in truth, there was nothing to test myself against, and no reward to be gained, only an ego to shed in the river of creation.

Removing my kurta and sandals and wrapping them in my towel, I crossed the concourse and climbed down the ghat to the waterline. The water was an opaque brown colour. Unable to see the steps just beneath the surface, I felt with my toes for a footing. Standing on the lower steps in front of me, partially submerged men, women and children saw me coming and made way, welcoming with broad smiles and hands clasped in namastes. Then I was among them, inhaling the fresh air of the morning and warmed by the sun. A pear-shaped man beside me recited a sonorous mantra, eyes tightly closed, and beside him, several women dunked themselves in their saris, arms drawn modestly across their breasts. Boys and girls lunged, splashed, and desperately dog-paddled.

Taking one step down, then another, I found myself waist-deep in the Ganga, only then realising that I hadn't the faintest idea what to do. There was no point just standing there. I couldn't remember the words of the Gayatri Mantra and, anyway, that seemed way too formal. I'd just have to wing it. Drawing my hands together, I clasped them tight in front on my lowered forehead, and turning towards the rising sun, I prayed. I prayed to the God of the Hindus and Christians, the God of Muslims and Buddhists, Jains, Sikhs and Zoroastrians.

'*Ishwar ek hai*,' I prayed. God is One.

Then I pinched my nostrils and plunged deep beneath the surface of the water once, then again, and then a third time. On the final dip I stayed under, watching the submarine light playing on the closed lids of my eyes, and when my breath was exhausted, sprang up from the water like a dolphin, no doubt startling people, and perhaps even a few dolphins.

It felt good to be home, good to be free. I would be keeping the name my parents gave me, the wisdom of India's sages, a healthy scepticism, and the secret of how a polluted river can make you clean, grinding it all down until it resembled something I could call my own.

Climbing the ghat back towards my bundle, and checking to see whether some thief had stolen my sandals, I dried myself in the sun, and sat for a while admiring the colour and beauty of the morning.

POSTSCRIPT

One hundred and fifty years since India's first attempt to overthrow colonial rule, and sixty years since it succeeded in doing so, India continues to make major strides in what Mahatma Gandhi might have called its experiment with freedom and democracy. India has retained its nuclear arsenal (as did Pakistan), but instead of becoming an international pariah, it is being canvassed as a potential member of the United Nations Security Council. With its economy growing by 8 per cent annually, it has become the world's tenth largest economy, with a seat at the annual G10 summit. The buzzwords of the new Indian economy — 'outsourcing' and 'information technology' — have assisted in the widespread perception that India's time has come. Capitalists see a fast-growing and liberalised economy; strategic analysts see a populous, nuclear-armed democracy capable of balancing the power of China and buttressing the fight against terrorism.

In October 2003, a memorial marking the spot where Rajiv Gandhi was assassinated was inaugurated at Sriperumbudur in southern India. Seven granite 'pillars of eternity' stand guard, topped by brass capitals representing *dharma* (righteous conduct), *satya* (truth), *nyaya* (justice), *vigyan* (knowledge and reason), *tyag* (sacrifice), *shanti* (peace) and *samriddhi* (abundance). The capitals take various shapes — a wheel of dharma, a bodhi tree, a *chhatri*, or protective canopy, a star, a flame, a lotus and a bushel of grain — and the pillars are carved in swirling patterns representing the seven sacred rivers of India. Along one side, a 35-metre-long stone frieze recreates scenes of everyday life:

women sowing rice, oxen ploughing fields, train travellers with their tiffin boxes. A spout at the feet of the river goddess Ganga dispenses water representing Ganga jal. Speaking at the opening ceremony, the President of India, Dr A.P.J. Abdul Kalam, read a poem he had composed for the occasion seeking divine guidance for India's religious leaders. 'Give strength to the people to combat divisive forces, guide my people to develop an attitude to appreciate different ideologies and transform enmity among individuals and organisations and nations into friendliness and harmony ... transform our country into a peaceful and prosperous nation,' he prayed.[1]

The pillars of eternity consciously recall the pillars of the Emperor Ashoka, whose edicts were carved on similar monoliths surmounted by capitals installed at locations across India in the third century BC. Rajiv Gandhi, the memorial suggests, belongs in the same company. There remains no national memorial honouring the Sikh victims of the 1984 pogrom in Delhi, to which Rajiv turned a blind eye.

On 15 August 2004, Dr Manmohan Singh became the first Sikh to address the nation as prime minister from the ramparts of the Red Fort in Delhi. That same year, speaking in parliament, Dr Singh apologised to the Sikhs on behalf of the Congress Party for its failure to prevent the 1984 riots, which claimed the lives of 3000 members of their community, saying that he bowed his head in shame and would pursue those named in a judicial inquiry into the riots. Within days, two of those accused, the Minister of State for Overseas Indian Affairs, Jagdish Tytler, and Sajjan Kumar, chairman of the Delhi government's Rural Development Board, resigned their posts, vowing to clear their names.[2]

Sonia Gandhi's 'renunciation' of power did not prevent her from exercising power. As the Singh government approached its second anniversary, the Italian-born widow was widely seen as the power behind the throne. Economic reforms continued, although restrained to a degree by the Congress's alliance with the communists for a majority in parliament. The coalition also included the Dalit politician Ram Vilas Paswan, who early on promised to extend job reservation for lower castes into the private sector.[3] Nevertheless, overjoyed to be back in power, the Congress celebrated Sonia's fifty-eighth birthday by sending her a 240-kilogram pineapple cake from a five-star hotel in the capital.[4]

In February 2004, the Delhi High Court exonerated Rajiv Gandhi of involvement in the Bofors corruption scandal. The following year, the court also quashed charges against the influential Hinduja brothers in a related case. However, the Hinduja verdict was being challenged in the Supreme Court, where action against the Italian middle-man and Gandhi family friend Ottavio Quattrocchi also was continuing.

Stripped of power by voters in 2004, BJP leaders including the former home minister Lal Krishna Advani were hauled by police before the courts to answer charges of inciting the demolition of Babur's Mosque in Ayodhya. The case was continuing, along with other litigation concerning the ownership of the disputed site, but Mr Advani was dumped as party president after the election defeat. Atal Bihari Vajpayee continued on as parliamentary leader of the BJP, defying calls from sections of the Sangh Parivar for his resignation for failing to implement the movement's core policies during his six years as prime minister. The nationalists' tilt at fundamentally altering Indian political culture had failed, but the challenge to secularism remained, mainly because of the political convenience of large, cohesive communities formed on the basis of caste, religion and language.

Thirteen years after it was established to probe the demolition of the Ayodhya mosque, the Liberhan Commission had yet to complete its inquiries. The Commission's original six-month timeframe had been extended repeatedly, during which period it held 350 sittings and examined 101 witnesses. As at February 2006 it had yet to report or recommend that charges be framed against any individual or organisation.[5] On 5 July 2005, the fears expressed by officials I met in Faizabad materialised when five Muslim militants stormed the makeshift temple erected on the ruins of the mosque in an apparent attempt to destroy it. All five were killed by security forces before reaching the idols, much to the relief of the authorities, who feared widespread communal violence had they succeeded.

In May 2005, the Orissa High Court commuted the death penalty awarded to Dara Singh for the murder of Graham Staines and his two sons, awarding him life imprisonment instead, after finding that the evidence was too 'weak and speculative' to hold him personally responsible for their deaths.[6] Eleven others had their convictions overturned. The Supreme Court said it would hear an appeal against the acquittals and sentence reduction lodged by the Central Bureau of Investigations, as well as an appeal seeking Dara Singh's exoneration and release. Earlier that year, at a ceremony at Rashtrapati Bhavan in New Delhi, Gladys Staines was awarded the Padma Sri, India's fourth highest national award for community service. In Baripada, the not-for-profit Graham Staines Memorial Hospital was fully operational, but Mrs Staines and her daughter, Esther, were by then living in Australia.

Eighteen months after the Staines killings, the Shankaracharya of Puri, one of Hinduism's four so-called popes, visited the village of Manoharpur to preside over the 'cleansing' of forty tribals who had converted to Christianity. Each of them was called forth to donate two goats, ten pots of country liquor, and 20 kilograms of rice for a community feast. Some were too poor to offer the restitution, but the ceremony went ahead anyway, conducted by the shankaracharya in Hindi, a language most of the Santhal tribal people of the area do not understand. At the end of the ceremony it was announced that they had 'reconverted' to Hinduism.[7]

In 2004, the US Commission on International Religious Freedom recommended that India be designated as a 'country of particular concern' in respect of its treatment of religious minorities, but in the following year, after the defeat of the Vajpayee government, removed it from the list.[8] The Sangh Parivar's 'religious' wing, the Vishwa Hindu Parishad, remains active among affluent, upper-caste, non-resident Indians living in the West, a key funding base for the nationalists. 'The VHP has established its branches in these countries and is promoting Hindutva politics among them,' observed Meenakshi Ganguly, a researcher with Human Rights Watch. 'It holds regular summer camps for the children of these non-resident Indians ... As [non-resident Indians'] Hinduism gets diluted in Western societies, they vehemently assert their Hinduness through Hindutva rather than Hindusim. The VHP has been thriving financially more because of these NRIs, especially in Gujarat.'[9]

In January 2005, P.V. Narasimha Rao died in New Delhi. Obituaries praised his free-market reforms and lamented his failure to save Babur's Mosque, the twin emblems of his rule surviving him. V.P. Singh was still dabbling in politics and regularly having his kidneys flushed at Apollo Hospital.

In March 2005, Tushar Gandhi led a re-enactment of his great-grandfather Mahatma Gandhi's 1930 Salt March. Almost half the Indian Cabinet were among those flagged off on the march by Sonia Gandhi, although most of them were seen returning to their hotels after walking a few kilometres. The procession took several hundred marchers through the heart of Gujarat's communal crescent of troubled cities three years after it was convulsed by the Godhra riots.[10] In August 2004, police arrested six Hindus in connection with the Gujarat riots of February 2004, but as yet there have been no convictions. According to The Economist, the Modi state government, which was quick to bring charges against 123 Muslims allegedly involved in setting fire to the Sabarmati Express, continued 'to act less like a scourge of illegal violence than its sponsor'.[11]

The hijacker Satish Chandra Pandey's early optimism that direct action could solve his — and India's — problems proved to be illusory. In 2006, thirteen years after his reckless mid-air seizure of a civilian passenger plane, his case was still before the Lucknow bench of the Allahabad High Court. Fearing the death penalty, which can be imposed in hijacking cases, Satish had ceased attending the court, and had been officially proclaimed an absconder, jeopardising the 300,000 rupees ($6500) relatives had provided as surety for bail. His expectation that Hindu nationalist rule would deliver him from justice and reward him for his commitment to the cause did not materialise. At last report, a warrant had been issued for his arrest, and he was penniless and in hiding in Allahabad. In his home village of Saraiya Maafi, Satish's reputation was ruined, as his much-vaunted political connections failed to deliver jobs and development to the area. His younger brother Girish, who never resorted to terrorism and remained working on the family farm, had opened Saraiya Maafi's first STD/IDD telephone booth, linking the village with the rest of India and the world, and supplementing his family's income.

In November 2004, Francis Wacziarg, Aman Nath and their guests celebrated the 540th birthday of the fort at Neemrana. At last report, Hari Lal Dhingra continued to ply his trade as a vendor of language services in New Delhi. The Mahant of Sankat Mochan Temple in Varanasi, Veer Bhadra Mishra, also continued his work aimed at cleaning up the Ganga, and taking his morning dip in the river at Tulsi Ghat every day. On 7 March 2006, his Sankat Mochan Temple was rocked by a powerful bomb blast that killed ten Hindu worshippers, including members of a wedding party. Thirteen others died in a separate blast at a city railway station. In the early hours of the following day, Sonia Gandhi visited Sankat Mochan to give her condolences to Mahant Mishra and the bereaved. The former BJP president Lal Krishna Advani blamed Pakistan for the blast, and announced yet another yatra to rouse Hindu pride and anger. But in a moving display of Hindu–Muslim unity on the day after the bombing, the renowed Muslim maestro Bismillah Khan gave an impromptu concert which included hymns in praise of Rama at the temple.

In November 2005, the United Nations Educational, Scientific and Cultural Organisation (UNESCO) officially recognised India's Ram Lilas tradition as a masterpiece of the world's Oral and Intangible Heritage.

ENDNOTES

Openers

p. v 'M.K. Gandhi, Hindu Muslim Unity', 15 May 1924, in Rudrangshu Mukherjee (ed.), *The Penguin Gandhi Reader*, Penguin Books India, New Delhi, 1993, p. 264.

1 The Hindi Lesson

1 Gurcharan Das, 'Licensing Blues', *India Unbound: From Independence to the Global Information Age*, Profile Books, 2002, p. 202.
2 *Ibid.*, p. 202.
3 M.K. Gandhi, *An Autobiography or The Story of My Experiments with Truth*, M. Desai (trans.), Navajivan Publishing House, Ahmedabad, 1990, p. 187.
4 Madhu Trehan, 'Portrait of a Revolutionary as a Young Woman', *Indian Express*, 15 January 2005, p. 9.
5 Bipan Chandra, Mridula Mukherjee & Aditya Mukherjee, *India After Independence 1947–2000*, Penguin Books, New Delhi, 2000, pp. 288–9.

2 Instant Karma

1 Dilip Bobb, 'Ordeal of Prince Charming', *Times of India*, 15 June 1991, p. 62.
2 T.V. Rajeswar, 'Police Apathy and Religious Bigotry: Dual Approach Primary Cause of the Crisis', *The Tribune* (Chandigarh), 6 March 2002.

3   *Times of India*, 15 June 1991.
4   Margaret & James Stutley, *Harpers Dictionary of Hinduism: Its Mythology, Folklore, Philosophy, Literature and History*, Harper & Row, 1977, p 75.

3 The Raja Remembers

1   M.K. Gandhi, Speech at Women's Conference, Sojitra, 16 January 1925, in Rudrangshu Mukherjee (ed.), *The Penguin Gandhi Reader*, Penguin Books India, New Delhi, 1993, p. 182.
2   Pavan K. Varma, *Being Indian*, Viking, New Delhi, 2004, p. 198.
3   *India Today*, 31 October 1992, p. 91.

4 Reflections on a Samadhi

1   M.K. Gandhi, 'Hind Swaraj', Ch XVII — Passive Resistance, in Rudrangshu Mukherjee (ed.), *The Penguin Gandhi Reader*, Penguin Books India, New Delhi, 1993, p. 47.
2   Harinder Baweja, 'Picking up the Threads', *Times of India*, 30 June 1991, p. 105.

5 Siege of the Red Fort

1   M.K. Gandhi, 'A Baffling Situation', in Rudrangshu Mukherjee (ed.), *The Penguin Gandhi Reader*, Penguin Books India, New Delhi, 1993, p. 271.
2   Ashok Malik, *The Indian Express*, 24 December 2004, p. 5.
3   Shekhar Gupta, 'On the Record: P.V. Narasimha Rao', *The Indian Express*, 13 May 2004.
4   Neerja Chowdhury, 'In the End, Chanakya's Pearl of Wisdom', *Indian Express*, 24 December 2004.
5   A.G. Noorani, 'Legal Aspects to the Issue', in Sarvelpalli Gopal (ed.), *Anatomy of a Confrontation: The Babri Masjid-Ram Janmabhumi Issue*, Penguin Books, New Delhi, 1991, p. 70.
6   Durga Das Basu, *Introduction to the Constitution of India*, Prentice-Hall of India, New Delhi, 1997, p. 27.

7 'Amnesty Report is Biased: Gujarat', *Asian Age*, 30 January 2005.

8 Aroon Purie, Letter from the Editor, *Times of India*, 15 February 1993, p. 1.

9 R.C. Dutt, *Ramayana, Epic of Ram, Prince of India*, Rupa & Co., New Delhi, not dated.

10 *Ibid.*, p. 337.

11 M.S. Golwalkar, *We or Our Nationhood Defined*, Bharat Publications, 1939, pp. 43–4. Nationalist claims that Golwalkar did not write this book, or later recanted his views, are demolished by Sitaram Yechuri in 'What is this Hindu Rashtra?: On Golwalkar's Fascistic Ideology and the Saffron Brigade's Practice', *Frontline*, Madras, 12 March 1993.

12 M.K. Gandhi, quoted by Jagmohan Reddy & Nusserwanji Vakil in the Judicial Commission Report on the Ahmedabad Riots, 1969, Sabrang Alternative News Network.

13 Quoted in Jyotirmaya Sharma, *Hindutva: Exploring the Idea of Hindu Nationalism*, Penguin Viking, New Delhi, 2003, p. 125.

14 Robert Marquand, 'India's Leader-in-waiting Fans Hindu Nationalism', *Christian Science Monitor*, 26 July 2002.

15 M.S. Golwalkar, *op. cit.*, p. 39.

16 Sitaram Yechuri, *op. cit.*

17 Jeff Penberthy, 'What I Saw at Babri', *Asian Age*, 15 September 2004, p. 1.

18 Akshaya Mukul, 'Intelligence Reports Try to Undo Them', *Times of India*, 17 January 2001, p. 7.

19 Ashis Nandy, Shikha Trivedy, Shail Mayaram & Achyut Yagnik, *Creating a Nationality: The Ramjanmabhumi Movement and Fear of the Self*, Oxford University Press, Delhi, 1995.

6 The Blood-Dimmed Tide

1 M.K. Gandhi, 'Democracy vs Mobocracy', 8 September 1920, in Rudrangshu Mukherjee (ed.), *The Penguin Gandhi Reader*, Penguin Books India, New Delhi, 1993, p. 138.

2 Press Trust of India, 'Provocative Speeches Led to Babri Demolition: CBI', *Hindustan Times*, 21 December 2004. Later the BJP issued a statement condemning the demolition.

3 Yubaraj Ghimire, 'The Rise of the Sadhus', *Times of India*, 15 January 1993, p. 61.

4 Lalit Vachani (director), *The Men in the Tree: Revisiting the RSS and Hindu Fundamentalism* (documentary film), Wide Eye Film, 2002.

5 *The Statesman*, Calcutta, 7 December 1993.

8 An Indian Wedding

1 Quoted in Lekha Rattanani, 'The Day of the Tiger', *India Today*, 15 February 1993, p. 18.

2 M. Rahman, 'Trapped in Uncertainty', *Times of India*, 15 February 1993, p. 16.

3 'Politics By Other Means: Attacks Against Christians in India', *Human Rights Watch Report*, Vol. 11, No. 6, p. 177; and Asghar Ali Engineer, 'The Politics of Arrest of Bal Thackeray', *Secular Perspective*, Centre for Study of Society and Secularism, Mumbai, 1–15 August 2000.

4 Ikram Ali & Srawan Shukla, 'Hijacker Surrenders to Vajpayee', *Times of India*, 23 January 1993.

9 Inhaling the Mahatma

1 M.K. Gandhi, Speech at AICC meeting, in Rudrangshu Mukherjee (ed.), *The Penguin Gandhi Reader*, Penguin Books India, New Delhi, 1993, p. 166.

2 Christopher Kremmer, 'India "Happier but Resentful" under the Raj', *Sydney Morning Herald*, 23 June 1997.

3 Catherine G. Corey, *India: Economic Growth and Poverty Reduction During the 1990s*, Summer International Center for Development Information and Evaluation, Working Paper No. 326, US Agency for International Development, Washington DC, July 2001, PN-ACP–030.

4 Tata Services Ltd, *Statistical Outline of India 2004–5*, Department of Economics and Statistics, Mumbai, 2005, p. 1.

5 Sharat Pradhan, 'Gandhi's Ashes Immersed at the Sangam in Allahabad', United News of India, 30 January 1997.

10 Diary of a Munshi

1   Quoted in Muzaffar Alam & Sanjay Subrahmanyam, 'The Making of a Munshi', *Comparative Studies of South Asia, Africa and the Middle East*, 24 February 2004, p. 62.

2   Ishwar Das Nagar, *Futuhat-I-Alamgiri*, Tasneem Ahmad (trans.), Idarah-I-Adabiyat-I-Dalli, New Delhi, 1978, p. 38.

3   W.E. Begley & Z.A. Desai, *Shah Jahan Nama*, Oxford University Press, Delhi, 1990, p. 553.

4   Masur-ul-Umra, quoted in Maharaja Lal, *A Short Account of the Life and Family of Rai Jeewan Lal Bahadur, Late Honorary Magistrate, Delhi with Extracts from his Diary Relating to the Time of Mutiny, 1857*, 2nd edn, IMH Press, Delhi, 1903, p. 94.

5   Memo of Colonel W.G. Waterfield, Commissioner and Superintendent, Peshawar Division, reproduced in Maharaja Lal, *op. cit.*, p. 131.

6   Maharaja Lal, *op. cit.*, p. 28.

7   Charles Theophilus Metcalfe, *Two Native Narratives of the Mutiny in Delhi*, A. Constable & Co., 1898, reproduced in Maharaja Lal, *op. cit.*, p. 159.

8   Carr Stephen, Preface to *Archaeology and Monumental Remains of Delhi*, quoted in *ibid.*, p. 60.

12 Cow Belt Cowboy

1   M.K. Gandhi, Speech at AICC meeting, in Rudrangshu Mukherjee (ed.), *The Penguin Gandhi Reader*, Penguin Books India, New Delhi, 1993, p. 164.

2   Siriyavan Anand, '"Holy" Cow and "Unholy" Dalit', *Southasian Himal*, November 2002.

3   Margaret & James Stutley, *Harper's Dictionary of Hinduism: Its Mythology, Folklore, Philosophy, Literature and History*, Harper & Row, New York 1977, p. 41.

4   Sutapa Mukherjee, 'Unholier Than Thou', *Outlook*, 17 January 2000.

13 Explosion of Self-esteem

1 M.K. Gandhi, Speech at AICC meeting, in Rudrangshu Mukherjee (ed.), *The Penguin Gandhi Reader*, Penguin Books India, New Delhi, 1993, p. 164.

2 Ram Mohan Roy, quoted in Romain Rolland, *The Life of Ramakrishna*, Advaita Ashrama Publications, Kolkata, 2003, p. 69.

3 Sri Aurobindo, quoted in Amartya Sen, 'The Threats to Secular India', *New York Review of Books*, 8 April 1993.

4 Amartya Sen, *ibid*.

5 Robert Marquand, 'India's Leader-in-waiting Fans Hindu Nationalism', *Christian Science Monitor*, 26 July 2002.

6 Nirapuma Subramanian, 'When the Pink City Ran Red With Blood', *Sunday Observer*, 28 October 1990.

7 Agence France Presse, 'New Delhi Charges Top Hindu Politicians With Mosque Razing', 5 October 1993.

8 Christopher Kremmer, 'Austere Militant Dreams of Hindu Raj', *Sydney Morning Herald*, 12 August 1997, p. 12.

9 'Advani Babri Yatra Ends', *Asian Age*, 11 April 2001, p. 1.

10 Praful Bidwai, 'From Pokhran to Gujarat', *Hindustan Times*, 17 May 2002.

11 George Perkovich, *India's Nuclear Bomb: The Impact on Global Proliferation*, Oxford University Press, New Delhi, 2000, p. 412.

12 Chandan Mitra, 'Explosion of Self-esteem', *The Pioneer*, 12 May 1998.

13 John F. Burns, 'At South Asia Summit: An Annual Economic Lament', *New York Times*, 3 August 1998.

14 Nick Hordern, 'Hindu Extremism in Powerful Hands', *Australian Financial Review*, 27 September 2003, p. 33.

14 Genesis in Oriya

1 V. Mangalwadi, V. Martis, M.B. Desai, B.K. Verghese & R. Samuel, *Burnt Alive: The Staines and the God They Loved*, GLS Publishing, Mumbai, 1999, p. 44.

2 *Ibid*., p. 46.

3 *Ibid*.

4 *Ibid*., p. 24.

5 M.K. Gandhi, *An Autobiography or The Story of My Experiments with Truth*, M. Desai (trans.), Navajivan Publishing House, Ahmedabad, 1990, p. 29.

6 Prabhu, Abhijeet, 'Christian Converts Forced to Return to Hinduism in India', Compass Direct Service, 22 August 2001.

7 Vincent A. Smith, *Asoka: The Buddhist Emperor of India*, Low Price Publications, Delhi, India, 1990.

8 James Ferguson, quoted in Thomas Donaldson, *Konark*, Oxford University Press, New Delhi, 2003, p. 1.

9 Christopher Kremmer, 'Papal Visit Fires up Hindu Hardliners', *Sydney Morning Herald*, 30 October 1999, p. 24.

10 Pope John Paul II, 'Ecclesia in Asia', New Delhi, 6 November 1999.

11 Cardinal Joseph Ratzinger, 'Notification Concerning the Writings of Father Anthony de Mello, SJ', Congregation for the Doctrine of the Faith, Rome, 24 June 1998.

12 Saira Menezes & Venu Menon, 'The Zealots Who Would Inherit', *Outlook*, 22 February 1999, p. 18.

13 Kalyan Chaudhuri, 'Another Victim in Orissa', *Frontline*, Vol. 16, Issue 19, 11–24 September 1999.

14 M.K. Gandhi, *Christian Missions*, Ahmedabad, 1941, p. 288.

15 'Politics By Other Means: Attacks Against Christians in India', *Human Rights Watch Report*, Vol. 11, No. 6, p. 215.

16 Ruben Banerjee, 'Burning Shame', *India Today*, 8 February 1999.

17 V. Mangalwadi et al., *op. cit.*, p. 34.

15 Seven Cities of Delhi

1 Times News Network, 'In-Migration Has a Long History', *Times of India*, 11 October 2004, p. 2.

2 Gurcharan Das, 'The Respect They Deserve', *Time Asia*, 29 November 2004.

3 Express News Service, 'Gates For Colonies: MCD Sets Conditions', *Indian Express*, 5 October 2004, p. 4.

4 David Cohen, 'Millions Go Mobile', *New Scientist*, 19 February 2005, p. 40.

5 Pallavi Majumdar, 'Govt. Needs to Invest in Public Transportation in a Big Way', *Times of India*, 11 August 2004, p. 5.

6 Tata Services Ltd, *Statistical Outline of India 2004–05*, Department of Economics and Statistics, Mumbai, 2005, p. 149.

7 *Times of India*, as quoted in Faisal Kutty, 'Taj Mahal or Tejo-Mahalaya?', Ummahnews, 12 January 2003; Vir Sanghvi, 'Chariot of the Frauds', *Hindustan Times*, 28 January 2002.

8 Rahul Pathak, 'A Tangled Web', *Times of India*, 11 January 1993, p. 64.

9 *The Hindu*, 14 December 1992.

10 Praful Bidwai, 'No Voodoo Archaeology, Please', Rediff.com, 26 March 2003, p. 239.

11 Hari Manjhi & B.R. Mani, *Ayodhya: 2002–03 Excavations at the Dispute Site*. Report submitted to the Special Bench, Lucknow of the Hon'ble High Court, Allahabad, Archaeological Survey of India, Janpath, New Delhi, p. 272.

12 'Yagna Outside Qutub Minar', *The Hindu*, New Delhi, 22 January 2003.

16 Virtual Reality

1 Sunanda Mehta, 'Bridegroom and Prejudice', *Indian Express*, 6 November 2004, p. 8.

2 Rafiq Dossani & Professor Martin Kenney, 'The Next Wave of Globalization? Exploring the Relocation of Service Provision to India', Berkeley Roundtable on the International Economy, Working Paper 156, September 2004, p. 11.

3 Bardhan & Kroll, Associated Press, June 2005, quoted in *ibid.*, p. 4.

4 Quoted in Rafiq Dossani & Professor Martin Kenney, *op. cit.*, p. 11.

5 Rafiq Dossani & Professor Martin Kenney, *op. cit.*, p. 31.

6 Joydeep Mukherji, 'India's Slow Conversion to Market Economics', Centre for Advanced Study of India, University of Pennsylvania, November 2002, p. 8.

7 *Ibid.*, p. 9.

8 Martin Jacques, 'With Strength in Numbers, China and India Will Become Superpowers', *The Guardian*, reprinted in *Sydney Morning Herald*, 28 October 2004, p. 17.

9 Dinesh C. Sharma, 'Shining India's Swanky New Sweatshops', *Hindustan Times*, 24 October 2005, p. 1.

10 Anuradha Verma, 'The God of Mall Things', *Times of India* (Delhi), 27 August 2004, p. 1.

11 Ashok Malik, 'Sonia as a Savarkarite Hindu', *Indian Express*, 27 September 2004, p. 8.

12 Satish Grover, Preface, *Buddhist and Hindu Architecture in India*, 2nd edn, CBS Publishing, New Delhi, 2003.

13 E.M.J. Venniyoor (for the Kerala Lalit Kala Akademi), *Raja Ravi Varma*, Government of Kerala, 1981.

17 The Temple of Justice

1 M.K. Gandhi, 'Hind Swaraj', Ch XI — The Condition of India, in Rudrangshu Mukherjee (ed.), *The Penguin Gandhi Reader*, Penguin Books India, New Delhi, 1993 p. 30.

2 IANS, 'Amartya's Nobel Challenged In Court', *Hindustan Times* (Lucknow), 9 October 2004, p. 11.

3 Justice R.C. Lahoti, 'When Judiciary Is Strengthened Quantatively and Qualitatively', *Indian Express*, 5 December 2005, p. 1.

4 'City Stinks, ANN Stir On', *Hindustan Times* (Allahabad), 12 October 2004, p. l.

5 *Hindustan Times* (Delhi), 6 October 2004.

6 Urvashi Gulia, 'Cheating Case Drags On For 28 Years', *Times of India*, 21 October 2004, p. 9.

7 M.K. Gandhi, 'Hind Swaraj', *op. cit.*, pp. 30–2.

8 Pratap Bhanu Mehta, 'Can Judges, Judge Themselves?', *Indian Express*, 28 October 2004, p. 8.

18 Return of the Hero

1 Sutapa Mukherjee, 'Unholier Than Thou', *Outlook*, 17 January 2000.

2 Rahat Bano, 'Slumming It', *Hindustan Times*, 12 October 2004, p. 8.

3 Rukmini Shrinivasan, 'Made Indian Woman Cry in 60 Secs', *Times of India*, 12 January 2005, p. 11.

4 Tata Services Ltd, *Statistical Outline of India 2004–05*, Department of Economics and Statistics, Mumbai, 2005.

5 *Babur-Nama*, Annette Susannah Beveridge (trans.), Low Price Publications, Delhi, 1989, p. 378.

6 *Ibid.*, p. 518.

7 Charu Lata Joshi, 'Like Jain, Like Liberhans', *Outlook*, 25 May 1998, p. 58.

8 Amartya Sen, 'The Threats to Secular India', *New York Review of Books*, 8 April 1993.

19 An Inner Voice

1 Sonia Gandhi, 'Making of a Leader', *India Today*, 17 January 2006, p. 63.

2 Sonia Gandhi, *Rajiv*, Penguin Books, New Delhi, 1992.

3 *Ibid.*, p. 3.

4 *Ibid.*, p. 9.

5 Neerja Chowdhury, 'Rao's Moment in Indian Politics', *Indian Express*, 3 January 2005, p. 8.

6 Sonia Gandhi, excerpts from an interview with Shekhar Gupta, *Indian Express*, 16 May 2004, pp. 6–7.

7 Sonia Gandhi, quoted in Prem Panicker, 'Campaign Trail: When the Fire of Communal Violence Was Burning Up Your Homes, the People Who Set It Ablaze Were Sitting Peacefully Inside Their Homes', www.rediff.com, 22 February 1998.

8 *Ibid.*

9 Christopher Kremmer, 'Another Gandhi on the Rise', *The Age*, 27 February 1999, p. 5.

10 Christopher Kremmer, 'A Road Warrior Driven by Nationalism', *Sydney Morning Herald*, 4 September 1999, p. 27.

11 Shefali Anand, 'Cult of the Cut', *Indian Express*, 26 September 2004, pp. 4–5.

12 'Politics By Other Means: Attacks Against Christians in India', *Human Rights Watch Report*, Vol. 11, No. 6, September 1999, p. 183.

13 'We Have No Orders to Save You', *Human Rights Watch Report*, Vol. 14, No. 3(c), April 2002.

14 Press Trust of India, 'Modi Sworn in Along With 9 Ministers', 7 October 2001.

15 Luke Harding, *The Guardian*, 16 December 2002.

16 Citizens' Initiative, Submission to National Human Rights Commission, New Delhi, March 2002, quoted in 'We Have No Orders To Save You', *op. cit.*

17 'RSS Chief for Replicating "Gujarat Experiment"', *The Hindu*, 21 January 2003.

18 Ramachandra Guha, quoted in Luke Harding, *op. cit.*

19 Pratap Bhanu Mehta, 'The Future of an Illusion', *Indian Express*, 24 November 2004.

20 N. Talwar, 'A Comment on the Indian Elections', Yahoo Geocities, www.geocities.com/aipsg/charcha/july2004/elections.html

21 Rajeev Shukla, 'Whither Shining', *Indian Express*, 17 April 2004, p. 3.

22 Alex Perry, 'Lie Another Day', quoted in 'In Black & White — Home Truths from Abroad', *Sunday Express*, New Delhi, 9 May 2004.

23 Edward Luce, 'A Matter of Faith', A Party in Waiting, Seminar No. 5, June 2003, www.india-seminar.com

24 Pratap Bhanu Mehta, *op. cit.*

25 Rajdeep Sardesai, 'Cattle Call,' *Hindustan Times*, 9 December 2005.

26 Prabhu Chawla, 'Sonia Strikes Back', *India Today*, 31 May 2004, p. 18.

27 Harish Khare, 'With Sonia Saying No, Manmohan is Set to be Prime Minister', *The Hindu*, 19 May 2004.

20 The Prince and the Pauper

1 M.K. Ghandi, 'Answers to Zamindars', in Rudrangshu Mukherjee (ed.), *The Penguin Gandhi Reader*, Penguin Books India, New Delhi, 1993, p. 238.

2 Quoted in Utpal Borpujari, 'Harking Back to the Gandhis, Again', *Deccan Herald*, 29 August 2004.

3 Harinder Baweja, 'In Cold Blood', *Tehelka*, 11 June 2005, p. 16.

4 Kaveree Bamzai, 'Club Class Notes', *Sunday Times of India* (Review), 17 December 2000, p. 1.

5 Press Trust of India 'Sonia 3rd on Forbes Power Women List', *Asian Age*, 21 August 2004, p. 1.

6 'Agriculture: Reinventing the Monsoon Economy', India Economic Summit, 7 December 2004, New Delhi.

7 Harinder Baweja, *op. cit.*

21 Opera in the Dust

1 Romain Rolland, *The Life of Ramakrishna*, Advaita Ashrama, Kolkata, 2003, p. 49.

2 *Ibid*, p. 49.

3 Christopher Isherwood, *Ramakrishna and His Disciples*, Advaita Ashrama, Kolkata, 2001, p. 113.

4 Romain Rolland, *op. cit.*, p. 55, quoting from 'The Gospel of Sri Ramakrishna', II, 17 and 248.

5 Romain, *op. cit.*, p. 55.

6 David Hume, 'Of Tragedy', *Essays Moral, Political, and Literary* [1777], Liberty Fund Books, 1987.

7 Radhakrishnan, *The Hindu View of Life*, Unwin Paperbacks, London, 1988, p. 19.

22 Swimming in Varanasi

1 Narsinh Mehta, 'Vaishnava Jana', National Gandhi Museum & Library, Raj Ghat, Delhi.

2 Huston Smith, *The Illustrated World's Religions: A Guide to Our Wisdom Traditions*, HarperSanFrancisco, 1994, p. 56.

3 Joydeep Mukherji, 'India's Slow Conversion to Market Economics', Centre for the Advanced Study of India, University of Pennsylvania, 22 November 2002, p. 9; and T.V.R. Shenoy, 'Faith and Two Democracies', *Indian Express*, 17 June 2004, p. 8.

4 *Bhagavad Gita*, Juan Mascaró (trans.), Penguin Books, Harmondsworth, 1987, p. 82.

5 *Ibid.*, p. 50.

6 *Ibid.*, p. 97.

Postscript

1 Nandini Mehta, *Rajiv Gandhi Ninaivakam: Pillars of Eternity*, All India Congress Committee, Delhi, not dated.

2 Sujay Mehdudia, 'Sajjan Kumar Quits as Rural Development Board Chief', *The Hindu*, (online edn), 12 August 2005.

3 Times News Network, 'Bill on Job Quota in Private Sector Soon', *Times of India*, 10 December 2004, p. 5.

4 Times News Network, 'Sonia Gets 240-kg Cake From Congress', *Times of India*, 10 December 2004, p. 5.

5 'Liberhan Commission's Term Extended by Three Months', *The Hindu*, 13 December 2005.

6 Press Trust of India, 19 May 2005.

7 Anant Kumar Giri, 'Love and Fire', *The Hindu*, 8 July 2001.

8 US Commission on International Religious Freedom, Annual Report, Washington, 2005.

9 Meenakshi Ganguly, 'Other Screams of Terror', *Asian Age*, 26 September 2005.

10 'Gandhi's 1930 March Re-enacted', BBC News Online, 12 March 2005.

11 'It Still Hurts', *The Economist*, 12 August 2004.

TIMELINE

3300–1500 BC★	Rise and fall of Indus Valley civilisation
1500–500★	Rise of Hindu civilisation in northern India
623-543★	Life of the Buddha, birth of Buddhism
400★	Panini compiles a Sanskrit grammar
327	Alexander the Great crosses the Indus River
300★	*Ramayana* composed by Valmiki
260★	Emperor Ashoka's conversion to Buddhism
50 AD★	St Thomas the Apostle visits India
240–550	Gupta empire, Hindu revival
630	Chinese pilgrim Xuanzang (Hsuan Tsang) visits India
711	Arab Muslim conquest of Sindh
800★	Rajput kingdoms formed in northern India
997	Mahmud of Ghazni raids into India
1192	Delhi sultanate brings northern India under Muslim rule
1225	Qutub Minar constructed
1336–1646	Southern Hindu kingdom of Vijayanagar resists Delhi
1398	Timur the Lame sacks Delhi, demise of Delhi sultanate
1526	Battle of Panipat, Babur founds Mughal empire
1600	British East India Company founded
1631	Shah Jahan begins construction of Taj Mahal

1639	Shahjahanabad (Old Delhi) founded
1674	Shivaji founds secular Maratha empire
1707	Death of Mughal emperor Aurangzeb
1757	Battle of Plessey, rise of British power in India
1828	Hindu reformist movement Brahmo Samaj founded by Ram Mohan Roy
1857	Indian Rebellion defeated
1858	Queen Victoria declared Empress of India
1875	Hindu reformist movement Arya Samaj founded
1893–1914	Gandhi in South Africa
1919	Jallianwala Bagh massacre at Amritsar, Sikhs join Freedom Struggle
1942	Gandhi launches Quit India movement
1947	Partition of India, independence for India and Pakistan
1947–1948	First India–Pakistan war
1948	Mahatma Gandhi assassinated
1949	Hindu idols appear inside Babur's Mosque at Ayodhya
1950	Indian Republic founded on the basis of universal suffrage; district judge in Ayodhya permits restricted worship of Hindu idols inside Babur's mosque
1962	China launches brief border war on India
1964	India's first prime minister, Jawaharlal Nehru, dies of heart attack
1965	Second India–Pakistan war
1971	Third India–Pakistan war; creation of Bangladesh
1974	India conducts 'peaceful' nuclear explosions
1975	Allahabad High Court finds Indira Gandhi guilty of electoral malpractice, bans her from contesting elections for six years; Mrs Gandhi declares state of emergency, suspends democratic rights

1977	Indira Gandhi calls elections, loses
1980	Indira Gandhi re-elected
1984–1985	Indira Gandhi orders Indian Army to crush Sikh armed rebellion at Golden Temple in Amritsar, she is later assassinated by her Sikh bodyguards; anti-Sikh riots in Delhi; Rajiv Gandhi wins landslide election victory
1986	Local magistrate allows unrestricted Hindu worship at the disputed site in Ayodhya
1987	V.P. Singh quits Congress Party and government, launches campaign against Rajiv Gandhi on Bofors corruption scandal
1989	V.P. Singh defeats Rajiv Gandhi at elections, becomes prime minister
1990	Student riots after government orders 22 per cent of public-sector jobs be reserved for 'backwards castes'; Muslim uprising in Kashmir challenges Indian rule
1991	Rajiv Gandhi assassinated by Tamil suicide bomber; Rao government launches economic liberalisation program
1992	Hindu extremists demolish Ayodhya mosque, riots follow
1998	BJP's Atal Bihari Vajpayee forms coalition government, conducts nuclear tests, declares India a nuclear-weapons state
1999	Australian Christian missionary Graham Staines and two sons killed by Hindu extremist-led mob in eastern India; Christians harassed elsewhere
2002	Fire kills fifty-eight Hindu militants aboard a train in Gujarat 2000 Muslims killed in reprisal attacks
2004	Vajpayee government defeated at the polls; Sonia Gandhi declines prime minister's post, which goes to Dr Manmohan Singh

* Some dates are approximate

GLOSSARY

accha — (UTCH-ha) good

achar — (ach-AR) pickle

adivasi — (ah-dee-VAH-see) tribal

Ahimsa — (ah-HIM-suh) doctrine of non-violence

aloo — (AH-loo) potato

amrit — (uhm-RIT) divine nectar

anand — (AH-nund) bliss

arre — (AH-ray) hey, so

arti — (AHR-tee) worship with fire

ashram — (ASH-rahm) dwelling, retreat or guesthouse

asrama — (ash-RAM-uh) Four stages of orthodox Hindu life

atman — (ART-mun) soul

avatar — (AHV-tar) incarnation, usually of a divinity

ayah — (EYE-yah) woman employed to mind children

azan — (aZAN) Muslim call to prayer

babu — (BAR-boo) Hindu gentleman, bureaucrat

baccha — (but-CHAR) child

bagh — (BAR-guh) garden

bania — (BUN-ee-yuh) trader

banyian — (bun-ee-YAHN) singlet

Bapu — (BAH-poo) father (in Gujarat)

barat — (bar-RAHT) groom and his wedding party

barfi — (BAR-fee) sweet

bastis — (BUS-tees) hutments, or squatter colony

ber — (bear) a fruit, jujube

Bhagavad Gita — (BHUG-vud GEE-tah) lit. 'Song of God', a Hindu religious text

Bhagwan — (bug-WAHN) God

bhai/bhaiya — (BUY-yuh) brother

bhajan — (BUD-juhn) hymn

Bhakti/*bhakt* — (BHAK-tee/BHAKT) Hindu doctrine of salvation
    through devotion/devotee

bhangra — (BUNG-rah) Punjabi folk music

bidi — (BEE-dee) cheap cigarette in rolled tendu leaf

bigha — (BIG-uh) five-eighths of an acre

bindi — (BIN-dee) decorative dot on forehead, usually worn by Hindu
    women

bokhar — (book-HAR) fever

Brahmin — (BRAH-min) Hindu priestly caste

Brahmo — (BRAH-mo) member of a Hindu reform sect who shuns
    idols

chai — (ch-EYE) tea, usually boiled with milk and sugar, and sometimes
    cardamom

chapatti — (cha-PAH-tee) flat bread

chappals — (CHA-puls) flip-flops, thongs

cheel — (cheel) hawk

Chennai — (CHEN-eye) official name of Madras

chhatri — (CHUT-ree) canopied kiosk on roof of a building

chikoo — (CHIK-oo) a fruit

chik — (chik) hanging shade screen, usually cane

chowk — (chalk) town square, crossing

chowkidar — (CHALK-ee-dar) watchman

crore — (ca-ROAR) ten million

cul — (cul) tomorrow and yesterday

'cyber coolie' — derogatory term for Indians employed in BPO
    enterprises

dacoit — (DAK-oit) bandit

dada — (DAH-dah) elder brother, or paternal grandfather

dalal — (dah-LAL) stock trader

Dalit — (DULL-it) lit. 'oppressed', collective term used to describe
    Untouchables and lower castes and tribes

darshan — (DAR-shan) viewing a revered person, deity, place or
    object

desi — (DAY-see) Indian, local or locally

dharamsala — (duh-rum-SHAH-luh) travellers' lodge

dhaba — (DUH-buh) food stall

dharma — (DUHR-muh) Hindu code of individual conscience and social obligation

dhoban — (DHO-bun) laundry woman

dhobi — (DHO-bee) laundryman

dhoti — (DOH-tee) loin cloth

Diwali — (dee-WAH-lee) Hindu festival of lights

Doab — (DOH-arb) land between two rivers

dom — (dom) attendant at funeral pyres

dupatta — (doo-PAH-tuh) headscarf

firman — (fur-MAHN) edict of a Muslim ruler

gaddi — (GUH-dee) seat/throne

gali — (GUH-lee) narrow passageway

Ganesh — (guh-NAISH) elephant-headed Hindu god, son of Shiva and Parvati

Ganga — (GUNG-guh) River Ganges, sacred in Hindu tradition

ghat — (ghart) a slope, usually stepped access to a water source

goonda — (GOON-duh) thug, robber

gopi — (GOH-pee) milkmaid

gora — (GORE-ruh) European, white person

gurdwara — (GURD-wah-ruh) Sikh temple

ha — (har) yes

Hanuman — (HUH-noo-mun) Hindu monkey god

Hindi — (HIN-dee) Sanskrit-based language of northern India

Hindustani — (hin-doo-STAN-ee) language mixing Hindi and Urdu spoken in northern India

Hindutva — (hin-DOOT-va) political ideology stating that Hindus form a nation

Holi — (HO-lee) Hindu festival of colours

hookah — (HOOK-uh) water pipe for smoking

howdah — (HOW-duh) elephant saddle

Ishwar — (ISH-var) God

jaggery — (JUG-ah-ree) unrefined sugar

jal — (jarl) water

jalebi — (ju-LAY-bee) a fried sweet

janeau — (jah-NOH) holy string worn by upper-caste Hindus

janmasthan — (jan-MUS-tahn) birthplace

jati — (JUH-tee) sub-caste, usually occupational

jhola — (JOH-lah) shoulder bag

-ji — (JEE) suffix used as sign of respect

jingchak — (jin-CHUK) showy, cheap

jnana — (GHEE-ahn) knowledge

kabari — (kuh-BAH-ree) junk, scrap

kar seva/sevak — (kar-SAVE-uh/kar-SAVE-uk) volunteer work/worker

karma — (KAR-ma) deeds, doctrine concerning spiritual consequences
    of earthly actions

Kayasth — (KYE-ast) Hindu scribe caste

khadi — (KAR-dee) handspun cloth

kisan — (KISS-arn) farmer

kajal — (KAR-jul) mascara

Kolkata — (KOHL-kut-tuh) official name of Calcutta

kot/kotla — (KOT-lah) citadel

Krishna — (KRISH-nah) Hindu god

Kshatriya — (SHUT-ree-yah) Hindu warrior and ruler caste

kund — (KHOOND) artificial lake, bathing tank

kurta pajama — (KOOR-ta puh-JAH-muh) overshirt and pants suit,
    usually in light cotton

kutcha — (KUH-cha) unripe, unmade

lakh — (LAK) 100,000

lathi — (LAH-tee) baton, stave

lingam — (LING-um) sacred phallic symbol

maha — (MAH-har) great

Mahabharata — (maha-BHAR-at) epic story of a war between two
    families set in northern India, contains the *Bhagavad Gita*

mahant — (mah-HUNT) head priest of Hindu temple

maharaja — (maha-RAH-jah) great raja

mahatma — (ma-HART-muh) great soul

maidan — (mair-DARN) open ground, plains

mali — (MAR-lee) gardener

mandir — (MUN-deer) Hindu temple

mantra — (MUN-tra) sacred phrase

masala — (muh-SAR-luh) spices

masjid — (MAS-jeed) mosque

maya — (MY-uh) illusion, Hindu doctrine that the entire physical world is an illusion; also a woman's name

mela — (MAY-luh) festival, party

moksha — (MOK-sha) release from the cycle of reincarnation

muezzin — (MEW-zin) person who issues the call to prayer from a mosque or minaret

Mughal empire (MOH-gul) line of seventeen Muslim rulers of Central Asian Turkic origin who ruled India in whole or part from 1526 to 1857

Mumbai — (MUMB-eye) official name of Bombay

munshi — (MOON-shee) clerk, secretary

murti — (MOOR-tee) statue, often an idol

nahin — (nuh-HEEN) no

namaste — (NUM-uh-stay) hello/goodbye

namaz — (nuh-MUZ) Muslim prayers

namkeen — (num-KEEN) salty snacks

nashta — (NUSH-tuh) breakfast

nawab — (nah-WAHB) Indian Muslim ruler, noble or wealthy landowner

neta — (NAY-ta) leader

padyatra — (pad-YAT-ra) *yatra* on foot

pagal — (PAH-gul) insane

panchayat — (punch-EYE-at) local council

panda — (PUN-duh) Brahmin who assists the faithful in rituals

pandal — (PUN-dal) tent

pandit — (PUN-dit) a Brahmin or learned Hindu man

paranthas — (par-RAHN-tuhs) flat bread

parivar — (pah-ree-VAH) family

Parsi — (PAR-see) Zoroastrian

peon — (PEE-on) messenger

prasad — (pra-SAHD) blessed food (Hindu)

puja — (POO-juh) Hindu worship, ritual

pujari — (poo-JAR-ee) Hindu temple priest

pukha — (PUK-huh) proper, right

purdah — (PUR-duh) seclusion of women in Indian Muslim and some Hindu communities

purohit — (poo-roh-HIT) Hindu family priest

raja — (RAH-jah) king

rakhi — (RAH-kee) protective amulet, often a thread blessed and tied on the wrist

Ram Lilas — (RAHM LEE-lahs) dramatic adaptions of the life of Rama

Rama — (RAH-mah) Hindu god, prince of Ayodhya

Ramayana — (ra-MAI-uh-na) epic story of Rama, the Prince of Ayodhya

Ramrajya — (RAHM RAHJ-yah) God-given government

rashtra — (RUSH-truh) nation

rishi — (RISH-ee) seer

roti — (ROH-tee) flat bread

sadhu — (SAR-dhoo) Hindu ascetic

samadhi (sum-AH-dee) cenotaph

sangam — (SUNG-um) confluence of two rivers

Sangh Parivar — (sung pari-VAH) 'family' of Hindu nationalist organisations under RSS guidance

Sanskrit — (SAN-skrit) classical Indo-European language of Aryan origin

sanyasa/sanyasi (sun-YAS-ah/sun-YAS-ee) final stage of Hindu life, renunciation/ renunciate

shabash — (SHAH-barsh) well done!

shamiana — (shah-mee-AH-nuh) large tent

shikar — (SHIK-har) hunting and fishing for sport

Shiva — (SHEE-vuh) Hindu god

shloka — (SHLOW-kuh) Sanskrit poetic verse

Shudra — (SHOULD-ruh) Hindu labourer caste

Sita — (SEE-tah) wife of Rama

stupa — (STEW-puh) dome-shaped Buddhist religious or funerary mound

supari — (soo-PAH-ree) areca, or betel nut

tabla — (TAH-bla) drum

takht — (tukt) raised seat or platform

tamasha — (tah-MAH-sha) spectacle, fuss

Thakur — (TARK-or) local chief, usually Kshatriya caste

thali — (TAH-lee) metal tray/plate, as well as the name for the food served on it

thana — (TAH-nuh) police station

tiffin — (TIF-in) lunch or nested metal containers for carrying hot food

tikka — (TIK-uh) small cube or piece, usually of food

tilak — (TIL-ak) blessing mark on a Hindu's forehead

tonga — (TONG-uh) horse-drawn conveyance

trishul — (TRI-shul) trident

tyag — (tuh-YAGH) sacrifice

Urdu — (AUR-doo) language of Northern India using many Persian
and Arabic words

vaastu — (VAH-stoo) creation of harmonious environment by reference
to the cosmic energy fields

Vaishya — (VAISH-yuh) Hindu producer caste

vakil — (vuh-KEEL) legal advocate

Vedas — (VAY-dahs) Hindu religious scriptures collated in four books in
Sanskrit in the first millennium BC

videshi — (vid-DAYSH-ee) foreigner

vihara — (vee-HAR-ruh) Buddhist monastery

Vishnu — (VISH-noo) Hindu god

wallah — (WAH-luh) person associated with profession or thing

yaar — (YAHR) mate, friend

yatra/yatri — (YAH-truh) journey, pilgrimage/pilgrim

zindabad — (ZIN-duh-bard) long life!

ACKNOWLEDGEMENTS

The events, meetings and observations in this book are drawn from my experiences in India during two periods of living there (July 1990 to September 1993 and January 1997 to August 2001). Additional material was obtained during the travels herein described as the yatra, which consisted of four separate visits to India in 2004–05. All the material presented is factual, and the main historical events appear in the order in which they occurred. However, for the sake of narrative coherence, some of my meetings with individuals are presented in thematic rather than chronological order. In some cases, I have combined several actual conversations into one. Similarly, descriptions of visits to important sites are in some cases based on several visits to the place concerned.

The journey with former Indian prime minister the late Rajiv Gandhi, from Haridwar to Rishikesh, took place on 2 May 1991, nineteen days before his assassination. The journey with his son, Rahul, in Amethi constituency, took place in September 2004, as did the interview with the journalist and Gandhi family friend Suman Dubey. Former Indian prime minister V.P. Singh was interviewed once while undergoing dialysis at Apollo Hospital, New Delhi, in 2004, with a follow-up interview by telephone in January 2006. Former Indian prime minister the late P.V. Narasimha Rao was interviewed in June 1991. Former deputy prime minister Lal Krishna Advani was interviewed on several occasions in the 1990s, but was unavailable to meet me for this book, nor was former prime minister Atal Bihari Vajpayee. The general secretary of the Samajwadi Party, Amar Singh, was interviewed in October 2005.

The journey to Rishikesh with Hari Lal Dhingra took place in May 2004. He told me the story of his daily prayers at a later meeting in Delhi, but I have him relate the story when we visit Rishikesh. The hijacker Satish Chandra Pandey was interviewed in Saraiya Maafi in February 1998, and his brother Girish spoke to me in August 2004. Gladys Staines was interviewed in Baripada in January 1999 and again in June 2004, when I also visited Manoharpur, where her husband and sons were killed. After that we emailed, and I spoke to her again by telephone in January 2006. Chapter 17 includes material drawn from three visits to Allahabad, the first in January 1997 when the Gandhi immersion took place, the second during the Maha Kumbh Mela in January 2001, and the High Court visit in October 2004. The events, descriptions and meetings in Ayodhya are based on numerous visits to the pilgrim town in the period 1992 to 2004. Chapters 21 and 22 are based on two visits to Varanasi, in October 2004 and November 2005. I am indebted to Sri Veer Bhadra Mishra, who in his role as Mahant of the Sankat Mochan Temple gave generously of his time and wisdom concerning the Bhakti tradition and the philosophy of Saint Tulsidas.

Deep Singh is a pseudonym, as is Gopiganj, the name used for the call-centre worker's village. Ravi Zakrias, the name used to describe the doctor quoted in Chapter 14, is also a pseudonym. All dollars quoted in the book are US dollars.

I am grateful to Shrimati Om Lata Bahadur for showing me her own unpublished manuscript, which uses some of the same material that I also obtained from *A Short Account of the Life and Family of Rai Jeewan Lal Bahadur, Late Honorary Magistrate, Delhi, with Extracts from his Diary Relating to the Time of Mutiny, 1857*. Also my thanks go to another neighbour in Civil Lines, P.N. Dhar, the eminent economist and principal secretary to the late prime minister Indira Gandhi, for sharing his insights on the Indian economy, some of which are to be found in his classic work *The Evolution of Economic Policy in India*. Thanks also to Chandran Mitra, for his permission to quote from his work in the *Pioneer* newspaper, and to use a headline from one of his stories, 'Explosion of Self Esteem', as the title of Chapter 13 of this book.

In addition to all the above, heartfelt thanks are owed to the following people whose work and friendship helped a poor student of India to lessen, if not entirely overcome, his ignorance on a variety of subjects: Manoj Mattoo; Jitendra Srivastava, whose knowledge of politics, the law and the Sultanpur and Amethi districts was of enormous help; Ram Jethmalani; Biraja Mahapatra; Brajeshwar Prasad Singhdeo; Chandra Kishore Mishra; Robin Jeffrey and Jan Forrester who kindly read early versions of the manuscript; Gauri Gill; Pablo Bartholomew; Satish Sharma; Ajay Desai and Yasmeen Tayebbhai; the Maharaja of Ayodhya, Bimalendra Mohan Pratap Mishra; Babu Lal Sharma of the Gandhi Peace Foundation; Swami Agnivesh; Tushar Gandhi; Tony and Alayne Eastley; Amanda Wilson and all at the *Sydney Morning Herald*; Professor Rana P.B. Singh; Shanta Anand; Prabhu Chawla and Rajesh Sharma at *India Today*; Alissa Mello; Pinku Pandey; Hemant Sarna; Rita Kumar; Geoff Thompson and all at ABC New Delhi; Mohammed Hashim Ansari; Mahant Gyan Das of the Hanuman Gari and Mukhya Archak Satendra Das in Ayodhya; Yashodhara Agrawal at Banaras Hindu University; Shashank Narayan Singh at Hotel Ganges View in Varanasi; Rakesh Singh at Harmony Bookshop in Varanasi; Sanjay Subrahmanyam; Rajdeep Sardesai; Sagarika Ghose; Romila Thapar; S.P. Gupta; Debjani Ganguly; Arundhati Roy and Pradip Krishen; Ramachandra Guha; Arun Kumar Sinha; Binod K. Singh; Francis Wacziarg and Aman Nath; C. Babu Rajeev at the Archaeological Survey of India; Nayanjot Lahiri; William Dalrymple and Olivia Fraser; Sharat Pradhan; Tony Hill; Sir Mark Tully; Bulu Imam; Deepak Puri; Robert Nickelsberg; Timothy J. Scrase; Peter Friedlander; Tony Herbert; Edmond Roy; Scott and Kashmira

Baldauf; the India Office Library in London, and the Nehru Memorial Library in New Delhi; and John Spence at ABC Radio Archives. A word of thanks, too, to Nigel Hankin for his wonderful glossary *Hanklyn-Janklin or A Stranger's Rumble-Tumble Guide to Some Words, Customs, and Quiddities Indian and Indo-British*, published by Banyan Books, which although is not the primary source of the glossary in this volume, did settle many a semantic dispute.

On the production side, my sincere appreciation goes to all at HarperCollins Australia and my literary agency, Curtis Brown. In particular, this book would never have been written without the unfailing friendship and support of my agent, Tara Wynne; publisher Shona Martyn; designer Marcelle Lunam; researcher Devahoti Hazarika; photographers Palani Mohan and Jason Michael Lang for their stunning images; and *mera dost* Sanjay Jha. If I can ever return the many favours you bestowed on me, I will.

Finally, I wish to express my gratitude to Maya and Krishen Bans Bahadur; my wife, Janaki; her brother, Siddhartha, and his wife, Tarini, and their family; the Downs family; and all the aunts, uncles, cousins, nieces and nephews, for their trust, patience, candour and generosity during many happy years of life with them; and to my Australian family, Ted and Marlene Kremmer and sister Melissa, for their forbearance with my long absences. Words, in this regard at least, fail me.

INDEX

Partition, 69, 71, 80
  Hari Lal's experience, 7–8
Paswan, Ram Vilas, 381
Patnaik, J.B., 294
Patwardhan, Sudhir, 241
pendency, 243, 246–7, 250, 253–4
Perkovich, George, 176
Perry, Alex, 299
Pope John Paul II, 190–1
Prabhakaran, Velupillai, 26–7, 35
Prakasan, S.S., 307
Pranapratishtha rite, 270
Prasad, Jitendra, 127
Prayag, 59, 60, 255, 257
Princep, James, 341
Punjab violence, 30, 94, 177

Q
Qazi Islamic law, 245
Quattrocchi, Ottavio, 293, 381
Qutub complex, 221–5

R
Radhakrishnan, 369
Raghunath, Raja, 132, 133–4
Raj Ghat, 55, 58–9, 125
Raja of Ayodhya, 278–9
Rajasthan, 100
Rajputs, 100, 102
Ram Bhakt, 161
Ram Lilas (Deeds of Rama),
  340–7, 385
Rama, 70, 71, 73, 74, 75, 76, 77,
  161, 216, 217, 219, 221, 269,
  273, 280, 281, 341, 343, 344,
  345, 346, 347, 355, 358, 365,
  369, 385

Ramakrishna, Sri, 335–8, 339,
  349
Ramayana, 19, 73–7, 269, 355
Ramcharitamanas, 77, 269, 356,
  359
Ramnagar, 340, 341
Ramrajya, 78
Rao, Narasimha, 67–9, 81, 90,
  91–2, 123, 164, 174, 291,
  383
Rashtriya Swayamsevak Sangh
  (RSS), 78, 79, 80, 83, 91,
  115, 171, 176, 190, 205, 296
Ratzinger, Cardinal Joseph, 191
Ravana, 344, 346
Ravi Varma Pictures Depot, 240
Red Citadel. see Lal Kot (Red
  Citadel)
Red Fort. see Lal Qila (Red Fort)
regional parties, 152
Rehman, Sheikh Abdul, 199–200
Reliance Industries, 295, 312, 315
religious politics, 318. see also
  Hindu nationalism; Hindu
  nationalists
renunciation, 19, 75, 303, 304,
  335, 336, 337, 380
Rig Veda, 22, 155, 369
Rishikesh, 21, 23, 24, 31
Rithambara, Sadhvi, 91
Rolland, Romain, 336
Roy, Edmond, 12, 13, 15
Roy, Ram Mohan, 98, 169

S
Sahara Group, 315
Saint Thomas, 186–7

Venz, Gil, 193, 194, 202
Vipal, 103
Vishnu, 217
Vishwa Hindu Parishad (VHP), 80, 273, 282, 382–3
Vivekananda, Swami, 78, 191
Vyas-ji, 358, 359

W
Wacziarg, Francis, 100, 103, 212, 384
Wolpert, Stanley, 163
World Hindu Council. *see* Vishwa Hindu Parishad (VHP)

X
Xuanzang (Hsuan Tsang), 20

Y
Yadav, Mulayam Singh, 313
Yadav castes, 158, 313
Yamuna River, 6, 10, 18, 55, 65
Yeats, W.B., 88
Yechuri, Sitaram, 80
Y2K, 228

Z
Zakrias, Dr Ravi, 183, 184, 185
Zia ul-Haq, 141

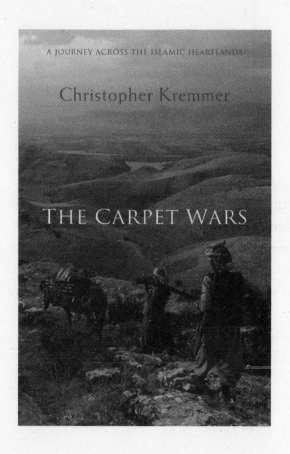

A JOURNEY ACROSS THE ISLAMIC HEARTLANDS

Christopher Kremmer

THE CARPET WARS

The Carpet Wars

A writer's true-life odyssey through a crescent of Islamic nations and regions. Following the historical and cultural threads of the oriental carpet, we plunge into a world where even the simplest motif on a rug can be filled with religious, tribal and political significance ...

BAMBOO PALACE

Christopher Kremmer

Bestselling author of *The Carpet Wars*

Bamboo Palace

Bamboo Palace begins as a travelogue, turns into a mystery and ultimately redefines a nation's history, as Christopher Kremmer journeys through Laos to uncover one of Indochina's darkest secrets.

For decades, the inscrutable leaders of the Lao People's Democratic Republic have deflected questions about the fate of the Lao royal family, traditional rulers of the 600-year-old Kingdom of the Million Elephants and the White Parasol, deposed by leftist guerillas in the aftermath of the Vietnam War. Now, the author of the international bestseller *The Carpet Wars* cuts through the bamboo curtain to reveal the shocking truth.

A timely reminder of the consequences of ill-considered war, *Bamboo Palace* takes readers from the jungles of South-East Asia to the north-western United States, where the author tracks down the last known survivor of the royal death camp. The former prisoner's testimony provides the definitive chilling climax.

An intriguing and at times disturbing portrait of a poor, landlocked country in the grip of tyranny, *Bamboo Palace* is also an extraordinary story of human endurance.